'This well-research   *Belfast Telegraph*

ssels;
now
d his
sorb-
is for
d the
sman

irous
n the
l the
of the
well
book
l add
to be
ibune

love
race).
gland
ffairs
with

rdian

hout
it is
not
s the
ship
Today

sting
ship-
by an
icent
and,
IFR

'As with his earlier work the author writes well and handles his material
adroitly'   *Contemporary Review*

Geoffrey Moorhouse is 'one of the best writers of our time' (Bryon Rogers, *The Times*), 'a brilliant historian' (Dirk Bogarde, *Daily Telegraph*) and 'a writer whose gifts are beyond category' (Jan Morris, *Independent on Sunday*). His *To the Frontier* won the Thomas Cook Award for the best travel book of the year in 1984. He is a Fellow of the Royal Society of Literature and for many years his home has been in a hill-village in North Yorkshire.

By Geoffrey Moorhouse

HISTORIES

The Missionaries
India Britannica
Hell's Foundations: a town, its myths and Gallipoli
The Pilgrimage of Grace
Great Harry's Navy

JOURNEYS

The Other England
The Fearful Void
To the Frontier
Apples in the Snow
OM: an Indian Pilgrimage

PLACES

Calcutta
Imperial City: the rise and rise of New York
Sydney

SOCIETIES

Against All Reason
The Diplomats

NOVELS

The Boat and the Town
Sun Dancing

SPORTING PRINTS

The Best-Loved Game
At the George

Great Harry's Navy

How Henry VIII Gave England Sea Power

GEOFFREY MOORHOUSE

PHOENIX

A PHOENIX PAPERBACK

First published in Great Britain in 2005
by Weidenfeld & Nicolson
This paperback edition published in 2006
by Phoenix,
an imprint of Orion Books Ltd,
Orion House, 5 Upper Saint Martin's Lane,
London WC2H 9EA

1 3 5 7 9 10 8 6 4 2

A CIP catalogue record for this book
is available from the British Library.

ISBN-13 978-0-7538-2099-5
ISBN-10 0-7538-2099-4

Typeset by Input Data Services Ltd, Frome

Printed and bound in Great Britain at
Mackays of Chatham plc, Chatham, Kent

The Orion Publishing Group's policy is to use papers
that are natural, renewable and recyclable products and
made from wood grown in sustainable forests. The logging
and manufacturing processes are expected to conform to
the environmental regulations of the country of origin.

This book is for
Kalyacitta, Andrew and Michael;
and in memory of their sister, Brigie.
In admiration, with love and gratitude.

'The trewe processe of Englyshe polycye. . .
Is thys, as who seith, south, north, est and west
Cheryshe marchandyse, kepe thamyralte,[1]
That we bee maysteres of the narowe see.'

The Libelle of Englyshe Polycye, a poem on the use of English sea-power, attributed to Adam Moleyns (Clerk to Henry VI's Council and subsequently Bishop of Chichester), 1436

'And though we haue not alwey werre vppon the see, yet it shalbe nescessarie that the kynge haue alway some ffloute apon the see, ffor the repressynge off rovers, sauynge off owre marchauntes, owre ffishers, and the dwellers vppon owre costes; and that the kynge kepe alway some grete and myghty vessels, ffor the brekynge off an armye when any shall be made ayen hym apon the see.'

Sir John Fortescue, *On the Governance of England*, 1471–6

'O eternal Lord God, who alone spreadest out the heavens, and rulest the raging of the sea; who hast compassed the waters with bounds until day and night come to an end; Be pleased to receive into thy Almighty and most gracious protection the persons of us thy servants, and the Fleet in which we serve. Preserve us from the dangers of the sea, and from the violence of the enemy; that we may be a safeguard unto our most gracious Sovereign. . .and a security for such as pass on the seas upon their lawful occasions. . .'

The Book of Common Prayer, 1662

'Under the providence of God The Safety Honor and Wealth of this Country chiefly depends on the Navy. . .'

Horatio Nelson to Henry Addington, 25 October 1802

---

1 'thamyralte' = the admiralty.

CONTENTS

ILLUSTRATIONS

Section One
Detail from *The Embarkation of Henry VIII at Dover* c.1520, artist unknown[1]
Henry VIII, c.1509, English School (16th century)[1]
Francis I of France, attributed to Jean Clouet[1]
Drawing of a 1470 carrack, by Master W.[2]
Thomas Howard, 3rd Duke of Norfolk, artist unknown[1]
William Fitzwilliam, 1st Earl of Southampton, by Hans Holbein[1]
John Dudley, Duke of Northumberland, by Richard Godfrey[3]
Drawing of a typical 3-masted merchantman c.1530, by Hans Holbein[4]
Thomas Seymour, Baron Seymour, artist unknown[3]
Sir George Carew, by Hans Hobein[1]
A model of James IV's *Great Michael*[5]
Leone Stozzi, engraving by Andre Thevet[6]
Claude D'Annebault, c.1535, attributed to Jean Clouet[1]
La Cordelière[9]

Section Two
Henry VIII, c.1542, artist unknown[3]
Henry Grâce à Dieu, from the Anthony Roll[7]
A model of *Mary Rose*[1]
The Encampment of the English Forces near Portsmouth, 1545, artist unknown[8]
The galleass *Anne Gallant*, from the Anthony Roll[9]
The rowbarge *Rose in the Sun*, from the Anthony Roll[7]
HMS *York*[10]

MAPS AND DIAGRAMS

FOREWORD

For those readers who are as interested as I am in the reasons why writers are attracted to their subjects, let me explain the genesis of this book. Having spent four years studying Henry VIII and his response to the great northern rebellion known as the Pilgrimage of Grace, I had become absorbed enough to want to stay in the period and find out more, so long as it didn't have much to do with Henry's domestic life, which has been greatly overwritten these past few years, to the point of anaesthesia. But what? The answer came to me, appropriately enough, in the bath one morning when I remembered that Henry was said to be the founder of the Royal Navy, in which I once served.

The sea, indeed, has been a recurring factor in my life since a very early age, though my first experience of it was not encouraging. As a small boy, I was taken out into Liverpool Bay in what was thought of as a 'pleasure boat' by my family, for what seems at this distance to have been an unwholesome wish to be thrilled by a tragedy which had just cost ninety-nine men their lives. The small craft which carried me and a dozen or so others probably belonged to an inshore fisherman making a bob or two on the side from day-trippers, and was shipping heavy spray from an increasing chop as we circled the buoy beneath which the sunken submarine HMS *Thetis* lay 150 feet under the surface. I remember the day as very grey and ominous, with me feeling slightly queasy and increasingly anxious as we lurched back to the safety of the land. Fortunately, the experience didn't do me any permanent damage, because two spells of serious seatime were to follow it – in one of His Majesty's light cruisers of the Mediterranean Fleet during my National Service, and later for a year I spent working as a deep-sea fisherman.

But I've also cruised the Atlantic coast of Europe a number of times, and circumnavigated the British Isles on several occasions, as well as traversing the Channel more often than I can recall en route to or from the North Sea, the Antipodes, the Canaries and various Continental ports. I have watched Stromboli erupt over the Tyrrhenian Sea from the deck of a four-masted barque, I have sailed the Aegean in a caique whose helmsman was called Themistocles, and I have felt very small indeed 150 miles offshore of Gloucester, Massachusetts, in the teeth of a Force 12 hurricane which hit us when we were hauling in our trawl on Georges Bank. Once, in mid-Pacific, the vessel that was taking me to New Zealand stopped off Pitcairn Island on a very black night punctuated only by tiny specks of light on the water, which materialised into long-boats coming out to sell us things. One of these craft was sending bananas and carvings up to an islander doing the commercial business on our deck faster than he could handle them, and he hailed his mates in the bouncing boat down below, telling them to slow up a bit. 'Tarry a little while, Clarence', was what he actually shouted – which took me straight back to the eighteenth century and the vernacular spoken aboard HMS *Bounty.*

Such was the background that pointed me to the topic of this book after I discovered that, although Professor Loades not long ago produced a fine study of the Tudor navies as a whole, and there have been umpteen volumes on Elizabeth's navy, no-one so far as I could tell had yet singled out Henry and his fleet for separate attention. I therefore decided to test the proposition that he was the founding father of the Royal Navy, accepted (cautiously) by some experts but rejected by others: a typically favourable response is that 'at some indeterminable moment between August 1535 and December 1538, very possibly the Royal Navy was born'.[1] On the first of those dates a bull of excommunication was drawn up after the Act of Supremacy made Henry head of the Church in England, on the second the bull was actually published; and the judgement is based on Henry's growing awareness that England might soon be facing inter-national aggression in support of the papacy, as a result of which he began

---

1 References to 'the Royal Navy' were unknown before the latter part of the eighteenth century. What had been 'the King's ships' in Henry VIII's time had become 'the Navy Royal' under Queen Elizabeth, and this term lingered until the Commonwealth. With the Restoration, 'His Majesty's Navy' became the common expression, and was still to be found in the nineteenth century. But in October 1761, the Lords of the Admiralty referred, in a despatch to Rear-admiral Rodney, to 'an Act for the Encouragement of Seamen employed in the Royal Navy &c' (though the Act itself spoke of 'His Majesty's Navy'). Queen Victoria's accession in 1837 saw off all masculine references to the Fleet.

a warship-building (or rebuilding) programme which within a decade had added more vessels to his fleet than at any other comparable period of his reign.

So here we are; this is the result. It suffers from the usual impediments to writing about the early Tudors: the maddening gaps in information, the contradictory sources, the unreliable and often elusive chronology. In particular, although there is almost a surfeit of some information (about ships, their tonnage, their captains and complements and, most of all, about the cost of everything, down to the merest nail), there isn't the extensively varied documentation that enabled N.A.M. Rodger vividly to reconstruct every conceivable aspect of the Georgian navy. We still know comparatively little about living conditions aboard ships in the first half of the sixteenth century, about the rhythm of a seaman's life as it alternated between ship and shore, about the ways men related to each other and their officers at sea, when the overcrowding must have been more than claustrophobic, about their morale when fighting their ships or facing destruction by the elements. There are no oral histories of the period to tell us what seafaring communities *felt* about the way of life that brought them their living, or their reaction to the tragedies that inevitably befell them year in and year out (and did the men who served in the King's showboat, *Henry Grâce à Dieu*, grumble about endless spit and polish, as naval ratings of my generation certainly would have done?).

There is sometimes little enough to inform us of what actually happened in some dramatic and well-remembered incident, such as Prégent de Bidoux's attack on Brighthelmeston (Brighton) in 1514, or what became of his treacherous nephew Pierre, who switched sides and served the English profitably in time of war, though we are informed about the Field of the Cloth of Gold (which involved Henry in person) in almost excessive detail. But we would know even less than we do about a whole range of nautical things if *Mary Rose* had not been raised from the seabed in 1982, to yield an archaeological treasure trove of artefacts, quite apart from a better understanding of how she was made and what she looked like when she was one of the two most cherished warships in Henry's fleet.

As an unreconstructed generalist, I am writing here chiefly for people who find history exciting for a variety of reasons – not least because it can help to explain us to ourselves by referring to our past – but are not professionally engaged in studying it. At the same time I should like to think that my book will pass muster with academic naval specialists, whose discipline borrows from mine the moment they put words on paper, just as mine borrows from theirs as soon as I begin to investigate their subject. Because I have always included historical background in my work, and sometimes placed history in the foreground, too, I have set the purely naval record of Henry's reign in the widest possible context, instead of relating it externally to nothing more than contemporary political – especially international – developments. For to treat any aspect of history without reference to conditions and happenings in adjacent fields has always seemed to me as inadequate (and, indeed, frequently misleading) as it would be to describe a room and its contents in detail without saying anything about the rest of the building or the community and environment in which it is set.

And so I have tried here to capture the essence of London at this time, not only because it was the capital, but also because in these years it supplanted Southampton as the South of England's most flourishing port; I have described the English fisheries in more detail than some would expect because of their vastly important role in England's economy and religious observance, and because they supplied much of Henry's naval manpower in time of war and required the protection of his fleet from pirates even in peace; I have reviewed the circumstances leading up to England's very first Parliamentary legislation to protect natural resources, because of its relevance to the great need for timber in shipbuilding; I have dwelt at some length on the history of maritime exploration in order to emphasise the limitations of the English world view when Henry came to the throne; and I have allowed myself to be diverted to the distinctiveness of Brittany, because it was closely linked to English maritime affairs, not least by supplying much of our navy's sailcloth. This approach, or something like it, has been most eloquently expressed by Professor Rodger in the second volume of his British naval history, which appeared just as I was finishing this book. Explaining his own attitude to the subject, he wrote:

> As far as the limitations of a single work and a single author will allow, this is meant as a contribution to political, social, economic, diplomatic, administrative, agricultural, medical, religious and other histories which will never be complete until the naval component of them is recognised and understood. By the same token it is an attempt to spread the meaning of naval history well beyond the conduct of war at sea and the internal history of the Royal Navy, and to treat it instead as a national endeavour, involving many, and in some ways all, aspects of government and society.

There has never been a more lucid expression of what I myself have always instinctively believed, what I have tried to achieve here.

I have just used the word tonnage, so this is the proper place to explain why I have rendered it as tunnage throughout my text, except when it has nothing at all to do with ships (e.g. with army artillery pieces, or with quantities of raw material). The point is that the measurement of ships in the sixteenth century did not follow the conventions of our own time, when calculations are made of a vessel's deadweight or of her displacement. The second of these indicates the weight of water displaced by the submerged part of a ship's hull, and therefore the weight of the ship itself excluding any cargo, and consequently it is used with reference only to warships. Deadweight (or burthen) is the measurement in tons of cargo capacity though, when it first became an issue at the beginning of the fourteenth century, as Edward I started to tax shipping, the reference was to volume, in the number of tuns of wine a ship could carry. A tun was a cask containing four hogsheads, or approximately 252 gallons. Ships were therefore sized according to their real or notional tunnage, even if they were non-cargo-carrying men o'war. My intention has been simply to remind the reader that a vessel rated at 500 tuns in 1509 is not the same as one of 500 tons in the twenty-first century; in the case of warships it was about half the size, though even that is misleading because it fails to take into account the difference between the weights of wood and metal, and 'size' can refer to a number of other dimensions. In further mitigation, I would plead that I'm only following the usage in the Anthony Roll, the great inventory of Henry VIII's navy at the end of his reign. In the same spirit I have reproduced (as Appendix II) the inventory of *Henry Grâce à Dieu* at her completion in 1514, to convey the meticulous nature of Tudor accountancy, to indicate the extreme complexity of such a vessel's construction and equipment, and to give the reader some flavour of the period by retaining the wildly inconsistent spellings of the original document. The introductory epigraphs, too, have been left as they were written. But in my main text I have, where necessary, transposed everything into modern English in the interests of clarity. For the same reason, the years are dated according to our own habit (beginning on January 1) to avoid the residual confusions of the sixteenth century calendar, in which years conventionally began on Lady Day (the feast of the Annunciation) on March 25 – an observance that would persist in England until the middle of the seventeenth century – while Henry VIII's regnal years were calculated from April 22 to the following

April 21 (but Edward VI's ran from January 28 to January 27 and Elizabeth's from November 17 to the following November 16).

This book is not, of course, all my own work any more than any other history is. The Bibliography indicates how much I owe to many writers before me, and I'm particularly thankful to whoever was inspired to commemorate the millennium by putting that incomparable source of information and learned analysis, *The Mariner's Mirror*, on CD-ROM, which enabled me to read at my desk the journal's full run, from its inception in 1911 to the end of 2000, thus appreciably reducing my workload elsewhere. As before, I'm greatly indebted to Jacqueline Whiteside and her colleagues in Lancaster University Library, where much of my research was carried out, especially into *Letters and Papers, Foreign and Domestic, of the Reign of Henry VIII* and other State Papers of the period. My thanks also to the Document Supply Centre of the British Library in Boston Spa for its efficient assistance on numerous occasions, and to the librarians of the National Maritime Museum for their unfailing courtesy and help when I was working in the collections there. Among individuals who have assisted me, I'm especially grateful to Dr Maria Hayward of the University of Southampton for some helpful suggestions, and to Michael and Marilyn Dugdale, both for their generous hospitality whenever I needed to be in Greenwich, and for their good companionship on several field trips to France: I'm much obliged to Brittany Ferries for facilitating one of our cross-Channel expeditions. As always, I'm more grateful than I can say for the back-up provided by my editor and publisher Ion Trewin; and by Anna Hervé, Linden Lawson, Helen Smith and Emily Sweet, whose skills and commitment have helped to make this book what it has become. And for the support of my children, to whom it is dedicated.

Gayle, September 2004

GLOSSARY

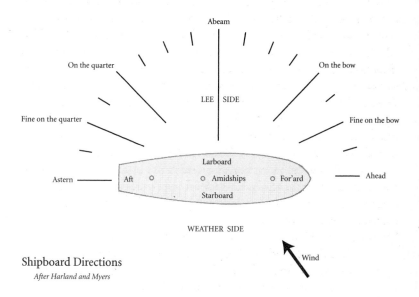

Shipboard Directions
After Harland and Myers

abeam, on the beam   At right angles to a ship.
admiral   (i) the officer commanding a squadron or a battle fleet at sea: (ii) the **Lord Admiral** was the senior naval officer, sometimes but not always seagoing; (iii) the **Vice-admiral** was a senior seagoing officer serving under him, and often there was more than one, with responsibility for different sea areas or separate task forces.
aft, abaft   Towards the stern or the after part of a ship.
amidships   The middle of a ship.
anchor   In its most primitive form a large stone, heavy enough to hold a ship's position when dropped overboard on the end of a cable. By the sixteenth century it had evolved into an iron shank with arms and flukes at the bottom. Ships carried several, of which the largest was the **sheet** (shot) **anchor** for use in extreme conditions. The **kedge anchor** was smaller, used for mooring and warping.
anse (*Fr.*)   Cove or bay.
astern   Behind a ship.

astrolabe   Navigational instrument for measuring the altitude of heavenly bodies and thereby calculating a ship's latitude.

balinger   Oared sailing vessel, usually single-masted, notable for speed and manoeuvrability.

ballast   Gravel, stones or anything heavy stowed as low as possible in the hold, so as to improve a ship's stability.

bar   Shoal across the entrance to a tidal estuary.

barge   Oared sailing vessel, either merchantman or man o'war.

bark   Any small seagoing vessel.

basilisk   A long heavy gun, usually breech-loading, firing shot of 15lb 4oz.

battened down   With hatches closed and loose gear secured, typically in bad weather.

beam   The width of a ship or at right angles to it: e.g. another vessel **on the beam** or one's own ship **abeam** of a navigational beacon.

beak, beakhead   A projection from the stem of a ship just above the waterline; its antecedents lay in the ancient ram used by the Greeks and Romans, but by the sixteenth century it was no more than a gesture in that direction.

bearing   A direction from a point of observation: e.g. the bearing of a headland in relation to an approaching ship, from which the observation is made.

beat, beating   To work a ship to windward by a series of tacks.

belay   Making fast a rope to a cleat or belaying pin, or (vernacular) to stop or cancel (e.g. 'Belay the last pipe' = 'Disregard the last order').

block   A pulley.

boatswain   Petty officer responsible for sails, rigging and ground tackle.

bonaventure (see **mast**)

bowline   A line attached to the vertical edge of a sail, to keep it tight when beating to windward.

bowsprit   A spar jutting from the bows, which carries rigging and sometimes sails.

braces   Ropes attached to all the yards of a ship, used to square or traverse the yards horizontally.

breast hooks   Timber put inside the bows to strengthen them, especially when a ship might be straining against its anchor cable.

breast ropes   A rope securing the yard parrels.

broadside   (i) The side of a ship; (ii) the guns mounted on one side or the other; (iii) to fire such guns independently or simultaneously.

buss   Small two-masted vessel, usually a fishing boat.

cable   (i) A rope not less than ten inches in circumference, usually attached to an anchor; (ii) a distance which was at first 120 and later 100 fathoms, or one tenth of a nautical mile.

caravel   Small seagoing lateen-rigged vessel.

carrack   Three- or four-masted vessel characterised by high super-structures fore and aft. Originally a type of merchantman found in the Mediterranean.

carvel   Method of ship construction in which the planks of the hull are laid edge-to-edge outside a skeleton framework.

caulk   To make seams watertight, usually with oakum and pitch.

chamber   The detachable breech of a gun, which contained the explosive powder.

chaser   Gun mounted in the bows (**bow chaser**) or stern (**stern chaser**) to fire ahead or astern.

clencher (see below)

clew   The lower corner of a square sail.

clinker   Method of ship construction in which the hull is made of overlapping planks built up from the keel. **Clench** nails were used to hold them in place. The method was eventually superseded by the carvel method of construction and **clencher** became the term used to indicate an old-fashioned (implicitly a worn-out) vessel.

close   To close a ship or a coast is to draw closer to it or to come alongside.

close-hauled   Steering as close to the wind as possible.

coble   A type of fishing boat found on the north-east coasts of England and Scotland, all with distinctive local differences in design. The Yorkshire version was characterised by high bows and bilge keels on either side of the hull.

cock-boat   Small ship's boat for use inshore.

cog   Single-masted vessel with a flat bottom and high freeboard, which had been the most common type of merchant ship from the thirteenth century but was fast disappearing by the beginning of the sixteenth.

commission, commissioning   The act of bringing a warship into service.

complement   The number in a ship's company.

convoy   (i) A fleet of merchant ships sailing under escort; (ii) the act of escorting them.

cordage   Rope or rigging.

corsa (*It.*)   Mediterranean pirates sponsored by the Muslim states of

North Africa, who preyed upon Christian mariners. There was a retaliatory Christian version of this operating at the same time.

course   (i) The direction a ship is sailing in; (ii) the foresail or mainsail, the lowest main sails.

coxswain   Petty officer in charge of a boat's crew.

crane lines (*cranelynes*, *cranelynnes*)   Small lines for keeping lee shrouds from chafing against the yards.

crayer   Small single-masted trading vessel.

cross-trestles   Timber supports to the tops of a mast.

culverin   Cast-iron gun of medium calibre with a long barrel, firing iron shot of 7lb 5oz–26lb 6oz.

curragh   Light Irish craft, its hull formed by animal skins stretched over a wooden frame, usually though not invariably operated by paddles.

curtal   Heavy gun with a large bore and short barrel capable of firing 40lb shot. Sometimes referred to as a **cannon**.

curtain wall   In military defence works, the wall connecting two or more towers.

dead-eye, deadman's eye (*dedemens hies/hyes*)   A round flat wooden block, pierced with three or more holes to receive a laniard; a component in a form of purchase.

deck   (i) A floor or platform in a ship, whose underside was the **deckhead**; (ii) **gun deck**, the deck on which the principal battery of guns was mounted; (iii) **half-deck**, the after end of the main deck, below the quarter deck; (iv) **main deck**, the uppermost deck running the length of a ship; (v) **quarter-deck**, a deck above the main deck aft; (vi) **weather deck**, the uppermost deck, exposed to the weather; (vii) the lowest deck of all was the **orlop**.

demi-culverin   A gun firing cast-iron shot of 10lb 10oz–14lb 14oz.

draught   The depth of water required to float a ship.

ebb   The falling tide.

falcon (*fawcon*)   Bronze or iron muzzle-loading gun firing cast-iron shot of *c*.2lb 2oz.

fathom   A depth (six feet) of water.

fetch   To catch, reach, attain.

fighting your ship   Handling the ship in combat.

fine   A point ahead or astern which is approximately 20° from the line a ship is sailing in: e.g. fine on the larboard quarter (see Fig. 1).

firth (Scot.)   Estuary.

fishing   A method of joining two spars together to make a longer one.

flat   A space inside a ship, especially one from which other compartments open.

flood   The rising tide.

flota (*Sp.*)   A fleet, especially applied to the convoys bringing bullion to Spain from the New World.

flotilla   A group of small warships, or warships of any size operating in coastal waters. The word is the diminutive of *flota*.

foist   A small vessel propelled by oars and sails.

footropes   Ropes suspended from the yards, on which men stood while working aloft.

forecastle   (fo'c'sle) Originally a fighting platform erected over the bows, later a deck built over the forward end of the main deck.

foremast (see **mast**)

forestay   A stay supporting the foremast from ahead.

freeboard   Minimum height of ship's side above the waterline.

futtock   A shaped piece of timber in the ship's frame at the bilge or side.

galleass   A usually three-masted warship propelled by oars and sails, with a gun deck above the rowing benches.

galliot   A small galley.

galley   (i) A warship propelled by oars and lying low in the water, originally in the Mediterranean; (ii) a ship's kitchen.

galleon   A medium-sized or large warship propelled by sails, with high upperworks but without fore- or aftercastles. They were longer and narrower than carracks.

goulet (*Fr.*)   The narrows of a channel.

grapnel (*crapnolles, grape irons, gravulles*)   A hooked or clawed piece of iron on the end of a line, used for grappling with an enemy.

grapple   To make a ship fast to another in order to board her.

ground tackle   Anchors and their cables.

gunport   An opening in the ship's side through which the gun could be fired.

gunwale   The timber beam running along the top of a ship's side and her bulwarks.

hackbut (*hakbusshes, hakebushes*)   A portable firearm, often attached to a ship's rail to support its weight. Sometimes called arquebus or harquebus.

halyard   A rope or tackle used to hoist a sail or yard.

handy   Manoeuvrable, a ship responding easily rather than sluggishly to the way it is handled.

hawser   A large (i.e. thick) rope or cable.

head sea   A series of waves and/or swell coming at a ship from ahead.

helm   The tiller (later, the steering wheel).

hoy   Square-rigged, single-masted sailing barge without oars.

hull   The main structure of a ship, to which masts, yards and all other external features are added.

hulk   A type of merchant vessel developed from the cog.

jolly-boat (*jollywat*)   The captain's small boat.

keel   The principal timber at the bottom of a hull and running the length of a ship. From it extends the rest of the structure.

keep   The innermost stronghold of a military castle.

kenning (*Scot.*)   The distance at which land can first be seen from the sea, usually reckoned at fourteen miles.

knee   An angled bracket installed to strengthen the intersection of other timbers in shipbuilding.

knights (*knyghtes*)   Pieces of timber bolted to beams, with a number of sheaves attached. A component of the tackle required to increase purchase or lifting power.

lading   Loading a ship's cargo.

laid down   The act of laying the keel, the first step in building a ship.

larboard   The left side of a ship looking forward. Eventually changed to 'port' to avoid confusion with 'starboard' when giving the helmsman steering orders in noisy weather.

lateen   A triangular sail with its origins in the Levant and set on an unusually long yard.

latitude   A position on a line parallel to the Equator, indicated by degrees North or South of that baseline.

lead   The weight on a marked line, used to take soundings: i.e. determine the depth of water beneath a ship.

league   A distance of three miles.

lee   (i) The direction towards which the wind is blowing; (ii) the water sheltered from the wind by the shore or the ship: hence (iii) a **lee shore** is one towards which the wind is blowing, a great hazard to any ship getting too close.

lerret   A double-ended fishing boat typical of the Dorset coast, with a sharp stem both fore and aft, propelled and steered by four or six oars.

lie-to   Holding the ship's position as a precaution in certain stormy conditions; e.g. when too close to a lee shore. Usually means dropping anchor if soundings suggest this is feasible.

lifts (*lyftes*)   Ropes extending from the masthead to the yard-arm.

line   (i) **line abreast** A formation of ships in which they sail side by side; (ii) **line ahead** a formation of ships in which one or more follows a leader and imitates his movements; (iii) **line of battle** a combat formation in which ships form a straight line which may be either line ahead or line abreast.

lodesman   Original name for a ship's pilot.

Low Countries   The Netherlands, the Spanish Netherlands (modern Belgium) and Flanders, which extended west from Antwerp to the edge of the Calais Pale.

luff   (i) The windward edge of a fore-and-aft sail; hence (ii) to **luff** is to turn into the wind; (iii) **luff hook** (*love hokes*), the hook by which a **luff tackle** – consisting of double and a single block – was secured to a strong point.

magazine   A storage space for explosives.

mast   A vessel might have anything between one and four of them: (i) **foremast**, the one nearest the bows; (ii) **main-mast**, the tallest and usually next behind the foremast; (iii) **mizzen mast** (*myson, mysson*), the one next behind the main-mast; and (iv) the **bonaventure mast** nearest the stern (see Fig. 2).

master   (i) the captain of a merchant ship; (ii) the officer responsible for navigating and sailing a warship.

meridian   The vertical lines on a chart, which cross lines of latitude and the Equator at right angles. They are more usually known as lines of longitude, and they indicate how many degrees East or West of Greenwich (and its meridian) a vessel (or anything else) is. Though Ptolemy's *Geographica* of AD 150 carried such lines, his understanding of them was limited. No certain way of establishing longitude was known until John Harrison's chronometer appeared; it was officially recognised as a vital instrument in 1765.

mess, messing   (i) A unit of men aboard a warship; (ii) the arrangement by which they receive their victuals.

miche (*myches*)   The mounting for a **base**, a small gun firing lead shot or iron shot encased in lead.

minion   A cast-iron or bronze muzzle-loading gun firing cast-iron shot of $3\frac{3}{4}$lb.

morris pike (*morys pycke/pyke*)   A staff of between sixteen and twenty feet long, with a sharp point and a blade on the end; a weapon for thrusting at an enemy. 'Morris' was a corruption of Moorish.

Four-masted ship *c.*1514

After Loades

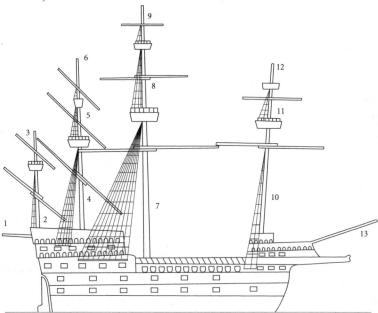

1. Outligger
2. Bonaventure/bonaventure mizzen mast
3. Bonaventure topmast
4. Mizzen mast
5. Mizzen topmast
6. Mizzen topgallant
7. Mainmast
8. Maintopmast
9. Maintopgallant
10. Foremast
11. Foretopmast
12. Foretopgallant
13. Bowsprit

murderer A gun firing various forms of shrapnel with the intention of killing and maiming crew rather than seriously damaging their ship.

muzzle-loader A gun loaded from the muzzle, as distinct from a breech-loader.

nautical mile 2,026 yards, compared with the 1,760 yards of a mile ashore. It varies in length fractionally, depending on its latitude, being shortest (as above) at the Equator.

neaps (see **tide**)

nef (*Fr.*) A vessel or ship.

oakum Rope fibres used for caulking.

onshore Towards or on the shore.

orlop (see **deck**)

parrel A loose collar of rope or iron which can slide up and down the mast, taking the yard with it.

pennant A long tapering flag, generally flown from the masthead of a warship.

pharos (*Lat.*) Lighthouse.

pinnace (i) A large ship's boat, usually towed astern when not in use; (ii) a small warship rigged like a galleon.

pitch (*piche*) Tar used with oakum for caulking.

poleis (*poleys, polies*) Pulleys.

poop, pooped The poop was a short deck built over the after end of the quarter-deck. If a huge sea came in over the stern a vessel was pooped and frequently sank under the weight of water.

prize A captured vessel. Prize money was distributed to the victorious crew according to a regulated allotment based on rank, and to the value of the vessel plus its cargo if it was carrying any. Admirals took their cut, too, even when they were not present at the capture.

purser The officer responsible for victuals aboard ship.

purveyor Official ashore who purchased provisions and other supplies on behalf of the Navy.

quarrel Otherwise known as a **bolt**, and fired from a crossbow.

quarter (i) The sides of a ship's stern; (ii) an indicator of anything lying outboard of that part of the vessel (see Fig. 1).

quartermaster The master of a ship's chief assistant in handling the vessel.

rade (*Fr.*) A roadstead, an anchorage; e.g. Rade de Brest, which is a spacious and sheltered anchorage outside that port.

ratlines Light lines strung horizontally across the shrouds, which can be climbed like a ladder, enabling men to go aloft.

rider An extra beam added to strengthen the internal planking in the hold.

rigging The ropes supporting and controlling the masts and spars.

roads, roadstead A usually safe anchorage just outside a port.

rope walk A building or space in which rope is manufactured.

rowbarge A small warship using oars as well as sail.

rudder Usually hinged on a vessel's sternpost, controlled by the helm to change the course of a ship.

run To sail with the wind behind you.

rutter (*Fr. routier*) Sailing directions, ancestor of the nautical almanack.

sail It may be set square, at an angle to the ship's sides, in which case she is **square-rigged**; or she may be rigged **fore and aft**, with the sails following the line between her stem and her stern. In a square-rigged vessel the (i) **foresail** is the lowest sail (the fore course) set on the foremast; (ii) a **headsail** is set forward of the foremast; (iii) a **mainsail** is the lowest sail (the main course) set on the main-mast; (iv) a **studdingsail** is a light sail set on booms projecting outboard; (v) a **topsail** is hoisted on the topmast above the main course; (vi) a **spritsail** is set on a yard below the bowsprit in order – as in the case of the studdingsail – to increase speed when yet more is required than a normal spread of canvas is producing. See also **lateen**.

saker   Cast-iron or bronze muzzle-loading gun, firing cast-iron shot of *c*.5lb.

serpentine   A breech-loading gun which came in different sizes, usually mounted.

shakedown   The period immediately following a ship's commissioning, when her crew familiarise themselves with her (and their) distinctive foibles. It usually occurs on a short cruise not far from the home port.

shallop   (i) A type of small warship; (ii) a type of ship's boat.

sheave (*shever, shivers, shyver*)   The wheel on which a rope runs in a block.

sheer   The upward curve of a ship's hull along her length, visible from her waterline.

sheets   Ropes attached to the bottom corners of sails to hold the clews in place.

ship   A square-rigged vessel with three or more masts.

shoal, shoalwater   A sandbank or dangerously shallow water.

shrouds   Stays supporting the mast from the sides.

slack water   The period between tides when little or no flow occurs. It lasts for about twenty minutes each side of low and high water.

slip   A surface sloping down to the water's edge, which allows a craft to be moved up and down for and after repair, or for any other reason.

soundings, to take   Ascertaining the depth of water by using a leadline.

springs (see **tide**)

spritmast   A small spar projecting from and above the bowsprit in order to carry some heraldic device.

squadron   The number of warships that can be comfortably commanded at sea by one senior officer. A battle fleet might contain two or more squadrons, with an admiral in overall command.

square-rigged (see **sail**)

starboard   The right side of the ship, looking forward.

stay   (i) An item of rigging which supports a mast from ahead or astern;

(ii) **to stay** is to tack: hence (iii) a ship **in stays** is pointing into the wind when going onto the alternative tack (going about); and (iv) to **miss stays** is to fail in the manoeuvre, consequently falling back onto the original tack.

stem   A timber rising from the keel and forming the centre of the bows.

sternpost   A timber rising from the keel at the stern, supporting the rudder and the rest of the stern's structure.

step   (i) A socket built on the keel, in which the base of a mast rests; (ii) the mast is **stepped** when its heel is fitted into the step and the entire spar is raised.

stockfish   Dried cod or other white fish. An alternative method of preservation was by salting them to produce **saltfish**.

stream   The tide or current.

strike   (i) To lower a mast or sails; (ii) to lower a ship's colours, signifying surrender.

supercargo   Strictly speaking, a merchant or someone else connected with a vessel taking passage for business or other reasons. Loosely used of any passengers in a vessel whose principal purpose is to transport cargo.

swell   A pronounced undulation of the sea caused by high winds, on a much larger scale than waves. Generally speaking, an ocean swell is even more impressive than one which develops in an enclosed seaway (such as the Channel). The ones in the great Southern Ocean are said to be often terrifying.

tack   (i) The act of changing a ship's direction so that the wind, having blown on one side of her, then blows on the other, this being a means of making progress to windward by sailing in a series of dog-legs; (ii) the course held by such a vessel beating to windward, on the starboard or the larboard tack.

tackle   (i) Rigging or gear generally; (ii) a purchase contrived with cordage and at least two blocks; (iii) **ground tackle**, anchors and their cables.

tall   (i) A **tall ship** was one with high fore- and aftercastles; (ii) **tall men** were stout-hearted, reliable fellows.

target   A small shield.

tide   (i) The regular rise and fall of sea level, with approximately twelve hours forty minutes between one high (or low) tide and the next; inland seas such as the Mediterranean and the Baltic, however, are virtually tideless; (ii) a **spring tide** produces the largest rise and fall of water; (iii) a **neap tide** produces the smallest tidal range. Both neaps and springs occur twice every lunar month.

tiller A bar issuing from the top of the rudder, by which a ship was steered.

top (i) A platform at the top of the lower mast, so as to spread shrouds running up to the topmast; (ii) **fighting top**, or **topcastle**, a platform (invariably with sides) from which marksmen could fire guns or arrows from a height at the enemy's deck; (iii) **topmast**, the extension of the foremast, main-mast and mizzen mast; (iv) **topgallant**, an extension of the foretopmast, maintopmast and mizzentopmast, or a square sail set on the topgallant mast above the **topsail** (see Fig 2).

trireme A Mediterranean fighting galley with three banks of oars; the classic warship of the Greeks and Romans among others.

waft To waft was to escort a convoy, the escort vessels being known as wafters.

waist The midships part of the main deck, not covered by either forecastle or quarter-deck.

warping A laborious method of getting a ship out of an anchorage with no wind or tide to assist her. It needed a lot of musclepower applied to ropes or oars, though anchors might also come into it, and progress was always very slow.

way The movement of a vessel through the water. A ship lost way as she slowed to a stop.

wherry (i) A passenger-carrying rowing boat on the Thames; (ii) a small and shallow-draught trading vessel plying the Norfolk Broads.

weather A reference to the direction from which the wind is blowing, the opposite of lee: hence (i) the **weather side**, on which the wind blows; (ii) the **weather gage**, the position always sought by ships engaging an enemy, to windward of him. To **weather** was to get to windward of a ship or other feature.

weigh The act of raising the anchor.

whipstaff The vertical bar attached to the tiller, which was attached to the rudder; the helmsman steered by moving the whipstaff.

wind Anything to **windward** is in the direction from which the wind comes.

wing The position taken up by warships on the flanks of a convoy or a battle fleet. They were the ones most exposed, deliberately, to hostile action.

yard (*yerd*) (i) A spar set horizontally on a mast to accommodate the spread of a sail: hence (ii) **yard-arm** at the end of a yard.

I

Business in Great Waters

They were keeping an eye lifted for the Scotsman, on a dirty July day off the Goodwin Sands. There, four miles out from Deal on the coast of Kent, was the most notorious hazard in English waters and one of the most treacherous anywhere; the ship-swallower, the widow-maker that every mariner feared. The Goodwins had two fathoms of sea surging over them at high tide on a calm day, but at low water they were exposed as a great and menacing obstacle, a little over four miles wide and just over ten miles long, riddled with narrow channels and little creeks where perverse tidal currents swirled; and if you walked across them before the sand had dried out, it felt as if you trod on a living creature, which would suck you into its depths if you stood still. In any conditions at all this place was lethally dangerous to all shipping, as the ribs and mast stumps of the principal victims, which were also exposed, forever testified. The most deadly thing of all was the storm coming at it from the east, at whatever state of the tide, when the great green seas would break upon the Goodwins and climb to the height of a mast, and vessels could be dragged for miles until – their timbers sprung by the impact, their sails torn to ribbons and cracking like whips in the howling wind, their spars hanging over the side in tangles of rigging – they fell off the edge of the sands into deep and raging water; and took their crews with them much more often than not.

Paradoxically, this deathtrap also provided the protection which usually made the Downs, the stretch of water between the Goodwins and the coast, a haven for shipping in filthy weather; but you needed to know this sea well, or at least have a good pilot aboard, to work your way carefully into its relative safety through the Gull Stream if you approached from the north, or round the South Foreland if you came the other way.

Yet even the Downs could be treacherous and no shelter at all, if an easterly gale was wild enough. The most characteristic sound anywhere in this corner of the Channel, except on an extremely tranquil day, was the thunder of a breaking sea, the dull, deep roar of the surf; the most visible signs of danger were the long lines of heavy rollers and the smoking clouds of spray, the sea curling and tumbling around the shoals. These were the things that told you to beware, because the Goodwins were only biding their time.[1]

Somewhere round here, the pursuers knew, they would find the Scot.

His name was Andrew Barton and they thought of him as a pirate, though his sovereign James IV rated him highly as one of Scotland's finest sea captains in peace and in war. He belonged to a distinguished and notorious family of mariners from Leith, whose long service to the Scottish Crown had earned them much favour and many rewards. There were three brothers, Robert and John as well as Andrew, and they owed their advantage in life to the favour their shipowning father John Barton had received in the 1470s from King James's predecessor, after one of Barton's vessels had been pillaged, and some of its crew killed, by a Portuguese squadron, which seized it homeward-bound from Flanders and made off with a cargo valued at £45,000, a colossal sum in the fifteenth century. The elder Barton had been given official permission to retaliate against any Portuguese shipping he came across and his sons had inherited this largesse, together with his great commercial interests ashore and afloat. They had also been granted privileges of their own that signified even more the high esteem in which they were held by King James. Robert Barton had lately visited the shrine of St James at Santiago de Compostela in north-western Spain, the holiest place in Christendom after Jerusalem and Rome, and there he had donated a silver ship and other gifts on behalf of his King. His brother John had been entrusted with transporting the monarch's illegitimate infant son to France in 1507, while Andrew had been granted considerable landholdings in Fife that had belonged to George Leslie, 2nd Earl of Rothes, from whom they were confiscated after he became a debtor of the Crown: Andrew was so much in the royal favour that he regularly played cards

---

1 The Goodwins were named after the Earl Godwine who supposedly owned land there in the eleventh century, which subsided into the sea. The Downs is thought to be derived from the French *Les Dunes*. The biggest disaster ever to occur here was in November 1703, when four warships and nearly a hundred merchantmen were wrecked, in the Great Storm that cost 10,000 seamen their lives around this country's coasts.

with his King. By now, still only a little way into the sixteenth century, all three Barton brothers were men of great prosperity: shipowners, shipbuilders and sea captains all.

The English, however, insisted that Andrew in particular was nothing better than an infernal pirate; and piracy was a topic that preoccupied anyone who had anything to do with the sea and shipping everywhere. It was practised by seafarers of every nation, often upon their own countrymen, and many other names besides Andrew Barton's were common currency along every European waterfront. The German Martin Pechelyn, from his base on the Baltic island of Fehmarn, was the greatest hazard faced by ships sailing between Bergen and Lübeck. The French Channel coast was ravaged by men like Philippe Roussel of St Malo, just as, in an earlier generation, the Coëtanlem family of Morlaix had crept out of that almost inland port to pillage an unsuspecting vessel which didn't sight them until it was too late to get away. Some reckoned that the English were the most pernicious pirates of all, and a name of theirs which still rang from the middle of the fifteenth century was that of Robert Winnington, a boastful man (and sometime Mayor of Dartmouth) who actually provoked a war between Henry VI and the powerful Hanseatic League. The Cornish coast was always dangerous to shipmasters, and Fowey in particular had long more or less lived off piracy: on one occasion which still rankled forty years after it happened, every shipowner and captain belonging to the town was arrested and had his property confiscated, but this only gave passing ships a temporary respite.

The big difficulty in dealing with piracy was that its boundaries were so vague. A pirate was not simply some swashbuckling individual with a fierce crew and a well-handled balinger – long the preferred craft of such men, with its origins in Basque whaling in the Bay of Biscay, highly regarded for its speed – and a recognised tariff of ransom money (20s for a sailor, twice as much for the master) for the unfortunates taken aboard as their prey.[2] A pirate might also be the captain of a well-loaded merchantman who, coming across what looked like a weaker vessel than his own, would decide to increase his profit for that voyage illegally. All merchant ships were armed to some extent and, while this was chiefly in order to protect themselves against predators, weapons also came in handy when the main chance turned up.

---

2 The balinger in time gave way to carvel-built vessels – just as popular with pirates – as shipbuilding techniques changed in northern Europe. See Glossary.

Another stereotype without foundation is that everyone involved in piracy was someone from the maritime version of the yeoman (or even lesser) class. One of Fowey's most notorious pirate vessels, *Mackerel*, belonged to the Duke of Exeter, who was Henry VI's Admiral of England at the time. Nor was what passed for piracy conducted wholly on the high seas. Many a ship was plundered of her cargo as she lay peacefully at anchor in harbour, by some gang putting out from the shore and helping themselves. This was a devilish difficult business to put down – Henry V was the only English King before now who had really repressed it – and part of the trouble was a totally inadequate legal system to deal with it. No man could be sentenced for piracy in England unless he admitted it in a civil action after an eyewitness had testified against him, which was traditionally the only means of redress a victim had until the fiasco was ended by Henry VIII's statute of 1536, which at last made piracy a common law offence and much more easily punishable, by death if the violation warranted it.

The Scots were no more piratical than anyone else, but it was true that Andrew Barton was not too particular about confining his depredations to the Portuguese shipping he was authorised to attack. He and Robert had effectively hired themselves out to King Hans of Denmark in his Baltic campaign against the Swedes and the Hanseatic merchant-barons of Lübeck, but Andrew had swindled the Dane by accepting his money and then stealing one of his ships. He was also on the wanted list of some Antwerp merchants after seizing a Breton vessel which was carrying their goods, and justified attacks he was beginning to make on anything that sailed, by claiming that they were all Portuguese. The English – traditional enemies of the Scots, after all – were not spared, and Barton had started to plunder their shipping along the east coast. Now, therefore, in the summer of 1511, Henry VIII of England decided that he had suffered this indignity long enough. So he ordered a naval operation against Andrew Barton, an escort which would conduct some English merchantmen safely to Zealand in convoy, a defensive tactic that had been adopted by many European nations for at least a hundred and fifty years: 'wafting', as it was known. If Barton were tempted to attack this appetising target and could be seized in the process, then so much the better.

The man entrusted with this task was Sir Edward Howard, the thirty-odd-year-old member of an aristocratic family which had a long association with the sea, both as shipowners and commanders: his grandfather

John Howard had been Richard III's Admiral of England from 1483 to 1485. The Howards were also to play an immensely influential part in Tudor power politics, being, among other things, related by blood or by marriage to two of Henry VIII's six Queens.[3] The curious thing about Edward Howard's appointment is that his elder brother Thomas, who would one day become 3rd Duke of Norfolk, was given only a subordinate role in the expedition. It was Edward who was paid £617 9s 9d from the Treasury for the fitting-out and victualling of two vessels for wafting. They were the *Barbara* (140 tuns) and the *Mary Barking* (probably smaller) and they now put to sea flying the Tudor colours of green and white, hired for the purpose from John Iseham and George Harward, their respective owners, because the King's own few ships had either been out on hire themselves to various merchants since April, or they were stuck in the royal dockyard at Portsmouth, undergoing refits or nearing completion.

Howard's tiny flotilla probably came upon Andrew Barton by accident, given that the Englishman's principal responsibility was to get the merchantmen across to the Continent without any trouble. The Scot would doubtless have been lurking somewhere in the vicinity of the Thames estuary, waiting for something profitable to emerge from or be heading towards the port of London. The sources for what happened next are sketchy, the principal one being Edward Hall's *Chronicle*, which was not published until thirty-seven years after the event. But Hall is adamant that Howard and his ships had been anchored in the Downs, that a storm was blowing and that, as a result, the Howard brothers were separated in their anchorage or shortly after leaving it. It was Thomas who spotted Barton first, smashing through the storm with two small ships of his own. One was the *Lion*, almost the same size as the *Barbara*, which Andrew and his brothers used in common whenever one or other of them needed her. The other was the even smaller *Jennet Pyrwin*, which was the ship that Andrew stole from the King of Denmark, who had been given it as a present by James IV. Hall's account, though flawed in some respects, is generally agreed to be basically accurate in its description of the engagement, so let us hear it in his words:

> The lord Howard [i.e. Thomas], lying in the Downs, perceived where Andrew was making towards Scotland, and so fast the said lord chased him that he overtook him; and there was a sore battle: the Englishmen

3 Anne Boleyn by marriage, Catherine Howard by blood.

were fierce, and the Scots defended them manfully, and Andrew ever blew his whistle to encourage his men yet, for all that, the lord Howard and his men by clean strength entered the main deck. Then the Englishmen entered on all sides and the Scots fought sore on the hatches, but in conclusion Andrew was taken, which was so sore wounded that he died there. Then all the remnants of the Scots were taken with their ship, called the *Lion*. All this while was the lord Admiral [*sic*]⁴ in chase of the bark of Scotland, called *Jenny Pirwine*, which was wont to sail with the *Lion* in company, and so much did he with other, that he laid him aboard, and fiercely assailed him, and the Scots as hardy and well-stomached men them defended, but the lord Admiral so encouraged his men that they entered the bark and slew many, and took all the other. Thus were these two ships taken, and brought to Blackwall the second day of August, and all the Scots were sent to the Bishop's place of Yorke and there remained at the King's charges, till other direction was taken for them.⁵

Hall reckoned that James IV, 'hearing of the death of Andrew of Barton, and taking of his two ships, was wonderful wroth, and sent letters to the King requiring restitution according to the league and amity'. This was scarcely surprising, given that the two nations were, for the moment, officially at peace, with a treaty to that effect. 'The King wrote with brotherly salutes to the King of Scots, of the robberies and evil doings of Andrew Barton, and that it became not one Prince to lay a breach of a league to another Prince, in doing justice upon a pirate or thief, and that all the other Scots that were taken had deserved to die by justice if he had not extended his mercy. And with this answer the Scottish Herald departed home.' There was another version of these events, composed by the Scotsman John Lesley, Bishop of Ross, which asserted that Barton had been peacefully making his way home when he was set upon by the English on Henry's orders, being caught unawares precisely because the two countries were not supposed to be at war and he thought he had nothing to fear. But it is Hall's account that posterity has preferred to accept.

There was a certain amount of tidying up to be done in the wake of this action, while the two sovereigns settled back into their fragile truce. Early in August one Richard Dyves submitted the expenses he had incurred 'by command of the lords of the Council, upon a Scot taken in

---

4 This is one of Hall's errors. Edward Howard was not made Lord Admiral until March 1513.
5 Yorke Place, Westminster, was the London home of Archbishop (subsequently Cardinal) Wolsey. It was later taken over by the King and thereafter was known as Whitehall

the Downs'. He billed Council for 'Hire of a horse to the Downs 8d, guide 4d, boat to go on board ship 8d. Three horses from Sandwich to Canterbury, Rochester and Greenwich, for self and guide and the prisoner 8s...conducting a Scot for six days 12s.' What became of the prisoner or his shipmates we do not know, but we must assume their lives were spared. The Howard brothers, meanwhile, returned to their homes and awaited further orders, which would not be long in coming. The captured *Lion* was incorporated into the English fleet but was sold on to some unspecified buyer a couple of years later, the *Jennet Pyrwin* sailing under Tudor colours until 1514, after which no more is heard of her.

Most importantly, however, Henry VIII of England had just laid down a marker to show everybody else that he meant business on the high seas.

II

THE INHERITANCE

Henry had only been on the throne two years when the Howards put Andrew Barton out of circulation. He was regarded as one of the most attractive monarchs in Europe, and a Venetian diplomat who saw him shortly after his accession on St George's Day in April 1509, prophesied that one day the whole world would talk of him.[1] The great Dutch humanist Erasmus, with whom Henry had corresponded regularly in Latin as a boy, was another admirer. In 1511 the King was still only twenty years old: handsome, slender, virile, accomplished, and quite a complicated young man. He was pious, attended Mass at least once every day, made the great pilgrimage to Walsingham barefoot for the last mile or two, believed in transubstantiation to his dying day, and had a taste for amateur theology which he was to air when Martin Luther (whom he detested) appeared on the scene. He was a gifted musician with a good singing voice, able to play the lute and other instruments much more than tolerably well, interested enough in the art to recruit the best singers in the land to the choirs of the chapels royal.

But there was an incongruously robust side to his nature that gradually dominated his life and his behaviour: a developing gluttony that would steadily transform the supple body of his youth into the bloated coarseness of middle age; a huge taste for roistering fellowship that fostered and was encouraged by his self-indulgence; and, of course, an appetite for women which the English would eventually remember above everything else. He

---

1 Four years later, another Venetian noted that 'when he moves, the ground shakes under him'. This diplomat was also much impressed by English gentlewomen: 'When they meet friends in the street, they shake hands, and kiss on the mouth, and go to some tavern to regale, their relatives not taking this amiss, as such is the custom. The women are very beautiful and good tempered'.

delighted in outdoor pursuits and in jousting most of all, and on at least two occasions came very close to death during bouts in the tilting yard. Such dedication was obviously related to his wider interest in military matters, but Henry was not the only monarch who attended to that. What set him apart from most other sovereigns was the intensity of his interest in guns and in ships. He wanted to know everything he could find out about them from experts, and he relished the company of those who could instruct him in the smallest details. In particular, he liked to hob-nob with seamen. He also liked to receive pictures of ships (and did so regularly), which were guaranteed a place on his palace walls; and he was the proud owner of a very rare European tidal almanack. Twice during his reign, he struck gold coins – a ryal and an angel – bearing images of ships.

He often left London in order to keep abreast of maritime affairs in various ports, where he could interrogate people whose profession was the sea, and observe for himself the conditions in which they served. Typical was his response to a decline in the annual visit of the Flanders galleys, the fleet of Venetian ships which, since the fourteenth century, had sailed each year from the Adriatic and the Mediterranean laden with spices and other luxuries obtained by the Serenissima's merchants from the East, which they then sold on in the markets of northern Europe. They were known as Flanders galleys because that was their principal destination, but they habitually put into Southampton en route, in order to make what profit they could out of Englishmen. So regular were their seasonal comings and goings that they obtained their own plot of land in the churchyard of North Stoneham, just outside the city, where any recently deceased Venetian could be given a decent Christian burial; and their sailors even did odd jobs around Southampton when local labour was in short supply. Almost exactly coinciding with Henry's accession, however, was the beginning of a struggle for the republic's survival against the forces of the Holy Roman Empire, and an early casualty was the Flanders voyage, which was discontinued until 1518. The first time the Venetians dropped anchor again in England, Henry was awaiting them, a gesture which was doubtless motivated by sound Tudor mercantile instincts. But the young King went further, and it is clear that his maritime interest was also aroused. 'He was banqueted on board the flag-galley, royally decorated with tapestry and silks, while the crews performed feats on slack ropes suspended from the masts for his entertainment, and fireworks were let off, *and at his request the guns were fired again and again to mark their range.'*

Henry made other excuses to get down to the waterfront. A little earlier, he had attended the commissioning of one of his own vessels, and there his great natural exuberance came bubbling to the surface. 'On the Thursday', reported the French envoy, 'the King acted as pilot, and wore a sailor's coat and trousers made of cloth of gold, and a gold chain with the inscription *Dieu et mon Droit*, to which was suspended a whistle, which he blew nearly as loud as a trumpet.'[2] Moreover, this sailor-sovereign liked to supervise naval matters personally whenever possible. A list of shipping which had been hired on his behalf in 1512 was corrected in Henry's own hand, but that was only one example of his tight control. A stream of orders invariably flowed from the throne whenever the royal ships were at sea, naval commanders being required not only to pay close attention to them but also to 'advertise the king's majesty' at every fresh turn of events – in modern language, to keep him directly informed.

One other thing was exceptional about Henry VIII. Towards the end of his reign he had acquired something of a reputation as a ship designer, though this talent may have been exaggerated (modern authorities are careful to insert 'allegedly' into the claim) by courtiers and others anxious to please. But Eugene Chapuys, the imperial ambassador at Henry's court in 1541, who had no reason to curry favour, informed Charles V that the King had sent to Italy for three shipwrights who were expert at making galleys, though Chapuys believed 'he will not set them to work as he has begun to make ships with oars of which he himself is the architect'. These were, in fact, rowbarges, vessels of only 20 tuns without an upper deck, commendable chiefly because they were more man-oeuvrable than vessels under sail in calm waters; and Henry was certainly an enthusiast for them.

Romantics with a weakness for astrology might have argued (and some doubtless did) that his wider enthusiasm for naval matters was inevitable, given that he was born beside the water in Greenwich. But what amoun-ted to at least a small obsession in the King did not at all follow from the circumstances of his birth. His father Henry VII was not destined to be remembered as a warrior king in the mould of Henry V even though, as Henry Tudor, he changed the course of the English monarchy for well over a century by defeating Richard III at Bosworth Field in 1485. The

2 The whistle, precursor of the 'boatswain's call' on which orders are piped aboard warships, was a badge of authority as much as anything, worn by boatswains and everyone else ranking above them.

Tudor family had its roots in Anglesey and the father Henry was born in Pembroke Castle, but he spent much of his adolescence and early manhood as a refugee in Brittany and Normandy, in order to escape the political machinations going on at home between the houses of York and Lancaster: it was from Harfleur that he set sail for the campaign that put him on the throne after the battle in Leicestershire. His reign was to be notable for fiscal policies which, among other things, laid the foundations for the meticulous accountancy of the Tudors, and he was above all attentive to his country's commercial interests: his only punitive expedition, to Sluys, which was the port for prosperous Bruges in the estuary of the Scheldt and which had become a piratical stronghold by 1492, was undertaken in the interests of English commerce; he was not belligerent on behalf of 'the realm' or to glorify his own reputation. But he was mindful enough that England's prosperity was uniquely related to the sea, to pay just slightly more attention to maritime matters than many of his predecessors: he encouraged the increase of merchant shipping by offering bounties when new vessels were built.

His most telling contribution was made ashore on the south coast. Kings' ships had used Portsmouth harbour since the twelfth century, and it had briefly been a galley base under King John, but Henry VII was the first monarch to spend much money on its defences, uneasily aware that any union of France and Brittany might increase the threat to his security, in which case it would be wise to have a fully functioning naval base on the south coast. In line with this thinking, he ordered the construction of its first dry-dock in 1495 on the south-western tip of Portsea Island. Traditional shipbuilding and repair had always been at the mercy of the tides. Ships were built above the high-water mark in creeks and estuaries throughout the land, and when they needed repair they were hauled as far as possible up the shore or the river bank just before the tide ebbed, the shipwrights operating only when they were high and dry, though eventually a temporary protective wall or dam was built around them at low water so that some work could proceed even during the flood. Henry Tudor, however, took this last device much further with the excavation of a permanent cavity below the high-water mark which was closed by dock gates, possibly removable rather than hinged, and certainly sealed with clay and stones; and these were supplemented by a primitive form of pump to get the water out, which may have looked like a bucket dredge powered by horses.

The work in Portsmouth was supervised by Robert Brigandine,

'yeoman of the Crown' and newly appointed Clerk of the King's Ships, an office that was once occupied by an archdeacon of Taunton and which went back to 1214, but so far without any permanency whatsoever: years might elapse with the post untenanted, depending upon a sovereign's interest in his ships, which was infrequently roused. Brigandine is thought to have taken advice on the construction from the architect Sir Reginald Bray, who had directed certain works at Windsor Castle and designed Henry's own chapel in Westminster Abbey. What made the dry-dock a matter of some urgency now was the need to repair two big men o'war, both of them carracks, with high superstructures towering above the bows and the stern: the four-masted *Regent* of 1,000 tuns, which had been laid down at Smallhythe in 1487 and completed within a couple of years, and the slightly smaller three-masted *Sovereign*, which had been commissioned in 1488. Under the old methods, they were simply too large to be hauled by horsepower up a shoreline and were therefore effectively irreparable if any major work needed doing to the hull below the waterline. But now the *Sovereign* could be overhauled and patched up by shipwrights operating for nine full months without interruption, and when the *Regent* followed her into the dry-dock she occupied it even longer.

These, and the three other much smaller royal ships that Henry VII left his son, – *Mary and John*, *Sweepstake* and *Mary Fortune*, the last two no more than 80 tuns apiece – were something of a start in life for the young man, but there was little sign of a sound nautical appreciation being passed from one generation to the next. The first Tudor had been so unaware of fundamental naval strategy that he left the Irish Sea unprotected and therefore failed to intercept the invasion fleet of the pseudo-Plantagenet Lambert Simnel, whose insurrection in consequence was not put down until he reached the English Midlands. Nor did Henry do much to secure the safety of the seas for mercantile interests apart from supplying wafters for Merchant Adventurer convoys, usually using someone else's vessels and charging the tradesmen for the privilege. It is quite possible that no royal man o'war fired a single shot in anger, or boarded any adversary, from start to finish of Henry Tudor's twenty-four years on the throne. What's more, in the eighty-seven years between 1422 and and 1509, only six new ships of any kind were built for an English monarch; but Henry VIII would do much better than that.

The father had amassed a personal fortune of £1,800,000 before he died and the younger Henry at once began to spend it, an appreciable amount being disposed of in the first ten years of his reign on his preoccupation with ships. By then he had already constructed seventeen new men o'war, with another dozen vessels bought or requisitioned for his naval purposes. One of his earliest acts was to pay John Hopton of London £1,000 for one vessel and £500 for another, but these were paltry sums compared with those he would disburse later, when he began to build ships of his own. *Henry Grâce à Dieu* which, together with *Mary Rose*, was to be his greatest pride and joy, was completed in 1514 after costing him more than £8,000. The running charges for every ship mounted up, too: it cost over £1,000 to keep the *Regent* going for three months.

Yet there is no evidence that Henry reached the throne with some grand design for the creation of a Navy Royal such as the English had never seen before, together with the apparatus to run it efficiently not only while he was in charge but for the benefit of his successors. Though both these things would come to pass in due course, and he would be responsible for them, they were neither premeditated nor were they accidental. They resulted from a fusion of Henry's deepest interests with his calculating, expansive, impetuous, opportunistic and incorrigibly ambitious nature. It is likely that he became King with only one thing clearly in mind apart from the dynastic imperative to father a son who would ensure that the Tudor bloodline continued to rule England. That apart, he wished, above all other things, to be the King of Kings in Europe; or, as one of his courtiers put it more preciously in those first heady days when the greyness of his father's reign was already beginning to fade in the dazzle cast by this bright new star in the firmament, he sought only 'virtue, glory, immortality!' His naval policies and passion for royal men o'war were merely means to this end.[3]

Above all, he wished to subdue the French, in the rivalry that had bedevilled the two peoples since the Norman conquest and settlement of England in 1066. For almost a hundred years after that, England was a Norman fiefdom, subject to all the codes and authority that regulated life in Bayeux, in Caen, in Rouen and elsewhere in Duke William's holdings across the Channel. But in time an acquiescent Anglo-French monarchy emerged from the early hostility and resistance of the native English. A pendulum then began to swing the other way when Henry

3 The courtier was Lord Mountjoy, Master of the Mint and Queen Katherine's Chamberlain, writing to Erasmus fulsomely. 'All England,' he added, 'is in ecstacies.'

II of England, the first of these hybrid monarchs to be fully literate, married the divorced wife of the French King Louis VII in 1152. She was Eleanor of Aquitaine, an independent-minded woman of great character, too vivacious and lively by far for the piously dull Louis (she once complained that she'd married a monk, not a king) and she conceived their son only after an anxious Pope – with allegiances and balances of power to worry about on his own account – had put pressure on both of them to perform.

Eleanor had one other great attribute in any suitor's eyes (and there were many eager candidates as soon as divorce was in the offing). She was the richest heiress in France and her union with Henry was therefore to increase his French possessions extravagantly. From his mother he had already inherited Normandy and Maine, from his father Anjou and Touraine, and from his new wife he now became ruler also of Poitou, Limousin and Gascony. Effectively, Henry II of England had also become sovereign lord of all western France from Normandy to the Pyrenees. And that would not be the end of English expansion. When the aggressive Henry V mounted the English throne in 1413 he at once claimed the French Crown too, and consolidated his position by military means, most notably at Agincourt, and by matrimony with Charles VI's daughter, Catherine. He did not long outlast this union, but by the time he was done in 1422, a very English King ruled over two-thirds of all geographical France.

Then the pendulum swung back again. The initial impetus came from another remarkable Frenchwoman, Jeanne d'Arc of Lorraine, whose reputation, including her betrayal and subsequent death, has been much glamourised by romantics but who unquestionably achieved two things: one was the defeat of the English at Orléans, at Patay and at Troyes; the other was the revival – some would say the birth – of French patriotism. As a consequence of this sterner and more belligerent nationalism, the English were obliged to make concessions with a Treaty at Arras (in 1435) and a truce at Tours (from 1444 to 1446) and, gradually, their French acquisitions reverted to the original owners. Brittany was lost in 1449, Normandy in 1450, Gascony (and its bountiful vineyards, *hélas!*) in 1453. That event saw the end of the intermittent Hundred Years War between the two nations – and the French were beginning to see themselves as a nation at last, instead of a parcel of principalities and dukedoms. Of that once tremendous Continental heritage, Henry Tudor was able to leave to his son nothing in France thirty years later but the Pale of Calais, which was not nearly enough to satisfy the younger man's appetites and ambitions.[4]

Mindful of illustrious precedents that Henry V had established, and with a temperament that would take second place to no man, the new English sovereign, scarcely out of adolescence, promised himself that he would restore some of his country's former glory on the Continent. He might even get Part II of the Hundred Years War going again. Making war, after all, was a principal business of Kings, as was the exercise of chivalry with arms. And then, as a Christian sovereign, he ought not to forget his wider responsibilities to the faith, to the threat from Islam, which might call for another crusade. This, or something like it, was how Henry's mind would have been working when he reached the throne.

Across the Channel, Louis XII of Orléans had been ruling the French for eleven years when Henry became King. One of his first acts had been to repudiate his Valois Queen of more than two decades and marry his predecessor's widow, the strong-minded and cultivated Anne de Bretagne. Her first marriage had been a political masterstroke by Charles VIII, for it brought together for the first time in their history the self-consciously Celtic Bretons and the much more diffuse French; among other things, this union gave the latter a direct naval and mercantile access to the Atlantic such as they had never before enjoyed. Far less astute was Louis XII's pursuit of the old French dream of expansion into Italy, with a particularly intense desire to possess Naples. There were competitors – or at least nay-sayers – so that at one time or another in a single generation the French were fighting the Papacy, the Milanese, the Venetians, the Swiss, the Spanish, the Flemings and the Holy Roman Emperor in their eagerness for this chimera. 'The old story repeated itself. Facile successes were followed by grave complications, by defeats in Italy, at last even by the invasion of France. Milan was conquered and lost, Naples was shared with Spain and then lost, Venice was driven from her mainland possessions by a league of France, Papacy and Empire, and then restored by a papal confederation against France. In the unstable atmosphere of Italian diplomacy the friend of today became the foe of tomorrow.' Europe at the turn of the fifteenth and sixteenth centuries

4 The Pale of Calais was an enclave of irregular shape which ran from the coast between Gravelines and Cap Blanc Nez almost as far to the south as the town of Ardres, some nine miles inland. It was about 120 square miles in area, with a population of 12,000. There was a similar Pale in Ireland attendant on Dublin, within which the English were most deeply entrenched. In both countries, those who dwelt outside these enclaves were therefore said to be 'beyond the Pale'.

was a messy place and Louis had managed to manoeuvre France straight into the deep end. Not that he didn't have something to his credit in these exchanges: he may have introduced rice-growing to the plains of Lombardy. And because France was not at odds with itself during his reign, as it too often had been in its past, because its agriculture prospered, its taxation was light and its justice appeared to be evenly applied, he was destined to be known by the laudable but colourless sobriquet '*le Père du peuple*'.

Henry VIII would have to take into consideration other big Continental players as he mounted the throne. No fewer than five Popes sat in Peter's place while he was King of England and all had roles to play in the wider politics of Europe, which no secular ruler could ever ignore. With three of them, however, Henry was to be on more intimate terms than the others. Leo X proclaimed him Defender of the Faith for Henry's attack upon Luther when he was still a scrupulously obedient Catholic of thirty. Clement VII was the less amenable pontiff, whom Henry petitioned for an annulment of his marriage to Katherine of Aragon; and Clement's successor Paul III it was who excommunicated him when the King went his own way regardless of the Pope's refusal to co-operate, married Anne Boleyn, and began building his own Church of England in defiance of and enduring separation from Rome.

Henry's rejection of Katherine inevitably antagonised another of Europe's big hitters, the Holy Roman Emperor Charles V, who happened to be her nephew. Charles had Castilian, Aragonese and Austrian Habsburg blood, was born in the Netherlands, and in his own right was heir to all Spanish possessions, including those recently acquired in Mexico and Peru. But he achieved his imperial role in 1520 in succession to his grandfather Maximilian I as a result of election by the seven leading princes – four secular and three ecclesiastical – of Germany, who had discharged this function since the middle of the fourteenth century. The position had been created, with Charlemagne as its first occupant, after the ancient Roman Empire collapsed into the Dark Ages and the Church found itself without a powerful guardian, such as it had enjoyed since Constantine the Great first championed Christianity in AD 313. Holy Roman Emperors were, quite simply, installed to protect the interests of the papacy by force of arms if need be, and many of their energies and resources were spent in doing so. Few positions can ever have bestowed so high a personal distinction under such a burden of expectation and responsibility.

There was one other figure whom Henry could scarcely ignore, and he was James IV of Scotland, the next-door neighbour with whom the English had been seriously at odds for two hundred years. Each nation had, in fact, been substantially changed by quite different events at almost the same moment much earlier in their histories. For the English, life was never to be the same again after the Norman Conquest, which added an extra element to an already rich mongrel mixture of people. For the Scots – another ethnic hotch-potch, of Picts, Scotti (who were Irish in origin), Britons and invaders from Scandinavia – the significant change had occurred nine years before the Battle of Hastings, when the Gaelic prince Malcolm Canmore defeated Macbeth at Lumphanan and triggered the social change from a tribal confederacy of clans in which kinship was the crucial element, to a feudal structure with a different form of hierarchy and the understanding that all land was royal land. Not that clan loyalties were dissipated by a nominal transfer of allegiance to the first King of Scots: the two fealties would always coexist uneasily and from time to time the clansmen fought the King's men. On one notorious occasion James found it expedient to take a castle belonging to the MacDonalds of Islay and install his own garrison, but the moment he was out of sight, the MacDonalds reoccupied Dunaverty and hanged its new royal governor. There were many elements in such animosities, including the bitterness of the poor and dispossessed for the high and mighty and securely remote. Somewhere near the bottom of it all was probably the ageless contempt of the Highlander for the Sassenach of the Scottish Lowlands.

For a while after the eleventh-century upheavals, the neighbouring countries lived more or less peacefully under separate monarchs until, in 1286, Edward II, the first English King to think seriously of expanding his realm to the north and the west, tried to make the Scottish sovereign his vassal and Scotland an English appendage. He got his comeuppance from Robert Bruce at Bannockburn in 1314; and thereafter the neighbours were at each other's throats more often than not. There were periods of peace, inevitably, for warfare requires energy, which is not inexhaustible: most recently there was a treaty of 1502 which promised indefinite peace, and twelve months later both parties were still warm enough to seal the bond with James's marriage to Henry's elder sister Margaret. But the majority of the sixteenth-century English saw Scotland 'as a country which they must patronise, a poor shabby sort of place whose ill-clad inhabitants turned a dishonest penny by robbing one another, harrying the Borders, and making dishonourable raids upon England in the interest of France'. And, indeed, the Scots did have their Auld Alliance with the French, which went back to the twelfth century, when both countries felt threatened by Henry II and his immediate Angevin successors. It had been renewed as recently as 1492.

The man who signed both these documents and then became Henry VIII's brother-in-law was the son of a Stuart King and a Danish princess, and he had come to the Scottish throne in 1488 as, in some sense, a fifteen-year-old regicide and parricide. As a much smaller boy he had been pitched willy-nilly into a dark family struggle for supremacy between his father James III and his uncle Alexander, Duke of Albany, the King's younger brother. Albany certainly coveted the Crown, which he was prepared to scheme for with English help, and in the untidy circumstances of the child's upbringing, not always or even very often under his father's roof, a suspicious James III came to believe that his son was under the thumb of the potential usurper; that the boy might be enthroned as a temporary puppet until Albany chose the moment to put him aside. The Scottish nobility took sides, the King's supporters hostile to anything that might allow the English to obtain a toehold in Scotland, a rebel faction becoming increasingly alienated from the King by what they regarded as high-handed vindictiveness. The matter was resolved in battle at Sauchieburn, almost within a bowshot of where Bruce had won his great victory, and the King was killed as he fled towards the Forth, where a ship was waiting to carry him to safety. Albany was no longer in the equation either, having been killed at a tournament in Paris three years earlier by, of all people, Louis XII of France.

So the adolescent James IV was secure in his new kingdom, his title ratified by his enthronement at Scone on the anniversary of Bannockburn, in a ceremony which incorporated St Fillan's bell, 'renowned for its efficacy in curing the mentally afflicted'. A few days later, he rode to Stirling to attend his father's burial in Cambuskenneth Abbey, where he undertook various penitential exercises, the most enduring of which was his acceptance of an iron belt that he wore for the rest of his life, with more weight added to it as every year passed. James was a young man of many parts, though in a rather different way from his English coeval. He eventually spoke five Continental languages as well as Latin, English and the Gaelic, attended regularly to his devotions and relished making pilgrimages, was open-handed, enjoyed music (but purely from the audience), was temperate in almost all his habits (but was a great womaniser), and a skilful jouster in the tiltyard; he was a good listener who grew into a sound judge of a counsellor's advice, and he was an extremely hard worker at everything he did, a man who attracted much loyalty. He was also very interested in ships, which may have had something to do with his maternal heritage. The first thing he did after mourning his father in Stirling, was to head for Leith to inspect the Danish vessels which his great-uncle Gerhard of Oldenburg had brought across the North Sea in at least tacit support for the rebel party.

Scotland was a nation whose destiny was as closely linked with the sea as England's. It could scarcely be otherwise in a small country with a disproportionately extensive seaboard, especially along its west coast, which was indented by a long series of sea lochs that might stretch as much as forty miles inland from the Minch or the Hebridean waters. From Sutherland, down through Wester Ross, along the length of Lochaber and Argyll, if you wished to travel more than a mile or two, then you did so by boat, just like the inhabitants of the inner and outer islands.[5] The Scots lived by the sea in another sense, fishing being a mainstay of their economy, accounting for one fifth of their exports at the start of the sixteenth century. There were therefore very good reasons why Scottish chieftains – clannish or royal – should pay attention to their shipping, both for trade and communications, and for potential hostility. And James IV was very mindful of this. Because Europe beckoned to the east of his country, whereas there was nothing but Ireland and the Atlantic Ocean to the west, most of his maritime initiatives, mercantile and naval, began in the North Sea, and Leith, nestling beneath the protective crag of Edinburgh Castle and somewhat shielded from the worst of the weather storming into the Firth of Forth, was his principal anchorage, as it had always been for his predecessors. But it had one big disadvantage apart from a degree of exposure, and that was a clutch of sandbanks across the entrance to the Water of Leith, which made the launching of large vessels difficult. So James first of all built a deepwater alternative a little further up the Forth, and for a while most of his east-coast shipbuilding took place at this Newhaven. Then a third dockyard at Pool of Airth, only eight miles south of Stirling and therefore much safer from attack, was constructed, commodious enough to handle the biggest ships afloat.

5 In the interests of clarity, topographical names recognisable today are used here. The boundaries of early sixteenth-century Strathclyde, for example, do not coincide with those of the Strathclyde which was resurrected nearly five hundred years later.

Yet even before these extensions, in 1494 he had begun making a western naval base at Tarbert on the Mull of Kintyre, and supplemented this by opening a new shipyard at Dumbarton on the Clyde. There were obvious advantages in having such facilities on both sides of the country, for they reduced the risk of Scottish seapower being totally crippled by an invader. But James's thinking also took account of the clansmen's unreliability. Once, they had exploited for their own ends the competition between the Scottish Crown and Norway to rule Shetland, Orkney and the Hebrides, and they were perfectly prepared to turn any Anglo-Scottish dispute to their own advantage, too: in 1462, John of the Isles had actually made a secret treaty with Edward IV, though he was eventually the loser and forfeited many of his lands as a result. But chieftains such as he required Kings to be always vigilant. They could drum up small armies of fiercely loyal warriors on any pretext they chose; and they had fleets of their own, galleys with high stem and sternposts which betrayed a Viking ancestry, quite unlike the generality of shipping which sailed in and out of the Forth, plying the North Sea, the Baltic and the English Channel in that last decade of the fifteenth century. And the clansmen who manned these Highland longships were the equal of any seamen in Europe.

In 1506, just four years into his perpetual peace treaty with England and three years after becoming the next English King's brother-in-law, James informed Louis XII of France that he was determined to build a fleet capable of defending Scotland against all-comers. An element in his thinking was doubtless the memory of 1502 when, in obedience to a treaty the Scots had made with Denmark, James sent some ships and troops to aid King Hans against a combination of Swedes and Norwegians, an operation that ended in humiliation. Ships that were supposed to sail were not readied in time, expected manpower never materialised, many Scots were killed in an assault on the Norwegian castle of Akershus, and James himself later admitted that his expeditionary force 'achieved less than it should have done and returned sooner than was expected'. His need to do better in future, however, was not wholly in order to erase the memory of this indignity. He had also promised Louis that the Scottish navy was at his disposal, prepared to sail anywhere at his bidding; James was becoming increasingly indebted to the French, one way or another, and needed to demonstrate his gratitude. Before long, he would be relying on them heavily for the fulfilment of his ambition.

The British Isles

N
W   E
S

0   50   100 miles

SHETLAND

Fair Isle

Kirkwall   ORKNEY

WESTERN ISLES (Hebrides)

The Minch

Pentland Firth

SUTHERLAND

Wester Ross

SCOTLAND
Lochaber

Atlantic Ocean

North Sea

Perth   Dundee   Musselburgh
Isle of May
ARGYLL   Dysart
R. Clyde   Kinghorn   *Firth of Forth*
Dumbarton   Newhaven
STIRLING   Dunbar
Tarbert   Edinburgh Leith
ROXBURGH   Berwick
North Channel   Tantallon Castle
Giants Causeway   Ayr   *R. Tweed*   Flodden Field

Carrickfergus   Kirkcudbright   Newcastle-upon-Tyne
Carlisle   *R. Tyne*
Belfast   Whitehaven   Whitby

Drogheda   Isle of Man   Scarborough
YORKSHIRE   *Flamborough Head*
Galway   Hull
Dublin   *Irish Sea*   Anglesey   LANCASHIRE
  Liverpool   *R. Humber*
IRELAND   Chester

ENGLAND   *The Wash*
Great Blasket Island   Birmingham   Lynn
  Waterford   Wexford   WALES   WARWICKSHIRE   NORFOLK   Yarmouth
R. Bandon   Cork   Worcester
  Kinsale   SUFFOLK
Bantry Bay   Milford Haven   ESSEX   Harwich
Fastnet Rock   Pembroke Castle   GLOUCESTER-   London
Dursey Head   *St. George's Channel*   Bristol   SHIRE   *R. Thames*
  R. Severn   Chatham
  Bath   *Weald*
  Bristol Channel   Lyme   Portsmouth   SUSSEX   Dover
  DEVON   Regis   DORSET   Ashburnham
  Exeter   Bridport   *FLANDERS*
CORNWALL   Plymouth   Swanage   Isle of
  Fowey   Dartmouth   Wight
Scilly Isles   The Lizard   *English Channel*

Channel
Islands   FRANCE

About the only thing he didn't need from them was a supply of fine sea captains. The Barton brothers may have been his especial favourites, but there were others in the same class: William Brownhill, David Falconer, William Merrymouth and John Merchamestone. Most feared of all on the high seas, with the possible exception of Andrew Barton, was Sir Andrew Wood of Largo, in Fife, whose ships had been waiting in the Forth to take James's father to safety, and who was to prosper more than anyone who switched sides after Sauchieburn. In consecutive years after that battle, he fought superior English forces in the North Sea for his new sovereign and beat them both times. In 1490 he had taken three English prizes into Dundee and subsequently used his captives to add some defensive works and other improvements at Largo.

When James told Louis of his plans, he was, in fact, well into a spending spree that was quite remarkable, given that his was a small country whose means were limited by a natural imbalance in its top-ography and its resources. There was fertile land down the eastern side of Scotland, and coal was mined there, while salt pans were worked along the shores. The extensive Highlands in both the east and the west, however, was intractable land on which nothing much would grow apart from heather and pasture of low quality. But in his first ten years James spent £1,482 on shipbuilding and repair, on purchasing vessels and on victualling. This seems only to have whetted his appetite, for in the year after he wrote to Louis, he spent £7,279 and, three years after that, the annual figure had risen to £8,710. Such was his enthusiasm for this form of expenditure that in a reign which lasted just twenty-five years, and which saw James's income trebled, his naval spending was sixty times greater at the end than it had been at the beginning. It had become easily the biggest drain on his exchequer.

By this means James acquired no fewer than thirty-eight ships, which could function if need be as men o'war. And he looked to France for vessels, for expertise and even for materials. He bought one ship from its owner in Le Conquet, and from the same small Breton port he ordered the building of another, which Robert Barton brought home from nearby Brest, where she was commissioned as *Treasurer*. There were not enough Scottish shipwrights to supply the expansion that James was aiming for, so he recruited three Frenchmen to direct operations in Leith, their first task being to find the necessary timber; but, the nearby Scottish forests lacking sufficient hardwood, much of the oak needed for keels and planking came from France, as did the canvas and the cordage. Within a few years, James would have three agents permanently stationed there, arranging naval stores and shipping for Scottish use.

James actually spent more than a quarter of his annual income on building the *Margaret*, a four-master of perhaps 700 tuns, completed (with a French keel) in 1505 and named after his wife. So thrilled was he by the evolution of this vessel on the stocks at Leith that he held periodic celebrations, with trumpeters and other musicians, to hail the raising of a mast, the flooding of the dry-dock so that *Margaret* floated at last: any pretext at all was good enough for a royal hurrah, vivid with gaudy draperies and gleaming with silver plate. James made his own decorative contribution to each occasion by presiding over the celebrations wearing a gold chain and a gold whistle, which was the particular insignia of an admiral among European mariners, for he liked to think of himself as such even though he does not appear to have been much of a sailor: trips down the Forth as far as the Isle of May, where the firth ends and the North Sea begins, seem to have marked the limit of his seagoing.

The year after the *Margaret* was completed in Leith, work began at Newhaven on the *Michael*, which was soon the talk of seafarers everywhere. By the standards of the time, the *Margaret* was a big ship, but *Michael*, at 1,000 tuns and needing a crew of 300 to work her, was one of the biggest vessels afloat when she was completed in October 1511. Scotland had been scoured for as much oak as possible, but a great deal of her timber had to be imported from Norway and Denmark as well as from France, which again provided most of what was needed by the Scots, including the principal shipwright, Jacques Terrell, who had directed the construction of Newhaven a mile west of Leith. But it was not simply the size of this warship that was remarkable: her armament, too, was incomparably superior to anything else in northern waters. For whereas the norm in men o'war was a few light guns and small arms to supplement bows, arrows, axes and other implements of hand-to-hand combat, *Michael* carried real artillery, such as soldiers conducting siege warfare might be familiar with. There were twelve pieces on either side of the hull, with two other heavy guns mounted in the bows and one in the stern; and these, at least, were wholly Scottish in origin, being cast by the King's Master Melter in Edinburgh. So huge were they that they needed six wagons apiece to get them down from the castle to the dock; and the ship carried 120 gunners to work them, in addition to her complement of seamen. The launching and fitting-out were memorable, with even more trumpeting and ceremony than had attended the

Margaret's commissioning. The King dined on board several times, at least once with his Queen, and stayed aboard when his Leviathan was towed out of Newhaven up to Pool of Airth for her final shakedown.

This was to be his crowning naval achievement and its import was not lost on James's brother-in-law. The English ambassador in Edinburgh, Lord Dacre, kept a close eye on proceedings as soon as it became obvious from the laying-down of *Michael's* keel that something extraordinary was happening here, and he sent regular progress reports to his sovereign: eight of her guns, he noted on one occasion, were three yards long and more, and 'will shoot a stone as much as a swan egg'. By the time she was finished, Henry VIII had come to the conclusion that he must match her with some uniquely marvellous warship of his own. He was also well aware by then that, though his principal quarrel would be with the French, the Scots would sooner rather than later revert to their historic role as a persistent thorn in England's side; they might even embark on some joint enterprise against England. The only question was, when would the peace treaty between the island neighbours, solemnised for the moment by fraternal matrimony, come to an end?

James IV and Henry VIII were almost alone in their shared fascination with ships, and in one other respect. European monarchs did not often build ships of their own, especially ships that were principally intended for war. Traditionally, 'the King's ships' might be wholly or only partly owned by a monarch, or even chartered by him to sail on his behalf, and were much more often than not intended to trade like any other merchantman, the profits going into the sovereign's own pocket and not into the national Treasury. If hostilities broke out between two countries, it was very easy to convert a merchant vessel into something that could fight another ship more or less effectively. Additional pieces of superstructure – castles, they called them, and they were often prefabricated ashore and stored until needed in action[6] – could be attached above the bows and the stern; and on these platforms would be placed guns and archers, leaving room in the waist of the ship for the marine soldiery who would engage in close combat when vessels grappled with each other, as they invariably did.

Rather than go to the great expenditure that King James lavished on his shipbuilding, therefore – and which Henry VIII would considerably

6 Hence *forecastle*, which was eventually shortened to *fo'c'sle*, the decking directly above the bows.

exceed – monarchs usually acquired whatever ships they needed by other means. Frequently they bought them second-hand, but hiring them was another common device, conducted like any other commercial transaction: the owner was paid according to the tunnage of the vessel and the length of time it spent in royal service. The rates were not generous. In 1512–14 Henry was paying 1s a tun per month and, given that he hired fifty-four ships for warfare in that period, at an average of 155 tuns apiece, it is clear that none of the shipowners was making a great fortune out of the deal. The rate was somewhat higher (15d a tun) if the vessel was a foreigner, as was often the case: in 1513 Henry recruited twenty-six Dutch hoys weighing in at between 80 and 36 tuns each. These payments were sometimes augmented in kind: the crew of a hired vessel might be provided with some extra clothing while they sailed as the King's men. And sometimes their usual shipmaster (who might well be the owner, or part-owner of the vessel, too) was allowed to continue his command; but as often as not some courtier – with or without any experience of the sea – was put aboard and in control. *Santa Maria de la Cayton*, a 200-tun Spaniard, hired at the same time as the Dutchmen, sailed on Henry's behalf with a Captain Baker in charge.

Such hirings were not by any means a one-way business: monarchs from time to time turned an honest penny by offering their own vessels for somebody else's trade. Towards the end of his reign, Henry Tudor hired out his *Sovereign* – lately overhauled in the new dry-dock at Portsmouth – to some merchants bent on a Mediterranean enterprise. She left Southampton with '469 pokes of wool, 16 bales and 7 fardels of various cloths, 1 barrel of pewter vessels, 2 barrels of tin in rods, 327 dozen calf skins and 555 tanned hides belonging to fourteen freemen of London'.[7] On a couple of similar voyages just before her refit, the same royal carrack had shipped great cargoes of wool owned by William Martyn, Thomas Wyndout, Christopher Hawes, William Herriot and various other London citizens. *Sovereign*'s principal purpose may have been to fight the King's enemies, but all shipping of this period was extremely adaptable. And it was made to work for its upkeep.

Vessels were sometimes pressed – otherwise known as being 'arrested' – into the King's service, however inconvenient their owners found it: as they obviously did, especially if the ship was lost and they received no compensation, which was the normal practice in such circumstances.

7 A poke was a bag or small sack; a fardel was a bundle or parcel. Their weights were variable.

Mostly, such shipping was used in transporting troops, horses and other animals, ordnance and other stores in time of war, though sometimes they were expected to turn to as fighting ships. The Mayor and brethren of Newcastle were once told 'to put ready four of their best ships', which were 'bound by indenture to be ready in six days, furnished, the *Elizabeth* with 50 mariners and carpenters, 40 soldiers and 20 gunners, and each of the others with 30 mariners and carpenters, 20 soldiers and 10 gunners, and with munitions and ordnance and one month's victuals; for which £200 is delivered to them in prest'. Such pressing was conducted very thoroughly, often over a wide area. In April 1513, 'Ships prested for the King in the West country by Anthony Carleton and Henry Calays' were taken from Poole and Topsham, from Dartmouth and Looe, from Lyme and Brixham, from Paignton and Dittisham, from Saltash and Fowey and elsewhere, including Totnes, which was situated on the southern edge of Dartmoor some ten miles from the sea. Between them, these places yielded thirty-nine vessels to the Crown, 2,039 tuns in all, and their owners were told to make sure they were in either Hampton (Southampton) or Sandwich by the end of that month. Or else... On another occasion when arrests were being made in the same counties, one of Henry VIII's court officials told the Admiral to keep the King informed how many of the pressed ships on his list turned up at the rendezvous as instructed, so that if any had slipped away 'to their own adventure' their masters could be punished on their return.

The Cinque Ports occupied a legendary role (now thought to be somewhat overblown) in the mobilisation of shipping by the Crown, certainly from the twelfth-century reign of Richard I and possibly earlier. The five Head Ports of the title were Hastings, Romney, Hythe, Dover and Sandwich, with the Antient Towns of Winchelsea and Rye as co-opted members from the beginning of the thirteenth century. By the time of the Tudors there were a number of subsidiary members – Folkestone, Lydd, Pevensey and others – and this entire bundle of Channel ports was under a collective obligation to supply the monarch with fifty-seven ships for a couple of weeks in the year, for whatever purposes he (or she) had in mind.[8] How and in what proportion each of the Ports produced vessels was up to them to work out between themselves. In exchange for this service, the Portsmen were allowed various benefits: exemption from certain taxation and a number of fishing rights (they

8 The Liberty of the Cinque Ports eventually included thirty-nine towns and villages, stretching from Seaford in Sussex to Brightlingsea in Essex.

were all communities that lived by fishing to a large extent); in addition to which, the Barons of the Ports – a lofty name for the shipowners – were granted the inestimable privilege of holding canopies over Kings and Queens at their coronations.

They were among the most belligerent of Englishmen, and they didn't need wars to provoke them to violence. In the fourteenth century, the men of Winchelsea and Rye once set about some ships from Fowey, because the Cornishmen would not doff their hats as they sailed by; and, at one time or another, the seamen from the Antient Towns and their shipmates from the other Ports had battled it out with vessels from Bayonne, San Sebastian, Rouen and St Malo which had been going peacefully about their lawful occasions until the Portsmen came along. But nothing could be compared to the everlasting feud of the Cinque Ports with Great Yarmouth, which had always been England's principal base of the herring fishery; its annual Fair, from 29 September to 10 November, when the fish were running most prolifically off the Norfolk coast, was even busier than Scarborough's (which lasted twice as long but was much farther from the capital), as hundreds of fishermen from all over the place landed their catches to supply the immensely profitable London market.

The origin of the feud with the Cinque Ports followed on from this. The Portsmen had been granted the right to dry their nets and salt their fish on the beach at Yarmouth, at some indistinct moment in their early days; also to send bailiffs to administer justice at the Yarmouth Fair. But as the small fishing village grew into a sizeable town, its own people resented this privilege for outsiders and hostilities began, in which the Portsmen usually gave much more than they got. Yarmouth houses were burgled, Yarmouth ships were seized (seventeen of them on one occasion, their crews finishing up in Winchelsea gaol), or else they were burned; and while inconclusive actions between the two sides were the common currency of this ongoing strife, killings were not a rarity. And even now, at the start of the sixteenth century, with the Cinque Ports well past their prime, the hostility between the two combatants still broke out from time to time, though Yarmouth boats were not the only ones that needed to look lively as they sailed along the Kent and Sussex coasts – where Henry Kite of Rye was a celebrated pillager of anything that came within reach, once disposing of cloth worth £300 that he had seized from some passing ship. He and others like him were still a force to be reckoned with.

But it is no longer as clear as it was once thought to be, what the Cinque Ports actually *did* to justify their exemptions and other privileges from the Crown. Part of the trouble is that, as was noted many years ago, 'The chroniclers of the Middle Ages generally passed over the Cinque Ports in silence.' Another is that the Portsmen's own records did not start until 1432 and suffer from a number of gaps, because some volumes have not survived the centuries: so virtually nothing is known of what they were doing to earn their tax breaks, for example, during the Hundred Years War. It has always been held that their official duty was to 'go on the king's service' and to 'keep the seas'; that is, that they were expected to offer some protection to Englishmen sailing within their range through the Narrow Seas, which stretched from the southern end of the North Sea down much of the Channel. But it now seems probable that vessels provided by the Ports were rarely employed as fighting ships (though they were when they raided Boulogne and Dieppe in 1340), but were recruited principally as transports or to do odd jobs. One of the few things we do know for certain is that thirty-three of these vessels sailed for Richard I on the Third Crusade in 1189; which would have exceeded their annual duty by many months. Another is that Dover and Sandwich were both required to supply twenty ships, each manned by twenty men (which does not suggest a military purpose), for fifteen days every year, and were also obliged to find passages (for twopence in summer and threepence in winter) when King's messengers needed to cross the Channel.

By the fifteenth century, however, the Cinque Ports were well past their collective heyday as important components in any naval strategy, and this was partly because some of the harbours – at Hastings, Winchelsea and Romney most conspicuously – were becoming more and more silted up as a result of the Channel's notorious eastward drift, or were already unusable. Such ports as were still serviceable when Henry VIII reached the throne were valuable chiefly because 'they were simply the nearest ports to France', and for that reason alone they might come in handy, as Sandwich still did for the mustering of pressed ships. But of them all, only Dover would ever figure vitally in Henry's naval calculations. The rest functioned most visibly in their dispensation of justice at special 'inquisitions'. Thus, in August 1517 at Winchelsea, a jury sitting under Sir Edward Poynings, Lord Warden of the Cinque Ports, considered 'nets called "flewys" and "tramells", fish called "cowngers", and a bale of "macez" found upon the seashore; a Flemish vessel unlawfully taken by John Morea; nets of fishermen maliciously cut; an assault; ballast thrown into the harbour; and extortion by Rauf Roo, searcher of merchandize'. The result of Sir Edward's deliberations is missing from the official transcript.

English Kings before Henry VIII were keen enough for their self-esteem to be acknowledged by foreigners at sea – from the time of King John at the end of the twelfth century, all alien vessels were required to lower their topsails as they sailed past English coasts – but scarcely any of them had any concept of a navy as we understand the word today; that is, as the seagoing arm of the nation's capacity to defend itself and/or attack its enemies. Various monarchs made small adjustments which had some bearing on naval affairs, such as the Admiral's Court which Henry I created to invigilate anything to do with foreign prizes, and to oversee litigation about maritime commerce; or the local functionaries known as Keepers of the Sea, who were required to levy merchant shipping on Henry III's behalf. Otherwise, Kings of England usually concentrated their belligerence and their self-interest on the land, and only demonstrated an interest in ships – except, of course, as a steady source of income – when it was absolutely unavoidable. Henry VI, indeed, was so uninterested in the topic that he sold off almost everything he had inherited and in one period of two years spent only £8 9s 7d on what was left.

Until Henry VIII came along, only three sovereigns out of the nineteen who had reigned since the Conquest did very much better than this. Richard I understood one basic element of naval power well enough to send a seaborne task force all the way from England to the far end of the Mediterranean, in which as many as 110 vessels may have set sail from Dartmouth; and they engaged in sea warfare when they reached the Holy Land: they were not just a fleet of landing craft. Nobody else for well over a century did anything comparable until Edward III gradually acquired a navy of forty vessels, which put the Channel out of bounds to anyone whom the English chose to exclude for the rest of his reign, after they had won one of the most significant of all naval victories at the Battle of Sluys in 1340, supposedly sinking no fewer than 190 French ships and killing 18,000 of the men aboard them.[9] But only one tenth of

9 It's curious that although the Royal Navy has named five warships to commemorate the Battle of Trafalgar between 1820 and our own times, in over seven hundred years only one vessel has ever been associated with the Battle of Sluys. She was a 'Battle' class destroyer, commissioned in 1945 and subsequently sold to the Iranian Navy.

Edward's navy was still in working order at the end of his life.

Towering above all the rest before the sixteenth century, however, was Henry V. It has been claimed that he was 'probably the first English king since Aethelred to have a proper understanding of the meaning of seapower'.[10] Not even Richard had such a grasp as Henry of seaborne invasion's tactical effectiveness, as he demonstrated by his surprise landing in Normandy in 1417, which was the springboard for his major conquests in France. He had his great sea battles, too: off Harfleur the year before, which lifted a French siege and made it possible for the invasion to take place; and then in the Baie de Seine twelve months later, when the French Admiral was captured, together with the money to pay his sailors for the next three months. But there were other things that set Henry apart from his predecessors: small, but not trifling things, like the building of a naval stores depot in Southampton; long-needed but hitherto neglected things, like his making piracy an act of high treason (and therefore carrying hideous penalties), which made home waters safer than they had ever been, or would be after him for a long time to come. He had his Big Ships, too; *Jesus*, which was a 1,000-tunner, and three other vessels of more than 500 tuns to provide the heavy punching in his fleet of forty or so. He also took delivery of *Grâce Dieu* from (probably) Southampton shipbuilders, and at 400 tuns she typified the backbone of his navy; but she put to sea only once and was accidentally destroyed by fire some years after Henry's death. And when he had gone, a familiar pattern repeated itself. Most of the navy was sold off to pay Henry's debts, the South-ampton stores depot was disposed of, the Clerk of the Ships retired and was not replaced. 'As far as the keeping of the seas was concerned, the victorious reign of Henry V was just another false dawn.' That would change quite drastically in the space of less than half a century.

---

10 Aethelred II (979–1016) is said to have mustered his navy to sail around the British Isles each year, perhaps the earliest version of 'showing the flag', and to have built up a fleet of over a hundred ships. Yet he was known as 'the Unready'.

III

A NATION DEFINED BY THE SEA

The whole point of navies was threefold. Warships existed to protect a country's interests from pirates or other predators, including invaders; they were required to convey and escort soldiers to warfare on somebody else's territory; and they added to a sovereign's 'virtue, glory, immortality' by their power, their efficiency, their achievements – and also by their capacity to make people gasp at their beauty, their resilience, their bravado in desperate circumstances, their tragedies. Of all these roles, the first was obviously the most important, and it was the island nation's maritime commerce, the principal source of its prosperity, which generally needed protection above everything else. The threat of full-scale invasion by sea was relatively infrequent (it had happened only eight times between 835 and 1485, though disruptive smash and grab raids were much more frequent), but the commerce was perpetually at risk, with all manner of enemies roaming the seas from one year's end to the next.

Much in need of naval sustenance, therefore, by the end of the fifteenth century England's commerce extended along all the coasts of northern Europe, as far as Iceland in one direction and the far end of the Baltic in another. It surged up and down the Atlantic coasts of France and the Iberian peninsula, and it went some distance into the Mediterranean. To and from most of these destinations, it was a demonstrably unbalanced trade, England's imports ranging across a wide variety of commodities, her exports being almost limited to the items of cargo carried from Southampton to the Mediterranean aboard *Sovereign* in 1505; the chief exceptions were stockfish (wind-dried cod or other white fish, which every European country traded in) and coal from Newcastle, which had been shipped to the Continent since the 1290s. By far the biggest English export at the start of the sixteenth century was wool in some shape or form, in bales of either fibre or cloth, the product of the commercial sheep farming which Cistercian monks had introduced from France in the twelfth century and on which a great deal of the national wealth was now based. At a purely local level there was prosperity, too, and none could have been greater than that enjoyed by John Winchcombe's operation at Newbury in Berkshire, which employed '200 women carders, 150 children pickers, 200 girl spinners, 200 weavers with 200 boys at the spools, 80 teasers, 50 shearers, 40 dyers and 20 fullers' in the production of kerseys, a kind of lightweight woollen cloth which was much sought after everywhere:[1] apart from direct supplies carried in English ships, German merchants would sell them on to Hungary, and Italians made a profit from them in Turkey and Greece. The foreigners, though, supplied the English with a wider range of cargoes than this – wines and spices, iron and timber, cattle and salt, rope and canvas and other necessities, as well as silks and a great variety of other luxury goods.

But the Iceland trade was unlike any other. It began with the arrival of a solitary English fishing boat in 1412, whose crew were so astonished by the quantities of cod and ling to be caught with hand-lines in those waters (especially around the Vestemann Isles), that twelve months later there were thirty boats, all frantically catching fish, then salting them so that they would survive the journey home and for some time after. The richness of these fishing grounds is suggested by the fact that Henry Tooley, an Ipswich worthy who was to prosper greatly from the Iceland trade, sent a boat up there equipped with 3,200 hooks: she was the *Mary Walsingham*, which he chartered out to fishermen for at least four seasons, despatching her to the Bay of Biscay in autumn, when the Iceland fishing was over for another year, to fetch quite different cargoes home. That English fleet of 1413 was accompanied by a merchantman, with the usual English cargo of textiles, and the following year five of these turned up, one owned by Henry V himself, who sent a bossy letter 'to the people and chief men of Iceland, to the effect that licence should be given to transact business, especially that relating to the king's own ship'. Within ten years of the inaugural visit by fishermen, the trade had become so attractive that the port of Lynn, on The Wash, had organised a guild known as The Merchants of Iceland, which was taxing its members. And

---

1 The relative prosperity was widespread except in the North of England, but Winchcombe's factory was a rarity, trade guilds opposing such concentrated operations until well into the eighteenth century. Over two hundred years earlier, however, his kerseys were thought to be the best that could be obtained anywhere.

what was so unlike England's export trade with other countries is that woollen goods, augmented perhaps by a few rods of Cornish tin and pewter vessels fashioned in London workshops and hides for leatherworkers, were soon not the only things she was selling there. Iceland was so impoverished of raw materials, including timber, having virtually nothing of her own but fish, that her people were open to everything the visitors offered.

The English boats began arriving laden with clothing, needles and thread, horseshoes, nails, pots and pans, swords and knives, pitch and tar, wax, yarn, paper, almost anything that was used in less isolated places; including foodstuffs. They brought barrels of wheat and meal, butter, honey and wine, malt for beer-making and beer itself from English breweries. There was a recognised barter rate going, in which three codfish (which are large) could be traded for a pair of cheap shoes. By the second half of the fifteenth century, the English effectively monopolised the Iceland trade, their fishing boats setting out from every east-coast port between Whitby in Yorkshire and Dunwich in Suffolk, which one day would vanish beneath the waves. The merchantmen sailed from Lynn, from Hull and from Bristol for the most part; and for all these mariners this trade was a very seasonal business because of the harsh Icelandic weather. Ships and boats left England in the spring and returned by autumn. The Bristol vessel *Ive* (Capt. John Gough) set sail for the northern waters with a mixed cargo on 14 February one year and was docked beside the Avon again, loaded with fish, on 18 July. Then she was off to the Atlantic coast of France, for further profit before winter shut down everything but short-sea voyaging.

Apart from cross-Channel traffic, which might convey anything from manufactured things to firewood (which Chichester and its adjacent creeks shipped out regularly), the biggest cargoes of all coming from France to England were casks (tuns) of Gascon wine, sent in great quantities from Bordeaux when each year's harvest was done, one of the splendid acquisitions resulting from Henry II's marriage to Eleanor of Aquitaine. Bayonne, too, in the Basque country which almost immediately continues from France into Spain, had a part in the early wine trade, but its lasting connection with the English was to be the building of ships for English Kings; some served Edward III in the Battle of Sluys and the Bayonnais were still willing to turn to on behalf of Henry V. The Bordelais, however, concentrated on their principal advantage, which was to reap the reward of vineyards that were fruitful along five different river valleys in the port's hinterland. Psychologically, they were much more in tune with this part of their heritage than with the Atlantic; indeed, because their river came from the south-east, beyond Toulouse, from a source just above the Golfe du Lion, in some ways they were more in harmony with the Mediterranean.[2] They were not themselves as committed to seafaring as the Bayonnais, who had a great reputation for catching whales and for lawlessness, whereas the Bordelais were never fishermen of any kind and only rarely resorted to piracy. As a result, the shipping of wine eventually became virtually an English preserve, which the Gascons were more than ready to support by waiving all river tolls along the Gironde, as well as other taxes. And this traffic continued, with occasional interruptions for war, after Gascony reverted to France, in a trade so important internationally that all ships were sized by how many tuns of wine they could carry, which became their recognised tunnage, as we know.

The great convoys – often well over a hundred vessels in the 1530s – would assemble off the Isle of Wight some time before the harvest was due, and come home from Bordeaux loaded to the gunwales with the claret that had become the English gentry's favourite tipple, bound for Bristol, Southampton, Hull, London or lesser anchorages like Topsham and Bridgwater, which might mean ten days' hard sailing from France. By the time they reached their home ports, the vessels would have been away for a couple of months. There were occasional exceptions to the normal pattern of this trade. In 1510 the *Magdalene* of Penmarc'h, and the *Lucas* of Crozon took Gascon wine to London, while the *Regnard* of Le Conquet shipped a cargo to Waterford, all three of them owned and manned by Bretons. A Bristol ship once returned from Bordeaux laden not with wine but with casks of woad for dyeing English wool blue, transported in dried balls from a different harvest around Toulouse, Albi and Montauban. And an archbishop of Bordeaux, not needing kerseys or any other English cloth for the time being, traded wine from the archiepiscopal vineyard for 1,000 red (that is, smoked) herrings from Cornwall, which he prudently stored in his pantries for Lent.

Woad was sometimes picked up by vessels trading with Spain as well, though in such cases it was being sold on from France. The Spanish had enough commodities of their own, without needing to rely on anyone else's to maintain their balance of payments. They produced good wine themselves, but the English took four times as much in their annual clear-out of Bordeaux. What the northerners were chiefly after from

---

2 Bordeaux is itself on the Garonne, just before the confluence of that river with the Dordogne to form the Gironde, which flows the remaining forty-seven miles to the ocean.

Spain was iron ore, mined in the Cantabrian mountains near Bilbao, and whale oil, which was in demand for lighting, preserving, soap-making and processing textiles. Sometimes they imported the Spanish by-products of these things, like 'smigmates', which was a form of soap regarded highly enough for the Prior of the Durham Benedictines to use, or crossbows, which were brandished regularly in Englishmen's wars, or anchors, which held fast many an English ship. Otherwise, they were in the market for citrus fruits, dates and the like, for a variety of other exotic foodstuffs such as saffron, for the finest leather from Cordova, olive oil from Seville (in big demand among English clothiers) and salt which was almost as highly esteemed as Brittany's.

One other striking traffic in these seas was that in pilgrims going to or returning from Santiago de Compostela on the Atlantic coast of Galicia, where the shrine of St James was venerated more than those associated with anyone but Christ himself and with St Paul. Pilgrimages to the Christian holy places were the only example of long-distance passenger sailings in the whole of Europe, throughout the Middle Ages and into the sixteenth century. The English pilgrims heading for Spain generally travelled as supercargo aboard vessels starting out from Bristol with their usual load of broadcloth, supplemented at times with dried herring and hake. Others were picked up in Plymouth until a limit of a hundred or so in each vessel was reached, braced for a four-day crossing across dangerous seas for the improvement of their souls.

The Portuguese, meanwhile, were England's principal source of cork; and of a desiccated insect (*kermine ilicis*) which thrived on Portuguese oak trees and was the origin of the cochineal dye that produced the vivid scarlet cloth so coveted by the English nobility. The English vessels headed for Lisbon to pick up their Portuguese cargoes, but they traded with many more ports in Spain, especially along her northern coast, which was overlooked by the mountains that yielded the iron and stretched along the waters that were home to the whale. A serious difficulty with that was the pirates who lurked in many a small gulf or slot along that towering coast; the Spanish voyage was reckoned to be the one above all others made by Englishmen, where piracy was a hazard rather more than less likely to materialise. Nor was it only threatened by Spaniards: men like John Hawley of Dartmouth – a seagoing owner who is thought to have been the model for Chaucer's Shipman – supplemented their legitimate incomes by preying on vessels sailing to Iberia or, more frequently, coming back. Yet the trade with Spain became a major enterprise in the last half

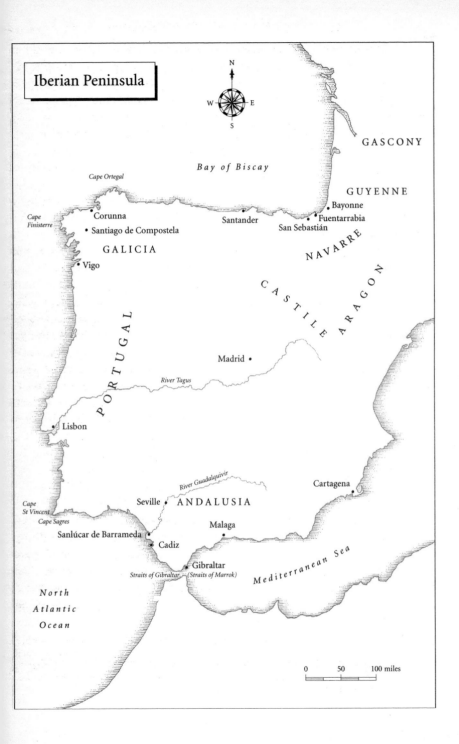

Iberian Peninsula

N
W — E
S

Bay of Biscay

GASCONY

GUYENNE

Cape Ortegal

Bayonne
Fuentarrabia
San Sebastián

Cape
Finisterre

Corunna
Santiago de Compostela

Santander

GALICIA

NAVARRE

Vigo

CASTILE

ARAGON

PORTUGAL

Madrid

River Tagus

Lisbon

River Guadalquivir

Cartagena

Seville

ANDALUSIA

Cape
St Vincent

Malaga

Cape Sagres

Sanlúcar de Barrameda

Cadiz

Gibraltar

Straits of Gibraltar
(Straits of Marrok)

Mediterranean Sea

North
Atlantic
Ocean

0   50   100 miles

of the fifteenth century and thrived even more in the early decades of the next. Much of it was conducted from Bristol, where at least one Spanish captain became a member of the Staple there. But Chester, the principal port of north-west England – with a population of 4,000–5,000 in 1506, when Liverpool had fewer than a thousand inhabitants – saw Spanish merchants as early as 1444 and was welcoming Spanish vessels by 1473. Local ships still dominated the trade, however, making round trips each year that lasted a couple of months. Then the silting process that finished the working lives of many an English seaport, in this case affecting the River Dee, meant that less and less sixteenth-century Spanish trade could be done with Chester, and the balance of north-western maritime power shifted to more fortunate Liverpool.

English shipping rarely ventured beyond what was then known as the Straits of Marrok and into the Mediterranean. Though a great deal of traffic came through the Straits to and from England, it was almost wholly Italian, either the Flanders galleys from Venice, or their rivals from Genoa or even, at one stage, the Florentines. The Genoese, in fact, were the first to make the Flanders voyage in 1277 and by the end of that century it had become an annual trip, with the Venetians quickly following suit (the Florentines did not join in for another hundred years and had mostly dropped out again by 1478). These were two well-organised maritime powers: it was the Genoese who helped the French to set up their Clos des Gallées at Rouen at the end of the thirteenth century, the Venetians whose Arsenal was the first naval shipyard in Europe, and who insisted that all their mercantile shipping should be inscribed with loading marks, hundreds of years before Samuel Plimsoll argued in the English Parliament for his famous line.[3] And they almost monopolised the seaborne trade with northern Europe in the merchandise that the well-to-do in London, Antwerp, Paris and other cities craved – everything from spices to silks, from precious stones to finely wrought weapons, from clocks to tennis balls – only some of which were the products of Italian craftsmen. A great many of these cargoes had been obtained in the Levant by merchants who sometimes overlanded them to the home ports of the galleys: seed-pearls from the Persian Gulf

3 Plimsoll, MP for Derby, campaigned against the dangerous overloading of ships. As a result, in 1876 an Act stipulated that hulls should be marked with a line indicating the maximum depth to which a British merchantman might sink in saltwater when loaded with cargo. It was enforced by the Board of Trade and in 1906 no foreign ship was allowed into British ports, either, unless it too was similarly marked.

that were crushed in wine to make a particularly intoxicating drink, rhubarb (which may have travelled from China along the Silk Road) for the apothecaries, pepper, saffron, frankincense and other fragrant substances that could have been grown anywhere between Palestine and India. On the return voyage, the Italian boats would be carrying, in addition to English woollens, other textiles, metalwork, haberdashery and even beds (for which Arras was famous) from Flanders.

The monopoly was only broken for a comparatively short time. In 1446 Robert Sturmey of Bristol sent his *Cog Anne*, loaded with wool and tin and 160 pilgrims for the Holy Land, the full length of the Mediterranean to Joppa, but she was wrecked off Greece on the way home. Eleven years later he tried again, this time despatching a small convoy of vessels, which were attacked by the Genoese and all sunk. Yet according to Richard Hakluyt's *Voyages*, which began coming off the presses in 1589, English merchants using English ships were trading with the Levant in the early years of the sixteenth century; Henry Tudor's *Sovereign*, as we know, was one of the vessels used. And Henry VIII was certainly being urged (by whom we do not know) to challenge the Italians point-blank. 'A remembrance for the advancing and setting forward of the King's ships' in 1511 expressed great concern at the prospect of English wool being shipped out 'by Venetians, Florentines and other strangers in galleys and other ships, to the decay of the King's navy'. The author of this document proposed cancelling all the licences which enabled the Italians to trade in Henry's realm and to license only English merchants to carry on eastwards beyond the Straits. He suggested that four ships of 200–300 tuns should set sail every year 'or at furthest every 13 or 14 months' and that they should have 'a place of resort and staple', preferably in Florentine Pisa, which they could use as a Mediterranean base. If Hakluyt got it right, then this may have been what happened, but he claimed that this particular trade ended about 1552. The Mediterranean was fraught with hazards other than those presented by tempests and the Genoese. The ferocious *corsa* of Tunis, Algiers and Tripoli were sworn enemies of all Christians and leapt at any chance of looting and sinking their vessels and taking the people in them captive. But there were slave markets on both sides of the Mediterranean.

The Baltic was another sea with particular difficulties for English traders. To some extent this was due to the political upheavals taking place in Scandinavia in the early decades of the sixteenth century. The rulers of Denmark-Norway had long held the whip hand in the region and, from 1501, King Hans, an ally of the Scots, had effective control of the Baltic, which he maintained with an efficient navy, including some of the biggest ships afloat. Not only could he blockade Sweden any time he chose, but he could also tax vessels of any nationality that sailed past his realm, because a toll had been imposed since 1425 for passage of the Øresund, the narrows separating Denmark and Sweden, which had to be negotiated in order to gain access to the great enclosed sea to the east. But in 1521 the Swedes under the young nobleman Gustav Vasa rebelled, and after two successful years against the Danes they elected him King. So turmoil, never conducive to stable trade, wracked the region. There was also the thrusting rivalry of the Hanseatic League to contend with. This was an association of German cities and merchants which stretched from the eastern Baltic down to lower Rhineland, and which had long enjoyed a monopoly in the commerce of its homeland and a dominating presence in the trade and finance of adjacent territories as well, with preferential treatment secured by a series of ancient charters for the merchants of the Hanse in a number of countries beyond, including England.

It was a superbly organised operation, with depots in various foreign cities to take care of Hansard interests there: at the Tyskebrugge in Bergen, the merchants' representatives arranged all movements in timber and fish; at the Peterhof in Novgorod they concentrated on furs; at the Assemblies in Bruges, dealings in cloth concerned them most. In London, Cologne had established its Guildhalla Teutonicorum as early as 1170, but as more and more Hansards became hungry for the commerce in wool and cloth and in what they themselves could bring across the North Sea, this became home to all of them and was known, from 1384, as the Steelyard. There, in a cavernous building that functioned principally as a warehouse with its own wharf on the Thames, they settled their Customs bills on cloth exports at a lower rate than Englishmen had to pay, which was only one of the privileges they enjoyed: in any sort of local trouble they were also beyond the reach of the city magistrates, answerable only to the King; and they were allowed to travel freely in England, as very few foreigners were. The building was topped by a little tower, from which the Hanse's London agents could go and look out for their ships coming up the river.[4]

---

4 In Braun and Hogenberg's pictorial map of 1572 it looks quite like the 'widow's walk' atop houses in Gloucester, Salem and other New England ports, where fishermen's wives went to look for their men's schooners coming home from Georges Bank. All too often, one or more of these failed to appear.

In its fourteenth-century heyday, the loudest voice in the policy-making of the Hanse was that of Lübeck, with Cologne and about a hundred other towns accepting the Lübeckers' lead; but since the 1470s, Hamburg and Danzig had become the most prominent, certainly in the English trade. This had once flourished along the length of the east coast until it was discontinued in Boston, Ipswich, Colchester and elsewhere, leaving Hull and, to a lesser extent, Lynn as the only ports north of London that had any part in it. Proud Lübeck had always distanced itself from the other Hansards even though it called their tune, which they had danced to because the Lübeckers possessed the greatest clout on land and at sea. Always, when friction occurred between anyone and the Hansards, Lübeck was most visibly in the thick of it. There had been the repercussions of Robert Winnington's attack on a Hansard convoy led by Lübeck ships, when they were bringing cargoes of salt home from Brittany in 1449, which led to a break in relations for nine years and then the full-blown Anglo-Hanseatic sea war which lasted from 1469 to 1474. This was preceded by an attack on English merchantmen riding at anchor while they waited their turn to pay the Øresund toll. There was periodically trouble ashore, too, generally arising from resentment at Hansard privileges: so much hostility in Hull that in 1488 the Hanse forbade its people to go into the Yorkshire port, for their own sakes; and riots outside the Steelyard in 1493 after a dispute between the Hansards and the London mercers. And now the Baltic had erupted again in 1510 in a war between the Danes and the Wendish towns to the south, which hampered all commercial traffic in the region.[5]

There was no question, however, of Henry VIII turning his back on the Hanse and its shipping. As he began to plan his own first war, he had to face the fact that most of the naval stores he required could only be obtained from this source – masts and cordage, pitch and tar, saltpetre for gunpowder and copper for the making of bronze artillery. At the same time – and in spite of their alliance with the Scots – he needed to stay on terms with the Danes, who could stop the flow of his naval supplies whenever they wished.

The fishing industry needed as much naval back-up as anyone, of course, and occupied as prominent a place as anything in the English economy of the time, apart from wool and its by-products. All of Europe

5 The Wends were originally Slavs, but were overrun by the Saxons in the early years of the Middle Ages. Their chief Hansa towns were Lübeck, Lüneburg, Hamburg, Stralsund, Wismar and Rostock.

had a big stake in fish, because ever since the fourth century the Church had decreed frequent and regular abstinence from red meat, which was thought to encourage carnal desire and its attendant vices. Well before the sixteenth century (when the Council of Trent reinforced the order), the result of this dictum was that people were fasting on Wednesday, Friday and Saturday throughout the year, together with the whole of Lent and Advent – a total of 186 days out of the 365 – with certain dispensations, naturally, for those who knew their way round the rules. As fish was excluded from the ban, it became a prominent part of the European diet, especially for the poor, who rarely managed (or could afford) to circumvent the rules. And this continued until the Reformation got into its stride, with the consequent rejection of many old imperatives among the emerging Protestants. It led to the vast importance of stock-fish, which would keep for weeks or even months if the preservation had been done properly: the Archbishop of Bordeaux wasn't the only person to buy his fish in autumn for use in Lent, or to make sure that it was well beaten before being served, so that it would be digestible.

Nothing was more sought after than the herring, which swirled in its myriads around the North Sea above all, attracting 40,000 fishing boats in one recorded season of the fourteenth century. And in 1535, there were 600 English boats alone after the herring in the Irish Sea, which was a profitable subsidiary source of supply. At the same time, methodical Dutch herring fishers pursued their quarry in what was effectively three distinct seasons as different streams of spawning fish swam past the British Isles from north to south. First they caught them in the waters off Orkney and Shetland between June and July, and the Dutch Bank up there still testifies to their long-departed presence; then they moved down the Scottish coast and that of Yorkshire and netted the creature throughout August, finally fetching up off East Anglia in autumn and selling some of their catch at the Yarmouth Fair. Most of it, however, went home, often conveyed by fast *ventjagers*, which bought the herring from the fishing boats while they were still at sea, so as to cash-in on the high prices that were going before the main landings began. The *Grands Pêcheurs* of France, for their part, made four separate trips a year, and two of these were for herring: one to the North Sea in the autumn and another in the Channel at the onset of winter. In spring they first plundered Irish waters of their mackerel, before doing likewise off the Normandy coast.

To a considerable extent, the English east coast especially depended on the herring for its survival, though not every coastal community dealt in this trade. In Yorkshire, Hull stuck to importing and exporting merchandise, while Scarborough, Whitby and some smaller villages concentrated on fish; likewise, Lynn was the big general trader along the Norfolk coast, leaving Cromer, Blakeney and their like to take advantage of Yarmouth's great fair as well as to keep their own people from starvation. For the West Country, which shared with the east coast England's greatest fishing tradition, the pilchard was the equivalent of the herring, so prolifically did it appear every summer. Then, all the headlands between Land's End and Dorset made perfect vantage points for the huers, who could see from up there which way the great shoals were swimming (their very density gave them away by turning the water a purplish colour), and who signalled the direction to the boats waiting with their seine nets offshore.[6] These were usually twenty feet long, sometimes constructed so that they could be launched from a beach when no quay was available, and they generally carried five men apiece. It was such a craft and its crew that in one sixteenth-century season off the coast of Devon was said to have landed 900,000 pilchards in Hope Cove. 'The commodity that ariseth of this silly small fish is wonderful', as someone writing of Cornwall a few years later remarked. But the waters off the West Country abounded in many other sorts of fish, too, eighteen species that were recorded at this time. Cornwall benefited from great landings of cod, ling, conger, mullet, herring and porpoise, as well as pilchard; the estuary of the Exe was rich in salmon, eels, mullet, mussels and oysters (which were so plentiful on many English coasts that they had little commercial value and therefore became a common item at the tables of the poor). When Henry's Lord Privy Seal, Thomas Cromwell, sent his commissioners round the country in 1535 to assess the wealth of the Church, including its tithes, it was found that among the most valuable fisheries in the land were those of Torbay and Start Bay.

There was great prosperity in fishing, though most of the money did not go to the fishermen themselves, who were often so poor that they subsisted only by having a bit of land on which they could do some small-time farming as well. They were much at the mercy of many factors well beyond their control: the weather most of all, of course, but also the wayward breeding habits of the fish, which might produce a glut in one season and almost nothing in the next, and the normal ups and downs of

6 The Old French verb *huer* meant to shout or cry. Nowadays, of course, it means to boo.

commerce which, among others things, meant that in the course of the sixteenth century Yarmouth's pre-eminence on the east coast was gradually overtaken by Lowestoft. In all circumstances, however, it was the merchants who made most of the profit, and this was not only an English predicament: fish landed in Dieppe had to pass through two different middlemen before it was even despatched to the Paris market. The incubus was not always bad news, however. Thomas Bodley of Exeter married into fish, as it were, and, on the wealth that his wife brought to their union, built up the great library in Oxford that bears his name.

So important were the fisheries to the economy at large, and so great was the international competition for what swam in English waters, that at the end of the fifteenth century the Crown was taking an active interest in affording protection to its fishing fleets, encouraging the skippers to sail and fish in convoys; and these had become very necessary by then, because sea fights sometimes took place between the English, the French and the Spanish fishermen in particular, though the English and the French were known to call a private truce when their countries were at war, so that they could get on with what mattered more to both of them: this happened in October 1542, when 'letters to that effect went from Dieppe and Calais to the King in London'. For any naval protection, naturally, Henry VIII exacted his price: the first people to come aboard when a fishing boat docked were officials who took a proportion of the catch – as much as 100 ling or 200 cod sometimes, or the equivalent in cash. This was not the only advantage of the fishing industry to him. As his reign progressed, more and more he expected it to provide much of the cannon fodder for his own developing fleet.

London was England's biggest fish market, of such importance that at the Lord Mayor's annual Feast, the Fishmongers Company (which had six separate halls in the capital) came fourth in order of precedence, behind the mercers, grocers and drapers, and before the goldsmiths, merchant tailors, skinners and fifty-odd other trade guilds. Somewhere down the list were the Merchant Adventurers, who tried (but never quite succeeded) to monopolise the export trade to western Europe in unfinished and undyed cloth, which they sold in Bruges and later in Antwerp to the Hansard merchants of Cologne, who then took their own cut from a cargo by distributing it throughout Germany. The Adventurers had smaller operations going in York, Bristol and Newcastle; but London was their headquarters and its Antwerp trade was their principal business. The most striking thing about the capital's commercial identity, in fact, is that it not only held a commanding position in England's domestic economy: it also dominated the national export trade. It was becoming the country's chief seaport, serving not only the markets overseas, but also occupying a decisive role in the coastal trade. There were several reasons for London's primacy and one very obvious result: the population of the capital, which stood at 60,000 in 1500, was to double in the next fifty years.

Tudor London was, in fact, in the process of taking over Southampton's role as the principal starting point and terminus of maritime commerce in southern England. The Romans had founded their Clausentum near the present location of the great Hampshire port, having discovered many advantages for seafarers. The anchorage was well sheltered by the Isle of Wight from the worst of the Channel weather; approaching enemies had to sail up a dozen miles of enclosed but deep water to get to it and they would be visible all the way; and there was also the phenomenon of the double tides, from which every generation since has benefited. The flood tide from the west divides when it reaches The Needles, the stream flowing inside the Isle of Wight giving the Solent its first high water. A couple of hours later the outer stream rounds the eastern end of Wight and pours in after it; and, as the fall between the two tides has been no more than nine inches or so, which is almost Mediterranean (and Baltic) in its reticence, the result is effectively two high tides before there is a swift ebb of all the tidal water back into the Channel again. This peculiar natural occurrence meant that medieval shipping had a much longer period than usual of slack water between the tides, when vessels could load or unload cargo without having to adjust their mooring ropes continually and without having to take account of strong tidal currents. If they were transferring cargo while at anchor instead of at a wharf, as was often the case, they even had longer available working hours. And on all these advantages, Southampton thrived from the thirteenth century onwards, as merchandise travelled backwards and forwards across its hinterland even as far as London itself. It came and went long-distance across this water and it also shuttled between Southampton and the Low Countries, France and Brittany, as well as around most of the English coasts.

The Italian ships, as we know, found it very much more convenient to drop by there on their way to Flanders, instead of having to sail round North Foreland and struggle with the complexities of the Thames estuary before they could reach the capital, even though that's where most of their pricier cargoes finished up. Besides, the Italians felt more welcome in Hampshire than they generally did when dropping anchor elsewhere in England: it was in London, not in Southampton, that there had been disturbing riots against foreigners in 1455 and 1456 and they were not the first. It was this factor, added to the navigational difficulties and the prospect of reduced costs, that had led foreigners to transfer their patronage from London to Southampton in the first place. And it was the fall in the important Italian trade that led to Southampton's decline from the back end of the fifteenth century. The Florentine galleys, which used to tie up at the West Quay, stopped coming after 1478. The Genoese carracks, which once rode at anchor out in the harbour, dwindled to nothing in the latter years of Edward IV. The Venetians, most tenacious of them all, abandoned this trade in 1509 because they were under attack at home. And when Henry VIII went down to welcome them back in 1518, it was almost certainly not because he fervently hoped it might help revive Southampton's prosperity. Much more likely, he wanted to run an appraising eye over their ships, and to see how their gunnery shaped up.

So London's connection with the sea was entering a new era, although it too had a Roman pedigree, and although Southampton was still its outport when Henry reached the throne. The changeover occurred gradually in the course of his reign because developments in ship design and improved aids to navigation (including a new guild of pilots in 1514, known as the Trinity House at Deptford Strand) made a passage up the Thames much less hazardous to strangers than it usually had been in the past; and because the considerable colony of London merchants who had settled in Southampton over the years and had become the most powerful group of traders in the town, decided to profit from the potential in these nautical improvements by returning home, where their costs would be lower and where they would still prosper so long as the foreign ships kept coming to them. There was some risk of the foreigners not co-operating, of course, but the Londoners counted on the contacts they had made seeing them through. And where they led, others followed, men who had come to work in Southampton from the Channel Islands and even from Calais, and men who were Hampshire born and bred, but who now felt it necessary to move on in pursuit of their trades; to sink or swim as a matter of choice. The Londoners calculated correctly, and not only the foreign shipping followed them back to the Thames, but vital components of Southampton's commerce fell into line, too. The Cornish tin trade, which was of enormous value to the middlemen wherever they might be based, was diverted to supply London's flourishing pewterers directly with one of their principal raw materials. Southampton was a bedraggled place by the time Henry's daughter Elizabeth became Queen. Not until the nineteenth century would it recover its old significance and its self-esteem.

The capital depended on and was characterised by its river. It was walled on three sides, while the Thames was its bastion to the south; also the regulator of much metropolitan life. Ten gates pierced the walls in Tudor times, closed every night when the curfew bell rang, at dusk or certainly not later than eight o'clock, to remain shut till sunrise or, in winter, till six. Then all manner of traffic could pass into and out of the suburbs – Clerkenwell, Poplar, Shoreditch and their neighbours – and on to the surrounding countryside, whose fields were divided by hedges in order to restrict the grazing horses and cattle, 'with brooks running through them, turning water-mills with a pleasant noise'; cornfields, too, and villages such as Islington and Tottenham. The walled city was really quite small, just over a square mile in extent, yet packed into it was not just by far the biggest population in England, but over a hundred churches as well, including the great Norman bulk of St Paul's, its massive tower extended by a spire added in the thirteenth century (which would be destroyed by lightning in 1561).

Within the walls, a few of the main streets were paved or cobbled, but most thoroughfares were ankle-deep in mud after more than a shower. All of them were narrow and tended to wind tortuously, so that strangers might easily get lost even in such a small space; and they were congested with traffic soon after the working day began, carters cracking long whips to urge their dray horses along, coaches galloping heedlessly whenever that was possible, but usually hampered by flocks of sheep and herds of other animals being driven to market, sometimes great distances from two or three counties away. Some of the buildings on either side of these lanes were made of stone or brick, but most of the houses, which could be as many as five storeys high, were timber-framed, infilled with lathe and plaster, wattle and daub. Fire was therefore a constant danger in London and its environs and frequently occurred, one of the most serious outbreaks damaging the Palace of Westminster in 1512. Westminster was where Parliament sat, usually at the sovereign's whim, where the Law Courts were situated, where Benedictine monks still sang Gregorian chant in another massive church. Between it and the walled city was no more than a downstream mile, and the two places were connected by the mansions of the rich and powerful, standing by or a little back from the riverside. But they might have been in different worlds.

The capital's prosperity came from within those walls or just across the river opposite. Here were the workshops of the craftsmen who created much of it, where two out of every three London men were apprenticed until they were anything up to their mid-twenties: the goldsmiths in Westcheap, the ironmongers in Old Jewry, the shoemakers in Cordwayner Street, the bowyers by Ludgate, almost every street loud with the sound of beating hammers or acrid with the smoke of industrial fires. Here were many markets: Smithfield for livestock, Leadenhall for meat and poultry, Cheapside for flowers and vegetables, Eastcheap for butchers, Queenhithe for grain, Billingsgate for many foodstuffs, especially fish – these were the most prominent. Here, too, was Blackwell Hall, the principal woollen exchange, where dealers from all over England disposed of their cloth wholesale. Southwark, facing the city, also had a great general market, and was where most of London's substantial population of foreigners dwelt, no less than five per cent of those 60,000 inhabitants at the turn of the century; and when, in 1510, 400 aliens were busy making furniture in London, most of them were settled in Southwark. That side of the river was also a great place for pleasure, not all of it wholesome. There was a cockpit in Smithfield for the commoners, and another for the nobility which Henry himself introduced to Whitehall, but if ordinary folk wanted rough pastimes, they usually made for Bankside, which lay beside Southwark. That was where men trawled through the stews in search of an affordable doxy, it was where they could repair to the bull pit or the bear pit; and close by each pit were the kennels where mastiffs were kept and trained to bait these poor beasts.

But there were only two ways to get to Bankside and Southwark from the city – or anywhere else south of the Thames until you were halfway to Oxford. You either did it by boat or you crossed London Bridge, which the Romans had built of wood but which was now a very permanent structure of stone, with twenty arches and a drawbridge closer to the Southwark than the city side, which was raised for the last time in 1500. Lining the roadway of the bridge on both sides were 'large, fair and beautiful buildings, inhabitants for the most part rich merchants, and other wealthy citizens, mercers and haberdashers', as John Stow would observe during Elizabeth's reign; also a chapel dedicated to St Thomas à Becket, which would finish up as a grocer's shop. Generally, the householders lived above their commercial premises, and most of the time they kept company with the rotting remains of some wretch who had been executed for treason, and whose head had been impaled on the drawbridge tower as a warning to all passers-by: that was to be the fate of Sir Thomas More, Lord Chancellor of England, after falling out with Henry over the King's breach with the Church.

If you wanted to get about London and its surrounding district, then the easiest and quickest way of doing so was to travel by boat. The Lord Mayor went upriver to Westminster for his swearing-in this way, as did attorneys from the Temple with cases to plead in the Law Courts; and many other citizens with day-to-day affairs to transact anywhere. Noblefolk and merchants kept their own gigs and barges at their beck and call, and a coxswain and his crew might have a device embroidered on the back of their coats, to advertise whose property they were, or sometimes the boat itself would be painted distinctively. Less important people than these used what a later age would recognise as water taxis; so that, one way and another, there were a couple of thousand rowing boats to convey passengers up and down the Thames in the sixteenth century. There were certain things they needed to be wary of, however. The watermen who manned the public wherries had a disobliging habit of changing the fare price once their passengers were midstream until, in 1514, Henry pushed a Bill through Parliament which regulated fares and stipulated penalties for extortion.

And then there was the hazard caused by the bridge's nineteen piers. The Thames was a great deal wider and shallower than we know it now, because it lacked all the embankments that Bazalgette built in the nineteenth century; which is why it froze over so much more frequently than it has done since then. The piers also had a dangerous effect on the river's flow when it came to London Bridge, for any craft trying to pass through its arches. A boat might get through them safely at slack water, but to make the attempt at other times could and often did lead to disaster. When the river was flowing strongly again, the obstruction of the piers produced a rapids in between each one of them which in extreme circumstances – with the ebb tide at springs, for example – would result in a difference of four feet between the levels of water above and below the bridge: to make the attempt then was madness. Although that water was grey because of all the silt washing up and down, it was clean enough to be fished profitably for anything from salmon to eels, from trout to shrimps; and people still spoke of the legendary time in the thirteenth century, when a pod of eleven whales was pursued all the way up the Thames as far as Mortlake before they became stranded and were killed.

Along the city's side of the river were the wharves that saw all the big trade come and go, most of them below the bridge. The country boats, bringing cargoes of timber or hay down the Thames to the capital, were unloaded above it, returning with whatever London had to offer the upstream shires. That's also where the Hansa cargoes were put ashore, at a wharf jutting out from the Steelyard, the closure of the drawbridge meaning that they had to be unloaded into smaller boats to finish their journey upstream. Below the bridge was the terminus for most of the merchantmen coming in from the North Sea: at Greenberries Quay, which took care of the French trade, Crown Quay for the coastal traffic in corn and wood, Gibsons Quay for lead, tin and other cargoes from around the English coast, Bear Quay and Youngs Quay, which welcomed the Portuguese, Old Thurstons Quay, where the Flemish cargoes arrived, Galley Quay, which was was the landing place for the Italians during their London days, and Billingsgate Quay, which lay well back from the riverline inside a basin big enough to accommodate the great traffic in herring-busses and other fishing boats. There were twenty landing places in all.

Many craft with shallow draught tied up at the wharves to discharge and load cargoes: hoys, small vessels whose principle trade was with the Netherlands, where they originated; shallops, ferrying cargo from larger vessels to dry land; and flat-bottomed plates with leeboards, ancestors of the Thames spritsail barge which is still (just about) with us.[7] And no two such craft, even sharing the same generic name, would be absolutely alike. Local idiosyncratic styles were a constant factor in medieval and Tudor constructions in every form, as local craftsmen took account of regional conditions, preferences and materials, as well as their own need to express themselves. A church built in Somerset in the Perpendicular style of the period would be strikingly different from one built in Suffolk, for in Somerset they went in for spectacular towers, in Suffolk for elaborate timber roofs. A farm wagon made in Herefordshire would be almost crescent-shaped in profile, curving upwards at both ends, but one made in Staffordshire would be level, from front to back, effectively rectangular.

7 The descriptive names given to shipping at this time can be highly confusing even to specialists, who have to pick their way through no fewer than forty-three different varieties which were recorded in Customs and other contemporary documents.

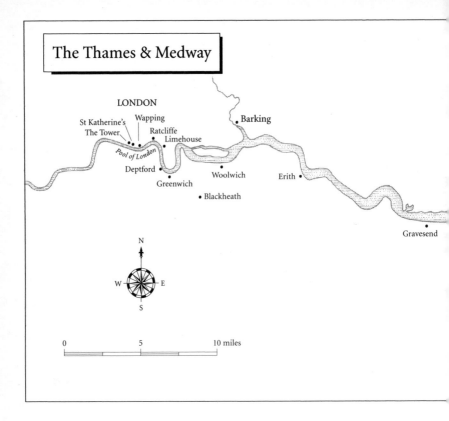

The Thames & Medway

LONDON

St Katherine's Wapping
The Tower Ratcliffe
Limehouse
Pool of London
Deptford
Greenwich
Blackheath

Barking

Woolwich Erith

Gravesend

N
W — E
S

0   5   10 miles

So it was with the building of boats, especially in the fisheries and the coastal trade. A Yorkshire coble, twenty feet long, with three oars and a sail, would have a high bow and two side keels so that it could be beached stern first and launched later into heavy breakers without waiting for the sea to calm down. In Dorset they had their lerret, of similar length and with a similar problem to be solved on Chesil Beach, but there they overcame it by making their craft double-ended, built the same way both fore and aft. It is largely because of such differences in design, from one place to another, that generalisations about fifteenth- and sixteenth-century shipping types can only be made in the broadest terms.

The deepwater vessels which traded all over Europe and any great distance round the English coasts generally offloaded after dropping anchor in the Pool of London, between the bridge and St Katharine's, just downstream of the Tower and its intimidating keep. A few old cogs –

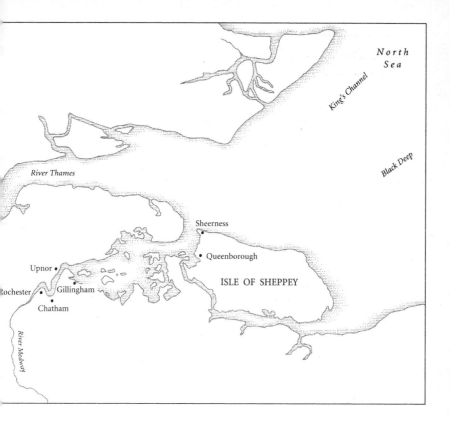

single-masted, square-rigged and tubby vessels which had been the maid-of-all-work throughout Europe since the thirteenth century – might still be seen there early in the sixteenth, but they were on their way out owing to changes in ship design. Sometimes in the Pool, with their broad and high bows and narrow sterns, were balingers, which carried up to 50 tuns of merchandise from the Low Countries everywhere as far as the Mediterranean, though they were found more often in the West Country ports than on the English east coast; and two- or three-masted crayers with quite complex sail plans for their time, usually owned by Englishmen, Normans or Bretons. There were barges (or barks; the words became interchangeable) which ran cargoes across the Channel as well as to Spain and Bordeaux; and the much larger carracks, which combined on their three masts both the traditional square rig of northern Europe and the lateen sails that originally belonged to the Mediterranean, and thus made them much more manoeuvrable in difficult circumstances. There might even be a Portuguese caravel, sometimes known as a carvel because of its construction, which was in the process of revolutionising ship design and performance everywhere.

Until the middle of the fifteenth century, ships in northern Europe had always been constructed from the keel upwards, with the planks of the hull overlapping each other, and were said to be clinker-built. But in the Mediterranean they had gone in for laying the planks flush with each other over a skeleton framework, because they had found that ships moved faster that way; such vessels were carvel-built. The design had been conveyed to northern Europe by the Italians (to a lesser extent by the Portuguese) and the northerners had been sufficiently impressed by it to adopt it in their own shipbuilding. A member of the Howard clan – Sir John, 1st Duke of Norfolk and Richard III's Lord Admiral – was probably the first Englishman to have a carvel-built ship laid down for him: the three-masted *Edward*, which was on the stocks at Dunwich in 1465–6. And so quickly did others follow his lead that by Henry VIII's time 'clinker-built' meant 'old-fashioned', and such a vessel was liable to be dismissed as a 'clencher' (which was the special nail required to hold the overlapping planks in place). For the new hull construction, together with the more sophisticated sail plans, was the answer to a seaman's prayer. It meant that ships which combined the two were much handier than before, either on a mercantile passage in a difficult seaway, or when mixing it with the enemy in a sea battle.

They needed to be when coming into the port of London, or when leaving it again. Having weighed anchor in the Pool, an outward-bound ship moved straight into the series of curves and bends – and one great loop – that characterise the Thames. For a good mile or so below the Tower, there were buildings along the north bank, cottages inhabited by victuallers, shipwrights and others who had a toehold in the business of shipping, before the vessel slipped past Wapping, where pirates were hanged in chains at the low-water mark and left there, drowned, until three tides had covered them. For some distance downstream, the spire of St Paul's would still be visible fine on the larboard quarter or dead astern, but once the King's birthplace at Greenwich was cleared and the vessel had turned and turned again through the loop to make Blackwall Reach, there was little to be seen on either side but marshland, broken by small hamlets and their invariable church, and the occasional riverside alehouse, where incoming sailors could refresh themselves after days or even weeks at sea, while their ships swung at anchor and waited for a berth in the Pool. Barking, tucked away up its creek, was passed and then, after two more sweeping turns in its course, the river brought the outward-bound crew abeam of Gravesend, where a ferry loaded with people and livestock might be setting off for London Bridge, and where ships leaving the great port had to stop until their Customs and other papers had been checked.

It was after this that the greatest hazards of the Thames revealed themselves, as the river gaped open into its estuary, with the mudflats of Essex on one side and the brooding saltmarshes of Kent on the other. There were certain well-known aids to navigating safely in these waters, passed down the ages by mariners before the Trinity House pilots took the responsibility upon themselves. As a seventeenth-century expert was to put it when advising masters about the best approach to London on coming in from the Channel and the North Sea:

> Sail on so west all along the shore until that the Reculvers (which are two steeples in one church) come one in the other and then you shall run in sight of the first buoy of the Lastes which lieth upon the aforesaid marks of the Reculvers; being by it you can also see the other buoy which lieth like the first on the north side and over against it on the south side standeth also a beacon; there you must sail through betwixt them both, leaving the buoys on the starboard side and the beacon over against it on the larbord side.[8]

One of the greatest tests of seamanship was moving a craft safely along a tidal fairway, when you had to assess more precisely and quickly than when you had plenty of searoom the wind and the current, decide what canvas to hoist and how to set it, whether it might be best to go through stern first with just enough sail to give steerageway and risk going aground (and possibly breaking up), or whether to drop anchor and wait for the tide to turn or the wind to change. There were no buoys to help with these manoeuvres until Trinity House laid them down, paid for out of the dues earned in pilotage fees. All the shipmasters had to go on before that was, effectively, the two steeples of Reculver church and a few other landmarks, all useless in fog, which frequently shrouded the Thames. That and very hard-earned savvy.

8 The two towers of Reculver church are said to have been erected at the behest of the Abbess of Davington, as an act of gratitude for surviving a shipwreck there. They were held in such esteem that passing ships used to dip their sails in acknowledgement

It was the great sandbanks of the estuary that shipping had to be wary of, sandbanks that might shift a little from tide to tide – Oaze Edge and Shivering Sand, Long Sand and the Girdler, the Knowles and the Kentish Knock, Maplin Sand and Black Tail Sand; these and many, many more, all waiting for the next victim to fall foul of them; and there were plenty of those over the years. The acquired knowledge that got you safely out of the Thames estuary, whichever way you were sailing, was priceless, as Henry VIII appreciated well. In 1540 he was to settle an annuity on Jean Bartelot, a hired Frenchman, who looked for and found a safe channel through the fearsome Black Deep. But even when your ship had come past all these obstacles, and was out into open water at last, there were other dangers to be faced, lurking upon the Narrow Seas and far beyond.

IV
THE ENEMIES

Warships were employed to fight seamen and other combatants in similar vessels, but most of the time they and all shipping battled with the elements, in an endless struggle unmitigated by the respite of peace treaties and exhausted warriors. Storms abated unpredictably in their own good time, and not because they had worn themselves out against an old adversary. No-one who has never faced a storm at sea can quite appreciate its limitless power and its capacity to subdue even the stoutest hearts, especially if they are aboard a small vessel in real danger of being overwhelmed by masses of water that tower above its decks one minute before crashing down, and then fling it high and out of control onto a precipice of swell; and we tend to overlook the fact that all ships of this period were really very small compared with what would gradually evolve over the centuries leading to our own.

Nor were the hazards these vessels faced confined to the weather as such, for a great deal depended on the condition of the craft itself, which as often as not was in sore need of an overhaul, if only to rid it of the weeds and barnacles that quickly accumulated on the hull below the waterline and made it sluggish and dangerously slow to answer the helmsman's touch; and there were other things that could go perilously amiss, such as anchors failing, cables parting, leaking timbers and defective pumps. But a storm could finish off the most well-founded ship, even a seaside community, with its own unaided power and ferocity: one wiped out most of Lyme in Dorset in 1377, taking with it fifteen ships and forty boats. Alonso de Chaves, a thoughtful Spaniard in the service of the Emperor Charles V early in the sixteenth century, put warfare at sea in such conditions in perspective when he wrote that 'if there be a storm, the same terror will strike one side as the other; for the storm is enough for all to war with, and in fighting it they will have peace with one another'. Everyone accepted the wisdom that it was madness to keep a fleet at sea during the winter, when the worst of the weather could be expected; with very few exceptions, naval engagements tended to take place between the onset of spring and the last days of autumn.

Even in that relatively benign period, the weather was often the decisive factor in what shipping did, and where and when. The high sterns that were beginning to come into naval architecture were largely down to a fear of being pooped: of having a sea come in over the stern, at least sweeping away everything in its path but more probably sinking the ship and its crew. A fleet might be landlocked for days or even weeks because the weather prevented it from putting to sea. A solitary vessel *could* get out of harbour in adverse conditions, but only by warping her, which was a tediously slow process requiring a great deal of musclepower and posts sunk deeply enough into the harbour's quays to take plenty of strain: the posts were used as a fulcrum, while men in boats, or heaving on a ship's windlass, hauled on hawsers to get the ship moving and then to control it when its momentum began to take charge. Or kedge anchors could be dropped ahead of the vessel to fulfil the same purpose as the posts. Or the ship could simply be towed out by a large proportion of her crew in small boats. But the idea of shifting an entire fleet in these ways was obviously impracticable (though it did perforce happen at least once, so that the English could get out of Plymouth to repulse the Spanish Armada in 1588).

Bad weather, therefore, usually had the upper hand. You could get from Paris to London in six days, but only if the weather in the Channel was behaving itself and favouring you; and it could take two whole months for a ship to sail from London to Berwick on the Scottish border because the winds were constantly changing, blowing the wrong way. A powerful sou'westerly once blew two fishermen, John Picheford and Ralph Geggs, from the east coast all the way across the North Sea to Norway, without their having the slightest desire to go in that direction. The sou'westerly was the prevailing wind at most times of the year in the Channel, which was why the coasts of Cornwall, Devon and Dorset, which took the full force of its blast, regularly endured the sort of battering that virtually destroyed Lyme in the fourteenth century. The climate, in fact, was on the change while Henry VIII was King, and had been for some time. It had been improving somewhat since 1450, people on the land enjoying mild, wet winters and dry, warm summers; and in the space of just over half a century only three years (and they were consecutive) brought disastrously bad harvests, which was exceptional. But from the 1530s onward, things deteriorated, producing what some would regard as the second ice age, which continued into the seventeenth century.

At sea, in all conditions during these generations, the mariner had none of the assistance which can be taken for granted in our own times and has been since long before us. The first barometer that might give some idea of impending storm would not appear for over a hundred years, and the Beaufort wind scale which measured velocity was not devised until 1806. Nothing remotely resembled meteorology, as we understand the science now, though there were many soothsayers who tried to prophesy what weather was coming and who so alarmed those in authority that their activities were prohibited in 1541 by an Act of Parliament directed against all forms of sorcery. These innocent people were simply using the lore handed down from one age to another verbatim ('Red sky in the morning...'), as did every seaman afloat. The Dutch Professor Buys Ballot would not enunciate his famous Law until 1857; but every master mariner knew, from what his predecessors had told him and from what he himself had long found to be true, that winds move anti-clockwise round the deepest depression in circular storms (and so they knew which way to steer to avoid sailing straight into the eye of the storm).[1] They knew that wind speed was greater at the masthead than it was at the waterline (which mattered in gauging how much and what canvas to hoist). Many of them had also discovered that an approaching waterspout would disintegrate if it was hit by a well-aimed cannon ball. These were rules of thumb to be applied in extreme conditions, which occurred often enough; but even in milder weather, the winds could be very contrary. Sir William Fitzwilliam was describing typical Channel weather in a signal he sent to the King from his anchorage in the Downs on a midsummer day in 1522. 'On Friday last...the wind changed to WSW and blew so hard that...obliged to go into the Downs and stay there all Saturday and Sunday. On Monday the wind changed to W by N. Started for Hampton, intending to have stopped at every flood, and gone in with the tide. Was obliged to put back to the Downs, as the wind went back to SW in which quarter it keeps still. Will go to Hampton by the next wind.'

1 That is the Buys Ballot Law as applied in the northern hemisphere. The reverse is true below the Equator.

The Narrow Seas in which these conditions prevailed were so called because they were, in greater or lesser degree, hemmed in by land, with more length to them than breadth. If you sailed down the North Sea and reached a line drawn from The Wash to Texel on the Dutch coast, there you were entering the Narrow Seas, and you did not leave them until you passed Cherbourg on your larboard beam with Portland to the north.[2] Beyond that was the Western Approaches and after it the vast Atlantic itself, where the seas could be even more treacherous with storm and, when a storm raged, with mountainous swells. Nothing, in fact, was more threatening to the seaman than the 350 miles of Brittany's coast, especially the coasts of Finistère and Morbihan, which were not only fully exposed to the worst that the Atlantic could do, but were jagged with rocks and reefs extending miles out to sea, sometimes visible only in calm weather at low tide – Le Corbeau and its close companion La Corneille, Le Bouc, Les Trois Cheminées, Les Pierres Noires and hundreds more – which meant potential disaster to any vessel that didn't have a local lodesman (pilot) on board.[3] Frequent fog there compounded the peril, and so did the strong tidal stream surrounding the Ile d'Ouessant which, combined with a stiff westerly, could carry the London-bound ship coming out of the Bay of Biscay much too far to the north than was intended, consequently piling her up on the Cornish coast, which was almost as dangerous as the Breton; yet it was important to make the Lizard after a day or two without the sight of land, so as to be sure of your position before you changed course through anything up to 90° for the eastward passage. But French waters generally were tricky for everyone who sailed in them, the entire Channel coastline of Brittany, Normandy and Picardy lying behind a long wall of sunken ledges, with very few anchorages easy for the stranger to approach (though one of Henry's commanders was of the opinion that Dieppe had 'a good road for westerly winds').

The English coastline was much more hospitable, with many fine natural harbours (Topsham, the port for Exeter, had room for 200 ships), though there were powerful tidal races to beware of, off the Lizard, Start

2 The extremities were redefined from age to age and for some the Narrow Seas were synonymous with 'the English sea' which, during the Anglo-Dutch war of 1674, was said to stretch from the Naze in Essex as far as Cap Finistère in Brittany.

3 An ominous Breton saying translates as 'No one passes the Raz without fear or harm'. A lethal and extensive archipelago of rocks and islets lies just off the Pointe du Raz, at the south-western extremity of the Baie de Douarnenez, and any north-bound vessel wishing to reach the port of Brest has to negotiate this obstacle.

Point, Portland Bill and St Albans Head. A shipmaster needed to be familiar with such things; needed to know that if you thought you were anywhere near the fearsome Eddystone rock off Plymouth, you had best make sure you had forty fathoms under your keel; needed to know that strange ripplings across calm water on a dark night often meant that you were closer to the French coast than you thought you were; needed to know the phases of the moon and the movement of the stars because both could tell you what tides to expect in the next hour or so; needed to know how strongly the tidal streams ran – from two to three knots along most of the Channel, but from six to eight knots around the Channel Islands – and how far the tides rose and fell (as much as sixteen feet at springs off the Low Countries, but a little less in the Scheldt estuary). There wouldn't be a lighthouse on the Eddystone until the very end of the seventeenth century, though a light shone from a hermitage on Plymouth Hoe and, at a number of other places round the English coast, people had erected some form of beacon to give mariners a helping hand.[4]

But if you were anywhere near land or a notorious sandbank, the most important thing was to take soundings at frequent intervals and, with luck and the right sort of weather, you might make twenty-four sea miles safely during a six-hour tide. The trouble with the Narrow Seas was that you could never rely on them for the right sort of weather or for anything else but waywardness. A great sandbank known as Scrotby lay just off Yarmouth and, one day in the sixteenth century, it rose so high out of the sea that grass and other vegetation started to grow on it, in which seabirds built their nests. The citizens of Yarmouth began to visit Scrotby for recreation, 'some feasting, bowling and using other pastimes there according to their several inclinations'. And then, one night, a couple of years after it had emerged from the waters, the sandbank disappeared beneath the waves during a strong easterly wind.

At the narrowest part of the Narrow Seas, two towns faced each other across what everyone called the Passe of Calais, both of them duty-bound to Henry VIII, each of them highly significant for different reasons. In Dover's case this was because of the port's long historical role as 'the very front door of England', in Matthew Paris's

4 The first Eddystone light, built of wood on a stone base, rose eighty feet above the rock. In 1703, three years after its completion, it was swept away in a storm, taking its designer, Henry Winstanley, with it: he had been supervising repairs at the time.

memorable opinion.[5] It lay between two massive headlands of chalk, where the trifling River Dour ended a short journey down its valley to the sea, the only gap in a dozen miles of cliffs over three hundred feet high. Iron Age people had been the first to fortify it against enemies by throwing up earthworks round their settlement. The Romans saw its strategic and maritime potential at once, making Dubris their chief port of entry to Britannia and their principal naval base after Richborough started to silt up. They built a lighthouse on each of the two headlands, the eastern pharos rising a good eighty feet from within the old Iron Age earthworks.

That was where Dover's next great development occurred, too, when Henry II started to build a castle of stone in 1168, to replace what was left of a timber structure the Saxons had bequeathed on the remains of the Roman *castrum*. He built it without the slightest regard to cost – in fact, he spent just under £7,000, when his total income was no more than £10,000 a year – and the result was magnificent as well as, to some extent, unprecedented. For although the keep was classic Norman in style – tall, rectangular, overwhelming – he surrounded it with a curtain wall, which King John later surrounded with another, which was provided with eleven defensive towers of its own. The idea of such concentric walls originated in Islam, reaching its most spectacular achievement in the walling of fifth-century Constantinople. The Crusaders brought it back with them to the West; but it was still uncommon for such a fortification to be built anywhere in Europe. John had put up the outer wall after the garrison surrendered without even retreating into the keep in 1203, and it proved its effectiveness thirteen years later when a French attack was repulsed.

And now, in the sixteenth century, the castle still stood mightily above the port, which was itself walled, with two jetties terminating in forts to form protective arms round the anchorage. It also overlooked the town's Maison Dieu, the refuge that took in the poor and infirm as a Christian duty, and allowed pilgrims on their way to Rome (or to Canterbury, if they had come from the Continent) to doss down for the night. Dover Castle was the very impressive home of its Constable, who doubled as Lord Warden of the Cinque Ports. But above all it was a bastion, a lookout, a warning presence to anyone approaching from the opposite

---

5 Matthew Paris (*c*.1200–59) was a Benedictine monk of St Albans and the abbey's annalist, who wrote a history of the world since the Creation, most of which was lifted from an earlier work by someone else. But he was a great traveller at home and abroad, and his later pages reflected a sharp and authentic observation of thirteenth-century life in England and elsewhere.

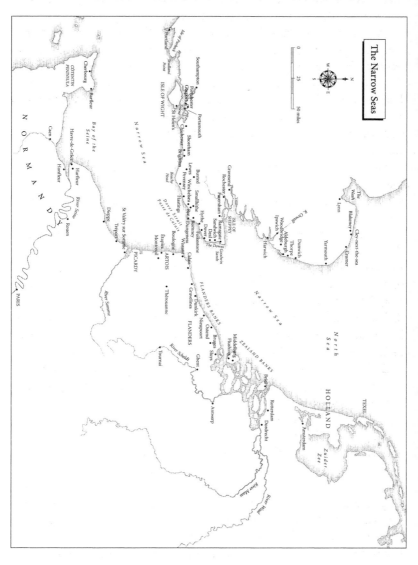

The Narrow Seas

N
W E
S

0   25   50 miles

NORMANDY

COTENTIN
PENINSULA

Cherbourg
Barfleur
Caen
Honfleur
Harfleur
Havre-de-Grace

River Seine

Rouen

PARIS

River Somme

Bay of the Seine

Portland Bill
Isle of Portland
Portland
Studland Point

Southampton
ISLE OF WIGHT
St Helen's
Chichester
Quarr
Wootton
Portsmouth
Shoreham
Brighton
Winchelsea
Lewes
Beachy Head
Pevensey
Rye
Hastings
Dungeness
Winchelsea
Romney
Hythe
Folkestone
Dover
Wissant
Boulogne
Calais
Gravelines
Dunkirk

Narrow Sea

Dover Strait
Pas de Calais

Dieppe
Trepport
St Valéry sur Somme
Etaples
Montreuil
PICARDY
ARTOIS
Thérouanne

FLANDERS BANKS
Nieuport
Ostend
FLANDERS
Bruges
Sluys
Ghent
Middelburg
Flushing
ZEALAND BANKS
River Scheldt
Tournai
Antwerp
Brielle
Rotterdam
Dordrecht
HOLLAND

Amsterdam
Zuider Zee
TEXEL

River Maas
River Waal

North Sea

Narrow Sea

The Wash
Lynn
Blakeney
Cley-next-the-sea
Cromer
Yarmouth
Dunwich
Thorpe
Aldeburgh
Woodbridge
Ipswich
R. Orwell
Harwich
The Naze
Goodwin Sands
Sandwich
Deal
Ramsgate
ISLE OF SHEPPEY
Faversham
Rochester
Gravesend

coast with ill intent. And the day would shortly come when a septuagenarian Italian with a lively imagination would suggest to Henry VIII that it might be an idea to position a giant mirror, which he himself would make, on top of the castle, so as to spy on all the ships leaving Dieppe. The French ambassador, in reporting this to a superior (the Constable of France), added 'Although that seems incredible, he has persuaded the King to provide money to make it, and left yesterday for Dover to fulfil his promise.'

There was no need to spy on Calais in the same way because it, too, belonged to the English Crown, perfectly situated to act as a spy itself upon what went on in the French hinterland; but there was a general understanding that anything said in the town was relayed very quickly to Westminster or wherever Henry was holding court, so that when a proclamation was made in Calais on a Saturday, 'the King's Grace had word of it by 9 of the clock on Monday'. Apart from its English connection, Calais was as unlike Dover as any other port could possibly be. It had its castle, true, but this did not dominate and was only one of half a dozen buildings, three of them churches, which competed for attention above the town walls. Moreover, it was perfectly flat, as was most of its surrounding Pale, which largely consisted of marshes, parts of which had been drained to make room for agriculture, while the rest were left in their natural state as an important defence against inland attack. Calais had a permanent garrison of 800 troops, but it was reckoned that if the Pale was flooded (and this could easily be done by manipulating a system of sluices and gates), the effect would be worth another 10,000 men on the strength. The town was further guarded by three other fortresses deployed across the Pale, at Hammes, at Guines, and at Newneham Bridge on the road to Boulogne, which controlled the causeway across the marshes to the west. And Calais had remained inviolably English since 1347, when Edward III seized it with an invasion fleet of 738 ships. As Henry VIII himself would proclaim, it had been 'of long time, and yet is, one of the most principal treasures belonging to this his realm of England'. He was thinking in particular of the town's value as a defensive outpost for his realm and its role in controlling the Narrow Seas, but it had a number of other virtues in English eyes: as a listening-post and a potential beachhead in frequently hostile territory, also being of considerable commercial value, not least because its ample harbour saw nearly 700 vessels come and go every year, not to mention 340 foreign fishing boats.

The population of Calais was not by any means wholly English in origin – Edward III had from the outset insisted that they should also include a mixture of Picards and Flemings – though all the dominant voices were, and Henry was very adamant about the position of Calisiens at large. He deemed it lawful for anybody who was 'mere English' to intermarry with anyone at all born within the Pale, in which case their children would be 'taken as mere Englishmen'; but if such people subsequently chose to move off somewhere else, then they forfeited their lands entirely, together with a quint (a fifth) of their moveable goods 'and they to be reputed and taken afterward as strangers forever. . .' Otherwise, Calais was run in exactly the same way as any community on the opposite side of the Channel, with a mayor and a town council, who functioned from their town hall, just across the market place from Calkwell Street. Twelve aldermen each represented a different ward in municipal affairs, while contentious matters affecting the parishes generally ended up on the Archbishop of Canterbury's desk.

The King's man in town was the Lord Deputy, who was attended by the small private army of his official Retinue, which included an individual known as a Spear, generally of genteel birth, who had already put in time at court as one of the King's élite bodyguard and who was doubtless planning the next upward move in his career. He might be aiming for a position on the King's Council in Calais, as Lieutenant of Guisnes, as High Marshal, Marshal or Under-Marshal, as Lieutenant of the Castle, Lieutenant of the Rysbank, Lieutenant of Hammes or Lieutenant of Newneham Bridge, as Treasurer or Vice-Treasurer, Comptroller or even as Knight Porter. And these men, operating under the Lord Deputy, were the penultimate voice of authority within Calais and its Pale. Only the King himself could countermand anything they ordered, which affected everything from the victualling to the protection of the town; also its punishments, which were not invariably as barbaric as was generally the case in the sixteenth century, or even unreasonably severe. If a member of the town watch was found asleep on duty three times in the same night (!), the next market day saw him suspended in a basket above the harbour, with a loaf of bread, a pot of beer and a knife to keep him company. And there he stayed, to the gratification of the market day crowd, until the beer gave him the nerve to cut the rope and pitch the basket into the water many feet below – where there was always somebody posted to fish him out.

The other important force was the Merchants of the Staple in Calais, an offshoot of the Company of the Staple which had been founded in London in 1343 with an exclusive licence from the Crown to sell wool in the Low Countries. The Continental Staple (that is, the London merchants' control point there) was in Bruges at first and prospered exceedingly, though a cloud appeared on their horizon in 1407 with the foundation of the Merchant Adventurers, who were granted a similar monopoly in unfinished cloth. The problem from the Staplers' point of view was that raw wool was very highly taxed, as cloth was not, and as a result the Adventurers steadily overtook the wool merchants in prosperity. As a way of solving the problem, the Continental Staple was moved in 1423 to Calais, where the Adventurers did not operate, and began to trade in cloth as well as in wool – and eventually in a number of other commodities, too: tin, lead, hides and butter. And in Calais the Staplers became a semi-autonomous presence in the life of the town, with their own council and aldermen based at Staple Inn, which included a chapel and a garden and was thought to be the most handsome building anywhere in the Pale.

Generally, the Staplers also provided the King's Council with its Treasurers and were always closely connected with the Crown: in their great days they regularly lent the King money, they took receipt of all tolls and Customs, and they accepted responsibility for financing the garrison, which cost them £10,000 a year. Their great days were, in fact, almost over by the time Henry VIII reached the throne, though they remained a significant presence in Calais until it was captured by the French in 1558, their trade being easily the most important element in the town's economy, well ahead of agriculture and fishery, which were its only competitors. But the substance they had accumulated in more than a century there was so drained by 1535 that they were forced to hand over their precious Staple Inn to the King, to pay off a debt they owed him. That was twelve months or so before Calais obtained its own seat in the Parliament at Westminster.

It was an expensive little colony to run, and the biggest and most regular expenditure of all was incurred in keeping its sea defences in good shape (a problem it shared with Dover, which also took a battering from every Channel storm). The sea-banks in Dykeland beside Newneham Bridge always needed fixing, and if it wasn't that, then it was a wharf by Beauchamp Tower urgently wanting repair, or the waterways of the Pale needed dredging, likewise the castle moat, or some sluices could do with mending, and something must be done pretty soon about that wharf beside the Lanterngate (which would require more than 600 tons of timber and £200 worth of ironwork to fettle properly)... The list of serious maintenance work to be done was endless at any time of the year. And all the raw materials had to be shipped over from England, the timber from the Weald of Kent, which was also the source of domestic firewood. But the expenditure was wholly justified in everyone's eyes because of what Calais meant to the English Crown and to several lower levels of English society: which was not simply a matter of national defence, of intelligence-gathering, or of convenience if an invasion of France was planned, but an emotional need after what had happened since Orléans in 1429, when the French began to reclaim what had been taken from them by the English across nearly three centuries. Calais was the only tangible reminder of the glory days, the last toehold (and barely that) in this bountiful land, whose destiny had been joined with England's since the autumn day in 1066 when the wind at last changed to favour Duke William's invasion fleet, which had been fretting for several weeks in the estuary of the Somme.

This relationship manifested itself in many ways, from the bits and pieces of Norman and Old French which had embedded themselves in the English language (words which became *peace, possible, pleasure, journal, sovereign, chivalry, felony* and many, many more) to the particular taste for claret which had been developed during the English acquaintance with Gascony.[6] For mariners, the most familiar legacy was the Laws of Oléron, a collection of maritime rules and regulations which were first codified in 1266 and which governed the rights and conduct at sea and in harbour of all who sailed the waters of north-west Europe. The Laws were associated with the Ile d'Oléron because all shipping coming out of the Gironde with its cargoes of wine from Bordeaux had to pass the island on its way home, and the rules had been promulgated because this traffic was so huge and in need of regulation. We have no idea who set down what was largely an accretion of old sea wisdom and custom, probably derived from several sources, but it was certainly sanctioned by the English Crown and accepted as basic sea law in the English courts. By the middle of the fourteenth century it had been incorporated into the Black Book of the Admiralty, which came in a mixture of English, French and Latin, with the original length of the Laws expanded from twenty-four to thirty-four articles.

6 But pendulums swing...and it has been estimated that one twentieth of today's French vernacular consists of *anglicismes*.

And a very wide-ranging document this is, covering all manner of topics, such as:

1 The master may not sell the ship without leave of the owners, but he may, if necessary, pawn her gear to obtain provisions.

2 The master must take the crew's opinion of the weather before sailing, otherwise he is responsible for the loss of ship or goods...

5 The crew shall not go ashore without leave from the master, but when the ship is moored with four cables they shall have the right to go ashore...

7 A man who gets ill on duty shall be put ashore and looked after at the master's expense...

12 Insults between the crew are to be punished by fines. A member of the crew may defend himself after one blow by the master. A mariner striking the master first is to lose 100 shillings or his hand...

22 If a ship is kept in port so long that the master runs short of money he may sell some of the merchant's wines. Such wines shall be reckoned at the same price as is fetched by the rest and the master shall have full freight for them...

The most striking thing about the Laws of Oléron is how very reasonable most of them were, even-handed to a fault, though hungry Bretons and thirsty Normans might not have thought so at the time. But typically, 'The mariners of Brittany ought to have only one cooked meal a day, by reason that they have drink going and coming. And those of Normandy ought to have two a day, by reason that their master only supplies them with water in going. But when the ship arrives at the land where the wine grows, the mariners ought to have drink, and the master ought to find it.'

The two nations had one other thing in common, and that was their indifferent historical naval traditions. For the French, even more than the English, had always believed that warfare was something to be conducted on land rather than at sea, that a battle wasn't really a battle unless horses were somehow involved, plunging through mud and galloping across acres of grass. For most of the time, therefore, the French did not have a fighting navy to speak of: before the sixteenth century, only Philip IV, two hundred years earlier, had shown any enthusiasm for acquiring a royal fleet; and it was he who first formed the Auld Alliance with the Scots, which would eventually have a naval element. By 1295 he had mustered a nucleus of sixty galleys and, though these were heavily outnumbered by his several hundred transports (which were, of course, for conveying soldiers and their horses from one battlefield to another) and other sailing vessels, that was many more warships than any other French monarch had commanded, either before or for a long time afterwards. Many of those galleys had been built in the great base he established on the left bank of the Seine at Rouen with Genoese help, and this set a pattern that the French had found difficult to shake off. They became obsessed with the galley, which, although it had something in common with the old Viking longship, was more at home in the Mediterranean than in the Narrow Seas; the Mediterranean, after all, was where its ancient Greek and Roman antecedents were.

Though the galley generally had masts and could sail, it was also propelled by oarsmen, sometimes as many as 150 of them, often in more than one tier; and this, together with its shallow draught, gave the galley its greatest assets, which were speed and manoeuvrability. With your sails lowered, you could spin a galley like a top if the larboard oarsmen pulled her in one direction while those on the starboard side backed water in the other; whereas a carrack, even when her sails were handled most handsomely, could only have made a lumbering attempt to achieve the same end and would have needed much more searoom in which to complete the manoeuvre. On the other hand, the galley was at a severe disadvantage in anything worse than moderate weather, a poor seaboat which could easily be swamped because its hull lay much closer to the water than a sailing vessel's of comparable size. But in advantageous conditions it could do very well for itself as an offensive weapon, using the beak projecting from low down on its bows to ram an enemy, or the guns which were eventually mounted fore and aft, capable of hitting at some distance anything almost dead ahead or coming up astern; and it was with galleys that serious naval gunnery began, in the Mediterranean. So much was that sea the vessel's true home, that the galleys based in Rouen were always repaired by shipwrights who had been brought the length of France from Marseille or Narbonne (or even from Genoa), where they had a specialist expertise that the northern artisans never seemed to acquire. And this was the case until Henry V's troops razed the Rouen dockyard in 1418 and put an end to its activities: a fate which in itself illustrates the inertia that generally possessed French monarchs when confronted with decisions about warfare at sea.

But at least Louis XII, who became King in 1498, took a step forward that none of his predecessors had dared for 150 years. His most notable inheritance from his distant cousin Charles VIII was the war in Italy with the papal Holy Alliance over who should control Naples; and, after his victory in Milan, Louis was ejected at some cost. He suffered setbacks to his Mediterranean galley fleet in the process, and this appears to have alerted him to a potentially wider crisis on all his coasts. Three admirals had been passed on to him to supervise naval affairs, such as they were, in Brittany, Guyenne and Provence respectively, and another who was grandly termed Admiral of France, though this officer's overall primacy was more nominal than practical. Apart from that, Louis had but a small handful of ships and a great reservoir of fine seamen, especially in Brittany, who could be tapped for royal purposes if necessary. So he began to build. One of the admirals, Louis de la Trémoille, was told to cut down as much of the royal forests as was needed for ships' timbers, but that was all the King was prepared to spend out of his own pocket. Artfully, he laid most of the responsibility for creating some semblance of a navy upon his subjects instead. Provinces and even individual cities were told that they must raise the funds to produce one or more vessels for their sovereign, and the tunnage of these ships would be related to the community's wealth. Languedoc and Provence, as a result, were each down for two *nefs* of several hundred tuns apiece; and many smaller vessels were launched bearing the names of the municipalities that had sponsored them – the *Nef de Dieppe*, the *Nef d'Orléans*, the *Nef de La Rochelle* – and others like them, which could put to sea if need be under the red and yellow colours of Louis XII. The French King could probably rely on one more naval dimension. When James IV told Louis in 1506 that he intended building a Scottish fleet that could take on anyone, he added that it would always be at France's disposal if she had need of it. This probably wasn't empty rhetoric, for James owed Louis a great deal in the creation of his own navy: French shipwrights, French timber and, above all, French money. The Scottish King was very mindful of this debt.

Across the Channel, the young Prince Henry of England was about to start flexing his own muscles as sovereign. His naval intent was clear almost from the moment he reached the throne in 1509, only months before work started on a new four-masted carrack, *Mary Rose*. His larger objective was revealed two years later, when he joined the alliance between Pope Julius II and Ferdinand of Aragon against the French; his quarrel with the papacy was still eighteen years away, when he sought a dispensation to have his marriage to Ferdinand's daughter Katherine annulled. Within weeks, on 25 January 1512, Henry's Parliament endorsed his desire to make war upon the French King and his dominions. And in planning this, his first thought was to make sure that his fleet was well prepared. By the end of that winter, a memorandum had been drawn up of things that needed organising for the navy before its campaign could begin. 'Indentures and instructions to be devised for the admiral and treasurer of wars... To ascertain the number of guns of every sort and the amount of shot and powder necessary; also the number of bows, arrows, bowstrings, "mares pyques" [a form of pike] and bills; that a substantial man may be appointed in every ship to have charge of them.' Nothing was overlooked; 'Places wherein provision of beer shall be made' included Windsor, Kingston, Putney, Staines, Wandsworth, Harwich, Ipswich and Colchester, 'and of ale at London and Deptford'. Already in the pipeline was a consignment of naval artillery, forty-eight pieces in all, from the famous Flemish gunfounder Hans Popenruyter of Malines, who had asked for 8,000–10,000lb of Cornish tin before he could make a start on the order, 'as the tin of England is better and cheaper than any foreign tin'. According to Lorenzo Pasqualigo, the Venetian consul in London, 25,000 oxen had been salted down for a forthcoming campaign, as a result of which the price of meat in the capital had risen from 1d to 3d per pound.

And now, the latest intelligence from France was collated, telling Henry that all the ships in Brittany had been placed on a state of alert, while all Norman vessels had been ordered to Honfleur to prepare for war, 'to the number of 100 or 120 which are all at the entry to the Seine, as yet unguarded, save that four great ships are being armed to put to sea and keep watch for ships passing'. It was suggested that the English King 'might easily burn them if he had 10 or 12 vessels of war ready', but Henry was advised not to think of an amphibious landing in Haute Normandie, Pays de Caulx, Abbeville or Picardy, because their defences were well prepared, and Louis XII intended to take charge in Normandy himself if it was attacked. Far better, it was proposed, to aim for the Atlantic coast, to target La Rochelle (being careful to avoid Bordeaux) and to let the King of Aragon's army overrun Guyenne and Languedoc from the south before the English joined forces with them ashore. Having digested this information, the English King on 7 April gazetted Sir Edward Howard, who had led the sally against the Scot Andrew Barton, 'to be admiral of the forces now to be retained for succour of Holy Church at the request of the Pope and Ferdinand King of Aragon'.[7]

Now, at last, Henry VIII was quite ready to go to war and cover himself with virtue, glory and immortality.

7 The office of admiral went back to 1295, though the word itself is of Arabic origin: *amir al bahr* meant 'prince of the sea' in the Mediterranean. Until the fifteenth century there was generally an Admiral of the North in England, who supervised naval affairs along the east coast, and an Admiral of the South, in charge of all Channel operations, and these men were not seagoing naval commanders but only overseers. In 1408 the first Admiral of England was appointed on a permanent basis with overall supervision and, sometimes, like Edward Howard, who was fully installed in March 1513, did command ships at sea. Later in the sixteenth century the title was enlarged to Lord Admiral and, in the seventeenth, to Lord High Admiral.

V

Disaster off Brittany

With an admiral's gold whistle of office hanging on a chain round his neck, and with his admiral's pay of 10s a day assured, Sir Edward Howard also received his instructions for the forthcoming campaign.[1] He was to set sail with eighteen ships under his command and 3,000 'men of war, over and above the 700 soldiers, mariners and gunners in *The Regent*', which had almost completed her great refit in Portsmouth. At 1,000 tuns, she was by far the biggest vessel in Howard's fleet. But because she wasn't quite ready to sail, he chose to fly his flag in the brand-new *Mary Rose*, which was but half the size or a little more, with only *Peter Pomegranate* (also just off the stocks) and three other vessels rated at 300 tuns or above. A couple of crayers were added to the fleet as supply tenders, to replenish the fighting ships with fresh water and any other necessities while at sea. In the first instance, Howard was told to cruise the Channel, from the mouth of the Thames round the coast of Brittany as far as the Trade. This was the name used by English mariners for the northern approach to the Rade de Brest, involving a narrow passage between the Pointe de St Mathieu and the isles and rocks which cascaded south-east from Ouessant, a prospect quite as hazardous as the southern approach to Brest past the Pointe du Raz. He was to stay on station for three months before returning to Southampton to revictual – and he must bear in mind that if his voyage was fruitful, 'half the prizes &c (are) to be reserved for the King'. Thus charged, Howard weighed anchor after taking his oath of office before Henry at Westminster on 11 April 1512.

For a couple of weeks, his fleet cruised the Channel and picked up a deal of plunder in the process, not always from French trading vessels he

---

1 Captains received 1s 6d a day, seamen 5s a month plus 5s for their victuals. The all-important lodesman (pilot) received 20s a month.

came across. Spaniards and Flemings also had reason to regret crossing his bows, and so did a hapless fellow from Lille, who was seized, compelled to sail on *Mary and John* (Capt. Sir Griffith Don) as a gunner, racked so badly that he lost a foot and then was imprisoned in Southampton, where he had his ears slit and was threatened with hanging – all on the pretext that he had planned sabotage, though Jacques Berenghier had done nothing more sinister than speak in his native tongue. But there were French vessels simultaneously acting as pirates on the high seas, too, including the bark *Rochellaise*, which belonged to the notorious Malouin Philippe Roussel, and which alone took a dozen prizes between Scotland and Ireland at this time.

With the aid of two lodesmen (who may well have been Bretons in English pay) to pilot his vessels safely through the most dangerous shallows off Pointe de St Mathieu, Howard reached the Anse de Berthaume, a wide cove preceding the extreme narrows of the Goulet de Brest, which formed the entrance to the spacious roadstead. There, on 6 June, he put ashore a great landing party, which chased a garrison out of their bulwark and then went on a rampage for seven miles inland, torching and despoiling a number of towns and villages, killing anyone who got in their way. After returning to the ships that night, the soldiers went back next morning to finish what they had started, attacked Le Conquet (which had supplied James IV of Scotland with one of his ships) and then carried on until they reached the castle at Brest, where they withdrew as before. The third day of this little expedition saw them ashore again, this time on the Crozon peninsula, which formed the southern side of the roadstead. The English were seriously challenged for the first time, by a number of Breton lordlings, who sent word that they were on their way and intended to do battle. According to the chronicler Raphael Holinshed – but not to any other commentators – the Bretons eventually turned up with at least 10,000 troops, to confront not many more than 2,500 enemies; 'and yet, when they saw the order of the Englishmen, they were suddenly astonished' and decided to retire.'[2] There followed a certain amount of parleying, in which Howard is supposed to have ticked the Bretons off for not having the stomach for a fight. 'And thus (making them a banquet), he sent them away.'

Something much more likely than that was in the offing, however. Howard patrolled the coast of Normandy on his way back to the Solent

---

2 Holinshed's *The Chronicles of England, Scotland and Ireland* did not appear until 1577, and Shakespeare relied on them for a number of his historical plots.

and Lorenzo Pasqualigo reckoned that the admiral reached his home port with twenty-six Flemish hulks and forty smaller Breton vessels in tow, which went down so well with his King that Henry hastened to Portsmouth on the last day of July and gave his captains a banquet before they set off again, with the *Regent* in fighting order at last. But this time there was to be no facile success for the Englishmen. Louis XII had at last gathered himself together for action, ordering a land tax to cover any expenditure that might now be incurred in warfare, and mustering twenty-two men o'war to confront the next English challenge along his Atlantic coast: they were placed under the command of Vice-admiral René de Clermont, flying his flag in *Louise*, his biggest ship (790 tuns). After that, his proudest vessel was one of four vessels that actually belonged to the Queen rather than Louis, the *Cordelière* (700 tuns), which she had built in Morlaix at her own expense and whose captain, hand-picked by Anne herself, was reckoned to be one of Brittany's finest seamen, Hervé de Portzmoguer, otherwise known as Primauguet.[3]

In company with the rest of the French warships, *Cordelière* had taken station in midchannel just south of the Berthaume bay, so as to guard the narrow entrance to the Rade, but on the morning of 10 August they were all dutifully celebrating the Feast of St Lawrence, the third-century Italian martyr who was roasted to death on a grille. Primauguet was a man who liked to live generously and in style, and he had invited members of his family together with some three hundred of the local gentry and their wives, including M. Cornanguel, the Seneschal of Morlaix, to a party on board his ship. They were just beginning to enjoy themselves when Sir Edward Howard and his twenty-five vessels rounded St Mathieu at eleven o'clock, so suddenly that there was simply no time to get Primauguet's guests safely ashore; they were about to have a unique view of what warships were really about. But how the French allowed themselves to be caught like that, given that the English fleet had been tracked by watchers ashore ever since they passed Dinard on the north coast of Brittany the night before, is beyond understanding.

Howard himself picked out the French flagship – it was unthinkable that an admiral should demean himself by choosing otherwise – and shot away her mainmast with one cannonade of *Mary Rose's* guns: the carrack carried seventy-odd pieces of various kinds, but the only ones capable of doing that sort of damage were five curtails which would fire 40lb of shot

3 The ship was, in fact, launched as *Marie la Cordelière*, but the longer title was rarely used.

each and a heavy murderer, so-called because it was loaded with fragments of iron which produced carnage on a crowded deck. What happened next depends on whose account you accept. The English version is that the effect of this salvo was to make de Clermont lose his nerve so badly that he put *Louise* about and headed back to Brest. Most of his fleet followed him, leaving only *Cordelière* and the much smaller (336 tuns) *Nef de Dieppe* (Capt. Rigault de Berquetot) to face the English. Some French sources insist that de Clermont in *Louise* stayed with these other two ships to cover the retreating vessels before clearing off. There is, however, no dispute about the substance of what followed. The 300-tun *Mary James* (Capt. Anthony Ughtred) made for the *Cordelière* rather than the Dieppe boat, in spite of the great difference in size, and loosed off a volley of ball with her curtals before falling away. The *Nef de Dieppe* found herself confronted by no fewer than five English vessels, and kept up a running fight which lasted until de Berquetot and his crew were 'at last rescued, about 7pm, by some Guérandais' from the far south of Brittany. If that account is even half true, it could only have been accomplished by superb seamanship which kept the *nef* at considerably more than arm's length from the English craft.

Regent's part in the action is unclear until the *Mary James*'s failure to make much impression on *Cordelière*. The newly refurbished English big ship was commanded by Sir Thomas Knyvet, who had been knighted on Henry VIII's accession, when he became Master of the Horse, and whose wife was Sir Edward Howard's sister, with whom Knyvet had four sons and a daughter. He had been preparing to join in the fight with the Dieppe boat, but changed course and headed for Primauguet's vessel instead. His intention was to carry out the classic and traditional naval tactic of flinging grappling irons onto his adversary until the two vessels were held fast together, then sending a huge boarding party over the side for hand-to-hand combat on the enemy's deck until there was surrender. The grappling was successfully managed, whereupon *Cordelière* dropped her anchor and swung with the tide to gain the weather side of *Regent*: an important advantage, because it meant that gunsmoke from small arms being discharged from *Cordelière*'s tops and castles would drift into English rather than French faces, and so would the smoke from any fire that was returned. Archers and crossbowmen were also hard at it in the effort to repel boarders, and in the melée Knyvet was cut in two by a ball, his second-in-command Sir John Carew mortally wounded.

Then, in the midst of all the confusion, noise, gunsmoke, flying bolts

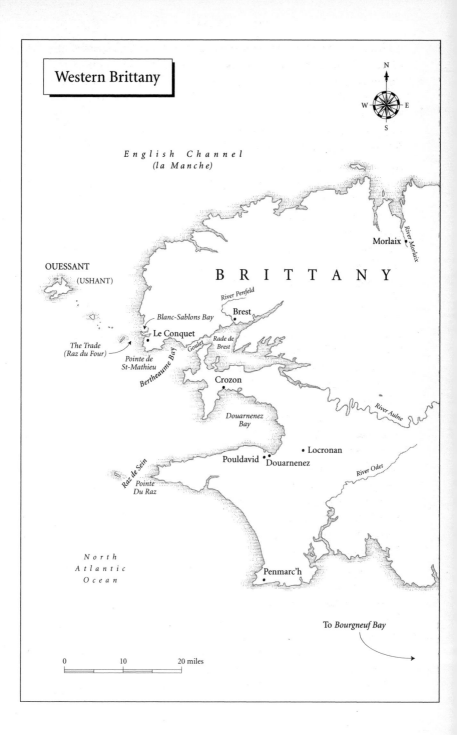

Western Brittany

N
W E
S

*English Channel
(la Manche)*

OUESSANT
(USHANT)

B R I T T A N Y

Morlaix

River Morlaix

River Penfeld

Blanc-Sablons Bay
Le Conquet
Brest
Goulet
*Rade de
Brest*

*The Trade
(Raz du Four)*
*Pointe de
St-Mathieu*
Bertheaume Bay

Crozon

River Aulne

*Douarnenez
Bay*

Raz de Sein

Pouldavid
Douarnenez
• Locronan

River Odet

*Pointe
Du Raz*

*North
Atlantic
Ocean*

Penmarc'h

To *Bourgneuf Bay*

0   10   20 miles

and arrows and other shot, there was suddenly a colossal explosion aboard *Cordelière*, an eruption of flame that quickly engulfed both vessels and, tethered together as they were, presently sent them to the bottom ('*la Cordelière* s'ouvrit comme un volcan, en lançant sur *le Regent* des torrents de flammes'). The *Regent*'s crew got off the lightest, with 180 of her 600 people saved, but Primauguet was killed, together with his parents, his grandfather, the Seneschal of Morlaix, his other guests and all but half a dozen of his men: almost eight hundred French were lost in the catastrophe.[4] What no-one has ever been certain about, however, is the cause of the explosion. According to some accounts it was an accident, a random shot or burning material that landed in *Cordelière*'s magazine. Others thought it was an act of desperation by Primauguet when he saw that he could no longer win the engagement but could take the English with him: 'The French were losing', reported someone in Venice, 'when one of them, who preferred to die a heretic, set fire to the gunpowder.' Certainly a poem was composed shortly afterwards, extolling their lost captain's heroism; and a legend developed among Bretons that, just before the explosion, Primauguet had exhorted his people to die bravely in the same way as St Lawrence. This is plausible.

That finished the action, though the English lingered off the coast for a couple of days before making sail for home. In the shock of losing his brother-in-law, Howard had sworn that he would not see the King again until he was revenged upon the French; and revenge of a sort he did take, burning twenty-seven small ships and capturing five, raiding ashore once more and bringing back a number of prisoners. But by the end of the month, much of his fleet was snugged down in their seasonal anchorages, sheltered from the onset of the dirty weather that made campaigns at sea in the autumn undesirable and in winter quite impossible. Some spent the whole winter at Dartmouth and Southampton, but at the end of September Henry decided that a number of vessels, including *Mary Rose*, *Sovereign* and *Peter Pomegranate*, should be brought round to the Thames as a precautionary measure: rumours had begun flying about French preparations to attack at various places.

Howard's reward for the Brittany action was a payment of £66 13s 4d for his services, and elevation from mere 'admiral of the forces...' to Admiral of England. His principal adversary became swamped by controversy, however. Rigault de Berquetot, who unquestionably had fought

4 Other reports at the time gave somewhat different tallies, but there are no serious discrepancies.

his ship as well as a man might, was so incensed by his own admiral's behaviour on the feast day of St Lawrence that he wrote to Louis XII, accusing de Clermont of cowardice. What's more, he was supported in his indictment by the other French captains, and the upshot was a vague official inquiry, which came to no public conclusions, though de Clermont was not seen at court (of which he had been an ardent *habitué*) throughout the following year, having been sent to reflect upon his behaviour in a minor posting to Rouen. His command was taken over by Guyon le Roy, Seigneur du Chillou, who thenceforth flew his own flag in *Louise*.

But why had these various engagements taken place in Brittany's Atlantic waters rather than, say, off Normandy or elsewhere in the Narrow Seas? A prime reason was that part of Howard's first commission was to escort English transports and an army led by the Marquis of Dorset, Thomas Grey, who, in spite of a twenty-year age difference, was close to the King and was his constant companion in jousting tournaments. The escorts would sail as far as the Trade, at which point Spanish warships would take over the responsibility and see the English troops safely across the Bay of Biscay to join King Ferdinand's campaign in Guyenne. But a factor governing Howard's second sally off the same Breton coast was almost certainly connected with the importance of Brittany itself, both as a maritime and a trading province of France. So far as we know, there were no orders to attempt an assault on Brest, but if that had been successfully concluded – and Howard did reach the city walls before turning back – it would have been a mighty blow to both the commerce and the prestige of the enemy. For this had been France's most valuable northern port since Anne de Bretagne married Charles VIII in 1491 and her duchy lost much of its precious independence to become part of the wider nation, though it was not to be a fully incorporated French province until 1532. Historically and culturally, it had little in common with France apart from the coincidence of geographical attachment.

The Bretons were a Celtic people, as unlike the French as the Welsh were unlike the English, and their native tongue with its four distinct dialects – all incomprehensible to the French – bore certain similarities to Welsh. The ancient name of Brittany, Armorica, meant 'land facing the sea' and this marked the Bretons as a people whose destiny was irrevocably bound up with seafaring. And daring with it, too: they had reached Ireland in skin boats (probably resembling the Irish curragh) in 600 BC, and they were fishing for cod off Newfoundland in 1509, many years before Englishmen or anyone else made for the Banks. They had, moreover, a merchant fleet four or five times bigger (in total tunnage) than that of Normandy in 1500: scarcely surprising when in no fewer than 200 Breton towns and villages, local families owned ships as well as providing the men to sail them. The importance of Brest, placed as it was in an innermost recess of perhaps Europe's most splendidly protected natural harbour (forty square miles of deep sheltered water), had been recognised since the third century, when this was the Roman Osismis and the first fortification was erected on a headland overlooking the Rade to the south and the narrow Penfeld River on its eastern side. Now, in the sixteenth century, Brest Castle was an ominous presence, its squat towers and curtain walls brooding massively over the quays where shipping tied up; with, facing it a few hundred yards away across the river, the tall, round Tanguy tower, in a balance which had guaranteed absolute security in the anchorage these past two hundred years. Brest itself was small – it wouldn't have 2,000 inhabitants until the beginning of the eighteenth century – but besides its value as a naval arsenal and ship-building yard, it was perfectly placed to keep a watchful eye on the overseas trade of Brittany, which was considerable.

Three Breton commodities were much coveted by everybody else. Salt was of inestimable value at this period of European history, useful in the preparation of leather, in soldering metals, in relieving toothache (and in a number of quack remedies), in making cheese and butter, but above all in the preservation of fish and meat: fish needed salting within twenty-four hours at the most if they were not to rot, and every Martinmas saw the great autumnal slaughtering of animals who could not be fed through winter but whose flesh would keep for months if properly treated.[5] Salt was produced in many places (in the Hanseatic town of Lüneburg they made it by boiling brine from local springs, and Lincolnshire's salt pans were indispensable when the east-coast herring season came round), but it was generally agreed that the finest salt came from warmer climates, where seawater was confined in ponds until it had evaporated naturally and relatively quickly, which produced smaller grains. And of all these salts, the harvest from the Baie de Bourgneuf, just below Guérande and the Loire estuary, was prized above all others, very largely because it was the cheapest salt available in northern Europe. Every year since the fourteenth century, great convoys, often of a hundred vessels and more just like the wine fleets, had sailed northwards loaded with Bay salt,

---

5 This problem would not be solved in England until 'Turnip' Townshend and Thomas Coke started growing root crops for winter cattle feed towards the end of the eighteenth century.

which was generally carried in bulk except when it was destined for Russia, whose regulations insisted on its being packed in sacks. Many of the convoys were organised by the merchants of the German Hanse, and it was one of these that the English pirate Robert Winnington had attacked in 1449 to provoke the Anglo-Hanseatic war. English and Breton vessels, however, tended to run a greater risk of piracy by sailing individually or in only small flotillas.

The other Breton commodities in great demand were also shipped from the bay, though that was only one of several local outlets handling them. They were a result of Brittany's generally poor and rocky soil, which didn't do much for agriculture except in the growing of hemp and flax, both of which thrived there. One of their by-products was domestic linen, which was as fine as anything made in Normandy or anywhere else in France: the Archbishop of Bordeaux (the one who anticipated Lent with Cornish red herrings) always insisted that his tablecloths should be made in Brittany, just as a Duke of Lancaster during the English occupation of France had invariably ordered his shirts, his underpants and his handkerchiefs from the same source. But canvas and other coarser textiles were at least as important to the Breton economy, which supplied foreign markets with everything from the fabric needed for packing raw wool, to the drills which made the most hard-wearing breeches. The production was a cottage industry in towns and villages throughout the duchy, each community having its own speciality: if you wanted good light canvas drill you turned to the weavers whose looms were in Vitré, Fougères and other villages round Rennes; but if you were after really stout sailcloth then you need look no further than Locronan, a small place above the Baie de Douarnenez which prospered as much as its contemporary Chipping Camden did from the farming and marketing of Cotswold wool (it even, in time, resembled the Gloucestershire town in its great houses and other buildings of substance, including its opulent church). Year in and year out, cargoes of Locronan sailcloth were sent forth from Pouldavid (which was a port some time before it was overtaken by adjacent Douarnenez), bound for destinations along the entire English south coast and beyond, but heading for Cornwall, Devon and Dorset in particular.[6] This commerce never flagged, except when hostilities between the two countries were at their height, and even then some cargoes were smuggled across. Henry VIII's navy would always be well spread with

6 In 1509–10, 6,330 pieces of this sailcloth were exported to Devon alone. In the same year, Topsham (the port for Exeter) took 340 tons of Bay salt.

Breton canvas, as were the navies of Scotland, Spain and France itself.[7]

Sir Edward Howard returned to Brittany the following year, with the rumours of impending French attack intensifying. A report had come in that thirty-five French men o'war and six galleys were preparing to set sail from Brest and would join up with sixteen vessels waiting in St Malo; and Sir John Wiltshire, the Comptroller of Calais, who informed the King of this, added that the English West Country should have its defences made ready, together with those protecting Southampton. A month or so earlier, there had been talk of fourteen French vessels making a risky winter voyage to Scotland laden with artillery for James IV to use in an invasion of England from the north. The possibility of England's being caught in a pincer movement could not be dismissed, and so Howard was ordered to make for the French coast again as soon as Easter was out of the way.

Vessels that came home from the Trade damaged at the end of August had been repaired in the six months since, and Henry even increased the size of the force at Howard's disposal in 1513: one of the first things the King did when the earlier campaign was over was to order four new ships to be built before March, and to buy 12,000 suits of armour 'from certain Staplers'. As a result, twenty-three of his own vessels were now ready, together with twenty-eight hired ships and the customary attendance of crayers for victualling. Three of the new craft were rowbarges, a small version of the classic galley and, bearing in mind the conditions off Brittany and their chances of survival there (which he appeared not to rate too highly), one of Howard's captains, William Sabyn, expressed the opinion to the future Cardinal Wolsey, who was already Henry's chief officer of state, that they should be manned by convicts and not by relatively honest seamen. Howard himself had other things on his mind, however.

The King had gone to see the Thames vessels during the third week in March, just before they set sail to rendezvous with the rest of the fleet, and in Howard's first despatch after *Mary Rose* and her consorts reached the Channel, the admiral had a familiar and frustrating story to tell: 'on Saturday morning, after the King had left the fleet...the wind veered from WNW to ENE and obliged them to anchor for the day...all Palm Sunday they stirred not, for the wind was E by S...on Monday the wind

7 In June 1513, with Anglo-French hostilities at their height, the English Treasurer at War, Sir John Daunce, took delivery of thirty-eight of bolts of 'poldavys', the name by which the Locronan sailcloth was usually known in England. They were obviously destined for the King's ships.

came WNW which was very good for us...', but then there were a dangerous few hours just off the Goodwin Sands. The ships had weathered everything well, however, and their admiral was proud of them: 'Such a fleet', he wrote, 'was never seen in Christendom.' He was particularly warm in his opinion of *Mary Rose*, 'your good ship, the flower, I trow, of all ships that ever sailed'. He begged to be excused for sending Henry such a long letter, 'but the King commanded him to send word how every ship did sail', and he had followed this instruction punctiliously. It was 5 April before Howard signalled from the Plymouth Road, where he was awaiting the arrival of the Southampton squadron and experiencing more trouble, most especially with the *Katherine Fortileza* (Capt. Flemming, 700 tuns) which Henry had just bought from the Genoese. For one thing, 'Bedell, the carpenter, bored so many holes in (her) that she leaks like a sieve', because the wretched man had forgotten to caulk. For another, the admiral was 'much troubled in victualling the *Katherine Fortileza*, no provisions having been sent for her'.

The victualling of the entire fleet had, in fact, suffered a serious breakdown. The naval pursers had been left behind in London to bestir the laggardly contractors and get things moving, but nothing much had happened yet and what started as an anxiety was rapidly becoming a crisis. In his very first signal to the King, Howard had said 'I pray God that he send our victual shortly' and by the time he reached Plymouth a note of real alarm could be heard. He begged Henry 'for God's sake, to make provision of biscuit and beer' so that they didn't have to return to the Downs and let any French task force heading their way escape. Still the provisions failed to show up, and they sailed from Plymouth on 10 April without them. Two days later the fleet had dropped anchor in Breton waters and it was 'Sir, I beseech you, let ships resort with our victuals into the Trade'. One other matter had been neglected, and on the same day the admiral brought it to the attention of Wolsey, who was the King's Almoner among other things. The fleet's money had almost run out, so that there wasn't enough to pay the next month's wages; 'Wherefore, send a proportion against the payment of the next month of £1,000 at least, and ye shall see that there was never penny laid out but of force it must needs be.' Both these failures, but the inadequate victualling above all, doubtless played their part in determining what happened in the next few days. For they represented at least one worry too many for Sir Edward Howard, when he was about to face a situation for which his earlier experience of the Trade had not prepared him.

When Louis XII was galvanised into action after the first of Howard's two sallies into his waters, one of his orders had been to summon France's most successful sea captain to the Atlantic coast in readiness for another bout with the English. This was Prégent de Bidoux, the Admiral of the Levant and Knight of Rhodes, whose exploits with galleys against Turks, Venetians, Spaniards and other enemies of France had won him a resounding reputation far beyond the Mediterranean, where all his fighting had been done so far; he was 'le magnifique capitaine' to all who were aware of his record. Word of him had reached the English, too, though they usually referred to him as Peryjohn, Prior John or variants of these names. He was now in his forties, a Gascon from Tarbes in the foothills of the Pyrenees, close enough to Louis to have been one of the envoys entrusted with obtaining papal permission for the King's divorce and remarriage.

Having received the order to sail to the Atlantic, Prégent paused en route in Portugal, where his galleys underwent a refit, perhaps to prepare them for action in northern waters, where conditions could be significantly different from those they were accustomed to. There were only six of these craft and it was understood that the Admiral of the Levant would have control of them independently of le Roy's overall command. His small squadron reached Brest at the end of October and, after discussing plans with the Admiral of France, Prégent and his vessels – whose oarsmen were convicts that Louis had released from prison for the purpose – continued northwards to the Channel, intending to raid the English coast somewhere in Devon or Cornwall. But the season of bad weather was well under way by then and it forced them to take refuge in St Malo, where they remained until Prégent was told that Howard and his ships were making for Brittany.

Reaching the Trade on 12 April, and just before he gained St Mathieu again, Howard came upon fifteen French ships, 'who fled like cowards' towards Brest as soon as they saw their enemy approach. Before he was able to round the point, however, the wind shifted ENE and prevented his fleet from sailing any nearer to the port than the narrows, though they could see well enough that about fifty French vessels in all were at the far end of the Rade. So the English dropped anchor and waited for the next day to come, bringing with it, if they were lucky, a favourable wind. It veered enough that night for an attack to begin in the morning, but this met with only limited success. A large French vessel lurking off the Crozon peninsula was set on fire and four small craft were taken,

with a cargo of Bay salt in one of them, which had a prize crew put
aboard to sail her to England, carrying Howard's latest despatch to the
King. So exuberant was the admiral at this easy triumph that he 'wrote
to the King to come thither in person, and to have the honour of so high
an enterprise'. And Henry was more than ready to go and join his fleet
in celebration, but his Council forbade it, 'for putting the King in jeopardy
upon the chance of the sea'; and he was still young and acquiescent
enough to pay some attention to what his principal advisers told him,
though it would not always be so.

A raiding party was sent ashore and burned some houses, coming close
enough to Brest to observe that the French had moored some hulks
across the entrance to the Penfeld River to prevent any of Howard's
vessels getting inside. The English then settled down to a blockade after
losing one of their own ships, the chartered *Nicholas* (200 tuns) of
Southampton, commanded by the middle-aged Arthur Plantagenet, who
was the bastard son of Edward IV and who had only joined Howard's
fleet in order to escape his creditors. Now he had grounded *Nicholas*,
which became stuck fast on a rock so immovably that her crew were
taken off and redistributed among the other vessels. Plantagenet himself
was sent home by his admiral, though this was done out of sympathy,
and not as a disciplinary measure. Howard, indeed, spoke most warmly
of him in his despatch to the King. 'I have given him liberty to go home;
for, Sir, when he was in extreme danger and hope gone from him, he
called upon Our Lady of Walsingham for help and comfort, and made a
vow that, and it pleased God and her to deliver him out of that peril, he
would never eat flesh nor fish till he had seen her. Sir, I assure you he
was in marvellous danger, for it was marvel that the ship, being under all
her sails ... brake not in pieces at the first stroke.' The unfortunate captain
would be a great loss to them, he added, and Howard recommended him
highly to the King. So Plantagenet was sent on his way, presumably with
the Bay salt, certainly with nothing much else to look forward to but the
hard tack of ship's biscuit until he had reached Norfolk and completed
his pilgrimage.

He had not been long gone when Prégent de Bidoux and his Mediterranean galleys, together with four foists, arrived from St Malo. The
galleys at least were heavily armed with basilisks, breech-loading guns
which could be anything up to twenty feet long and weighed over five
tons; and which could fire either 'diced iron' and inflict terrible casualties
on a mass of men, or 15lb of stone cannon ball at a ship's hull and very

seriously damage it. It is quite likely that English seamen had never seen such a weapon before, and they were certainly outgunned by Prégent's squadron that day. They were about to be given a lesson in naval warfare that none who survived it nor their sovereign master, Henry VIII – would ever forget. The Gascon first of all swept down on and through the fleet at great speed, sinking a Bristol vessel, the *Trinity* (Capt. Anthony Poyntz, who survived to be knighted afterwards) and holing the King's new *Less Bark* (Capt. Sir Stephen Bull *c.*200 tuns) in seven places so badly that she was put out of action and barely stayed afloat, while the French lost one of their foists. Possibly because they also sustained casualties and needed to regroup as much as anything, Prégent took his squadron into the wide and shallow Anse des Blancs Sablons, between two headlands just above Le Conquet to the north of St Mathieu, where you were often lucky to find a couple of fathoms under your keel and where many acres of the white sand were exposed at low tide. But if this was simply phase two of the Gascon's overall strategy, then Sir Edward Howard fell for it completely.

Next day, on Sunday, 24 April, he first thought of landing troops and artillery to come upon Blancs Sablons from behind and bombard Prégent's galleys from there, but he abandoned this idea and decided to attack from the sea instead. So he shipped his flag out of *Mary Rose* and transferred it to the rowbarge *Swallow* (Capt. Cooke), which was rated at no more than 80 tuns and consequently had a much shallower draught than the flagship. Accompanied by the similar *Sweepstake* (whose Capt. Tooley was replaced by Lord Ferrers for this occasion) and a medley of other craft, he entered the bay, leaving the rest of the fleet four miles away to continue the blockade. He was going to board the French galleys and overcome them in close combat, even though he would be facing overwhelming superiority in firepower. It was a reckless decision, and we can only conjecture on Howard's principal reason for it, there being several factors that needed taking into account. He had been worried about feeding his fleet, for everyone under his command had been reduced to one meal and one drink a day for well over a week. A convoy of victuallers had, in fact, at last arrived in response to his pleas, relieving that pressure briefly, but everything they brought had been consumed and the fleet had no more than three days' provisions left when nine more crayers turned up that Sunday. With one or other of these convoys, there apparently came a caustic letter from the King (which has not survived), impatient at all the complaints he had received from Howard and 'commanding him to accomplish that which appertained to his duty. Which caused him to adventure things farther than wisdom would he should...' Howard would be disgraced and his sovereign would never forgive him, if he withdrew and sailed for home to avoid another crisis with the victuals: inescapably, he must attack or suffer these consequences. But this enterprise was also in the admiral's nature, for he firmly believed that 'never did seaman good that was not resolute to a degree of madness.'

That afternoon, at four o'clock, Howard and his flotilla began their attack. Edward Echyngham, captain of *Germyn*, which had escorted the first convoy of victuallers from England, subsequently gave Thomas Wolsey an eyewitness account of the way things went. The French galleys, he wrote, 'were protected on both sides by bulwarks planted so thick with guns and crossbows that the quarrels [crossbow bolts] and the gunstones came together as thick as hailstones'. Nevertheless, Howard made for Prégent's vessel and, lacking the necessary firepower himself to do otherwise, tackled her in the old-fashioned way by coming alongside and grappling. After securing one of the ropes to his capstan in order to hold the two vessels together, the English admiral leapt aboard the Frenchman, accompanied by sixteen of his own men and Alfonso Charran of the *Sancho de Gana*, one of half a dozen Spanish vessels that had been incorporated into Howard's fleet.[8] Suddenly, the rope parted and *Swallow* began to drift away from the galley, leaving Edward Howard marooned on its deck. Echyngham wasn't at all sure who was responsible for this: he believed that 'the French hewed asunder the cable, or some of our mariners let it slip. And so they left this noble Admiral in the hands of his enemies'.

Howard was waving frantically at *Swallow*, shouting 'Come aboard again! Come aboard again!' but there was no response from the English vessel, 'which, when my lord saw they could not, he took his whistle from about his neck, wrapped it together and threw it into the sea'. When last seen, Howard was pinned against the rails by men armed with pikes: then he disappeared from view. For a little while, the action continued, the vessels commanded by Lord Ferrers, Sir Thomas Cheyne, and Sir John Wallop firing sheaves of arrows at the French galleys, while Sir Henry Sherburn and Sir William Sydney attempted to ram Prégent's craft and succeeded in smashing some of her oars. They only broke off the engagement when they realised that Howard was gone and, later that

8 According to Prégent de Bidoux, however, he was attacked by thirty ships and twenty-five or thirty barks, and Howard boarded him with forty-five or fifty men.

day, Wallop and Cheyne took a party ashore under a flag of truce to make enquiries of the French. They met Prégent himself and he told them 'Sirs, I assure you I have no prisoners English within my galley but one and he is a mariner, but there was one that leapt into my galley with a gilt target on his arm, the which I saw cast overboard with morris pikes; and the mariner that I have prisoner told me that that same man was your Admiral.'

It was the end of the Brittany expedition, which had turned into a nightmare. Including Howard himself, the English had lost 120 men in the Anse des Blancs Sablons; and almost as hard to bear was the thought that some had failed in their duty by abandoning their leader. He had, of course, finished up in the sea, though whether he fell or was pitched overboard has never been quite clear; whichever it was, the weight of his armour would have made it certain that he would drown even if he wasn't dead when he hit the water. Four days later, the body was recovered and taken to Le Conquet, where Prégent had it disembowelled and salted as a preliminary to embalming, while he waited for Louis XII to tell him where it was to be buried. He sent Howard's gold whistle of office to Queen Anne and the Englishman's clothes to the Princess Claude, and promised that he would have the scene of the action painted for the royal family. He had one request to make for himself (apart from the small matter of overdue pay): he would like to keep Howard's heart as a personal trophy.

The English had withdrawn by then, reaching Plymouth on the last day of April, with many of their people sick or wounded; some had died of measles en route and Edward Echyngham said that two men dropped dead the moment they were taken ashore. In his letter to Wolsey, he made one or two sharp points about the future conduct of naval affairs. If there was to be any hope of English galleys or rowbarges doing damage to the French, 'the King's noble Grace...must put into them some gentlemen that is of good courage' and the rowers must be chained to their benches; moreover 'they that shall be captains and mariners of the said galleys, ye must give them great reward if they do well'. The implication was unmistakable: too many of Howard's people had failed to perform as they might have been expected to under fire, lacking the necessary courage in command and simply abandoning their posts if they came lower down the natural order of things.

The criticism was made more pointedly by Howard's elder brother Thomas, who was sent down to the West Country to take Edward's place as Admiral of England. He informed the King from Plymouth that Prégent's ordnance, 'if it be such as they report, is a thing marvellous' and that the action 'was the most dangerous enterprise he ever heard of, and the most manly handled'. He was doubtless referring to Edward, because in a letter to Wolsey he took a different line. After mentioning that the captains had been greatly disheartened by the King's criticism and could do with some encouragement, Howard said that he intended to punish two men who 'did their part very ill that day my brother was lost: the one was Cooke, the Queen's servant in a rowbarge and the other Freeman, my said brother's household servant'. The first of these was the same Cooke who captained the *Swallow* in the fight with Prégent, and Howard obviously felt that he had left his younger brother in the lurch. We have no idea what Freeman's failure was, but it may be that he did not board the French galley with his master, which would make him, too, guilty of cowardice.

The King wanted his new admiral to get the fleet to sea again as quickly as possible and back to Brittany in order to repair the damage done to English honour – which, in Henry VIII's terms, meant never being seen to give way to anyone else and punishing any challenger – and to Henry's own reputation in particular. But Thomas Howard had quickly recognised the despondent mood of the fleet; he was ever a realist, as well as a devious man much given to concealing his self-interest, so that no-one was ever quite sure what he really believed about anything. On this occasion, however, his instincts were beyond reproach. Having listened to what his captains had to say about the humiliation they had suffered, and especially to their descriptions of Prégent's firepower, he told Wolsey the blunt truth of the matter. 'Never man saw men in greater fear than all the masters and mariners be of the galleys, insomuch that in a manner they had as lief go into Purgatory as to the Trade.' He didn't understand their unwillingness to return to Brittany, he said; which was either a platitude or a failure of the imagination. But, then, he had not himself been in the shallow bay with the white sands, had not seen what Prégent de Bidoux and his basilisks could do.

VI
A QUEST FOR GLORY

❧

Henry needed something to salve his injured pride. His obstinate wish to punish someone for the affront to his majesty, and to exact the punishment in Brittany above all, caused him to persist in his demand that Howard must lead the fleet back to the Trade, whatever awaited them there. In 1513 the King had, in fact, suffered two simultaneous indignities, in Brittany and in the far south, where the Spanish had badly let him down. The southern campaign was supposed to have been a signal moment in Henry's drive for European supremacy: not since 1453 had an English army established a new presence in France in order to retrieve old possessions; in effect it would be a renewal of the Hundred Years War. But the first phase of the master plan had become a discreditable mess soon after Edward Howard's escorts handed over their responsibility for convoying Thomas Grey's army to amalgamate with Ferdinand of Aragon's. The English soldiers were seriously seasick crossing the Bay of Biscay and the English seamen manning their transports had consumed the victuals that the military could not for the moment get down. On arrival in San Sebastian, on Spain's northern coast, Grey's troops were supposed to march to the border town of Fuentarrabia, where ordnance and horses would be awaiting them. Ferdinand's people had arranged nothing, however, and refused to co-operate when Grey suggested crossing the border and attacking Bayonne, which would make an excellent base for further excursions into Guyenne. Ferdinand, it turned out, was not very interested in the agreed plan of campaign, his own ambition being simply to annexe the ancient Pyreenean kingdom of Navarre, which would bring the Basque people entirely under his control.

So the English remained isolated in Fuentarrabia, waiting for something and somebody to turn up, increasingly demoralised as none of the support they had been led to expect appeared. Steadily, everything in the enterprise fell apart. It poured down day after day and, with not enough tents to shelter in, among other things, the archers' weapons became soaked and therefore useless. Grey bought 200 mules to serve instead of the horses they didn't have, and then discovered that the animals had never been broken in. The food and the beer were running out, and the English troops didn't much care for the local drink. As the weeks passed, the sick list lengthened and then desertions began, followed by the looting of civilian properties. Mutinous quarrels were growing among the men and even the officers were at odds with each other. Grey himself fell ill, beginning to lose control, and by the time just about everyone under his command made it clear that they had had enough, he had become incapable of salvaging anything. So the English army sailed for home ignominiously, and Henry did not spare Grey and the other commanders his wrath when they arrived. By the time they were received at court, Ferdinand had compounded his duplicity by accusing the English of everything from incompetence to unhelpfulness, even of timidity, which upset Henry so much that he deliberately humiliated his officers in front of the Spanish ambassador.

He needed a bigger scapegoat than them, however, yet he could hardly make war against Ferdinand, who was not only supposed to be his ally still, but had also become his father-in-law when Henry married Katherine. As the pressure on Thomas Howard increased, so for a while he went through the motions of preparing the fleet for more action in Brittany. On 13 May, Henry instructed him to start 'making an enterprise as well by land as by water for the distressing of the navy of France now being in Brittany'. Troops were to join the admiral in Southampton and then would sail to Plymouth or Dartmouth to meet up with the fleet, and there Howard must discuss with the military commander, Charles Brandon, the newly created Lord Lisle and a boyhood friend of the King's, the best course of action. Howard, however, was already in Plymouth aboard *Mary Rose*. Having received the King's instructions, together with a great deal of logistical detail about who was to take part in the expedition, he wrote from there, 'Sir, I doubt not, God and the wind serving, you shall obtain the destruction of the French navy and a great part of the coast of Brittany.' But he quickly added a rider: Plymouth Sound, he said, was 'the most dangerous haven in England' for even the number of ships now gathered there, without the addition of military transports, 'and when the wind is southwards it is impossible to leave'.

It didn't make sense for Brandon and his army to come there from Southampton (which 'would be clean out of his course') and if a south wind blew when he got to Devon it might keep him there in harbour until all his victuals were exhausted, and would thus frustrate 'your noble pretended enterprise'. Instead, he suggested, 'if wind serve, I will draw to the Isle of Wight and ride before Portsmouth. . .we can also make shift to take in some of my cousin's men if he lack shipping and I undertake that at Hampton none of our company shall come on land'. He then underlined the point: 'If the coming forth of the French is unlikely, as I wrote yesterday, our remaining here is useless.' He finished with a typical Thomas Howard emollient. 'Your letters directed to Lord Ferrers and other captains have marvellously rejoiced them.'

Next day, he told Wolsey that he intended sailing to Southampton and repeated his dislike of Plymouth: 'this is the worst haven in England to get out of. . .no wind but North can bring all forth without warping'. He prayed that the wind would shift from the south, where it now was. On the 15th he reported that he was still windbound in Cattewater, the eastern arm of Plymouth Sound, 'which prevents him from following the King's pleasure', and hinted at disciplinary problems in the fleet: he had set up a pair of gallows at the waterside, 'where some will "towter" tomorrow,' Twenty-four hours later, the news was no better: 'this day at 10 o'clock, when most of the ships in the Sound were ready to weigh anchor', the wind, which had gone to the west, suddenly came from the south again 'and blew so rudely' that all the ships were forced to belay the order to move. He told Wolsey that he feared 'ye be weary of my writing, but I had rather be judged too quick than too slow'. On the 18th, still stuck in Plymouth, the admiral wrote to the King again with more bad news. Not only had he and his fleet been standing by to leave for six days, but the wind had blown so fiercely that they had been forced to lay out shot anchors and had broken many of them, with many cables parting under the strain.[1] 'Your new cables are of the worst stuff that ever man saw. At my coming to Hampton, I will send you an example.' As for Plymouth, 'I pray God defend me for ever coming again with such a royal army.' Still it went on. On 20 May, a full week after receiving Henry's instructions, he told Wolsey that it looked as if he could only leave Plymouth by 'warping with much pain from Cattewater to the Sound', and Wolsey replied that when Howard and his ships reached the

---

1 A shot anchor was one on the end of two cables spliced together, which made a ship ride easier in strong winds.

Isle of Wight, he didn't doubt that the King would be with them soon; and he repeated that Brittany was still the target for naval and land warfare.

It's unclear when Howard did, in fact, get out of Plymouth, for his next communication to Wolsey was from Southampton and is dated 5 June. The admiral wrote that he had 'found him so kind, he can do no less than write to him from time to time, as never poor gentleman was in greater fear to take rebuke than he'; which was another piece of ingratiating humbug, for Howard above all the rest of the nobility loathed Wolsey as a jumped-up commoner (he was a butcher's son from Ipswich). The King had evidently been and gone from Hampshire before the letter was written, but while he was there, Howard said, it had been debated 'whether he should burn the ships at Brest Castle or destroy the haven there by sinking ships; and the King bade him spare not to enter the great water of Brest'. After Henry had returned to London, however, 'the Lords Winchester and Lisle have, in the King's name, countermanded the order'.[2] This was an early taste for Thomas Howard of the sudden changes of plan that would recur throughout Henry's reign, to the despair of all English commanders. Henry had, in fact, been seriously considering an attack on Picardy since the first week in May, when he discussed with two of his advisers whether Dunkirk was a better place for mustering an invading army than Gravelines 'or some town nearer Bruges'. His mind appears to have been made up no later than 17 May, when a Royal Proclamation announced that Henry was going to lead his army across the Channel in person. Why Howard had reason to believe for so long after that in the possibility of Brittany as an option, is something that no surviving document has ever made clear.

On 6 June, the Admiral wrote to Wolsey again that some French fishermen, who had been taken off the coast of Normandy and questioned, said that in the past couple of weeks eighteen ships had arrived in Honfleur from Brittany and that their sailors and soldiers had gone home, 'saying they will no more go to the sea this year without the Scots and the Danes come, whom they look daily for'. They were looking in vain. It would be several weeks more before the Scots set sail to fulfil James IV's pledge that his navy was at France's disposal, and even then their assistance came to naught. It wasn't until 25 July that the Scottish fleet left the Firth of Forth, James going with them as far as the estuary

2 Richard Fox, Bishop of Winchester, was also Keeper of the Privy Seal and a key figure in Henry's government.

in his great ship *Michael*. She and the other vessels then turned north, so as to avoid any English guardians of the Narrow Seas, and sailed round Scotland westabout between Orkney and the mainland, which meant that they had to get through the Pentland Firth, one of the most difficult stretches of water in northern Europe, full of rip tides and treacherous currents. They then set course for France by way of the Hebrides but, as they were approaching the Irish coast, the fleet's commander, James Hamilton, Earl of Arran, decided to sail into Belfast Lough and bombard the English stronghold of Carrickfergus, either as an act or bravado or because he believed that was what his King would wish him to do. If he intended to take the town he failed, and had to retire to Ayr in order to revictual and get more ammunition before he could continue the voyage. This delayed him even more and, if the weather in the Western Approaches that summer was as perverse as Thomas Howard implied, he would be facing contrary winds for much of the rest of his voyage: it was to be September before the Scots reached France, and by then Brittany had been long discarded as a theatre of war.

Not that this was entirely apparent to the English Admiral even by the middle of June. Two days after informing Wolsey of the latest French intelligence, Howard was writing to the King's Council in reply to a message from them which gave him reason to believe that he was after all bound for Brest. But he had bad news for the government: a lot of the people who were supposed to be sailing in his fleet had apparently deserted (Hereford gaol was said to be full of them) and Lord Ferrers had found at a muster of the forces under his command that 100 of his troops and sailors were missing. Howard vowed that any who had gone without permission would be hanged on the morrow and advised that 'The King should command some of them to be executed, and others to be brought hither against my return to be executed here.' There was also a delay in loading the beer, though he thought the local brewhouses were the goodliest he ever saw and already brewed 100 tuns a day. 'As there is no place to store it but the streets, where hot weather would destroy it, he has commanded William Pawne to have great trenches digged and covered with boards, turf and sedges.' He was, however, in better heart than he had been for some time, when he scribbled a message to Wolsey and Fox from *Mary Rose* which, by 13 June, was anchored off the Mother Bank in Spithead, just below the Cistercian abbey of Quarr, and its beacon to assist mariners. 'We are here strong enough', he wrote, 'to encounter the whole fleet of France.' Had the wind served, he added, they had been gone towards Brest before this. But he was destined to fight elsewhere, and it would be ashore.

An English invasion fleet started taking soldiers across the Channel on 6 June 1513.[3] The army of 30,000–40,000 led by the King himself and with Charles Brandon as his second-in-command, would go into action in the three traditional battle formations of fore-ward, middle-ward and rear-ward, and it was logistically convenient to convey them over the water in the same pattern. The fleet was supposed to have sailed three weeks earlier, but the planning wasn't all it might have been, or the response to the timetable of some people who had crucial roles in the project (which was perhaps pardonable if Thomas Howard was not the only one who didn't know whether he was coming or going by then). It took four days to get the fore-ward over, but by then the middle-ward were also on their way and the rear-ward were beginning to embark. Given that they had to contend with typical Channel weather, even if it was approaching midsummer, the shipping of the invasion was conducted with reasonable despatch, though not without loss.

Towards the end of the month, with the business of supplying the army with victuals and other necessities only just beginning and bound to go on indefinitely, a sudden storm blew up and wrecked one of the English transports off Wissant, a short distance out of Calais on the way to Boulogne; the vessel was plundered by the townspeople, who took the crew prisoner. In reprisal, some English men o'war sailed into the shallow ellipse of the Baie de Wissant and put ashore a landing party, which looted the little town and destroyed it with fire. Even some of their compatriots thought the invaders had gone too far with this, and saw divine retribution in the loss of five English ships outside Calais a few days later. The weather had worsened, the seas had become colossal, and the vessels went down with all hands, the seamen perishing 'after long struggling with the waves'. Watching the disaster from the town walls was John Taylor, Parliamentary clerk, King's chaplain and Rector of Coldingham in Lincolnshire, who took the commendably balanced view that the Almighty had not approved of what had been done to Wissant.

With the army assembling, augmented by 4,000 German infantry supplied by the Emperor Maximilian, the 12,000 men of the fore-ward moved out of Calais on 13 June, followed by the rear-ward of 7,500 three days later. As they marched off to the west of the town everyone assumed

3 This was 431 years to the day before another invasion fleet crossed from England to France for the D-Day landings in Normandy. On both occasions, the weather was dangerously erratic.

they must be heading for Boulogne, but unaccountably (there is no surviving documentary evidence) they turned south-west about fifteen miles outside the English colony after holding a council of war. They were now in enemy territory and came under fire while the English officers were deliberating in a tent what to do next; whereupon a bullet came through the canvas and killed the old soldier Sir Edmund Carew as he sat at the council table. The commander of the rear-ward, Lord Herbert, took a philosophical view of his colleague's death, which, he said, 'was a chance of war, if it had hit me you must have been content, a noble heart in war is never afraid of death'. And on they went until they reached the outskirts of Thérouanne, a small town in Artois which the English had once possessed. There they made camp outside the walls, knocked some of the houses about with their artillery, and waited for their commander-in-chief to arrive.

He had not, of course, travelled with the hoi polloi of his army, but had waited until they were out of his way before making his grand entrance in France. There was a mystique to be preserved, an image to be maintained, all to do with majesty and a higher plane of being than anyone else could aspire to. If Henry's Council entertained any doubts about the wisdom of his personal involvement, as they had when strongly advising him not to go to Brittany in April (obviously a sound judgement on that occasion), they could be more easily overridden this time. It might be argued that the King could be evacuated more expeditiously from Picardy than from Brittany in the event of a disaster. Communications would be better if he was present in person, instead of some days away in Greenwich. The troops would be invigorated by having their King lead them in the field. After one English failure on the land that year, and another at sea, Henry would be the best person to put heart into his army and make sure there wasn't another setback in 1513. His delay in leaving England was quite in the natural order of things, though it is possible, in view of the turbulent weather, that one other factor counted. It certainly wouldn't have done for this monarch, above most others, to be seen being seasick on his way to France.

Henry and his escorting vessels arrived at Calais on a sparkling and relatively calm 30 June, a fleet 'such as Neptune never saw', according to John Taylor. Henry came in great grandeur, of course, and with a retinue of well over eight hundred: there were knights and squires, ushers and sewers, grooms and pages, bedmakers and dressers, 115 members of the King's chapel and a solitary lute player, eight trumpeters, ten minstrels –

and 276 people whose sole function was to provide the King's food and cook his meals. He would also have 2,000 personnel of the middle-ward at his beck and call, men who would never have been in France if a mere nobleman had been the field commander. One of the items in his extensive wardrobe was a superbly wrought suit of armour made of almain rivets, which were small overlapping plates of metal designed to give the person inside something approaching normal movement, which was never remotely possible in the customary armour of the day. Henry wore this outfit under a gold tunic decorated with St George's cross, and St George himself was depicted on a brooch pinned into the crimson satin attached to his hat. The faint echo of Henry V before Agincourt was almost certainly calculated.

As he stepped ashore, a little stiffly perhaps, the King was received by the Lord Deputy of Calais, Sir Gilbert Talbot, who had just spent a fortnight in bed suffering from the nervous strain of anticipation, and who now handed the town keys to the reason for his anxiety. Then the royal party crossed the garden named Paradise, where ninepins and other pastimes were regularly enjoyed just under the town walls, before passing through the Lantern Gate, everyone on foot apart from Henry and his sword-bearer. They made straight for St Nicholas's church, where a Mass was said and Te Deum was sung; and then Henry was conducted to Staple Inn, where he was to stay while he was in town. His first night's sleep was disturbed by the pandemonium raised when 300 French managed to wade past the outlying Rysbank fort at low tide to attack the massed ranks of tents just outside the walls, but the watch spotted them before they could do damage – no-one would have dared to nod off once on this night, let alone three times – and they were driven away by English bowmen.

Henry remained in Calais for three full weeks, while he demonstrated his royalty and his prowess ostentatiously. He discussed plans with his Council at some length. He met the ambassadors of the Emperor and others on numerous occasions: three of them arrived while he was 'practising archery in a garden with the archers of his guard. He cleft the mark in the middle and surpassed them all as he surpasses them in stature and personal grace'. He led a large body of worthies back to St Nicholas to hear a Mass in the chapel where Sir Edmund Carew's funeral had been held five days before Henry arrived. He ratified his agreement with the Emperor before the high altar of St Mary's. He went to church regularly and always put 6s 8d in the collection, though none of it came out of his own pocket but was extracted from the campaign funds as one of the legitimate expenses of war. And all this time the middle-ward of 16,000 or so were kept hanging about just outside the town walls, because they had been singled out for their sovereign to lead them personally in the direction of battle.

They finally moved off on 21 July, with Henry at their head – in a manner of speaking, for he was, in fact, at a healthy distance behind an advance guard, the sergeant of tents, the victuallers, and the master of the ordnance, who were required to protect the King's Grace or to have everything properly arranged for him before he arrived at any halting place in a day's march. Part of the ordnance moving behind the column were some pieces of heavy artillery which were Henry's particular joy. A dozen of them had been cast in bronze in Flanders especially for this campaign and were known as the twelve apostles, after whom each of them was named. It was more than a setback when St John the Evangelist, weighing three tons, capsized into a stream and had to be left behind before it had fired a round at the enemy, while the middle-ward marched on, leaving a hundred men under the master carpenter of Calais to try to get the thing back on the road on its wheels: they were in the middle of this labour, their comrades well out of sight, when a detachment of French turned up and killed the lot of them. Meanwhile, Henry and his troops plodded on, for this was not a swift advance, with the heavy guns each needing twenty-four great Flanders horses (much more powerful than English mares) to haul them; while even the four-wheeled wagons carrying stores might require seven. It was not until 4 August, therefore, that the column finally caught up with the fore- and rear-wards beneath the walls of Thérouanne, in vile weather that had the soldiers up to their knees in mud and damply miserable even in their tents. Henry, it went without saying, was sheltered in more lavish accommodation – a pre-fabricated timber house, set within 4,000 square feet of canvas, which included a porch, three pavilions, two marquees with connecting galleries; and a discreet little room which a much later generation would recognise as a thunderbox.

The French had been in no mood to surrender, which was brave of them, given that they could not expect a lot of help from any other quarter, with most of their army fighting in faraway Italy. There was now a pause in the train of events, though it was not without incident. Maximilian arrived for a council of war ('He is of middle height, with open and manly countenance; pallid complexion; has a snub nose and a grey beard') and John Taylor, understandably vigilant where the English episcopate was concerned, noted that the Bishop of Winchester was kicked by a mule and 'for some days he could neither sit nor stand'. The outcome of the discussions with the Emperor is hard to understand when the invaders had bombards as well as three-ton apostles between them quite capable of smashing Thérouanne's walls to bits.[4] The evidence for the number of pieces is contradictory but even if the three wards between them had only half a dozen named after saints (the lowest estimate we know of), they and the other big ordnance should have been enough to breach the defences. Nevertheless, mining was tried in preference, and when that failed because the French detected and then blew up the mines, it was decided to starve the garrison into submission. Once again, planning controlled by Henry was in a muddle, and nothing was properly deployed until Maximilian arrived and started giving orders, thinly disguised as suggestions, which the King seems meekly to have accepted: this was the Holy Roman Emperor after all, and he was old enough to be the young Englishman's father. And suddenly an air of urgency swept through the army, when news came in that a column of French cavalry was on its way with much-needed victuals (sides of bacon, in fact) for the garrison. Some of the horsemen were told to drop these supplies swiftly beside the town walls, where the defenders could retrieve them after dark, and then they were to withdraw as quickly as possible. The last thing Louis sought was a pitched battle with only a depleted army at his disposal.

The engagement that day would be much dressed-up as the Battle of the Spurs, when it was nothing more than a brief encounter, a skirmish at most. Henry, surrounded by a bodyguard of mounted archers, and the Emperor rode forth with their troops to block the French column, which came to a standstill when it saw what was awaiting it. English archers posted behind some hedges (the Emperor's idea) then let fly, which caused the French, sides of bacon and all, to turn round and gallop away in great confusion as fresh detachments arrived in the path of their headlong retreat, so that there were collisions all over the field. Pierre Terrail de Bayard, whose name would eventually become a byword for French courage and chivalry ('le chevalier sans peur et sans reproche'),

---

4 Bombards, sometimes known as cannon, were huge guns employed in siege warfare: they could project an iron ball of 260lb , which needed 80lb of gunpowder behind it, and for various technical reasons they could be fired only five times a day. The twelve apostles could each fire a 20lb ball thirty times a day.

mounted a small rearguard action but he and his men were then cut off and forced to surrender. And that was the end of the so-called battle, which was given its name not because it was where Henry VIII won his spurs (he hardly did that), but because the French cavalry dug their heels into their horses in their haste to get away. He, of course, was wont ever afterwards to see in a grander light a trifling military incident which may have cost as few as forty casualties. Not even his own chaplain thought it worth extolling in the journal he kept of the campaign, which then involved the capitulation of the Thérouanne defenders, and the demolition of every building in the town apart from the cathedral and the houses of the clergy next to it. After that, the English struck camp and marched on eastwards towards Lille and Tournai. It was the second of these that they were interested in because the first was an imperial possession and therefore friendly. Tournai was of some importance because of its strategic position on the River Scheldt, right on the border of France and the Low Countries, but while subject to Louis XII in 1513 it led a largely independent existence. The citizens were defiant when the invaders turned up and many of them remained so even when a bombardment of their walls began on 16 September, overseen by Henry in person.

He was in fine fettle, ready for more action, having spent a few days of rest and recreation at the court of Margaret of Savoy (Maximilian's daughter) in Lille, where 'girls offered crowns, sceptres and garlands' to their honoured guest, where tapestries were hung from the houses, where 'histories of the Old and New Testaments and of the poets were acted' and where the Emperor presented Henry with a full-grown ox for roasting. For his part, the English King gave Margaret and her ladies a great deal of expensive jewellery. Back with his army and determined on another moment of glory, Henry ordered the bombardment of Tournai to continue nonstop even when Clarenceux Herald was sent to parley with the citizens about surrender, which meant that the poor man was in as much danger as any of them while their talk was going on. The herald quickly realised that he was negotiating with a town divided between wealthy people who wanted to do a deal and those who didn't have much time for the rich and preferred to fight. But after five days of ceaseless cannonfire, everyone was ready to call it a day and the surrender of a very badly damaged Tournai took place on pretty stiff terms. Its people were given to understand that they were now an English possession, subjects of Henry VIII. They were obliged to hand over £10,000 at once to defray

English expenses incurred in the siege. In addition to the £1,200 per annum they had paid Louis, they must now find another £800 each year for the English monarch. In return, they were merely promised the retention of all the rights and privileges they had enjoyed under the French, which included not having to put up with a garrison. At least they were spared the violations of looting and rape, which were almost invariable when armies were let loose on foreign soil: throughout the 1513 campaign, the English troops behaved with notable discipline, for which Henry must be given credit as the author of a strict code, promulgated at the outset, that also prohibited gambling – except between the King and his closest officers.

It remained only for the customary panoply of formal occupation and celebration to run its course, followed by the installation of an English garrison of 5,000 men (so much for promises), the establishment of a new administration and the start of a considerable rebuilding programme. Among the new appointments, Thomas Wolsey was made absentee Bishop of Tournai, to add to his growing list of titles. The recently shriven Arthur Plantagenet was dubbed a knight for services rendered as a captain of the middle-ward. But the town was not a particularly convenient acquisition to Henry, situated as it was in isolation a hundred miles from the nearest English outpost, and it has been argued that the money spent in acquiring it would have been far better used in the improved fortification of Calais. The cost of the campaign had been exorbitant, even by Henry's prodigal standards. Lorenzo Pasqualigo reckoned that 'artillery and other camp furniture' alone were paid for by enough gold to fill a well. Another Venetian claimed that the King had travelled with fourteen wagons laden with gold coins and another four with silver, 'facts which sound like tales of romance but are nevertheless true. The King has also innumerable other riches.' Expenditure of that magnitude was one reason why the army began the long march home after Tournai. Another was that October had arrived and the weather would soon put a stop to campaigning on land as well as at sea. In any case, no other feasible and suggestive target was anywhere within range. But the clinching argument for withdrawal may well have been that Henry had achieved what he wanted most of all, which was victory in the art of warfare conspicuously tucked under his belt for all at home and abroad to see and admire. So he left Tournai on 13 October and embarked for Dover a week later (after a hitch with the shipping, which wasn't ready for him when he arrived in Calais).

He also had more pressing business to attend to elsewhere, though it had already been capably supervised by his wife while he was away. Back in August, when Henry was being given tactical tips by Maximilian outside Thérouanne, the Scottish Lyon Herald arrived post-haste from Edinburgh with a message from James IV saying that if his brother-in-law didn't withdraw from France immediately, the eleven-year-old Anglo-Scottish peace treaty would become a dead letter, because James would invade England in order to support his French ally. Quite apart from being angry at what he regarded as a treacherous threat, Henry was also in something of a dilemma when this intelligence was delivered. If he stayed in France and James invaded, there was some risk of his losing much more at home than ever he could hope to gain here; but if he withdrew and went back to deal with the Scottish problem, it would probably be interpreted as weakness on his part. That was something Henry's nature could not countenance and, with the possibility of longed-for glory within his grasp here, it doubtless made up his mind for him, and so he sent Lyon Herald home with a flea in his ear. It was true that Henry had the best part of his army with him in France, but there were enough good men still in England to repulse an incursion from over the Border; and he trusted Katherine of Aragon, who was acting as Regent in his absence as well as captain-general of his forces at home, to accept the advice of the best military minds still in the country. These included most especially the Earl of Surrey, who had served the state in various capacities on and off the battlefield since the time of Edward IV, was well accustomed to dealing with the Scots and, though he was approaching seventy and suffered badly from rheumatism, was not only a member of the King's Council but Henry's lieutenant-general in the North.

James had, of course, been preparing for war for some time, as the build-up of his navy clearly indicated, and in recent months a variety of munitions had been reaching Scotland from France and elsewhere in Continental Europe. What prompted him to threaten Henry at this stage we can only guess, but it was probably because the Englishman was otherwise engaged and was likely to stay that way, given the part that vanity played in every decision he made, as James understood very well. So at the same time as sending his envoy to Thérouanne, and within days of bidding his fleet Godspeed on their long voyage to France, the Scottish monarch on 26 July ordered a full muster of his army in Berwickshire, at Ellem ten miles from the Border. The sixteenth-century code governing such matters meant that he could do nothing more until Lyon Herald

The embarkation of Henry VIII at Dover for the Field of the Cloth of Gold in 1520, with the King standing exuberantly amidships of *Henry Grâce à Dieu*, according to the unknown artist who painted it many years after the event.

The only thing wrong with this is that Henry and his Queen, Katherine of Aragon, sailed for France in a different vessel.

Left Henry VIII in 1509, the year he came to the throne, when everyone thought him an extremely attractive young man, the most promising prince in Christendom.

Right Francis I of France, Henry's great rival in European politics.
They were alike in their arrogance, their vanity and their ambitions, though Henry was the more complicated of the two. But whereas Francis was a significant patron of the French Renaissance, Henry was culturally more limited.

A medieval carrack, drawn *c.*1470 by an artist generally known as Master W (who may have been the Flemish engraver Willem Cruce). This typified the deep-sea merchant-man increasingly seen all over Europe in the late fifteenth and early sixteenth centuries. The two 'sentry boxes' overhanging the stern were probably lavatories.

Three men who became successive
Admirals of England during Henry VIII's
reign: (above) Lord Thomas Howard,
later 3rd Duke of Norfolk (1513–25);
(top right) William Fitzwilliam, 1st Earl
of Southampton (1536–40); (right) John
Dudley, Viscount Lisle, 1st Earl of
Warwick and subsequently Duke of
Northumberland (1543–47).

Drawing by Hans Holbein of a typical merchantman *c.* 1530.
Although the figures are not to scale, they give an idea of how very small and cramped
most shipping of the period was.

Thomas, Lord Seymour, Admiral of England (1547–49), and brother of Henry's third wife, Jane Seymour, eventually husband of his widow, Catherine Parr.

Sir George Carew, the Vice-admiral who flew his flag in the ill-fated *Mary Rose* and went down with her off Portsmouth in 1545.

A model of James IV of Scotland's *Great Michael*, launched in 1511 and the biggest warship in northern Europe for a while. Her building caused Henry VIII to lay down *Henry Grâce à Dieu*, spurred by a pathological need to outdo every other rival monarch. His own great warship was finished in 1514.

Two of Francis I's most prominent naval officers: Leone Strozzi (above) was a notable galley captain from Florence, who served France in the English Channel and in Scottish waters; Claude d'Annebault (below) was no seaman at all but was nevertheless appointed Admiral of France. His lack of experience and commitment wrecked Francis's plan to invade England in 1545, but he later sailed up the Thames to the sound of English saluting guns during a peaceful interlude between the two countries.

The French warship *La Cordelière* (foreground) and the English vessel *Regent* (behind) blowing up during their engagement off Brest in 1512. Many Frenchmen believed that *Cordelière's* captain, Primauguet, deliberately fired his magazine when he realised he was losing the fight. Both vessels sank with huge loss of life.

returned some time in August, but he would then be well prepared for a showdown if it came to that. There was, in fact, an excursion into Northumberland led by Lord Home, but it was unauthorised by James, who was nowhere near at the time, and it was quickly seen off by Sir William Bulmer with heavy Scottish casualties and the loss of some plunder. The majority of James's army of perhaps 40,000, which was the biggest Scotland had ever raised, was still converging on Ellem during the third week of August, with a great deal of heavy artillery in tow: some 400 oxen were said to be hauling the guns along. With the news fresh in from Thérouanne, this force, led by the King himself, crossed the Tweed into England between 22 and 24 August. At once it began marching along the south bank of the river towards Norham Castle, long-standing stronghold of the Prince Bishops of Durham which, twice in the previous half century, had withstood Scottish assaults. This time, it fell in five days and James set about demolishing parts of it to make a point. He left a great deal of Norham standing, however, because he intended to defend it until the bad weather at the back end of the year ruled out further military action before the spring, what time it would stand as an assertion of Scottish prowess and strength. This was a significant prize, second only to Berwick Castle further down the river at the mouth of the Tweed, as England's most important Border fortification.

The stronghold fell largely because no English force ever appeared to relieve its defenders. The Earl of Surrey's headquarters were at Pontefract Castle, down in the south of Yorkshire, but James did not doubt that as soon as word of events in Northumberland reached him, Surrey would be hastening towards the Border in order to recapture the episcopal fortress; so the Scots took up a defensive position on high ground in order to repel the English when they arrived. They settled themselves just below the summit of Branxton Hill, along Flodden Edge, which overlooked the River Till on the northern side of the Cheviots. And there they waited, while Surrey and his force struggled up northern England in dreadful weather; with him rode his son Thomas Howard, the Admiral of England, who had been obliged to relinquish *Mary Rose* for the time being, in order to act as commander of the fore-ward. Gathering up contingents from the Yorkshire dales and beyond, Surrey first made for Durham, where he appropriated the banner of St Cuthbert from its usual position above the high altar of the Benedictine priory (which was also a Cathedral): an important talisman, because it was said never to have flown above the scene of an English defeat. With this streaming above his standard-bearer, he marched on to Newcastle, where he heard that Norham had fallen, and not Berwick, which is what he had been expecting. Meanwhile, some of the Scottish army began to desert, as they grew tired of the waiting and, above all, of not being paid for it, unlike the gunners and the wagon drivers, for the footsloggers were required to put in forty days' service at their King's command, gratis, and to provide their own victuals while they were about it.

Nevertheless, there was still a formidable force entrenched along Flodden Edge when the English at last turned up on 5 September; it has been estimated that the armies were approximately of the same strength when they finally clashed. But this didn't happen until certain pre-liminaries had run their course. For the one thing wrong with the defen-sive position occupied by James is that it was far too good to tempt an enemy to attack it full-on, which would have meant climbing 300 feet up a very steep hill. So a ritual of challenges broke out, each side sending a herald to within hailing distance of the enemy, with messages of defiance. This went on for several days before the next stage of acceptable behaviour was reached. What Surrey obviously wanted was to entice James onto lower ground and so, in order to provoke this, he moved his soldiers in a great encircling movement, which would cut off Scottish retreat in any direction. With the enemy now at his back as well as on every other side, James took his troops to the top of Branxton Hill, to forestall any attempt Surrey might make behind him to take it himself, which would give the English a distinct ground advantage over the Scots. Even James's heavy artillery was manhandled to the summit ridge to avert this, a task so obviously preposterous that it beggars belief. Moreover, at that height above the enemy, the guns could not be depressed enough to have any significant effect on what was happening below them.

The battle began on the afternoon of Friday, 9 September and, in spite of the assortment of Scottish nobility and leaders on both sides who were mounted, Flodden was principally fought by infantry. It was singular in that archery played almost no part in it, nor did either side's gunners: 'the contest was hand to hand…a most exceptional phenomenon', as a military historian eventually assessed it from the nineteenth century. James's soldiers were deployed in five columns, each mustered from different parts of Scotland and led by its local noblemen, but organised by French captains who were serving James on detachment from Louis. The King himself commanded 8,000 or so Lowlanders, positioned with two other columns on either side of them. His army would also copy other traditionally Continental methods of warfare, including the use of heavy pikes between eighteen and twenty-two feet long, which the Swiss had more than once used to devastating effect. For their part, Surrey's troops were armed with halberds, an eight-foot spear-axe which could go through armour and bisect the man inside it; but they also included their usual contingent of archers. They were arranged not in the three customary English battle formations, but in smaller and thus more man-oeuvrable units, which would have a better chance of successfully crossing the marshy ground that initially lay between them and their enemy.

But at the outset, the Scots appeared to have gained the upper hand, when they began to descend the slope, one column after another in a highly disciplined full battle order. The first ones down, Borderers and north-eastern Highlanders under Lord Home, fell upon the English right flank, led by Thomas Howard's younger brother Edmund, and wiped out the best part of it. But they squandered their advantage by lingering to seize what plunder there was, allowing Surrey's main force the time to reinforce Thomas Howard and gain an advantage that they never lost. In the end, the battle was settled by the difference in weapons. For it soon became obvious that the long pike, which could be murderous in a rapid and tight general advance over firm terrain, was quite useless in the hand-to-hand combat that quickly developed across the marshes at Flodden: it was simply too long and too heavy for agile close action on wet and slippery ground.

The carnage among the Scots was dreadful. Whereas the English lost no more than 400 men, the Scots suffered 10,000 casualties as they withdrew and scattered in all directions, relentlessly pursued by the enemy. The majority of the dead were, of course, the rank and file of soldiers, but what stunned the Scottish nation even more is the fact that most of its hierarchy was destroyed that day, together with its King. 'No great man of Scotland has returned, except the Chamberlain (Lord Home)' according to a contemporary chronicler. An archbishop, two bishops, two abbots, nine earls and fourteen lords of parliament were lost at Flodden Field. James himself fell near his banner, hacked by a halberd only the length of a spear away from where the Earl of Surrey had been. His body was not recognised at once because of the treatment all the fallen received from the victors. Thomas Ruthal, Bishop of Durham, who was there, reported that his fellow countrymen 'did not trouble themselves with prisoners, but slew and stripped the King, bishop, lords and nobles, and left them naked on the field. There might be seen a number of goodly men, well fed and fat, among which number was the King of Scots' body found, having many wounds and naked.' Naturally enough, the Bishop took the view that the great triumph had been won by the mysterious power exerted from beyond the principal grave in his cathedral. 'This victory', he declared, 'has been the most happy that can be remembered. All believe it has been wrought by the intercession of St Cuthbert, who never suffered injury to be done to his Church unrequited.' As for James, his body was taken to Berwick, and his tunic was sent as a trophy of war to Katherine of Aragon.

His fleet finally arrived in French waters at about the same time as the Battle of Flodden was fought, and the two allied navies took station off Normandy while they waited for news of a successful Scottish invasion, and also for word that the King of Denmark's ships were on their way. When neither of these prospects materialised, Admiral Louis de Rouville, commander of the Franco-Scottish naval forces, decided that his best course was to intervene in the English expedition to Picardy, possibly to attack Henry himself when he was crossing the Channel, homeward-bound at the seasonal end to his campaign. But, once again, the weather played a decisive part in naval strategy. A series of storms disrupted all the preliminary movements, and an exceptionally violent tempest in October caused the ships to scatter and make for any haven that offered protection from the weather. In the course of this withdrawal, King James's *Michael* ran aground and was all but lost. She was left behind, together with two other men o'war, when the bulk of the Scottish fleet sailed for home in November. Refloated and repaired, she was bought by the French for 40,000 francs to replace *La Cordelière* as flagship of the Brittany Squadron. The only action she had seen on behalf of the King who built her at exorbitant expense, was the bombardment of Carrickfergus on the outward passage from Leith.

VII
CREATING A FLEET

With the immediate threat from north of the Border removed, Henry was able to concentrate on other matters when he returned from France. He did not delude himself that Scottish hostility to England would be deadened by the disaster of Flodden, but it would obviously take time for the Scots to regain their strength. The heir to the Scottish throne, James IV's boy, was but eighteen months old when his father was killed and his mother (Henry's by now estranged sister Margaret) was proclaimed Regent until she married again in 1514, when she was replaced by John Stewart, 2nd Duke of Albany, who served until the child came of age to be crowned. One of Albany's first acts was to reaffirm Scotland's commitment to the Auld Alliance with France, which meant that the danger of joint action against the English would one day recur. But at least, for the time being, a recent pressure had been eased and Henry was determined to profit by it. He would get on with the task of improving and expanding his navy, by following where James IV had led. It is doubtful whether this already arrogant young man saw things in that light, but imitation is exactly what he had begun some time before he invaded France. Though he would never be caught admitting it, grudging envy would have been his response when James attracted so much attention by launching his great ship *Michael*. Well, Henry VIII of England would show them all that he, too, could spend freely on naval expansion, that his own English shipwrights (not hired Frenchmen) could build him the greatest warship afloat.

He had started ambitiously with the creation of *Mary Rose*, which was begun so early in his reign that some authorities have wondered whether Henry inherited plans made by his father, a question stimulated perhaps by the fact that Henry Tudor's Clerk of Ships, Robert Brigandine, stayed on for many more years of service under Henry VIII and so administered the shipbuilding at Portsmouth. But even if that were so, there is no question that it was the second Tudor monarch who actually had the vessel built. She and her sister ship *Peter Pomegranate* (450 tuns) appear to have been laid down in January 1510 – that is, nine months after Henry was enthroned – and they were completed in the midsummer of the following year.[1] *Mary Rose* was rated, in the rather haphazard measurement of the time, at between 500 and 600 tuns and, apart from the novelty of her hull's carvel construction, she and her consort were also the first English warships to be endowed from the outset with gunports, which are generally reckoned to have been introduced to naval warfare by a Breton, the appropriately named M. Descharges of Brest. Not that (until she underwent extensive reconstruction in 1536) *Mary Rose* took full advantage of this innovation for, of the seventy-seven guns shipped at her launching, only half a dozen or so were of sufficient calibre seriously to damage another vessel. But firing any heavy guns from somewhere below the weather deck through ports cut into each side of a ship was considered a very serious (even daring) departure from traditional design and practice in 1511. *Mary Rose* had two such lower decks: the main, where four big guns were housed, where sleeping accommodation was provided for both officers and men, and where the ship's surgeon dealt with his patients; and the orlop underneath it, which was a compartmentalised storage space and may also have been used for sleeping in. Below that was the hold, where the gravel ballast was spread and where the four masts were stepped; it was down there, too, that a brick oven was built amidships, with a form of lead-lined chimney taking the smoke and fumes of cooking up to the weather deck and the fresh air. Hatches up there, which could be battened down in a storm, were the chief source of ventilation for the decks below.

The principal masts – fore and main, mizzen and bonaventure – all carried topmasts, and the mainmast also flourished a topgallant above that. With the heights of these four-masts extended, more sails could be set, more speed and manoeuvrability be placed at a shipmaster's disposal.

1 The names of both ships are intriguing. The symbolic pomegranate of Granada appeared prominently in Katherine of Aragon's personal insignia, and the Tudor rose was part of Henry's. But rather than his favourite ship being named after his favourite sister, as has always generally been assumed, it is quite possible that the exceedingly pious young King wished to acknowledge the Virgin Mary, who was sometimes referred to as 'the Mystic Rose' (as she still is in the hymn 'Crown Him with many crowns'). There is, in fact, no documentary evidence for either proposition.

The highest form of seamanship was displayed in the skill with which the choice and arrangement of canvas was made in any given circumstance, an outlandish and vastly underrated business, described in a jargon utterly incomprehensible to anyone with no experience of the sea. The complexities of ship-handling were fully explained with great clarity (though not until 1620) in Sir Henry Mainwaring's *Seaman's Dictionary*, the first authoritative work on seamanship published in English. Considering how a ship could best beat to windward by tacking, he wrote:

> Before the ship can be ready to be tacked, she must come *a-stays* or *a-backstays*; that is, when the wind comes in at the bow, which was the lee bow before, and so drives all the sails backward against the shrouds and masts so that the ship hath no way, but drives with the broad side. The manner of doing it is at one time and together to put down the helm, let fly the sheet of the foresail, and let go the fore bowline, and brace the weather brace of the foresail; the same to the topsail and topgallant sail, only they keep fast their sheets. If the spritsails be out, then they let go the spritsail sheet with the foresheet and brace the weather brace; [the tacks, sheets, braces, bowlines of the mainsail, main topsail and mizzen standing fast as they did]. Sometimes by the negligence of him at the helm, sometimes if it be little wind and a head sea on the weather bow, a ship may miss staying; that is, to fall back and fill again. The best conditioned ships are those which stay with least sails, as with two topsails, or fore topsail and mizzen, but no ship will stay with less sail than those, and few with so little.

The master mariners serving in *Mary Rose* and other vessels of Henry VIII's navy would have found nothing unfamiliar to them in Mainwaring's text. They, too, would know that although setting the spritsail might give you a bit more speed, and helped in bringing your ship's head round, it also had a tendency to bury the head in the waves if any sort of sea was running. They understood well that you hoisted your heaviest canvas on the lower courses, and only used lighter material for your topsails. Automatically, as a long-conditioned reflex, the whipstaff by which the helmsman exerted leverage on the tiller attached to the rudder – the steering wheel did not arrive till 1704 – was unshipped in foul weather and the tiller was secured by tackles.[2] And all such adjustments, of sail, of spars, of steering gear, all the handling of canvas, of guns, of rigging, of blocks and the scores of other components of a sixteenth-century man

---

2 A great advantage of the steering wheel was that it doubled the arc through which the rudder could be turned, which in the whipstaff's case was only about 7° either side of amidships.

o'war, were not only executed with an uncommon degree of manual dexterity and hard-won knowledge, but often enough with one other quality as well. For even if there were no enemy in sight or within a hundred miles, it took a great deal of courage to perform some of the necessary tasks aboard a ship. This was never more obvious than when men had to go aloft to take in sail, which meant crawling along the yards without benefit of footropes (they were not introduced until 1642), so that you had to hang onto a length of timber grimly with whatever limbs you could spare for the purpose, while at least one of your hands was managing the operation you had been ordered to perform; all this carried out quite possibly in a heavily rolling ship, whose masts and yards would be careering from side to side in tremendous and gut-wrenching arcs. The fittest of men could, and quite often did, fall to their deaths in such conditions: that is one reason why the sea was so conspicuously a young man's profession.

Such was the vessel designed to carry some 400 Englishmen to war, about half of them seamen and gunners, the rest soldiers to lead the hand-to-hand fighting between ships as well as to engage the enemy ashore. *Mary Rose* sailed on her maiden voyage under her first master, Thomas Spert, from Portsmouth to London sometime after the beginning of July 1511, which is when she was certainly afloat and preparing to move to the Thames. Her guns were not shipped until she reached the capital, where she took delivery of them from Cornelius Johnson, the King's gunmaker, but otherwise everything necessary was in place and looking extremely smart, including the crew, some of whom had been issued with coats in the Tudor livery of green and white for the occasion. There seems to be no record of Henry's welcoming her in person to London, though it is inconceivable that he didn't, given his usual readiness to inspect his ships and also the fact that at that stage *Mary Rose* occupied a unique place in his affections. So conscious of this were the first men to command her that they went out of their way to extol her qualities, even at the risk of strict accuracy, in order to please their King. Sir Edward Howard had spoken fulsomely of her in one of his despatches to the King from Brittany; and some years later Sir William Fitzwilliam, flying his Vice-admiral's flag in her, put her sailing qualities ahead even of Henry's other great favourite. *Henry Grâce à Dieu*, he said, performed better than any other vessel in the fleet 'and weathered them all save the *Mary Rose*. And if she go by a wind, I assure your Grace there will be hard choice between the *Mary Rose* and her...' This sounds like a man hedging his bets so as to stay on the safe side of his sovereign.

It has long been understood that a new royal dockyard at Woolwich 'grew up round the *Henry Grâce à Dieu*', and certainly that is where the ship was laid down and where she was launched in 1514. Quite when the first timber was transformed into her keel is undocumented, but work probably began some two years earlier; that is, when Sir Edward Howard was preparing to engage the French off Brittany and only a few months after the almost finished *Michael* went down the slips in Newhaven. Although she would more than fill the hole left by the loss of *Regent* in the explosion with *Cordelière*, it seems unlikely that her planning did not begin sometime before that fateful day in August 1512: the Scottish 1,000-tunner is a much more probable catalyst. We know that at Woolwich a smithy and a long thatched storehouse were built for the undertaking, as well as the docking itself, but at about the same time similar facilities were going up downstream at Erith, halfway to Gravesend. Both sites would expand in the next few years but with somewhat different functions. Erith was to be linked with Deptford from 1514, when John Hopton, who had been working with Robert Brigandine (and would eventually succeed him as Clerk of the King's Ships), was appointed Keeper of the Storehouses in both places, and it appears to have been the headquarters of Henry's naval administration, such as it was during his novitiate, until his final reforms were made towards the end of his reign.

Like Woolwich, Deptford, a little upstream of Greenwich, would grow as a shipyard, especially after 1517, when Hopton was charged with 'the making of a pond wherein certain ships of our Sovereign Lord...shall ride afloat'. The pond was 'to be made and cast in a meadow next adjoining unto the storehouse of our said Sovereign Lord at Deptford Strand, at the west end of the said storehouse, a good and able pond... (with) sufficient head for the same pond, and also certain able sluices through which the water may have entry and course into the foresaid pond, as well at spring tide as at neap tide'. It was to be enclosed within an oak pale, one inch thick and seven feet high, and was expected to accommodate the King's five biggest vessels at one and the same time. Henry (who was always careful with his money when it wasn't being spent on his own person or in gifts to people he was hoping to impress) included in the contract a clause which stipulated that if Hopton failed to deliver in any particular, he would have to repay the 600 marks (about £400) that had been provided for the work. Deptford, however, was not in the running for the *Henry Grâce à Dieu* contract, though she was one of the five ships it was designed to handle. Erith might well have been chosen – and, indeed, coped with no fewer than thirteen vessels in four months during the winter of 1512–13 in its capacity as a maintenance depot. Woolwich may have been given the nod for the shipbuilding because it was situated at a less exposed stretch of the Thames than Erith. Though both sites were on the river's south bank, Erith took the full force, as Woolwich did not, of strong north-westerly winds, which would have put the construction of a huge vessel at some risk; moreover, until the problem was fixed in 1521, its storehouses were flooded to a depth of two feet at every high tide.

So the work began on Henry VIII's pipe dream. She was the fourth English man o'war to be named after the monarch's formal style and title 'by the Grace of God', Henry V, Edward IV and Henry VII all having had a *Grâce Dieu* in their service before her. *Henry Grâce à Dieu* would, in fact, as often as not be known as the *Great Harry*, which was a popular nickname for the King in his early years, when he was held in some affection by his people, and in which he rejoiced. And such a ship she was, at 1,500 tuns the biggest the English would see for another two hundred and fifty years and more. Brigandine and Hopton, naturally, had some part to play, though it was no more than keeping an eye on the accountancy. Otherwise, the work was taken in hand in the almost comically inexpert fashion of the day. The victualling of the 1513 campaign in France was put into the hands of the Bishop of Winchester and the Southampton Customs officers; the supervision of Henry's great ship took this amateur approach a stage further, with the appointment of William Bond as the paymaster who signed the bills, before he was promoted to Clerk of the Poultry in the royal household; and that of William Crane, Gentleman of the Chapel Royal, to oversee the work itself, a function he discharged until returning to his true profession as Master of the Choristers.[3]

It is one of the small but regrettable deficiencies of history that we shall never know who was the master shipwright, the highly skilled craftsman who actually told the workforce how to shape that piece of timber and where to put it (as regrettable as it would be not to know who were the master masons who built the great churches of England and of whose names we generally do have some idea, largely because each

---

3 The Poultry was one of sixteen departments in the royal household which concentrated on the supply, preparation and cooking of different foodstuffs. In this case it handled mutton and lamb as well as fowl, and these formed a significant part of the royal diet.

one left his distinctive mark on the cut stone). Some shipwrights were celebrated from much earlier times, like Henry Hellewarde of York at the end of the thirteenth century and John Hoggekyn of Southampton in the fifteenth, while the great Pett dynasty was beginning to emerge from East Anglia at the beginning of the sixteenth.[4] But the first salaried Master Shipwright in the royal service, James Baker, was not appointed until the last decade of Henry's reign. Whoever *Great Harry's* principal shipwright was, it is quite likely that he was not a Londoner, for there was such a dearth of experienced shipbuilding craftsmen in the capital at this time that, in order to recruit the 252 hands required for the work, it was necessary to scour the entire country: they came from Plymouth, Dartmouth, Bere Regis, Exeter, Saltash, Bradford (on Avon), Bristol, Southampton, Bodmin, Exmouth, Poole, Smallhythe, Ipswich, Brightlingsea, Yarmouth, Hull, Beverley, York and elsewhere, with the Exe ports, Smallhythe, Ipswich and Dartmouth supplying the biggest quotas.

They were all paid conduct money of a halfpenny a mile to cover their food and lodging while in transit to and from Woolwich, and while they were on site the going rate was variable, according to the crafts they were skilled in. Shipwrights received between twopence and sixpence a day, sawyers, caulkers and pumpmakers twopence to fourpence, smiths twopence to sixpence and mere labourers from twopence to fivepence. In addition, everyone was given free board and lodging while on the Thames, which was a rather better deal than they would have had from Henry's father, who expected them to find and pay for their own accommodation when he wanted shipbuilding done. In 1512–14, however, they were quite lavishly given cooked meals of beef, ling, cod, hake, herring, pease and oatmeal, as well as doles of bread and beer. We don't know just where they were housed, but they slept in beds which sometimes had mattresses, bolsters and even sheets as well as blankets: the beds were made to hold two or three men 'and in at least one instance ten men were packed into three beds'. These may sound like spartan conditions at this distance, but they were a great deal more comfortable than anything sixteenth-century seamen knew. Sailors didn't have a 'chamberlyn', as these shipyard workers did, to make their beds while they went about their daily business.

4 The first of them was William Pett of Dunwich, who died in 1497, while two Peter Petts became successive Master Shipwrights at Deptford during the sixteenth century and the most famous member of the clan, Phineas Pett, was Master Shipwright at Chatham in the seventeenth. Others of the Pett dynasty served in the same office at Limehouse, Wapping and Woolwich at various times.

Everything about the *Great Harry* was on a grand scale, her size most of all, which was so considerable and unprecedented that the ship was unable to use the harbours at either Dover or Calais, because she drew far too much water to get into them; which suggests that Henry never thought of such a difficulty when he placed his order for the vessel, or that it was of less concern to him than the impression he wished the sheer size of her to make. We have no measurements for her apart from her tunnage, which was reduced by one third when she was rebuilt in 1539. But she had, at the outset, more decks than anything built before her, 'seven tiers, one above another', according to the Emperor's representatives who visited her on completion, though it is not clear how they arrived at that figure: she had two decks above the waist in both the stern and the forecastle, and at least three decks below that above the waterline. The costings for the vessel show that 1,752 tons of timber were ordered for the work, and of this six oaks weighing sixteen tons went into making the keel alone. As in the *Mary Rose*, there were four masts and the main-mast at least was a quite complicated structure, with a central core of fir (almost certainly imported from somewhere bordering the Baltic), surrounded by numerous thinner and interlocking lengths of oak to strengthen the base, which were held in place as a kind of cladding by heavy metal bands. She needed no fewer than nine anchors (and at least the same number of spares) so that she could be sure of holding her ground.

Where Henry's first great ship had only eight gunports, his second boasted half a dozen on each side, and the ordnance was massive by the standards of the day. *Henry Grâce à Dieu* carried twenty-one heavy guns, of which the biggest were her two breech-loading iron stern-chasers, respectively 22ft and 20ft 6in long. She shipped 128 other iron guns as well as twenty-one of bronze, and she had 100 hand guns on top of all that. Stowed aboard in barrels were well over twenty tuns of gunpowder for these pieces. Then there were the weapons that needed no explosive – 500 bows of yew, 200 Morris pikes and the same number of bills, and 4,320 'darts', which were small arrows that could be fired or flung down by hand upon the enemy by men posted up in the ship's eight tops.[5]

With a full complement of 700, the new vessel was intended to include as many soldiers as the entire ship's company of *Mary Rose*, but in addition

5 The full inventory of the ship's 'stuff tacle and apparell', amounting to 316 different items, appears as Appendix II on p. 326. It is an exhaustive testimony to the meticulous efficiency of Tudor accounting.

she was manned by 260 seamen and forty gunners. The most important man aboard, as always, was the master, for he was responsible for the navigation and the ship-handling, based upon extensive experience and a lot of seatime. The captain was in command of the ship, he alone privy to his admiral's and his sovereign's wishes, making the immediate decisions about whether or not and how to engage the enemy; but very few of them at the start of the sixteenth century were qualified to challenge a master's decisions when it came to seamanship, though that situation would change as Henry's reign progressed. *Henry Grâce à Dieu's* first captain was very typical of the men who had always been given such commands, with nothing much behind them but breeding and influential connections, though in this case he had at least been to sea before. He was Sir Thomas Wyndham, whose mother came from the noblest family in Norfolk, which meant that he was first cousin to both Edward and Thomas Howard. Wyndham was knighted by Edward on behalf of the King after taking part in the destruction and capture of the French ships off the Crozon peninsula in April 1512, when he was second-in-command to Howard in *Mary Rose*. His own first command, of *John the Baptist* (400 tuns), came the following year and at the same time he was made treasurer of Thomas Howard's fleet, becoming Vice-admiral within another six months.[6] This was a striking ascent, given that his father Sir John Wyndham had been executed for treason in 1502 (which is why Thomas did not inherit the title), and the fact that he had never been to sea before 1510.

It was a background quite different from that of *Henry Grâce à Dieu's* first master, the man who had brought *Mary Rose* from Portsmouth to the Thames on her maiden voyage, Thomas Spert. For Spert was very typical of the seaman-shipowner who formed the backbone of Henry's naval officer class in the early years of his reign. He had the sea in his blood, being descended through several generations of mariners from Devon: his father had been master of the *James of Topsham*, which saw service under Henry Tudor. Thomas, too, had served with distinction under Sir Edward Howard off Brittany, but he also owned at least two vessels of his own, the *Valentyne of London* and the *Mary Spert*, and he would go on to become an important figure in naval and maritime affairs, though in his case a knighthood didn't happen until a few years before

---

6 He was succeeded as captain of *John the Baptist* by Sir Ralph Ellerker from the East Riding of Yorkshire, another member of the landed gentry with connections at court but no experience of the sea.

his death in 1541. Beneath Wyndham and Spert came the rest of their new ship's hierarchy: the master's mate and the quartermasters, all experienced shiphandlers; the boatswain and his mate, responsible for the sails, the rigging, the anchors, their cables and other tackle; the coxswain and his mate, who supervised the ship's boats and their crews; the master carpenter, his mate and the under-carpenter; the caulkers, who made sure the vessel was watertight by plugging all her seams with oakum and pitch; the purser, who was never held in high esteem aboard any ship because he was usually suspected of shady dealing with the victuals he controlled; the surgeon, who also served as the ship's barber; and so on, down to the lowliest seamen, who were often highly skilled, but who feared the idea of responsibility much more than they were scared of a tempestuous sea or any enemy they might come across.

Characteristically, as soon as his great ship was finished, Henry threw a tremendous commissioning party on Tuesday, 13 June 1514. Describing the event, the Emperor's men reported that on that day *Henry Grâce à Dieu* was 'dedicated with great triumph. Met the Queen, the Princess Mary, the Pope's ambassadors, several bishops, and a large number of nobles. Were most honourably received, and conducted by the King through the ship, which has no equal in bulk, and has an incredible array of guns. In the scuttle on top of the mainmast are 80 serpentines and hackbuts.' Doubtless the ship's trumpeters were heard from time to time, and almost certainly the guests were invited to admire the sails, which were made of gold cloth, the belfry with its great brass bell for striking the hours, and the crowned orb which was perched on a little spritmast at the end of the bowsprit.

This was a well-decorated ship, though it's unlikely that all her gaudy trappings were displayed except on special occasions. But when dressed overall she had long streamers flying from all her masts, the longest of them fifty-six yards, with nothing less than twenty-eight yards, and there were eighteen banners fringed with silk as well, all these fabrics bearing a variety of emblems in many colours; there were also 100 'little flags'. The national totem of St George's cross figured prominently several times (there was even a small pennant on the bowsprit emblazoned with it) as did the Tudor rose and Henry's own heraldry (including his dragon badge), but there was also a portcullis (which signified control of the straits of Dover) and other devices worked into the bunting or decorating the targets ornamentally arranged along both sides of the poop, all gleaming with new gold and scarlet and blue and yellow paint, but mostly with the green and white of the Tudors. And when all this had been absorbed by the visitors, when all the diplomatic pleasantries had been exchanged, when the King had finished being hospitable and gracious at the top of his most jovial form, when selected members of the ship's company (also there to create an impression) were probably beginning to wilt a little after several hours of being on their exceptionally best behaviour as inconspicuously as possible – it was time for the last and very typically Henrician flourish. 'On the ambassadors leaving the ship, a salute was fired from all the guns.'

Had the commissioning taken place just a few weeks earlier, they might by now have been fired in earnest, for in April there had been a new action in the Channel. Prégent de Bidoux and his galleys had spent the winter in Dieppe, following the failure of the combined Franco-Scottish fleet to engage with the English during the Picardy campaign. With the arrival of spring, however, thoughts turned to battle stations again and Prégent's first notion was to make for Calais and burn some English ships entering and leaving the port, but instead it was decided that he should launch an attack on the English coast, and Brighthelmeston became the target. In 1514 it didn't remotely resemble the Brighton it would eventually become. It was simply a fishing community at the mouth of the small River Wellesbourne, though to call it 'a poore village', as Edward Hall did during Edward VI's time, was misleading, for here was one of the more important fishing fleets along the south coast, thriving on plaice and mackerel as well as herring and cod, and holding four local fairs of its own every year, as well as sending its boats up to Yarmouth in the autumn to make some money there.

The town was sustained by rope walks in addition to the fish and was appreciably larger than the average early sixteenth-century village. Several rows of houses formed three sides of the market place, with the sea at the other end but with a number of additional houses situated after an interval just above the beach, all lying beneath the great sweep, rising to 500 feet, of the South Downs. In total, there were ninety-six dwellings, which meant that the population was about six hundred, living in the shadow of the manor whose tenants most of the householders were. Nearby was the smaller Hove, also endowed with a church, and from both these places roads led to Lewes and elsewhere in Sussex and beyond. One thing Brighton didn't have in 1514, however, was a harbour, which would be of no consequence when fishing boats along that stretch of coast were commonly launched from the beach; but it meant that this was not a port for any other sort of craft, though it would become one in a modest way before the end of Henry's reign. Quite why Prégent went raiding there is something we do not know, though the driving force was obviously Louis XII's pride, which had been bruised by the English on both land and sea in the previous two years and was sorely in need of a tonic.

According to Edward Hall, who left a sketchy account of the raid but the one written closest to the date of the action, Prégent and his ships arrived in the night and, before the town watch spotted him, set fire to buildings and made off with some of their goods. Before the French were able to regain the beach, the clifftop beacon – an iron basket full of wood and hanging from a tall post – had been lit and the six armed members of the watch, together with other locals, were pursuing the raiders: 'which seeing, Prior John sounded his trumpet to call his men aboard, and by that time it was day', he himself wading out to his own galley. The archers followed him and his shipmates into the water and during a brisk exchange of fire a number of the French were killed before the galleys withdrew into the Channel. Prégent himself was hit in the eye by an arrow 'and was likely to have died', but survived, and in gratitude 'he offered his image of wax before Our Lady in Boulogne, with the English arrow in the face, for a miracle'.

Towards the end of May, Thomas Howard, now restored to the sea and *Mary Rose* after his efforts at Flodden, led a squadron out of Dover, bent on retaliation for the injury done to Brighton, and with him was 'my cousin Wyndham' who was flying his new Vice-admiral's pennant in the ageing *Trinity Sovereign* (600–1,000 tuns, Arthur Plantagenet her captain) before taking command of *Henry Grâce à Dieu*. Prégent with a number of French ships were discovered at anchor five miles on the Calais side of Boulogne, evidently bent on pursuing the action they had thought of in the first place; but at the sight of Howard and his English vessels, they 'fled with sails and oars, and got beyond reach'. In his despatch reporting the matter to the Privy Council, Howard explained that he then summoned reinforcements, and ordered Sir Henry Sherburn, *Mary Rose*'s captain, to put her and some other vessels between Boulogne and the French galleys, while Edmund Wisemen in *Mary George* (300 tuns) led another group of ships out from Calais to intercept them. If only he had 2,000 or 3,000 soldiers such as were then in Calais, said Howard, to add to the 3,000 who were already aboard his ships, he believed the galleys could be taken. The response of the Council to this call for reinforcements has not survived, but in any event nothing came of Howard's proposal. Instead, the retribution was exacted by Sir John Wallop in *Great Barbara* (400 tuns) leading a flotilla further along the coast beyond the estuary of the Somme, where landing parties went ashore at a chine in the seacliffs of Normandy to burn twenty-one villages inland and to destroy boats caught in the fishing harbour at Le Tréport.

That was the last Prégent de Bidoux saw of action in northern waters. In August, he and his galleys were sent back to the Mediterranean to resume their campaign against the assortment of France's enemies there. Louis had lately received bad news from the South, after the loss of the French holding in Milan and a new threat to him from the combined forces of the Holy League, and he needed his southern fleet reinforcing by its most illustrious commander. But Prégent would also find himself fighting for the Knights of Rhodes, the military religious order to which he belonged and which had promoted him to the rank of Prior. He was present at the siege of their citadel on the island in 1522 by the forces of the Ottoman Sultan Suleiman (the Magnificent), which would subsequently enjoy an astonishing progress from Constantinople along several hundred miles of the Danube – during which they captured Hungarian Budapest – to the gates of Vienna itself.[7] And it was the Turks who would do for Prégent a few years later. In August 1528, he attacked a Turkish galliot off Marseille in order to free 150 Christian slaves who were chained to its rowing benches, but he was mortally wounded in the attempt and, though his men managed to get him ashore, he died on them in Nice shortly afterwards. His death ended a conspicuous career at sea, which would be surpassed in the sixteenth-century Mediterranean only by that of the even more durable Genoese admiral Andrea Doria, who also battled against the Turks on behalf of Christendom and was for a time in the service of France. He was still putting to sea against Barbary pirates when he was eighty-four years old and did not hand over his command until 1555, only five years before his death at the age of ninety-four.

Louis had been able to release Prégent from further service in the Channel and the Atlantic without worrying about the hole he would leave in the naval defences there, because the French and the English came to terms with each other on 6 August. Louis was weary of fighting simultaneous wars at the top and bottom of his country, and Henry was

---

7 The Knights of Rhodes were otherwise known as the Knights of St John of Jerusalem (the Knights Hospitaller) and their other great stronghold, to which they completely withdrew in 1530, was Malta.

doubtless glad of the reduction in his military expenditure, which had mounted alarmingly in the previous two years. What happened next was very typical of European monarchies in general, by whom marriages were always made for dynastic or strategic purposes, and in which royal women were invariably disposed of as a matter of political advantage and convenience to everybody but themselves. On this occasion, the sacrificial victim was Henry's younger sister Mary, who was then eighteen years old. A contract for her marriage to Prince Charles of Castile had existed for several years until both were considered old enough to fulfil it, though she was now thought to be in love with Henry's closest boyhood friend, Charles Brandon, the Duke of Suffolk, whose domestic life was notoriously complex. And while Thomas Wolsey was secretly negotiating the peace with Louis on Henry's behalf in the summer of 1514, her betrothal to the Spaniard was formally renounced because something more useful to the English King had presented itself. In January, Louis' second wife Anne de Bretagne had died, leaving him a widower in less than the prime of his life at fifty-two. So the main chance was seized on both sides of the Channel and, just over a week after the peace agreement, young Mary Tudor was married by proxy at Greenwich to a man thirty-four years older. The Duc de Longueville stood in for the absent Louis, exchanged vows and rings and chaste kisses with the bride before a great gathering of courtiers and, after a banquet and hours of dancing, they both briefly went to bed where, in the presence of William Warham, Archbishop of Canterbury, each bared a leg to the thigh so that their flesh symbolically touched.

For the next few weeks, preparations for the real thing went ahead: the accumulation of a trousseau (it included thirty gowns), the exchange of various gifts, including a huge diamond with pendant pearl from Louis, and the despatch of a painter from the French court so that the groom would have a better idea of what was in store for him. And on the second day of October, Henry bade farewell to his sister, the reluctant and protesting new Queen of France, at Dover, where a fleet of ships had been mustered to take her to her destiny; most of them were hoys hired to transport the great retinue waiting on the still-virgin Queen, together with its army of servants and its 232 horses and other necessities. The biggest vessel to sail out of the harbour that day was the *Great Elizabeth* (900 tuns) which Henry had recently bought from the Hanse in Lübeck, but *Henry Grâce à Dieu* was waiting just offshore to give the voyage a bit of real class – and to show the French what he was now capable of at sea.

Mary Rose was not part of this marine cavalcade, however, because as soon as hostilities ceased she had been taken to Deptford with a handful of other warships and decommissioned for the sake of economy, which meant dismantling her masts and rigging and much else that was placed in store until needed again.

A week after the Channel crossing, Mary and Louis were united in Abbeville and crowned together at St Denis the next month. But mercifully, the marriage that she had been dreading was not to become the ordeal it might have been. Exhausted by his latest bout of matrimony, as waggish historians are liable to point out, Louis expired on New Year's Day, leaving Mary free (her brother had promised this) to marry whomsoever else she chose. He was Charles Brandon, and she made him the King's brother-in-law by exchanging Queen of France for Duchess of Suffolk at a secret ceremony in Paris not long afterwards; which infuriated Henry, who liked to be in control of everything and who might well have executed anyone but Brandon for a presumptuous insolence amounting to treason. For once, however, he checked his natural instinct for punishment; and in due course, Brandon was restored to the royal favour again.

VIII
THE GUNNERY REVOLUTION

Warfare at sea had reached a turning point some years before Henry became King, in the crucial matter of weapons and battle tactics. He would make no truly original contribution to this, but he certainly pushed the English into the future by his perception of what was happening elsewhere and by his appreciation of artillery in every shape and form. It helped that he never lost his juvenile fascination with guns and what they could do; and the noisier they were the better he liked them, whether they deafened people on land or at sea. Part of him would always be the enthusiastic child who jumped up and down with glee at the sheer explosive spectacle of it all. With a passion for ships just as great, he was therefore better equipped by temperament and by inclination than any of his predecessors to set the King's navy on a ballistic course which would lead to the Kentish Knock, to Finistère and ultimately to Trafalgar.[1]

When men first began to fight each other at sea in the Pharaonic centuries long before Christ, they did so in ways which complemented each other and which were no more than extensions of warfare ashore. As soon as they came within range they fired arrows until they were able to engage in hand-to-hand combat with their vessels right alongside, so that the combatants could surge with their knives, their axes, their spears and their other hand weapons across the two ships. The only significant difference between such an action and one taking place on land was that

---

1 In the 1652 Battle of the Kentish Knock, off the sandbank of that name, an English fleet under Robert Blake severely mauled a Dutch fleet with their gunfire and caused heavy casualties at little cost to themselves. In 1758, off Finistère, the heavily outgunned *Monmouth* nevertheless did more than four times as much damage to the *Foudroyant* as she received, forcing the Frenchman to strike his colours: the success was due to a much higher rate of British fire. At Trafalgar in 1805, de Villeneuve saw seventeen of his French and Spanish ships taken or sunk, while not a single vessel in Nelson's fleet was lost.

the sea fighters couldn't rely on the ground not shifting beneath their feet. Another method of attacking a naval enemy made its appearance sometime between 850 and 750 BC, using your own vessel as a battering ram which, instead of smashing through a door or a wall, made a hole in your adversary's side which allowed the sea to rush in and sink him. The triremes of the Greeks, the Romans and the Phoenicians were designed and built with this purpose as much in mind as the method by which their ships could best be propelled, which was principally by banks of oarsmen, with sails having only a supplementary role to get a vessel to the prospective scene of action; then they came down and the rowers took over. The prow of such a vessel ended in a sharp and sturdy point at the waterline, generally clad in plates of bronze, and this was probably a Greek (though just possibly a Phoenician) invention.

In a subsequent refinement, after a number of ships had become wedged in the hole they had made and found themselves in difficulties, too, the ram was made blunt with stubby fins projecting from its sides so that, instead of piercing a hole in the enemy, you gave his hull such an almighty thump that the seams along the whole of that side sprang open and the boat began to sink anyway while you safely withdrew. In both its forms, the ram's introduction necessitated a change in battle tactics, with the rowers more important than ever, for the crux of such an engagement was a captain and his crew's skill in manoeuvring for position before going in for the kill. 'Victory would go to the crew so trained that it could respond instantly and accurately to command and drive its ship to that point from which a blow of the ram could be launched at the enemy's vitals. . .sea battles became more and more contests in manoeuvering, the captains using the oars as, centuries later, men-of-war were to use their sails to attain the proper position for a broadside.'

The ram had a very long run to the onset of the Middle Ages, though never north of the Mediterranean. The boarding party's history would be much lengthier than that, for it continued everywhere, though in an increasingly modified form, even into the faraway nineteenth century.[2] While it was still recognisably in its original shape, as it was when Sir Edward Howard tried to employ it off Brest in 1512, a number of ancillary tactics were devised to make such close combat more effective. One was to fling buckets of soft soap onto an enemy's deck so that men skidded

2 It can even be followed as far as 1940, when a boarding party from HMS *Cossack* rescued 299 British merchant seamen imprisoned aboard the German supply vessel *Altmark*, which was at anchor in Jossing Fiord on Norway's west coast.

and fell over and, if they were wearing armour, found it difficult to get up again. Caltrops, more usually a threat to horses' hooves than to seamen, might also be showered on an adversary to crippling effect, particularly to anyone who trod on them with bare feet. It was even known for quicklime to be thrown into the enemy's faces provided the wind was in the right direction, and to board him while many of his crew were blinded. Another form of damage was sometimes done by the use of sharp shear-hooks projecting from the yardarms, which could rip the enemy's sails or cut down his rigging and immobilise him: Henry VII's *Grâce Dieu* carried four of these blades on its yards and two more on one of its forestays.

Ballistics involving missiles other than arrows (which were used from the very beginning) came into the reckoning very early on. In 306 BC an action took place off the Cypriot city of Salamis between a Greek fleet of 190 ships under Demetrius Poliorcetes, and an Egyptian force of 140 galleys and 200 transports, commanded by King Ptolemy himself, which was intended to lift the siege of the island that Demetrius was conducting. In the bows of each Greek trireme was mounted a catapult for firing arrows, but these galleys also carried similar appliances which hurled stones at the enemy, and the Egyptians were armed with comparable weapons. The engagement began with something not at all unlike a headlong cavalry charge by both sides, after suitable prayers had been said to a selection of deities, and after trumpeters had tantivied to signal that battle should commence. As soon as they were within range, both fleets fired their missiles and, as they closed with each other, men on both sides flung javelins at their enemy before the moment of impact between two vessels which, until the final deft manoeuvre by the oarsmen, had been rushing towards each other head-on. The action was eventually won by superior Greek seamanship and tactics, which entirely broke Ptolemy's right wing of about fifty ships and thus left the rest of his fleet exposed. And Demetrius went on to other triumphs, in which he used ships built to carry even bigger stone-throwing appliances adapted from the warfare he more frequently conducted on land and for which he was eventually known as Besieger of Cities.

Most feared projectile of all (because it involved the mariner's ever-lasting nightmare of combustion at sea, which almost no wooden ship ever survived) until long-range guns appeared in the fifteenth century was the substance known as Greek Fire. The Greeks and Romans spent centuries experimenting with ways and means of setting enemy ships on fire, including pots of blazing material suspended from long poles projecting from your bows, which you released onto the enemy's deck if he got too close: the independent island of Rhodes, a maritime power in the eastern Mediterranean quite disproportionate to its size in the third and second centuries BC, won a number of great victories against Levantine pirates and others by the skilful use of fire pots. The most effective substance for producing such combustion was based on what the ancients called naphtha, which was nothing less than crude petroleum oil, frequently lying in surface puddles throughout the Near East and therefore easily obtainable. You had to mix this with other ingredients such as sulphur, pitch, resin or quicklime (there were several different formulae), which would give you a healthy blaze, but the big breakthrough in the mixture's use as an offensive weapon did not come until it was discovered that the addition of saltpetre would produce spontaneous combustion. The man generally credited with this discovery was Callinicus of Heliopolis, an engineer who fled to Constantinople in AD 673 when the Arabs invaded the Nile Delta. The invention had very long-term effects, but immediately 'it not only saved the Byzantines...but provided them with their chief weapon for the future; merely by keeping it a secret from the Arabs they were able to hold a clear advantage on the sea for centuries'.

New naval weapons were developed almost at once. The catapult which so far had fired only arrows and stones now threw with equal force improved versions of the old fire pot, which shattered on impact and burst into flames that spread rapidly. Much more sophisticated was a sort of incendiary rocket which could be launched from the deck of a ship. A reed filled with the Greek Fire mixture was loaded into a bronze tube with a fuse that could be lit after the tube was sealed. When the gases inside ignited, the flaming reed shot out of the tube and with average luck started a fire on a vessel some distance away. Just as eerie to anyone contemplating these weapons after a twentieth century that has seen both rockets and flamethrowers used to dreadful effect, was the employment of Greek Fire in close combat. A large and bronze-lined wooden tube packed with the flammable mix and with an air pump attached to its nether end, was mounted on deck and trained on an approaching enemy. Just before he was about to board, the mix was ignited, the air pump was started – and a great sheet of flame shot out into the faces of the boarding party. There was a powerful belief for a long time that Greek Fire could only be extinguished by sand, vinegar or urine, which is clearly a nonsense in the case of the last two, for they would simply cause flames to spread;

only the sand would have any quenching effect upon a mixture based upon petrol. All manner of protection for ships was tried, including large sheets of hide or felt soaked in liquid and hung about the vessel; but it is doubtful whether any of it really served the purpose.

The fire-making was introduced to northern Europe as a result of the Crusades, and it was known in England no later than the end of the twelfth century. That is but a couple of generations before the first date we have for the existence of gunpowder in Europe, in the formula that the Oxford Franciscan (and alchemist) Roger Bacon hit upon in 1260: seven parts of saltpetre to five of young hazelwood charcoal and five of sulphur.[3] Guns inevitably followed soon after but for a long time they were small pieces firing shot the size of pebbles, capable of injuring or even killing a man but doing little or no damage to his property. Moreover, their range was so limited that it would not be until quite late in the fifteenth century that the gun was regarded as potentially more useful at sea than either the longbow or the crossbow, both of which continued to have their champions, who used them enthusiastically well into the sixteenth century. The gun would not become the undisputed weapon of first choice until the time of the Spanish Armada. The first recorded instance of a gun's being installed in an English King's ship was in Edward III's *All Hallow's Cog*, whose inventory for 1337–8 included 'a certain iron instrument for firing quarrels and lead pellets, with powder, for the defence of the ship'. This is believed to have been no more than a foot long, and it is difficult to make any other assessment of that particular 'instrument': not for well over another century would it be quite clear what anybody meant when he referred to a cannon or a gun, because such names were used indiscriminately and could mean one thing or another in several variations.

When guns designed to be fired from some sort of mounting appeared they came in iron until, a little later, they were also made of bronze. Iron ordnance was much cheaper to make than anything comparable in bronze; but it corroded more easily and was much more likely to be flawed when it came from the furnace, which could lead to explosions when in use. The first of these pieces was simply a tube of wrought-iron strips bound together with iron hoops, like an elongated version of a cooper's barrel but forged by a blacksmith, and it was open at both ends. The cannon

3 By the sixteenth century this had evolved to a balance closely resembling the modern formula: seventy-five per cent saltpetre, fifteen per cent charcoal and ten per cent sulphur. The crucial element is saltpetre (nitrate of potash), which has a phenomenal oxygen content.

ball (the expression is used loosely) went into and came out of one end, projected by a powder charge packed into a special chamber which was jammed into and closed up the other end, so that the explosive gases would travel in only one direction and fire the shot: this method was known as breech-loading. Alternatively, a gun might be cast in bronze, by men who had acquired the skill of moulding molten metal into a single entity when making church bells, in which case it would be open only at the firing end, into which both powder and shot had to be inserted in the method known as muzzle-loading. The bronze gun was a distinct improvement on the built-up iron barrel because it was stronger and could therefore take a heavier charge of powder. The firing procedure, however, was exactly the same for both types of gun. A small hole was drilled into the loaded end of the bronze barrel, or into the breech chamber of the iron weapon, and powder was dribbled into it to function as a fuse: a match was put to this and – Bang! – off went the shot.

That at least was the theory behind the first steps in naval gunnery. In practice, many problems had to be overcome by long trial and error before any really telling gunnery was seen. It was particularly important to get the relationship between the diameter of the shot, the calibre of the gun and the quantity and tight packing of the powder just so. If the cannon ball was appreciably smaller than the barrel, leaving an inordinate amount of clearance between them (the technical term was windage), then the muzzle velocity of the discharge would be so reduced that the shot would curve in a gentle downward arc soon after leaving the gun and fall harmlessly into the sea. If, on the other hand, the windage was almost non-existent (or if the ball actually jammed because it was not perfectly spherical) and the powder was inexpertly loaded, the explosion would very probably burst the gun and kill its crew. All guns for centuries were not only clumsy and inaccurate, but downright dangerous to their own people as well.

As in so many naval matters, it was the Venetians who led the way in the early years of the fourteenth century. Their ships were carrying heavy basilisks by the 1470s and the habit had spread to other Mediterranean seapowers. These were mounted for'ard in a timber bed which didn't permit any recoil or any elevation, and in time they were flanked by smaller, swivel-mounted guns (sakers) to increase the arc of fire over the bows. At some time in the fifteenth century, guns were being carried by merchantmen to protect themselves against pirates, as well as by men o'war, and they were as common in the waters of northern Europe as they had been in the south. What's more, they seem by then to have been shipped in other parts of the vessel, as well as in the bows or in the stern. A celebrated drawing of a merchant carrack by an almost anonymous Flemish artist (who identified himself only as 'W') in about 1470 shows five guns ranged down the larboard side between the mizzen mast and the stern – and there were presumably five similar pieces on the starboard side as well. The mountings are not visible but it is thought that they were probably swivels rather than anything more substantial; which means that the guns were comparatively light according to the standards that would evolve from the sixteenth century on. They may have been serpents (or serpentines), firing a ball of half a pound: if so, they were capable of killing men on the deck of an enemy and of destroying his rigging, but not much more. They would clearly be brought to bear on a vessel which was in pursuit of the merchantman and proposing to attack.

The developing importance of gunnery aboard warships in the fifteenth century is well illustrated by a comparison between vessels launched at either end of that period. Henry V in 1416 began building his *Grâce Dieu*, which was not much smaller than *Henry Grâce à Dieu* would be almost a century later, yet she carried only three guns. In 1489 Henry VII built the *Regent*, which was little more than two-thirds the size of *Grâce Dieu* but shipped 225 guns, admittedly serpents of small calibre. In explaining this glaring discrepancy, a historian of naval gunnery has pointed out that Henry V's ship was so outgunned by Henry VII's much later vessel because *Grâce Dieu* shipped a formidable number of archers with longbows, on which the King knew he could rely for extremely effective firepower in the traditional way, and he didn't feel any need to experiment with this new-fangled contraption about which he had probably heard very mixed reports. 'As so often, the excellence of the existing weapon may have been the chief obstacle to the development of the new.' But develop it did, though it would be some time yet before the traditional weapons were totally abandoned in favour of their successors.

By 1495, the *Sovereign* carried sixteen guns above her forecastle, forty-four inside the aftercastle and twenty-five in the flat above it, plus twenty more in the poop above that, with eleven more guns deployed elsewhere in the same part of the ship and with four stern chasers mounted right aft on lower decks either side of the sternpost. In other words, she was massively armed towards the stern, which was built exceedingly high at least partly to accommodate all that ordnance. But there were also some light guns in a smaller castle above the forecastle, and thirty-one heavy pieces firing stone shot from the waist between the castles. When Henry VIII rebuilt the ship in his very first spasm of naval enthusiasm, he added four iron breech-loading curtals, which had evolved for siege warfare ashore, and three bronze muzzle-loading culverins which were long guns that fired a 7lb ball (though there were versions capable of firing much heavier shot) with great velocity and increasing accuracy as gunners became more expert in their craft. By the time Henry was well established on his throne, such men were regarded as an elite with a completely different set of skills from those of the professional seaman.

In the early days of English gunnery, most of these specialists were recruited from Flanders and elsewhere, like the ordnance itself, because Continental Europe was just that far ahead of the insular English in this as in many other respects. But the islanders learned fast once they had grasped the significance of what they were being asked to imitate. Seamen to start with – no shipboard soldiers ever handled the guns – they became as expert as anyone in such arcane matters as training and laying the weapon with the required degree of elevation or depression, in deflection as well as windage and in muzzle velocity. They discovered all there was to know about gunpowder and its different properties, appreciating that the earliest and fine-mealed form (serpentine powder) absorbed moisture easily, which could render it useless, and was liable to produce problems even when it was bone-dry if it wasn't tamped down precisely; whereas the improved corned powder came in grains of uniform size which had been specially glazed to stop damp getting in.

As they became more confident of their craft, and found out by trial and error what worked best in given circumstances, the gunners often designed their own gun carriages for the ship's carpenter to make. The immovable timber cradle of the first experimental days gave way to forms of gun carriage that would permit recoil, which put much less strain upon the deck. Some of *Mary Rose*'s guns lay upon timber beds with grooves extending backwards to allow for 'give', but others seem to have been mounted on low and heavy four-wheeled carriages, which thereafter became the preferred method of gunners right up to Nelson's day. They probably came in at about the same time as the gunport, because that innovation meant guns had to be run in and out repeatedly for the loading and cleaning stages of gunnery. The cast guns were also provided with trunnions, two stubby bars projecting from either side of the barrel, which rested upon notches in the carriage and so made it possible for the weapon to be swung through a small arc in elevation and depression. Heavy ropes were also necessary for safety reasons, to lash things tightly in place so that they wouldn't buck up and down or sideways dangerously, and in order to control recoil.

There was plenty of scope in all this for the gunner to display his own ingenuity in getting the best results. His ingenuity as well as his additional craft skill was why he collected special allowances over and above the current rate of ship's pay. In 1513 a seaman's wage was 5s a month (and it would stay the same until 1545), but a gunner earned 6s 8d – a master gunner 10s – and could expect other bonuses: in 1514, Thomas Howard authorised his cousin Wyndham, captaining *Mary Rose*, to pay Andrew Fysch, one of the gunners, 'by the way of reward to heal him of his hurts – 13s 4d'. This sounds as if it was a form of shipboard danger money, *post hoc* perhaps, after one of the guns blew up or burst free of its lashings and damaged poor Fysch. No ordinary seaman seems ever to have been treated with such generosity after suffering from the inherent dangers of his job.[4]

The full significance of Prégent de Bidoux's attack on Edward Howard's fleet off Brest on 22 April 1513, is that the loss of the *Trinity* that day is thought to be the first time in the history of naval warfare that a ship was actually sunk by the use of gunpowder, instead of being merely damaged by gunfire. It is clear from the abysmally low morale Thomas Howard inherited when he took over his brother's command, that Prégent had seriously put the wind up the Englishmen with his gunnery: the dumbfounding spectacle of *Trinity*'s sinking (and the crippling of the *Less Bark*) would alone have been enough to send the fleet home subdued even if Edward Howard had not also been lost. So another new era began, in which fresh battle tactics slowly emerged with the use of bigger guns, heavy ship-smashers, pointing outwards from a vessel's sides and mounted as near to the waterline as possible for the sake of stability, so that the vessel would not become top-heavy and be in danger of turning over. Instead of ships attacking each other head-on, or catching up and attacking from astern, the important thing now was to get to the weather side of your enemy (they called it having the weather gage) and then fire at him from your maximum range – 100 yards or thereabouts at the start of the sixteenth century, but 350–400 yards in the 1540s; though, typically, the Venetians could do significantly better than that. You fired your guns thus with the largest possible target to aim at, the full length of his vessel:

---

4 Skilled workmen ashore, such as bricklayers, plumbers and joiners, earned 6d a day during spring and summer, but only 5d a day in the months when shortened daylight reduced the working hours.

his broadside. For most of Henry VIII's reign this would be regarded as a softening-up preliminary to the traditional business of grappling and boarding and taking him for a prize, but as the guns grew bigger and the charges more explosive it became an end in itself because of the damage it could inflict. At first, during Henry's reign, firing from the broadside was done by individual guns separately, but eventually the guns would often be fired simultaneously. So began the Royal Navy's great reputation for devastating broadside gunnery.

These developments had an impact ashore, well beyond the range of any naval gun, for they affected significant areas of the nation's economy, its craft skills – and also its environment (a word no Tudor ever knew, or anyone else until the early years of the nineteenth century). As the size of the guns and the number of ships carrying them mounted during Henry's monarchy, so the demand for raw materials and manufactured items grew prodigiously, and the chain of supply was extended far beyond previous necessity. The thing about ships in general and warships in particular is not only that so many different parts went into their creation, as the inventory for *Henry Grâce à Dieu* clearly shows, but that they were required in such quantity. An endless supply of timber was at the very top of shipbuilding priorities, but even before the matter of ordnance was attended to, the industry also consumed vast amounts of iron: Henry V's *Grâce Dieu* had seven and a half tons of metal built into her merely in the shape of clench-nails, bolts and chains; and then there were the ropes and the canvas, the oakum and the pitch and the paint and even the bricks that were sometimes called for so that some cooking could take place. Nor was any of this simply a one-off requirement, for wooden ships needed regular and extensive maintenance if they were to remain seaworthy; normally, they had to be recaulked and repaired every two years even if they had not been damaged in action.

All this was a perpetual drain on the national resources but, while emergencies were not uncommon, just occasionally there was a gratifying windfall. For a long time, the copper needed to make bronze guns (in an alloy that also contained tin, generally from Cornwall) was imported by the merchants of the Hanse who, in October 1509 alone, saw twenty tons carted off to the Tower of London from the Steelyard. But the day came in the last years of Henry VIII's reign when the Privy Council authorised 'the conveyance hither of such bell-metal as lieth ready at Boston...to be employed here about the affairs of the ordnance'. The Dissolution of the Monasteries had just been completed, yielding plunder galore, and for many years to come there was no shortage of bronze for gunmaking or any other royal purposes.

For the production of guns since at least the middle of the fourteenth century, English Kings had looked to the Tower and its Master of Ordnance, who supervised not only the storage of weapons but also a certain amount of manufacture, though this was never the Ordnance Office's principal function. In 1496 its Master, his clerk and his yeoman were in charge of sixty-three guns of various kinds and 406 barrels of powder; but they were also the custodians of 9,253 bows and 27,804 sheaves of arrows. This balance was to shift appreciably in the near future and, though it is not clear how many guns were actually fashioned in the Tower's foundry, references to Cornelius Johnson, resident gunmaker, repeatedly occur in the early records of Henry's reign: in October 1511 he was paid £20 'towards new stocking and repairing divers pieces of ordnance in the King's ships now in the Thames'. Humphrey Walker was a colleague of Johnson's, and the names of Herbert and Tyler also appear. But such were Henry's ambitions that the Tower alone could not possibly keep up with his immediate demands, and he looked to the Continent for ordnance that would serve both in his armies and his ships. Hans Popenruyter of Mechlin (Malines), as we already know, seems to have been the favoured source of supply, but there were others, and some foreigners were brought over to England to apply their specialist skills here. One of these was Hans Wolf who, in April 1515, was appointed 'one of the King's gunpowder makers in the Tower of London and elsewhere. He is to go from shire to shire to find a place where there is stuff to make saltpetre of'; and wherever he and his labourers had to do any digging to obtain what they were looking for, Wolf was to compensate whoever owned the ground.

In 1511, Henry established a new gunfoundry in London at Houndsditch, subsequently known as the Barbican, where crossbow-makers used to ply their trade and have target practice. But the most notable advance was made elsewhere, again with foreign assistance, in the Weald of Kent and (especially) Sussex. This thickly forested area between the North and South Downs (which the Anglo-Saxons called The Wild) had known iron-working since the time of the Romans and even before, because it was rich in the two necessities for such production: substantial deposits of ore in the clay and ragstone lying beneath the surface there, and hundreds of square miles of woodland from which charcoal could be made. There was a well established local industry in

1253, when the Sheriff of Sussex was required to provide 30,000 horse-shoes and 60,000 nails for the horses of Henry III's army, and this became much more sophisticated with the introduction of the blast furnace, which may have been invented at Namur, Flanders, in 1340. The manufacture of iron was a very simple matter originally, by what was known as the direct or bloomery process. You placed several alternate layers of charcoal and ore on a hearth and covered it all with clay, set fire to the charcoal and pumped up the heat manually with one or more bellows; a lump of impure iron resulted, full of cinders which needed beating out of it, but it was enough to provide bars of metal which could be hammered into a variety of implements. The blast furnace produced much higher temperatures by using water power to work the bellows and, consequently, the metal emerged as a fluid with a scum of cinders that could easily be skimmed from its surface. Then you could cast the molten metal into a required shape or you could allow it to solidify before treating it as you would do by blooming.

The use of furnaces spread across continental Europe, with France taking the lead in the production of cast iron from the beginning of the fifteenth century, the Italians specialising more in bronze. And it was the French who brought the casting process to England before that century was over: in 1493 one Pieter Robert, alias Graunt Pierre, was running an iron mill at Hartfield in the Forest of Ashdown, and he was only one of many compatriots who began to settle down in England and provide the early skills of the newly sophisticated Wealden iron industry. Eventually, well into Henry's reign, there would be between three and four hundred Frenchmen resident there, the years between 1514 and 1530 seeing especially heavy immigration. Although the French industry was first established in the Massif Central, it had moved north to Normandy, to the Pays d'Ouche west of the Seine, and to the Pays de Bray between Dieppe and Beauvais, and it was from Bray that most of the migrant workers crossed the Channel in search of work. There seem to be several reasons for their move: local wood stocks were beginning to run out early in the sixteenth century, the Norman landowners were increasingly tempted to invest in textile manufacture instead of iron, the workers were finding it harder to obtain small holdings that would supplement their iron-working wages, there was a disastrous harvest in 1521, and the plague reappeared around Rouen about that time, which is when emigration to England reached its height. The iron industry of Kent and Sussex, on the other hand, was expanding and the attraction would have been irresisitible, especially after the English and French made peace in 1514. Furnaces were springing up in many places apart from Hartfield: at Buxted and Newbridge, at Wadhurst and Pashley, at Robertsbridge, Panningridge, Mayfield and elsewhere.

Bronze was still the principal metal for cast guns in England, the iron-manufacturing on the Weald being limited to making the joined-together, open-ended breechloaders until 1543. But in that year at Buxted, the first iron muzzle-loader was cast by a curiously assorted trio. One was the overseer of the operation, William Levett, otherwise known as 'Parson' (he had been Rector of Buxted since 1533) and the other two were Ralph Hogge and the Frenchman Pierre Baude. 'Hogge was the owner of the furnace, and Baude was one of the founders of bronze guns in the service of the King... Hogge knew how to work a furnace and could furnish the molten iron; he knew nothing about guns or the preparation of the moulds for gun-founding. Baude, on the other hand, was an expert gun-founder and was learned in the proportions of the various pieces.' So pervasive had the French become in the English industry long before then that in 1537 John and Robert Owen, who usually worked alongside Baude at Houndsditch, felt it necessary to make a point about their own nationality when casting a gun for the rebuilding of *Mary Rose* that was then under way. Its bronze barrel bore the defiant inscription that the Owen brothers had been authentically 'born in the City of London, the sons of an English'.

Nothing was needed in building the King's navy nearly as much as timber in quantities that, by the end of Henry's reign, were threatening to outstrip the supply, though never as starkly as was the case later on, when a real crisis developed in the eighteenth century. Wood was required for some of the Tudor shipboard armament – yew for longbows, poplar for arrows, elm for gun carriages – but the biggest drain on timber resources was obviously the creation of the ship itself. When Henry V built his *Grâce Dieu* and a couple of balingers early in the fifteenth century, 2,591 oak trees and 1,195 beeches had to be felled for a start, before all the other timber he required. How much more exorbitant were Henry VIII's demands may be gauged from the fact that he either built from scratch or virtually reconstructed from keel to topgallant no fewer than seventy vessels before his death in 1547.[5] In the last twelve years of

5 Another guide to naval consumption of timber is that in 1796, to build a seventy-four-gun ship of anything between 1,550 and 1,830 tuns, you needed 2,000 trees of about two tons each. Wastage was unavoidable.

his reign, more oaks would be felled than in any previous half-century, a particularly damaging removal, given that the oak is a notoriously slow-growing tree which takes anything between eighty and 120 years to reach its full potential. Two varieties of timber were almost invariably imported – generally from the Baltic and especially from Scandinavia – and they were spruce, whose long trunk had the perfect straightness and supple strength necessary for making masts, and pine, which was the preferred timber for the yards and other spars; but everything else effectively was homegrown.

England still had extensive forests and woodlands at the start of the sixteenth century, though they were but a remnant of what had been when the Romans arrived in Britannia and began to clear the land in order to make room for settlements; until they turned up, most of England had been covered by trees in varying densities.[6] The steady reduction of woodland since then was caused above all by every kind of building, of houses and other premises most of all, but also by the requirements of agriculture and other industries, which needed farm wagons, waterwheels and similarly cumbersome wooden tools. The endless demand for fuel also contributed to the dwindling stocks, though for domestic and some other purposes such as charcoal-burning, 'underwood' – that is, lesser branches and immature growth, often in the shadow of prime trees – was taken rather than mature trunks. Nevertheless, it all mounted up, to a degree reflected in the demands of England's principal salt manufactory at Droitwich, where brine had to be heated over a furnace; there were 360 of these and, in the course of a year, they consumed 6,000 wagon-loads of wood. The naval responsibility for the reduction of English woodlands in this period has been the subject of much argument in recent years but it seems clear that, although royal shipbuilding was not the principal reason for the early signs of famine, it certainly had more and more to answer for as Henry's reign progressed.

The naval requirement above all was for oak because of its toughness and durability, though its endurance was not much more than that of other ship's timbers if it was not carefully prepared, installed and maintained.[7] Trees were always felled in winter for preference because

6 The difference between 'forest' and 'woodland' was more than semantic. The first referred to royal hunting preserves, with or without trees, where infringement of any kind was drastically punished. Woodland meant all kinds of arboreal landscape.
7 It has lately been suggested that oak was used more than any other timber 'simply because it was so easily available'.

the sap was down then, which meant that the timber would season quickly, whereas wood that had not been seasoned properly and was still green when installed was very likely to rot undetected in the airless bowels of a ship. Among other marine hazards, none was greater than *Teredo navalis*, the wood-boring shipworm found in all warm waters, which attacked a hull from the outside, seriously weakening it and producing leaks; 'they enter in no bigger than a small Spanish needle, and by little and little their holes become ordinarily greater than a man's finger. The thicker the plank is, the greater he groweth; yea, I have seen many ships so eaten that most of their planks under water have been like honeycombs...' This problem would not be fully solved for another two hundred years, until ships were habitually sheathed in a protective layer of thin copper plates below the waterline. What the government purveyors were looking for when they scouted out a tract of woodland that might yield serviceable timber, were trees that had mighty trunks, from which the ship's main planking could be hewn: this was usually anything up to six inches thick for much of the hull, but even more for the keel which, in the case of *Henry Grâce à Dieu*, as we know, was assembled from six full-grown oak trees. But the King's men also wanted so-called 'compass timber', the heavy branches which were anything but straight and from which angled pieces of wood could be cut to provide some of the smaller structural parts of a ship: the futtocks and the riders, the breast hooks and the knees. The dearth of good compass timber eventually became such (though not in Henry's time) that efforts were made to grow trees with unnaturally pronounced curves or angles, by pruning them expertly at various stages of their development.

Bronze was not the only raw material to be snatched from the monasteries at the Dissolution, to finish up in Henry VIII's navy. By the sixteenth century, the religious houses of England had accumulated a great deal of wealth: although it was unevenly distributed, between them they owned approximately one third of all the land in the country, and it was generally very well wooded. How well is indicated in a survey made by Thomas Cromwell's commissioners at the Benedictine abbey of Abingdon in Berkshire, which was ranked sixth in income (£1,876 per annum) among the houses of its order. Reporting on the abbey's resources in March 1538, they noted that on 1,197 acres there were 12,712 trees, which they valued at £2,948 15s 4d. It had been known in the past for monasteries and other religious houses to give timber to the Crown for shipbuilding purposes in order, presumably, to ingratiate themselves as much as anyone else who bestowed lavish gifts upon the monarch. When Henry V's *Trinity Royal* was being built at Greenwich in 1413–16 it was necessary to find 349 oak trees, some of which were felled in royal parks and woodlands, but 184 of them were donated gratis by eight religious houses in Kent, Essex and Hertfordshire.

What happened at the Dissolution, however, between 1536 and 1540, was in no sense a donation but barefaced seizure of all the accumulated monastic and conventual assets in every shape and form: precious metals and jewels were either sold off or reassembled in different artefacts, bells were melted down for gunmetal, roofs were stripped of the lead that could be otherwise used as waterpipes or moulded into small shot, walls were demolished to provide building stone – and timber was taken to be sold and replenish the royal coffers or to be used directly for whatever Henry had in mind, with shipbuilding high on his list of priorities. And for a while there was a glut of ship's timber as a result, though this was pretty short-lived in the face of increasing demand: of the seventy vessels that Henry built or rebuilt during his reign, twenty-five were finished between 1536 and 1545, with another eighteen appearing in the two more years before his death. Suitable oak, which had cost between 12d and 18d a load in his first few years, was worth 10s by the end. Scarcity, real or threatened, was beginning to find its level in the market place.

Expressions of concern about woodland stocks had been heard from very early in Henry's reign, when the Prior of Christ Church in Canterbury (which would shortly become Canterbury Cathedral in Henry's new Church of England) instructed his agent Humphrey Gay to convey to Robert Brigandine, Clerk of the King's Ships, a worry about tree-felling on the Benedictine monastery's land, saying that he 'has viewed the timber felled here for making the King's ship and finds that by the indiscreetness of the fellers much young wood is destroyed'. The ship in question was probably *Mary Rose*, the timber was possibly one of the aforementioned gifts to a sovereign, and the royal loggers were obviously more enthusiastic than competent or far-sighted. A few years later, in 1523, a Bill was brought before Parliament whose intention was to 'restrain waste of the King's woods'. It stipulated that people licensed to cut and sell such wood must fence out cattle for seven years after felling, 'to allow the spring to grow'. This was a form of legislation that had recurred periodically since the twelfth century, whose principal object was to protect the sovereign's private interests on his own land. Where it referred to woodlands generally, all early legislation concerned access or other rights, but never was it a precautionary measure against depredation unless the King's property was involved. Typical was Edward I's forest ordinance of 1305, which insisted that 'They whose woods are disafforested shall not have common or other easements in the forest.'[8]

But in 1543, Henry took a completely radical step forward when he caused Parliament to pass an Act for the Preservation of Woods, which originated in his realisation that if consumption went on at its current rate, the timber stocks of England would, sooner or later, run out. There is no reason to suppose that his concern was merely to guarantee a continuing supply of ships' timber, but that consideration was well to the fore in his thinking, as the opening words of the Act make plain:

'The King our Sovereign perceiving and right well knowing the great decay of timber and woods universally within this his realm of England to be such, that unless speedy remedy in that behalf be provided, there is great and manifest likelihood of scarcity and lack, as well of timber for building, making repairing and maintaining of houses and ships, and also for fuel and firewood for the necessary relief of the whole commonalty of this his said realm.'

From Michaelmas 1544, the eighteen clauses of the Act would be enforced with a number of stiff fixed financial penalties for infringements: 40s a year per acre was the going rate for converting woodland into pasture or tillage, and it would cost 3s 4d per rood (a quarter of an acre) per month if you failed to fence off recently felled coppices and underwoods for a period of four years so that the new growth could be 'saved and preserved from destruction by any manner of cattle or beast'; while anyone damaging such fences could be fined 10s. One of the provisions was of particular importance for the future of ships' timbers, because it specifically referred to oak trees. This was the first priority in the Act, and it began by stipulating that when trees of twenty-four years old or less were felled, twelve oaks had to be left standing – these were known as standils – in every acre where felling had taken place, but if there were not enough oaks to achieve that target 'then there shall be left so many of other kind, that is to say, of elm, ash, aspen or beech.' The Act then went on to amplify this by insisting that such standils 'shall be preserved and not felled or cut down till they and every of them shall be of ten

8 Easement was a right of way over adjoining property.

inches square within three foot of the ground'. Defy that ordinance and you would be 3s 4d out of pocket for every standil you failed to preserve.

But Henry's new Act, while rigorous in its general approach to the matter, was not unsympathetic to local needs. In certain circumstances, the standils could be felled by their owners: in order to repair their homes, their fences, 'and for the making and repairing of waterworks dampness, bridges, floodgates, making, repairing or amending of ships and all other vessels, and for all other things concerning their own uses or affairs...' This loophole could (and probably did) lend itself to abuse that undermined the effectiveness of the Act, which was obviously weighted in favour of property owners. Nevertheless, it may properly be regarded as the first time in English history that the Westminster Parliament legislated in favour of the environment in general, based upon a recognition of the fact that the nation's timber resources were not inexhaustible. It would also be the cue for Henry's daughter to think of conservation as well; and Elizabeth in due course would follow suit with an Act in the year she reached the throne, prohibiting tree-felling in order to produce charcoal for making iron, though the woodlands of the Kentish Weald and Sussex were excluded from its provisions.

Two things besides timber and metal were necessary for building a warship: sailcloth and cordage. As we know, sailcloth was almost wholly an import from Brittany and would remain so until the year of Henry's death, when Breton canvas-makers were recruited specifically to teach Englishmen in East Anglia how to make serviceable poldavys; as a result, by 1558 there would be two native operatives in Suffolk and eventually the Woodbridge and Ipswich districts became celebrated for their quality sailcloth, once the Ipswich weavers had overcome an early tendency of their material to mildew easily. The manufacture of cordage, on the other hand, had a long pedigree in England, particularly in Dorset, with minor operations developing later in other parts of the country: there was a small rope and thread industry in early fifteenth-century Lynn, for example. But in Dorset they had been growing rope's raw material, hemp, for several hundred years by then and Bridport had become the principal centre of rope manufacture. Although it was but a tiny place at the time of Domesday, it is thought that the transformation of 'neck-weed' to a spun rope had already begun, because the local rating was so high that only a significant commercial enterprise could account for it. There was certainly a thriving business in 1211, when King John ordered 3,000lb of hempen thread for making ships' cables, and came back for more two years later 'to cause to be made at Bridport, night and day, as many ropes for ships both large and small as they could, and twisted yarns for cordage'. And although Bridport supplied other derivatives of hemp – it made excellent wicks for lanterns and torches, and the hangman's rope so notoriously came from there that it became known as a Bridport dagger – shipping was by far and away the town's principal customer. From the heaviest cables used in mooring a vessel (which, in *Henry Grâce à Dieu*, were seventeen inches in circumference), to the hawsers needed to lash down its biggest guns and to the slimmer ropes required for ratlines, shrouds and other rigging, Bridport was the leading manufacturer.

Rope-making was a convoluted process, in more than one sense. The hemp which was grown locally was sent from Bridport to Plympton in Devon, there to be made into rope yarn, which was restored to Bridport to be spun into rope; and finally this was returned to Devon as a finished article, for use by the navy in Plymouth, though other orders were carted even more expensively to London. Bridport's part in the sequence took place in its rope walks, which at first were long – sometimes half a mile long – avenues shaded by trees, though low buildings were subsequently built for the purpose, which seem to have been short on natural light: one of them was reputed to be so dark that the spinners had to walk backwards and forwards with lighted candles on their shoulders. And the spinners did have to walk many miles a day, much of it backwards, twisting the yarn continuously as they retreated from the hook embedded in a tree or wall, which anchored one end of the emerging rope. Someone would one day describe the process vividly: 'The whole effect of the spinner moving slowly backwards in the dim light of the rope walk is that of a spider weaving a web in its lair.' And the effect of this trade would leave a lasting mark on Bridport, in its unusually wide main streets and in the back gardens of the houses lining them, which were exceptionally long in proportion to their width, giving away their original function as places where rope was made in the open air.

Bridport may have been the principal rope-making town in sixteenth-century England, but it was never the sole source of supply. In the fifteenth century much rope had been imported from Genoa and Normandy and, in 1545, the keeper of the King's storehouse at Deptford, Richard Howlett, took delivery of ten cables and twenty-seven hawsers which had been shipped to the Thames from Danzig, while the Normans still sold to the English, as did the Bordelais and the Hollanders. The

Dorset town didn't even enjoy a monopoly in its own county, for there were also rope walks in Poole and in Burton Bradstock, which was only three miles away; and so jealous of their neighbours were the burgesses of Bridport that they petitioned Henry to protect them from these rivals because, they argued, the artisans of their town had, for as long as any man could remember, made 'the most part of all the great cables, hawsers, ropes and all other tackling as well for your royal ships and navy as for the most part of all other ships within the realm'. And Henry duly obliged with an Act 'for the true Makynge of great cables, hawsers, ropes and all other tacklings for ships in the Borough of Bridport in the County of Dorset'. This forbade anyone living within five miles of the town from selling hemp except at Bridport market, adding that 'no person or persons other than such as dwell and be inhabitants within the said town, shall make. . .out of the said town any cables, hawsers, ropes, traces, halters or any other tackle'. An effect of this legislation was to cause other rope-makers to move away from Dorset, and a number of them consequently migrated to Yorkshire. And yet, in spite of the royal patronage, Bridport appears to have gone into an economic decline in the 1530s, when its trade was described as 'much decayed'; and the cause is thought to have been increasing competition from Danzig and Lübeck.

As for its sovereign, however, he was just getting into his stride.

IX
HENRY MEETS HIS MATCH

The new French King, Francis I, another Valois like Louis of Orléans, but from the alternative branch of Angoulême, was the perfect match for Henry VIII when he reached the throne at the start of 1515. He promised a vigour that had been missing from French affairs during the previous reign, and the death of Louis was the first occasion when the cry '*Le roi est mort, vive le roi!*' rang round the realm in anticipation. Francis was but two years older than Henry had been at his own accession and their rivalry was to be a principal feature of European politics until they died, within a few weeks of each other, in 1547. As a young man, he had some of the same impressive physical build as the Englishman, tall and broad-shouldered, though with a head that was not so finely proportioned, dominated by an excessively long and sharply pointed nose; but whereas Henry only lost his shape as middle age approached, the Frenchman appears to have had a pot belly above spindly shanks even when young. There were striking similarities of character, however, most notably a vaunting ambition to be a ruler whose name would ring throughout the world, to be a commander who would lead his soldiers to great victories in battle, to be noticed in everything he did by people everywhere. Francis shared some of Henry's robust inclinations, especially in the chase and in the tilting yard; he was also a great womaniser, though he embarked on matrimony only twice, which was paltry compared with the Tudor King's recurring need for new wives.

The two monarchs also cultivated the arts but, whereas Henry's taste rarely strayed beyond music and then only in the direction of marine painting and his own portraiture, Francis was much broader in his sympathies. He is justly regarded as a significant figure in the French Renaissance because of the patronage he dispensed in many fields. He

encouraged the almost indecently versatile Leonardo da Vinci, the architect Sebastiano Serlio, the goldsmith Benvenuto Cellini (who presented
him with an elaborate salt cellar in gratitude), the writer/philosopher
Guillaume Budé and many others in every field almost the only creative
mind which eluded him was that of Erasmus, whom he tried but failed
to attract to Paris. There, he had the ancient Louvre – which had started
life as a twelfth-century castle – renovated, and made another of the
talented Budé family Master of the King's Library, from which in due
course emerged the Bibliothèque Nationale. It has been said that only in
the atmosphere of intellectual freedom which Francis nurtured, did it
become possible for Rabelais to write his great satires. And yet this King
believed as much as any predecessor in the theory and practice of absolute
monarchy. Like his coeval across the Channel, he was quite a complicated
fellow as well as, from the outset, a swaggering and self-centred young
man.

He was a great builder of palaces which are now regarded as glories of
that period of architecture. In the Loire Valley he completed the Château
de Blois and saw the Château de Chambord through from start to finish,
both of them celebrated for, among other things, their ingenious spiral
staircases: the one at Blois rose airily up an open tower in a corner of the
courtyard, the Chambord version being even more elaborate because
people could ascend and descend it simultaneously without being able to
see each other. Francis then went on to create his Palais de Fontainebleau,
notable for its interior decoration, in which both Cellini and Serlio had
a hand, and where Leonardo's *Mona Lisa* was hung shortly after the
Italian finished it. It became his particular pride among the royal buildings, occupying a place in his affections comparable to that of ships
(which Francis did not find intrinsically so fascinating) in Henry's. He
was forever showing it off to distinguished visitors, much as the English
King liked to take such people aboard his men o'war, and all seem to
have been enormously impressed by it. According to one of them, the
English ambassador Sir Thomas Cheyney, who was invited to inspect it
in the peaceful midsummer of 1546, Fontainebleau was 'to me a thing
incredible, only I had seen it myself' and he was especially envious of
the monarch's privy, 'which was so cold and fresh as could be devised,
considering the time of the year'.

Francis did not often appear in Paris itself, and when he did it was
with some particular advantage in mind, to bully or cajole the city's
Parlement into lending him money for the pursuit of war or some other

expensive ambition. Fontainebleau was a safe thirty-six miles from the capital's smells and other contaminations, and there Francis generally held court when he wasn't enjoying one of his other properties or absent from the region altogether on one of his military campaigns. Like Henry, he appreciated his food, though never on the same gormandizing scale, needing not much more than half the kitchen staff that Henry employed to cater to his appetite: he was much more mindful of household economy than the Englishman. Another difference was the ease with which anyone at all respectable could gain access to him, which excluded virtually no-one above the level of artisan. Tudor Kings lived in very formal and extensively private surroundings, the public held always at a remote and extremely well-controlled distance. But at Fontainebleau the French sovereign's only sure retreat was his private chamber, essentially his state bedroom, and even there a great deal of public business often took place.

The English were warm in their acknowledgement of the new monarch, for Henry set great store by the niceties of whatever he defined as chivalrous behaviour and Thomas Wolsey was beginning to enjoy his excursions into foreign policy, though there were those at court, including Thomas Howard's father, now the Duke of Norfolk, and other members of the old nobility, who viewed any French alliance with suspicion. An English embassy, arranged by Wolsey but led by Charles Brandon – Mary Tudor's secret lover, shortly to become her second husband – crossed the Channel to present Henry's congratulations, at which the conventional platitudes of such an occasion were exchanged, though Francis discomfited Brandon in private (it's said he actually made him blush) by revealing that he knew all about the illicit affair because Mary had told him herself. The upshot of all that was an angry Henry, who promptly demanded from his younger sister a return of all that he had bestowed upon her in dowry on her marriage to Louis – £24,000 to be repaid at £1,000 a year – as the price of his accepting her remarriage to Brandon; he also wanted all the jewels that Louis had given her. As a penance, Brandon himself was charged with extracting this last demand from the French, who had their own price for compliance: the restoration of Tournai in a formal renewal of the recent Anglo-French peace. After long and not always diplomatic negotiation, from which no-one got everything he wanted, Tournai was restored, though not for another three years, by which time Mary was authentically installed as the Duchess of Suffolk. There would be no genuine reconciliation with her brother, although Henry and his Queen Katherine did attend the official marriage ceremony at Greenwich in May 1515, and he sometimes enlisted her for diplomatic purposes. But he insisted that she pay every last penny of what he reckoned she owed him.

Francis had made his official entry into Paris within a few weeks of becoming King, 'a sight very gorgeous to behold' according to an eye-witness, who was particularly taken by the new sovereign's showmanship, which made him conspicuous in the great column of archers, foot soldiers, members of the *Parlement*, pensioners, trumpeters, princes, gentlemen of the King's household (200 of those), other functionaries, and ecclesiastics, who wound their way through the crowded and cheering streets. Francis came 'armed, upon his barbed horse, wholly accoutred in white and in cloth of silver. The King did not keep under the canopy, but displayed his horsemanship by continually curvetting and prancing. And there were good horses and riders who did marvels to attract the notice of the ladies...' That was on 13 February, and he was already planning his first move in the great ambition to leave his mark on the world outside France. She had suffered humiliating setbacks in Italy in Louis' waning years and as a matter of national honour, as well as a quest for personal glory, Francis would re-establish her dominion on the peninsula. He first of all made a treaty in March with Charles of Burgundy (who would succeed Maximilian as Holy Roman Emperor within a few more years) in order to secure his flank for an invasion of Italy, and at once set his artillery on the road to Lyon and Grenoble, so that they would be well placed to continue into Italy, which they did in June.

And he began brilliantly by doing the unexpected to get across the Alps, over a pass which was supposed to be impassable to anything bigger than a mule train; but Francis in person led foot soldiers, horsemen, heavy guns and baggage train, 30,000 troops in all, so impressively that the surprised population of Turin wondered whether they had flown over the mountains like birds. These then marched on to their principal target of Milan, which was defended mostly by Swiss mercenaries, much better fighters than the native Milanese. On the afternoon of 13 September, battle was joined beside the village of Marignano, running on through much of the night and into the next day, producing fearsome casualties on both sides. Francis himself might have been one of them, for he was in the thick of things throughout and took a thrust from a pike that penetrated his armour and the buff coat he wore underneath. But it was the Swiss whose nerve uncharacteristically went first, starting them on the long march home and leaving the Duke of Milan to make his own surrender terms with the French. This was the first great defeat inflicted by anyone on Europe's most sought-after mercenaries, and it produced another reversal of tradition. As a result of Marignano, the Swiss made their separate peace with Francis and offered their services to him. Henceforth, they would for several years be his most reliable fighting allies, even more efficient at their trade than the German *Landsnechts*, to whom he had turned in this first campaign.

What made both the Swiss and the Germans such formidable warriors, feared by everyone who came up against them, sprang from the fact that warfare was their sole profession, which could not be said of any other soldiery in Europe. The Confederacy of Cantons in Switzerland had been a source of supply since the fourteenth century, because the Swiss had no great territorial ambitions of their own and so they made the manpower that might have fought for their expansion available to the highest bidder. Their mercenaries became notable for two things – their deadly use of the long pike in highly disciplined infantry formations, and their refusal to accept anyone else's terms for doing their business: if their monthly pay didn't turn up precisely on time, they simply packed up and left the battlefield; and they were self-confidently independent enough to make up their own minds whether an action should be fought this afternoon or tomorrow morning, whoever nominally commanded them. The German *Landsnechts* had been formed by the Emperor Maximilian as recently as 1486 in imitation of the Swiss, because he wanted a standing army that would fight imperial battles, which were not necessarily the same thing as battles on behalf of any of the German states from which they were recruited. But if you were in alliance with the Holy Roman Emperor, whoever you were and whatever your cause, you could draw on his *Landsnechts* and be sure of good value for money. Like the Swiss, they trained themselves to become an irresistible fighting force, practising tactics and the use of their weapons, taking care of their equipment, including their body armour and other distinctive gear. They, and the Swiss, looked like professional soldiers. The contrast between them and the various national militias of Europe could not have been greater.

Like most monarchs and their parliaments, Henry VIII could not countenance a standing army in England because the cost of having one was prohibitive, and could not even be justified on the grounds of usefulness when such a force might have been idle for years on end between hostilities. Occasional forays abroad such as the ill-fated exped-ition to Guyenne and the limited successes at Thérouanne and Tournai (when *Landsnechts* joined up with Henry's force) sometimes included mercenaries, partly because the cost of transporting Englishmen across the Channel in quantity was generally even more expensive, and certainly more disruptive to the cycle of agriculture in which a majority of English troops were normally engaged. For the defence of the realm depended upon the extremely part-time services of every able-bodied man in the country between the ages of sixteen and sixty. Details of each man and his fighting potential – does he have a horse, a harness (body armour), a pike, a bill? – were carefully noted on muster rolls, which were kept up-to-date by the Lords Lieutenant of each county. These functionaries ordered a muster of the local manpower at least every three years, more frequently in time of trouble, at which every man was required to drop whatever he was doing for a livelihood and fall in at some appointed place locally. There they were counted off against the rolls and amendments were made if necessary, manoeuvres were held over several days, at which defects might be exposed and could be remedied; and then the men were sent home and back to work again till the next time or until they received the call to arms in earnest. And that was where the weakness in the militia system was exposed as something very inferior to the military strength of the foreign mercenaries. Not only did English soldiers bring their own weapons with them, with the exception of artillery, but they were rarely paid on time by a sovereign whose demoralising stinginess in such matters became a regular cause of complaint among his commanders. As a result of these and other impediments, his troops simply could not be compared to the Swiss and the Germans in any particular.

> Beyond that of keeping their arms and implements in full trim, war was their [the mercenaries'] only employment. Whereas the national militia – and that of England especially, taken from the plough-tail at few and irregular intervals for muster, clothed in ill-fitting and old-fashioned habiliments which descended from father to son, badly cleaned and scarcely ever complete – must have presented a spectacle more ludicrous than formidable, as they took the field in rusty head pieces and cumbrous body armour, hastily patched together for the occasion.

That is a severe judgement from the nineteenth century, but it is undoubtedly a reasonable one.

Both Henry and Francis, coexisting peacefully for the moment, had to adjust their ambitions to the wider realities of European politics. So predictably fundamental to this was the fact of political inconstancy, that it is doubtful whether anyone was ever surprised when a ruler broke his word or if a nation switched from one alliance to another and ranged itself against an old friend. Monarchs who could behave impeccably in what they conceived to be personal matters of honour, simply did not recognise the same code when it came to international affairs: all that mattered then was advantage, victory, profit. Henry had already broken a peace treaty when he joined Ferdinand of Aragon and the Pope in alliance against France, simply because the moment seemed opportune to realise one of his ambitions, only to have the plan backfire when Ferdinand then left him in the lurch after Navarre had been gained. Worse, his father-in-law had then proceeded to make a surreptitious treaty with Louis XII, based upon the prospect of a marriage between the houses of Orléans and Aragon, from which Ferdinand, father of the potential groom, hoped to acquire all existing French rights in Italy as dowry. That was the common and cynical currency of European politics, and both Henry and Francis would have thought the other lacking in kingly virtue if either had ever passed up the chance of national success or personal glory merely to keep his word to his rival. The great victory at Marignano incensed Henry because it glorified Francis and put his own performances at Thérouanne and Tournai in a much dimmer light; and it became imperative that he should regain what he perceived to be the upper hand with some coup that would diminish the Frenchman's achievement. The pressure was only increased when, early in 1518, the Emperor, France and Spain made a pact whose principal purpose was to partition Italy between them. Although the English had never had anything but a trading interest in the peninsula, Henry saw this as another personal setback which intensified his need to reassert himself.

And he did just that – or, rather, Wolsey did it for him – with a bout of brilliant diplomacy that took advantage of Pope Leo X's announced desire for a crusade against the Turks. As a result of Wolsey's manipulation, this was transformed in the autumn of 1518 into the much more ambitious Peace of London (a 'perpetual' peace, according to the signatories) which was concluded between all the major European powers, who vowed not only to unite in their solemn Christian duty but to gang up against any aggressor who threatened any one of them. The treaty, far from being perpetual, lay in ruins within four years, but for a moment it produced the grand illusion throughout Europe of Henry the great reconciler. This built upon the opportunity which had presented itself twelve months earlier when Martin Luther nailed his ninety-five theses to the church door at Wittenberg, the first act in the evolution of Protestant Christianity, loudly deplored by Henry before he went on to compose a tract condemning Luther, which so commended him to the Pope that Leo proclaimed him Defender of the Faith. Henry the Peacemaker and Defender of the Faith: that certainly put Marignano in its place. It also caused Henry to think in terms of his being elected the next Holy Roman Emperor, the Vatican's official protector of all that was sacred throughout Europe.

Another king who fancied himself in this role was, inevitably, Francis, who subsequently admitted to having spent three million crowns among the German electors in his attempt to persuade them of his suitability. But when the position actually became vacant, on Maximilian's death in the summer of 1519, neither the English nor the French sovereign had ingratiated himself enough with the Archbishops of Mainz, Cologne and Trier, the Count Palatine of the Rhine, the Duke of Saxony, the Margrave of Brandenburg and the King of Bohemia, in whose collective gift the imperial crown lay. The new imperial leader was Maximilian's grandson, Charles of Burgundy, a charmless and ungainly young man of nineteen with a great jutting Habsburg jaw, who now became the Emperor Charles V – Charles-Quint, as the French would always refer to him. But a disappointed Francis regarded him much more petulantly, as an 'idiot, ill-intentioned, ignorant and lacking in courage'.

Wolsey more craftily sought to co-operate with the new Emperor at once, without shutting the door on the French; and this was part of a double game, whose whole object was to bring an end to the rapprochement with France – but only if the way was clear, which meant having imperial support. In the first glow of their amity, both Henry and Francis had agreed that they must meet at the earliest opportunity and thus share an encounter which should have taken place under the provisions of the Anglo-French peace of 1514, but which the death of Louis had frustrated. Typically, both men made the same dramatic gesture to indicate their eagerness: Henry declared that he would neither rest nor shave until they had come face to face, whereupon Francis announced that he would grow a beard, too. Arrangements had been put in hand for this rendezvous to take place in France in June 1520. The Lord Chancellor took the view that it would be an advantage if Henry and the Emperor got to know each other even before the French meeting, and in this he had the connivance of Queen Katherine – by now mother of a four-year-old Princess Mary, though as yet unable to give Henry his all-important son and heir – who was Charles's aunt and no great lover of the French. Nor was Charles himself, who rather hoped that he might dissuade Henry from seeing Francis. It was decided that Charles would cross the Channel en route from his first visit to Spain, the land of his mother and her ancestors, to the Spanish Netherlands (roughly coinciding with modern Belgium), where he had been born and which he still regarded as home; that he and Henry would confer before the date set for the Englishman's journey to France. Just in case the French meeting then went ahead, Wolsey also laid plans for another meeting between his sovereign and the Emperor once Henry's conversations with Francis were out of the way. Whatever had been settled then, he reckoned, could always be corrected elsewhere shortly afterwards.

It had been agreed that Charles would arrive at Sandwich in the middle of May, but the weather played havoc with his projected voyage from Corunna to England, and he was kept waiting ashore for four weeks before a stiff nor'easter at last blew itself out and he had a favourable wind from Galicia. Late on 26 May he landed at Dover, having already picked up Wolsey as a kind of diplomatic pilot in mid-Channel, with a large proportion of the English fleet standing by to fire the appropriate number of guns in salute. Henry was not there to receive him but travelled in the darkness from Canterbury to greet him in his bedchamber at the castle, just as Charles must have been thinking of going to sleep. To Canterbury next morning, which was Whit Sunday, the pair of them rode to attend High Mass in the cathedral, to pray together at the shrine of Thomas à Becket and to examine various relics associated with the saint whom one of Henry's predecessors had caused to be murdered before the altar of St Benedict. Tears were shed at the meeting of Charles and Katherine of Aragon, who had never seen each other until that day. Other intimacies were exchanged at a dinner attended only by Henry, Katherine, Charles, and Mary Tudor, Duchess of Suffolk (whose husband, however, was allowed to hold a basin in which Henry could wash his hands before eating). More general merriment followed at a banquet attended by a host of people of various nationality, who ate and danced their way through another evening, and indulged in alternative preferences: a visiting Spanish count was observed dallying with an Englishwoman so ardently that he fainted away and had to be carried out into the fresh air to recover. Henry, of course, was in his element; at table, in the dance, in all forms of that night's roistering, a loud centre of attention whatever was happening. Charles, however, did nothing but sit and watch what everyone else was doing, and exchange polite conversation, especially with Thomas Wolsey. But most of all he just watched.

The two rulers parted after a couple of days together, having agreed that they must do this again in the very near future. Charles then left for Sandwich and the completion of his voyage home. Henry set off for Dover and his own Channel crossing on his way to meet Francis, and a considerable fleet of hoys and other vessels weighed anchor on the morning of a calm last day of May, to accompany the King and his Queen over the water: *Mary Rose* and four other men o'war were given a particular escort duty, being ordered 'to scour the seas from time to time during the passage'. In command of the King's ships on this occasion was Sir William Fitzwilliam, descendant of an old Yorkshire family and another of Henry's boyhood companions, now a rising star in the Tudor firmament. He had been injured by a crossbow bolt off Brittany in 1513 and knighted for his part in the siege of Tournai, after which he was made Vice-admiral; one day, he would become Lord Admiral of England in spite of having been close to Wolsey before the Cardinal was banished from court in disgrace.

There is a famous painting ('after Holbein') commissioned by the King himself, which shows Henry standing exuberantly amidships on *Henry Grâce à Dieu*, surrounded by a number of other vessels which are about to leave Dover harbour across some distinctly frisky-looking waves. This was pushing artistic licence some distance beyond its limits because the *Great Harry*, as we know, could not have been there on account of her excessive draught; and the sea was so tranquil that morning that the convoy was in Calais by noon. Henry and Katherine, in fact, sailed aboard a small bark, the *Katherine Pleasance* (100 tuns), which had not long been launched at the recently appointed Deptford dockyard (where a stable had to be demolished so that she could slide down the slips and into the Thames). She appears to have been built chiefly in order to serve as a royal yacht, long before that expression was ever recognised.[1] Apart from all the absolute necessities that went into the vessel's construction – '8 loads of knees from Danbery Common', 56 tons of ballast in her hold, thirty iron chains for the shrouds, and scores of other things – no effort had been spared to make her fit for a King and his Queen; and to look

---

[1] The first royal yacht to be known as such was the *Mary* (also, coincidentally, of 100 tuns) which was presented to Charles II by the Dutch in 1660; and it was through her that the word 'yacht', which derived from the Dutch verb meaning to harry or hunt, entered the English language.

the part. One Godfrey had supplied 100 wainscots 'for making cabins and chambers for the King and Queen', a dozen 'joined stools' had been shipped for Katherine's cabin, a smith in Whitechapel had made special 'hinges, locks and staples for the doors of the King's chamber', 112ft of glass for glazing the cabins had been ordered, and 10s had been paid to 'John Wolffe, for painting and guilding the "collere" of the *Katherine Pleasance*'.

The logistics of the impending event had been formidable. Henry was taking more than five thousand people with him, together with enough horses (2,865) and carriages to convey them from Calais to the rendezvous, with hundreds of tents and pavilions, tons of plate, cutlery, glass and cooking utensils, and staggering quantities of food and drink, much of it still on the hoof or wing when it left England. There were 2,200 sheep, 1,300 chickens, 800 calves, 340 beefstock, twenty-six dozen heron, thirteen swans, seventeen bucks, 9,000 plaice, 7,000 whiting, 700 conger eels, four bushels of mustard and vast quantities of spices, sugar, cream, wine and beer – £8,839-worth of victuals in all – and every creature and every other item had to be shipped across the Channel (Wolsey had spent hours working out whether it would be more expensive to purchase flour for bread and cakemaking at home or over the water). Since March, 2,000 English craftsmen had been busy making the French accommodation for Henry and Katherine and Mary Tudor (paraded here not as Duchess of Suffolk, but as Queen Dowager of France in a sly hint at Henry's proprietorial assumptions), for Wolsey and their principal people-in-waiting; and shipping the materials for that had been a preliminary transport nightmare in itself: some timbers required for the temporary royal palace had been so large that they could not be loaded in any existing vessel, and so they had to be towed as rafts to Calais.

The foundations were of brick but the rest of the building was of wood and canvas, of such extensive and sumptuous fantasy that it became known as the palace of illusions. It had its own ornate gatehouse and battlements, and the canvas was painted to look as if it were brickwork, masonry or slate. There was a dining room whose ceiling was made from green silk studded with gold Tudor roses, and all the private apartments were splendid creations with gold cornices, priceless tapestries, Turkish carpets and other eye-catching objects; they were also provided with genuine stone chimneys just in case the nights became sharp enough to warrant a fire. There was a chapel, decked in much gold cloth and velvet, with gold statues of the twelve apostles beside ten candlesticks and a large gold crucifix on the altar. On the lawn in front of the gatehouse was a fountain which poured forth not water but white wine, Malmsey and claret, with silver drinking-vessels provided for the thirsty – but discreetly tethered to the fountain so that they could not be taken home as souvenirs by the unprincipled. The whole object of this extravagance, of course, which extended to all that happened through most of June, was to demonstrate that everything Henry put his hand to was richly incomparable. Which was no less than the truth on this occasion. Francis and his entourage made camp much more simply in a great spread of 400 elegant tents – though he was lodged in a pavilion 'as high as the highest tower' – and he spent nothing like as much as Henry (£15,000 in all, the equivalent of £4.5 million in today's currency) in ostentatious display; but it still took him a decade to clear off his debt.

The place chosen for the meeting between the two sovereigns was the Val d'Or, which lay nicely between the English outpost of Guînes on the edge of the Calais Pale, and Ardres, the first town in French territory: Henry's palace was put up close enough to Guînes Castle to be attached to it by a long corridor, while the French made their encampment in a watermeadow just outside Ardres.[2] But the name of the meeting-place is not why the encounter would be known forever as the Field of the Cloth of Gold: the fact is that the entire event, eighteen days from start to finish, was smothered in gold cloth, which provided clothing, horse blankets, tents, tapestries and sundry other trappings, on top of which came any number of baubles, platters and pieces of cutlery made of gold itself.

The Kings set eyes on each other for the first time on 7 June, which was the Feast of Corpus Christi, after artillery in both Guînes and Ardres had fired salvoes to announce their approach. Preceded by courtiers who, in Henry's case, included 'fifty gentlemen, his ushers, bareheaded and bearing gold maces as large as a man's head at one end', the monarchs rode towards each other. Henry was heavy with jewellery, pinned and dangling about his gold cloth tunic, with a long feather in his black cap, riding a great bay girt about with gold bells which jangled as it moved. Francis was in gold and silver cloth with precious stones stitched into the fabric, 'the front and sleeves set with diamonds, rubies, emeralds and large pearls, hanging loose,' and he sat astride 'a beautiful charger'. According to a French eyewitness, the two kings stopped 'at about two

2 Coincidentally, golden maize has been the most abundant crop grown along the shallow slopes of the vale in recent years.

casts of a bowl [i.e. *boule*] from each other...when silence was made on both sides. Suddenly the trumpets and other instruments sounded, so that never was heard such joy. After it was over, the Kings spurred their horses fiercely and embraced each other two or three times on horseback, bonnet in hand; then dismounting embraced again.' This was not the only felicity of that afternoon, as people began to mingle and introduce themselves. Francis received the principal English courtiers gracefully, and Henry warmly welcomed the French. 'Both hosts were well supplied with barrels of good wine and drank together, repeating several times the toast "Good friends, French and English".'

Exquisite and formal courtesy was the order of the month. On Sunday, 10 June the two monarchs simultaneously paid their respects to each other's wives, Francis riding to Guînes to see Katherine of Aragon, Henry trotting over to Ardres to present his compliments to Queen Claude. Dressed in a double mantle of cloth of gold, a head-dress of gold cloth and a great deal of jewellery – he had spent a large fortune in assembling his wardrobe for this trip – the Englishman first ran the gauntlet of the Queen's ladies, 'the most beautiful that could be', before being conducted to the *salle* where Claude awaited him. 'The King, on entering, made reverence to the Queen, who rose from her chair of state to meet him. He then kissed her, with one knee on the ground and bonnet in hand, and afterwards kissed Madame the Duchess and all the other princesses and ladies of the company. This done, he returned to the Queen, who took him by the hand and made him sit beside her.' A meal of many courses was then consumed while musicians played 'all sorts of instruments' in the background. It was noted that 'The King of England is a very handsome prince...in manner gentle and gracious, rather fat and with a red beard, large enough and very becoming.' When the meal was over, the tables were removed and the Queen led Henry into a high room 'richly adorned with tapestry of cloth of gold, and carpeted with crimson velvet, where they talked at leisure. This done, he took leave, and on mounting his horse gave it the spur, and made it bound and curvet as valiantly as a man could do.' French artillery let loose a parting volley, which was echoed by another one issuing from Guînes, where Francis was leaving after his own hour or two with Katherine of Aragon, whose reception was 'not inferior' to the one across the vale. The two Kings 'met each other on the way, and embraced, asking each other "What cheer?"'

Any formal business between them seems to have been confined to a single meeting, though there are conflicting reports of when that was, and none at all of what took place. Otherwise, the whole of this excursion was spent in various forms of recreation. There was much dancing and other merriment, one overwhelming feast after another, and something that John Fisher, the Bishop of Rochester, referred to obliquely as 'midsummer games'. These may have included the fancy-dress entertainment, for which Henry 'retired to the Admiral's tent, where he and 30 gentlemen disguised themselves in the costumes of *Landsnechts*, Albanians &c'. There was a tricky moment when, after watching some of his Yeomen of the Guard wrestling a team of Bretons, Henry challenged Francis to a bout and was tumbled in the dust for his over-confidence, though Francis went to great pains afterwards to make up for his discomfiture, and Henry was able to reassert himself by beating his rival at archery. Most of all, however, there was jousting in a tiltyard encircled by galleries for spectators within a high wooden fence, in which 300 armour-plated horsemen spent eleven full days in the lists according to a comprehensive set of rules drawn up by an Anglo-French committee, which combined both the English and the slightly different Gallic way of doing these things:

1. In consequence of the numerous accidents to noblemen, sharp steel not to be used, but only arms for strength, agility and pastime.
2. The challenge to commence 11th June and continue for a month, or so long as the two Kings shall be together, when the said gentlemen will answer all corners with blunt lances in harness...without any fastening to the saddle that might prevent mounting or dismounting with ease. Each challenger to have eight courses, with middle-sized lances or greater, if any of the comers prefer it, between one hour after dinner and 6pm...
7. On the 6th June, a tree shall be chosen, bearing the noble thorn entwined with raspberry, and on it shall be hung the shields of the challengers, and below them three escutcheons, black and grey, gold and tawny, and the last silver. Tablets, guarded by heralds, shall be hung below these for the names of the comers.

There was an interruption in the programme on the first day when the wind blew so strongly, with so much dust flying in everyone's faces, that jousting became even more dangerous than usual, but gradually the programme was completed, although 'Many persons present could not understand each other, and were obliged to have interpreters.' The two Kings, naturally, were the centre of attraction in all this, but very tactfully contrived not to tilt at each other; and both emerged more or less in one piece, Henry merely damaging his hand and Francis getting a black eye. One French knight, however, did die of his wounds at the Field of the Cloth of Gold.

Only two notable events remained after that. The day after the tournament, the tiltyard was transformed into a great open-air chapel, 'a fathom and a half [nine feet] high on pillars'. And there, surrounded by the two Kings (sitting together) and Queens (who did the same, but apart from their husbands), the nobility of both countries, the Archbishops of Sens and Canterbury, and a dozen or more other prelates who served at the altar as acolytes, Cardinal Wolsey led a Solemn High Mass. An introit was first sung by an English choir from the Chapel Royal, accompanied on the organ by an Englishman, then another followed with choir and organist supplied by the French. The pyx containing the Host was taken to the Kings for reverencing, and each sensitively tried to give way to the other in kissing it first; it was then taken to the two Queens, 'who also declined to kiss it first and, after many mutual respects, kissed each other instead'. After Wolsey had given the Benediction, there was an oration in Latin which enlarged upon the blessings of peace, and the announcement of plenary remission by the Pope for all who had taken part in the Mass, which meant a lot less time than some of them had been dreading in Purgatory. It had been planned to end the long festivities with a fireworks display, but something went amiss with one of the set pieces, which featured Francis's personal insignia, the salamander. This was accidentally launched while the Gospel was being read, a fizzing thing that resembled a dragon, 'four fathoms long and full of fire [which] appeared in the air from Ardres. Many were frightened, thinking it a comet or some monster, as they could see nothing to which it was attached. It passed right over the chapel at Guînes, as fast as a footman can go, and as high as a bolt shot from a crossbow.' Everything was bound to be anti-climax after that.

Then it was time for a last round of courtesy calls, a last feast, a prize-giving for all who had excelled in the lists, and the Field of the Cloth of Gold passed expensively (and almost supernaturally) into history. If it was notable for anything more than its wanton extravagance, then this was the atmosphere of concord between Henry and Francis, which both worked very hard to maintain throughout the eighteen days. But an astutely observant Venetian reckoned afterwards that it had all been show, that they really disliked each other cordially. And October had

scarcely begun before Francis was writing irritably to Wolsey about the
seizure of a French vessel, owned by a merchant of Paris, which had been
driven ashore on the Scilly Isles and there plundered by an English pirate
named Robin. M. du Moustier had lost goods to the value of 3,000 *livres*
but had been awarded only half as much in compensation by the English
court, which had then compounded its failure in justice by refusing to
return the document which attested to the value of the cargo. The letter
was the second that Francis had written to the Cardinal about this matter,
but there is no record of any reply. This was a much more reliable
weathervane than any of the forced *bonhomie* that, for best part of three
weeks, had coated the garish diplomacy in the Val d'Or.

X

A SMALL WORLD

It was a very small world that the English inhabited when Henry VIII came to the throne, much smaller than that of some other Europeans. The northern seas were familiar enough to them, the Mediterranean rather less so, but they had scarcely acquainted themselves with anything that lay beyond. Not until 1481 had they sailed as far south as Algeria, and no English vessel would cross the Equator until 1526. It was 1497 before they got right across the Atlantic to make landfall on the other side, probably in what is now Maine. That was John Cabot's second attempt at voyaging westwards from Bristol, and it qualifies as an English undertaking only because of Henry VII's very lukewarm patronage of a mariner who was Genoese in origin, and a certified citizen of Venice at the time. There had been an attempt in 1480 by two native Bristolians, the shipowner John Jay and his pilot Thomas Lloyd, to reach Brazil, a land whose name referred to a species of dyewood found there, so much esteemed as a textile-colouring agent that it would eventually fetch £10 a ton on the London market. Jay and Lloyd sailed in a ship of only 80 tuns – on the small side for such an ambition, even by the heroic standards of the day – though their knowledge of what they were aiming for was limited to the fact that it was somewhere west of Ireland; which is where they finished up after being driven back by mid-Atlantic storms.

Cabot's son Sebastian was the next man to try his luck westward, again from Bristol in 1508, when he persuaded a company of investors to back his attempt to find a way to an even more exotic destination than Brazil by sailing perversely in what might now seem the opposite direction. John Cabot, in fact, had supposed his North American landfall to be the fabled Cathay (China), and the son was simply trying to discover another route to the Pacific Ocean and what lay beyond. His instinct told him that there must be some route round the top of the American land mass that was navigable; as indeed there was, though only with great difficulty and for a very limited period each year. It would later be identified as the Northwest Passage and it would not be forced, after countless similar efforts had also failed, until the beginning of the twentieth century; but in reaching Hudson's Bay, as he may well have done a hundred years before Henry Hudson himself, Sebastian Cabot registered a notable if (again) only nominal English success.

These, however, were almost paltry achievements when placed against the long-distance voyages and discoveries of mariners sailing out of southern Europe. The Genoese had a long pedigree of nautical exploration, often (like the Cabots) in the name of somebody else. The Vivaldi brothers in 1291 had set sail from Spain in search of India, which they supposed to be on the other side of the Atlantic, a quest from which they never returned. Lanzarotto Malocello raised the flag of Castile in the Canary Isles in 1330 and was able to tell his Spanish patrons about it. Most celebrated of them all, Cristoforo Colombo sailed to Ireland and possibly Iceland in 1477 in a Genoese vessel, before offering to find Cathay and Cipangu (Japan) on behalf of the Portuguese in 1484. He was rebuffed by King João, who had not much idea of the distance involved (well over ten thousand miles) but was advised that Colombo's estimate (2,400 miles) was hopelessly inadequate, and that accepting it would only lead to problems of shipboard victualling and discipline. Colombo therefore peddled his idea over the next few years to several other monarchs – including Henry VII of England – before selling it in 1492 to Katherine of Aragon's parents, Ferdinand of Aragon and Isabella of Castile, the joint rulers of Spain, and embarking on the westward voyage that saw him make landfall first in the Bahamas, then in Cuba and finally in Hispaniola (Haiti) before turning for home. Next year, he sailed to the Leeward and Virgin Isles and to Puerto Rico, and a third voyage in 1498 added Trinidad and Venezuela to the bag. He still believed that he had reached an extremity of Cathay in Cuba, that his further excursion as far south as the Orinoco River was to India, and he set off from Cadiz a fourth time in 1502 with these illusions still intact. This time he coasted past Nicaragua and Costa Rica and actually spent Christmas anchored off the Panamanian isthmus, without ever realising that the Pacific Ocean was almost within walking distance. He was still unaware of this when he died at Valladolid in 1506, just as he remained ignorant of his real achievement, for which he would in time be remembered and revered as Christopher Columbus.

So began the Spanish engagement with the Americas, which Spaniards themselves swiftly joined. One of them was Vicente Yañez Pinzon, who had captained the *Niña*, one of the vessels with the *Santa Maria* on Columbus's first voyage; and who, on his own account at the end of 1499, took four caravels across the Atlantic to reach Brazil and discover the Amazon estuary. Another was Vasco Nuñez de Balboa, who in 1513 did what Columbus might have done, by leading Francisco Pizarro and a thousand natives on a twenty-four-day trek across the isthmus until he beheld the Pacific, which he formally annexed on behalf of King Ferdinand, so gratifying the King that he was proclaimed *Adelantado* (Admiral) of the Great South Sea on his return. It was on this expedition that Pizarro heard tell of an incredibly rich land much further south, which was the Inca kingdom of Peru and which, nineteen years later, he invaded and pillaged before transforming it into a Spanish dominion. Balboa had spoken of the rivers of gold that were waiting to be tapped in Darien, where the isthmus joined the South American mainland, but he didn't know the half of it. The entire region was thickly veined with precious metals in abundance, far beyond anybody's dreaming of it, and this was to be the basis of the Spanish empire in the New World; this, and a great traffic in slaves. The Spanish were not at all interested in trading with their trans-Atlantic possessions, but only in what they could take out of them. The seapower that Henry VIII's younger daughter Elizabeth would have to contend with much later in the sixteenth century, was built upon a need for fighting ships that would escort bullion safely back to Europe, across an ocean that an entire generation of English pirates (regarded indulgently for the most part by the English Crown) by then cruised hungrily.

The Portuguese were the voyagers who outdid everybody else. If there was a genesis to their remarkable achievements it lay in the fascination with geography and navigation of a prince, the Infante, with English blood in him, which came from his maternal grandfather John of Gaunt. Prince Henry had distinguished himself in a number of military campaigns as a young man, but his life's work awaited him in the Algarve, whose Governor he became in 1438. For the last twenty-two years of his life he made his home in Sagres, close by Cabo de São Vicente, where Europe turns sharply from the Atlantic to face the Mediterranean. And there, on a clifftop with a commanding view of sea and ocean which sweeps through 270 degrees, he established his school of navigation, the Vila do Infante.[1] He gathered together the best mathematicians he could attract from anywhere, many of them Arabs, whose people had pioneered celestial navigation since the eighth century, building on what they themselves had learned from Phoenicians and Greeks, and giving their names to Al Na'ir, Shaula, Aldebaran, Alkaid and many other heavenly bodies. He employed them and other experts to teach his sea captains all they knew of astronomy, navigation, cartography and mathematics; and he expected his captains in return to pause at Sagres on their way home to the Tagus, and give him a detailed description of all they had experienced and discovered in the course of their voyage. He thus built up a formidable, possibly unique, deposit of knowledge about ways and means of crossing the seas. The Portuguese had discovered the Azores just a few years before Henry the Navigator arrived in Sagres, and had quickly settled in the islands; but it was his work that provided the impetus for their further explorations. The school survived Henry's death in 1460 and at least one Englishman, John Borough, who later supervised the harbour works at Dover, studied there early in the sixteenth century.

The Portuguese had felt their way along the West African coast as far as Elmina, in the Gulf of Guinea, by 1471, and each year after that saw them push the boundary of their knowledge a little further down the continent. At the beginning of 1488 Bartholomew Diaz established the southern limit of Africa by rounding the Cape of Good Hope, before the crews of his three ships became so alarmed by the intimidating strangeness of their surroundings that they forced him to turn back. Vasco da Gama then took up the challenge and sailed on up the east coast as far as Malindi, above Mombasa; and from there in the spring of 1498, with the aid of a pilot from Gujarat, he crossed the Arabian Sea and reached Calicut on the Malabar coast of southern India. He had unwittingly come across one of the world's great sources of spice, and in doing so he started a maritime trade between India and Europe from which the English, the French and the Dutch would one day profit hugely. There was a follow-up voyage a couple of years later, on which Pedro Alvarez Cabral took da Gama's advice to sail westwards from Lisbon for a start, in order to pick up helpful south-east trade winds; but instead of reaching India as intended, he was blown straight across the Atlantic to Brazil,

1 The seacliffs at Sagres are something over two hundred feet high and the locals nowadays fish from them with rod and well-weighted lines, which they cast into the surf far below. It seems at least possible that their ancestors did the same thing in the fifteenth century.

which eventually became a Portuguese fiefdom, in spite of a Spaniard's having got there first.

Cabral's countrymen were more preoccupied for the time being with the East, however. By 1505 they were in Ceylon, four years later they were settled in Goa, and by 1511 they were deep into the East Indies at Malacca. By the middle of the sixteenth century the Indian Ocean would be as familiar to them as the Atlantic, and they were running annual convoys from Lisbon as far east as Maçao and Nagasaki, on the edge of an ocean that was twice the size of the Atlantic. Meanwhile, the greatest of all their navigators, Ferdinand Magellan, had also found his way to the Pacific, but by sailing westabout, and by doing so in the service of the newly crowned Emperor Charles V after falling out of favour with the Portuguese King. He led five ships out of San Lúcar (the port for Seville) in the autumn of 1519, crossed the Atlantic to Brazil, then crept down the coast of South America until he rounded its tip through the straits that ever afterwards bore his name. From there he went on across the full breadth of this new ocean until he came to the Philippines in March 1521, where he was killed by the islanders, as were many of his men. Only two of Magellan's ships managed to escape and of these only one, the 85-tun *Vittoria*, returned to Seville by sailing on westwards round the Cape of Good Hope. In doing so, Juan Sebastian del Cano and his crew had managed to complete what Magellan had started. Theirs was nothing less than the first authenticated circumnavigation of the globe.

A recurring denominator in all this maritime exploration was China, the mysterious Cathay of which Europe had been particularly aware since the Venetian Marco Polo's extended stay there at the end of the thirteenth century. Its existence had been known long before any European visited it, however, because it was the eastern terminus of the ancient Silk Road, along which the dried roots of rhubarb (highly esteemed for their laxative properties) and much else had been travelling to the Mediterranean and beyond as early as 114 BC, and maybe for two thousand years before Christ. But Marco Polo's account of his long journey to, and time in, China had excited Europeans with its vivid description of things that were novel to them. He told of bark from mulberry trees, especially 'the thin inner rind, which lies between the coarser bark and the wood of the tree...being steeped, and afterwards pounded in a mortar, until reduced to a pulp, is made into paper'. He outlined the Chinese process for making the finest porcelain, which began when they collected 'a certain kind of earth, as it were, from a mine, and laying it in a great heap, suffer it to be exposed to the wind, the rain and the sun for thirty or forty days, during which time it is never disturbed. By this it becomes refined and fit for being wrought...' He spoke of plentiful gold, of the great traffic in merchandise to be seen every day in the city of Kanbalu, which was the Great Khan's winter residence – 'no fewer than a thousand carriages and pack horses loaded with raw silk make their daily entry; and gold tissues and silks of various kinds are manufactured to an immense extent'. He mentioned many other opulent things, and strange phenomena, and outlandish customs, and teeming hordes of people everywhere he went, not just in China itself, but in the adjacent lands through which he passed on the way from and back to his own land. The tales he had to tell were not only exciting but totally compelling. From then on no European entrepreneur of substance, no mariner with a sense of destiny, was going to rest until a sea route was established to this fabulous place, by which bulk cargoes could be conveyed in both directions. Then indeed there would be a commerce to overshadow mightily any trade that had ever gone before.

Marco Polo was interested in ships (he was a Venetian, after all) and he took careful note of vessels that the Chinese had built for their trading voyages to India.[2] He mentions four-masted ships which could also be propelled by oars, with sixty small cabins to accommodate merchants, and with watertight compartments 'to guard against accidents which may occasion the vessel to spring a leak, such as striking on a rock or receiving a stroke from a whale, a circumstance that not infrequently occurs'. They were double-planked for additional protection, 'that is, they have a course of sheathing boards laid over the planking in every part'. They were caulked, as was the custom at home, but instead of using pitch to seal the seams packed with oakum, they mixed quicklime with chopped-up hemp and with oil 'from a certain tree, making of the whole a kind of unguent, which retains its viscous properties more firmly, and is a better material than pitch'. Such vessels as these were crewed by anything between 300 and 150 men, they held five to six thousand baskets of pepper and other spices in their cargo space, and they might have on board as many as ten small boats for fishing, carrying out anchors, or other purposes. Marco then drops a clue to the range of the Chinese mercantile fleet, telling how they were usually repaired after 'having been on a voyage for a year or more'. Where such a voyage took them apart from India is

2 A legacy of their Indian presence is the many surreal contraptions that still catch fish at the entrance to Cochin harbour in Kerala.

almost anybody's guess; but what is perfectly clear is that Chinese ships at the end of the thirteenth century were appreciably more sophisticated and a lot bigger than any vessel sailing under European command. And their people had by then been developing an ocean-going fleet for four hundred years.

By the time of the fifteenth-century Emperor Zhu Di (the Son of Heaven), the Chinese were building very large vessels indeed, and a prodigious number of them. They were a completely self-sufficient and proud people who had always cut themselves off from the rest of the world, both known and unknown, except on their own very strictly exclusive terms, but Zhu Di had a proselytising streak and decided that the time had come when his navy must 'proceed all the way to the end of the earth to collect tribute from the barbarians beyond the seas. . .to attract all under heaven to be civilised in Confucian harmony'. He embarked on a shipbuilding programme to augment the navy he had inherited, a programme of such magnitude that it would be quite unbelievable were it not for the fact that it has been attested to by, among other scholars, the great sinologist Joseph Needham. As a first step, the principal existing shipyards were doubled in size, until they covered several square miles on the Yangtze River near Nanking, with the addition of seven new dry-docks big enough to allow simultaneous work to be carried out on three ships apiece, all fashioned from teak in the style that the West has always thought of as the junk, with lugsails generally made of cane matting.[3] When the construction of these 1,681 new vessels was finished, the Emperor's navy

> consisted of some 3,800 ships in all, 1,350 patrol vessels and 1,350 combat ships attached to guard stations or island bases. A main fleet of 400 large warships was stationed at Hsin-chiang-khou near Nanking and 400 grain transport freighters. In addition there were more than 250 long-distance 'treasure ships', or galleons, the average complement of which ranged from 450 men in c.1403 to over 690 in 1431, and certainly overstepped 1,000 in the largest vessels. A further 3,000 merchantmen were always ready as auxiliaries, and a host of small craft did duty as despatch-boats and police launches.

The missionary enterprise was entrusted to the Emperor's Grand Eunuch Zheng He, who was made commander-in-chief of the 3,500 vessels

3 'Junk' is derived from the Portuguese adaptation of *djong*, the Javanese word for ship.

which set sail in March 1421 from Tanggu on the Yellow Sea. His command was, in fact, subdivided into five fleets, which would sail on in different directions once they reached the Indian Ocean, but the composition of each was effectively identical. They included the great treasure ships, 250 of those in all, which spread their sails on nine masts, carried 2,000 tuns of cargo in their holds, and were immense in many other ways. Both they and the other great ships were about 480ft from stem to stern and 180ft in the beam, and they shipped rudders that were 36ft high.[4] Much of the cargo carried both in the treasure ships and the merchantmen was designed to sustain during their infancy the colonies that the Chinese intended to establish wherever they went, but otherwise it consisted of presents with which to impress local potentates and goods for trading with native peoples. A great variety of Chinese flora was included, for planting out in the various destinations. Animals were carried in other vessels for colonial breeding purposes as well as for victualling the fleet, but hundreds of concubines travelled comfortably in the treasure ships, for they were meant for pleasure while at sea, later for doing their bit to populate the colonies. Also luxuriously accommodated were interpreters in seventeen different Indian and African languages.

It has lately been suggested that this enterprise took the Chinese to the Americas seventy years before Columbus, to the Antipodes three and a half centuries before James Cook, and perhaps even to the Antarctic land shelf four hundred years before any Westerner; that one group of ships all but circumnavigated Greenland and sailed home by way of the Arctic Ocean, the Bering Strait and the North Pacific; that the only significant part of the globe one or other of the fleets didn't reach and make maps of was Europe; and there is a certain amount of circumstantial evidence for this. What seems unquestionably true is that Zheng He's expedition ended in disaster for about three-quarters of the people who embarked on it, as ships foundered in tempests or were wrecked on dangerous shores, and as people who were landed in scattered settlements far from home and told to get on with it were abandoned by fellow countrymen who had promised to return with replenishments, but never did.

It was no more than a token squadron of ships that began returning to China during 1423, to find a homeland whose outlook had been

4 In other words, these ships were about 50ft longer and 135ft wider than the biggest modern British destroyers, while the height of their rudders was almost as much as the overall length of the *Niña* in Columbus's first voyage.

transformed while they were away. Some very troubling signs of divine displeasure had manifested themselves almost from the moment Zheng He's 3,500 vessels weighed anchor in the Yangtze estuary. Lightning had set fire to and destroyed the Forbidden City, 174,000 people had died in an unidentifiable epidemic, there were grave economic problems, Zhu Di had been thrown from his horse and was humiliated by impotence, increasingly mocked both by his concubines and by the old mandarin aristocracy, who had never approved of his expansive plans anyway. He died a few months after the battered ships returned and his son, Zhu Gaozhi, on succeeding him, announced that any future naval programme must be abandoned at once, shipbuilding and repair discontinued, with cargoes and other shipboard goods handed over to officials supervising internal affairs. All government employees who were in foreign lands were to return home immediately. China would now retreat into isolation once more, henceforth relying on its Great Wall and natural impediments to keep the rest of the world at bay.

Laggardly is the word that springs to mind when considering the English contribution during these centuries to the great increase in humankind's knowledge of the world it inhabited, though their failure to engage much in these matters was no greater than that of the other seafaring nations in northern Europe. There may have been a psychological block for the northerners in the last years of the fifteenth and the early years of the sixteenth centuries, essentially to do with proximate latitudes and not straying too far away from the familiar. In northern seas, moreover, there was never the slightest risk of running out of drinking water, because there was always plentiful rain, not something that could be relied on elsewhere. The Englishman's world had moved on a bit by the time Francis Drake made his great piratical circumnavigation in 1577–80, and it was considerably different when Cook was sent to observe the transit of Venus from Tahiti in 1769. The mindset of the early Tudor voyagers was certainly conditioned by the limits of their navigational abilities, which were considerably behind those of the Mediterranean and especially the Portuguese seafarers; the French, too, were somewhat ahead of them in this respect, and so were the Scots.

The Phoenicians had regularly sailed to Cornwall for its tin as early as 600 BC, but even in 1509 relatively few English seamen were confident that they could make their way safely to the eastern end of the Mediterranean, and the North African *corsa* were not the only reason for their nervousness. They were uneasy when they could no longer see land they recognised, and their habitual method of sailing from one place to another was by sighting familiar headland after headland until they reached their destination. The tradition for getting to Bordeaux and its wine was that you crossed the Channel at some place you already knew, sailed within sight of France right round to Pte de St Mathieu, and then hugged the Atlantic coastline until you reached the Gironde estuary. A direct sailing route from the Thames to Bordeaux would be about seven hundred nautical miles, but getting to Gascony by way of Plymouth and St Mathieu would make it almost half as long again. It was thought vital to stay 'in soundings', which is why the medieval English mariner relied more than anything upon the lead and line, which might be up to a hundred fathoms long and which, cast overboard, told him how much water was under his keel and what kind of sand or gravel or shell or mud was on the seabed there – or whether there was nothing but dangerous rock.[5] But the leadline became useless once a ship had sailed beyond the edge of the European continental shelf, and this extended only a hundred miles into the Atlantic, west of Penmarc'h in Brittany. Chaucer's Prologue to *The Canterbury Tales* summarised the approach of the medieval mariner to finding his way across the seas, in its description of the Dartmouth Shipman:

> As for his skill in reckoning his tides,
> Currents and many another risk besides,
> Moons, harbours, pilots, he had such despatch
> That none from Hull to Carthage was his match,
> Hardy he was, prudent in undertaking;
> His beard in many a tempest had its shaking,
> And he knew all the havens as they were
> From Gottland to the Cape of Finisterre,
> And every creek in Brittany and Spain. . .

There were much more sophisticated navigational aids than the leadline, memory and pilots with local knowledge, however, but it took the English a while to catch up with some of them. They relied on their acquired wisdom of natural phenomena; not only knowing the pattern of the night skies (they had been using the Pole Star for guidance at least since the ninth century) but also paying attention to the direction in which birds

5 The end of the 14lb lead billet was concave to accommodate a good smear of tallow, which picked up whatever substance it landed on. A line of only twenty-five fathoms was used in shallow water.

were flying, and to the distinctive pattern and length, smell and colour of waves, which changed as you moved from shallow to deep water: a mile offshore of the Seine estuary wasn't at all the same sea that you encountered on the far side of Ouessant.

They were familiar with one or two instruments that enabled them to be even surer which way they were heading. The forerunner of the compass, the magnetic lodestone and its accompanying needle, had been around since the twelfth century, a hundred years after the Chinese had discovered its apparently magic properties. The astrolabe, precursor of the sextant, is thought to have been used in the Mediterranean as early as 1295. The cross-staff, a cruder device for measuring the altitude of a heavenly body, was first described by a Provençal Jew, Levi ben Gerson, early in the fourteenth century. Then there were the written aids to navigation, based on the accumulated experience of seafarers – an important supplement to the fairly crude charts that existed before Mercator revolutionised cartography in the second half of the sixteenth century – but the English came very late to these. There had been sailing directions of a sort since AD 60, when the 'Periplus of the Erythraean Sea'[6] was composed by an anonymous Egyptian Greek to assist captains (often the merchant owner of their ship, with no seamanship skills) in coming to terms with the Red Sea and the Arabian Gulf; it covered a number of topics, from distances to natural hazards, from weather to commercial prospects ashore, but it was not comparable to the nautical almanacks that eventually evolved from it.

A rudimentary map for use in the Mediterranean had appeared c.1275, the 'Carta Pisana', which took account of scale and showed which way the predominating winds blew, in a diagram that anticipated the compass rose. From it, other such maps were developed, illustrating not only the Atlantic coast of Europe but the Channel and the Narrow Seas off Flanders. They were commissioned and probably drawn by Venetians, whose trading interests had expanded to northern waters, and they may also have owed much to information supplied by Genoese fighting for the French against England's Edward I. The next great breakthrough did not come until 1400, when a tremendous discovery was made in Constantinople. This was a copy of Ptolemy's treatise and world atlas known as the 'Geographica', which he had produced c.AD 150 and which had then been lost for almost a thousand years after the fall of the

---

6 Periplus, meaning both circumnavigation or the account of a coasting voyage, is a transliteration of the Greek word Περιπλουσ.

Roman Empire. It was an imperfect depiction of the known world in the Egyptian's day – for one thing, it understood a degree of latitude to be fifty rather than its true sixty miles – but in its projection of meridians and parallels, in its allocation of latitudes and longitudes to no fewer than eight thousand locations, it was an eye-opener which, taking advantage of the printing press that Gutenberg invented at Mainz in 1440, stimulated all the cartography that followed it.

It influenced, as did the 'Periplus', the sailing directions which began to appear towards the end of the fifteenth century and which the English knew as rutters.[7] The first and most famous of these was composed in manuscript by Pierre Garcie, a seaman from St Gilles sur Vie, between Nantes and La Rochelle, in 1483–4 and printed in Rouen sometime between 1502 and 1510. It was entitled *Le routier de la mer*, an expanded version of which appeared ten years later as *Le grand routier*. Garcie was writing particularly for the men who sailed in the small Breton vessels which traded along the Atlantic coasts of France and Spain, carrying salt from Bourgneuf Bay and wine from Bordeaux, and who faced the same hardships and hazards he himself was familiar with every time they put to sea. From the outset, the *routier* described tidal streams, gave the bearings of places, noted suitable anchorages and distances between them, together with the depths and nature of the seabed. It also included relevant 'Judgements of the Sea' from the Laws of Oléron; and there was an appendix which told how the movable feasts of the Church – by which many secular as well as religious events were regulated – could be determined, in case any Christian mariner found himself trading in some Muslim land which paid little heed to Easter or the Epiphany. The additional information of *Le grand routier* extended Garcie's range to include all the Channel coast westward from the Scheldt, and came to a conclusion at the entrance to the Mediterranean. Another new feature was the woodcuts which showed in outline what certain coastal features (headlands and islands in particular) looked like, for rapid identification. All through the text runs a powerful awareness of danger, as in a passage referring to the southern end of Biscay:

> You will see south of Le Boucaut and close to the sea, a thicket of trees, it is closer than all the others and close to Le Boucaut. And you will find close along the shore a cannon shot distant 20 and 24 fathoms, and there is neither an anchorage nor refuge there, except with a breeze from the

7 A corruption of the French *routier*, meaning route book.

land, then you will find it in 24 or 25 fathoms. But remember that every vessel which gets embayed is cast away on the coast and is totally lost and her crew drowned; the bodies of the men are always washed up on this shore and never elsewhere, there is no escape except by God's Grace.

An Englishman sailing in the wine fleet picked up a copy in Bordeaux and took it home to London, where Robert Copland translated it into English and published it as the *Rutter of the See* in 1528. This was itself expanded within a few years by the addition of the *Rutter of the Northe*, which had been composed in manuscript by some anonymous fifteenth-century English seaman and was now printed by Richard Proude: it extended the scope even more by starting at Berwick-on-Tweed and continuing clockwise round the English coast until it came to Dartmouth and then crossed to the Scilly Isles.

In spite of that anonymous English manuscript, the French distinctly had the edge in these matters, not only in the production of their *routiers*, but in the Breton tide charts which were drawn at some point before the English lost Bordeaux in 1453 and which have been described as 'perhaps the most remarkable contribution of north-west Europe to navigation'; for they enabled the seaman, finding himself anywhere between Finistère and Flanders, on either side of the Channel, to know what tidal conditions to expect on any day of the year, provided he knew the phases of the moon, which came as second nature to every mariner. It was Copland's translation of Garcie, however, that marked the beginning of a strangely close Anglo-French relationship in navigational matters, which flour-ished throughout the remaining years of Henry VIII and even survived a period of war between the two countries. Some of this is traceable to the school of navigation which was founded at Dieppe early in the reign of Francis I and thereafter produced most of the French seamen who ventured to the other side of the Atlantic south of the Newfoundland Banks: men like Guillaume le Testu, who sailed not only to South America but to Africa, and in time became *pilote royal* in the port of Havre de Grâce after producing a world atlas of fifty-six maps, decorated with detailed drawings of seventy-two different sixteenth-century ships he had met on his travels, which have been priceless source material for naval historians ever since.

Another product of Dieppe was Jean Rotz, who entered the English King's service in 1542 as Hydrographer Royal on £40 a year. Rotz's great contribution to Henry's naval appetite was his *Boke of Idrography*, a collection of charts and a treatise, written in an idiomatic form of English which gave away his ancestry: though born in France, he was the son of an emigré Scot, David Ross. The book was probably prepared before Rotz came to England and, after he had presented it to the King, it led to his being granted denization (something less than full citizenship, something more than mere permission to live in England) together with 'Coleta his wife and their children' within a couple of weeks; also permission to trade on his own account with Morocco. But the compilation was not the only service he offered the Crown, for he would act as navigator during Henry's terminal war with Francis, by which time no fewer than sixty French pilots were working for English pay. Another of them, also Dieppois, was the Jean Bartelot who was awarded an annuity of £20 'for the safe conduct and piloting of the King's ships through a place called "le Blakedepis" and for his labour and skill in finding a new channel there by which many serious dangers are avoided in navigation'.[8]

The oldest surviving chart by an Englishman was made in 1540 by Richard Caundish of Suffolk, who mapped the complexities of the Thames estuary after long and assiduous labour with his leadline. But London's river had inspired much earlier than that a most important step forward in the matter of pilotage. In March 1513, a group of shipmasters and seamen presented Henry with a petition which bemoaned the fact that it had become customary for foreigners to bring their ships into and out of the port, this giving them 'knowledge of the secrets of your said river' which might prove costly in time of war: a calculated suggestion which was bound to weigh with the bellicose Henry, who had recently lost the *Regent* in her action with *Cordelière* and was planning to lead his troops personally against France. They asked that, instead, pilotage in the Thames should be exclusively an English preserve, pointing out that this would also mean that 'fewer ships or none should perish in default of lodesmen as now of late have done'.

Twelve months later, having returned from his war. Henry authorised the revival of a medieval seamen's guild on the Thames, which henceforth became known for its attachment to the Church of the Holy Trinity and St Clement at Deptford Strand. Its express purpose was to foster navigation, and to maintain an almshouse for old sailors, and only

---

8 The Black Deep became one of three recognised estuarine channels into and out of the Thames. The others were the King's Channel and the Barrow Deep.

Englishmen could be admitted to it.[9] One of the leading figures in the revival was Thomas Spert who, although he was away on active service aboard *Mary Rose* when the petition was presented, was one of those who drew up the regulations for Trinity House in his capacity as its first Master. These insisted that nobody 'shall take upon him to be a lodesman within the said River of Thames without he be a Brother of the said Fraternity', though an exception was made for pilots from Sandwich, Dover, Harwich and Orwell, who were allowed to bring vessels up from those ports. The closed shop was even more firmly bolted by a clause which forbade the Brethren from discussing Trinity House business with anyone but colleagues; there were fines for speaking ill of another member; and everyone was expected to turn out for a fellow-pilot's funeral. Most of the guild's income came from fees paid by shipowners for the pilotage, and from a levy on ordinary seamen, who were deprived of the money they had been accustomed to receiving over and above their pay, for helping to load or unload their ship. If that seems unreasonable, at least the cash was put back into an apparatus that existed for their benefit, for it subsidised, among other things, the provision of buoys and other navigational aids, which began to be laid along the Thames in 1538, followed soon afterwards by similar protection for most of the principal ports and harbours. One day the Brethren would be responsible for the upkeep of all lighthouses, lightships and other safety devices around the British coasts.

Though they came late to ocean voyaging, the native English began to catch up with the foreigners (and with the alien Cabots) after Henry had been on the throne for seventeen years. An attempt to cross the Atlantic in 1517 scarcely counts because it was almost stillborn after Sir Thomas More's brother-in-law, the London printer (and man of many other parts) John Rastell, had commissioned two vessels for the voyage; but they had barely cleared Ireland before his shipmasters refused to go further west, preferring the certainty of Bordeaux wine in their holds to the imponderables of the New Found Lands. But in 1526, the Bristol shipowner Robert Thorne, whose father had sailed with John Cabot, sponsored a voyage whose intention was to reach the Moluccas with a view to gaining an entrée to the spice trade. It was led by two friends of his, Roger Barlow and Hugh Latimer, who were both described as 'somewhat learned in Cosmography', Latimer being also known as 'the

---

9 Five other seamen's guilds had been founded at various times in the fourteenth and fifteenth centuries, in Bristol, Lynn, York, Hull and Newcastle.

English pilot' in Spain, where he had lived for a number of years doing business. They never arrived at their intended destination, possibly because of the same mischance that had frustrated Pedro Cabral in 1500, but made landfall instead in La Plata, at the lower end of South America, whence they returned to Europe a couple of years later.

Barlow, another Bristolian, was obsessed with the idea of sailing east, however, and eventually (anticipating Jean Rotz's artful tactic) presented the King with a learned account of his navigation to and experiences on the other side of the Atlantic, which included descriptions of the natives he encountered, the local fauna, the fishes that swam in those waters, and all he had heard there about the existence of gold. This was, in fact, the very first description of Brazil in the English language, but it failed to engage Henry's attention; worse, the King, for some reason that was never documented, forbade Barlow to have it printed. And so it did nothing for Barlow's wider ambition. Other ventures did take place, however, and the first of them certainly enjoyed royal favour. Also in 1526 John Rut, a seaman with naval service behind him, took two vessels to the Caribbean and Newfoundland, one of them being the King's own ship *Mary Guildford* (160 tuns) which had been built only two years earlier; but nothing appears to have come out of the voyage and the other vessel was lost on the way back. Henry was certainly not indifferent to potentially profitable maritime enterprise (which makes his rejection of Roger Barlow all the more mystifying) because in 1541 he tried to obtain permission for English vessels to sail with the annual Portuguese fleet to India, 'to adventure there for providing this realm with spices'; but he failed, doubtless because by then he was a seriously lapsed Catholic, excommunicate into the bargain, and out of favour in the wider Europe. So the big success of his reign in this respect was to be his tacit approval of the formidable William Hawkins.

Hawkins came from a long line of Devon farmers from Tavistock, who had prospered greatly from the land. In a fairly turbulent life, he had been Collector of the royal subsidy for Devon, Treasurer and then Mayor of Plymouth, in spite of having been tried for beating up a John Jurdon, which only encouraged their fellow citizens to ask Hawkins shortly afterwards to organise Plymouth's defences against possible attack by the French. He subsequently fell foul of Cardinal Wolsey's successor Thomas Cromwell, who disbarred him from Plymouth Corporation; but Hawkins survived this setback to become Mayor a second time, and a Member of Parliament and, what's more, an ally of Cromwell. He married into the

Trelawnys, who were Cornwall's leading family, and with his Joan he produced two seafaring sons, one of whom became the Sir John Hawkins who not only pestered the Spanish on behalf of Queen Elizabeth but also made much money for himself out of the slave trade. The father's mercantile interests appear to have been less tainted than that, and William made several ocean voyages between 1530 and 1540 that did something to enrich the reign of Henry VIII. There is a celebrated passage about Hawkins – touching, saddening and reassuring in turn which conveys the impact of the earliest confrontations between Englishmen and people of different colour and race. It was set down after his death by Richard Hakluyt, based on what he had been told by Sir John Hawkins – so some allowance should be made for filial piety when reading it:

Old Mr Hawkins of Plymouth, a man for his wisdom, valour, experience and skill in sea causes much esteemed, and beloved of King Henry VIII, and being one of the principal seacaptains in the West parts of England in his time, not contented with the short voyages then made only to the known coasts of Europe, armed out a tall and goodly ship of his own of burthen 250 tuns, called the *Paul* of Plymouth, wherewith he made three long and famous voyages unto the coast of Brazil, a thing in those days very rare, especially to our Nation. In the course of which voyages he touched at the river of Sestos upon the coast of Guinea,[10] where he trafficked with the Negroes, and took of them Elephants' teeth, and other commodities which that place yieldeth; and so arriving on the coast of Brazil, he used there such discretion, and behaved himself so wisely with those savage people, that he grew into great familiarity and friendship with them. Insomuch that in his second voyage, one of the savage kings of the Country of Brazil was contented to take ship with him, and to be transported hither into England: as a pledge for his safety and return again, one Martin Cockeram of Plymouth. This Brazilian king being arrived, was brought up to London and presented to King Henry VIII, lying as then at Whitehall: at the sight of whom the King and all the nobility did not a little marvel, and not without cause: for in his cheeks were holes made according to their savage manner, and therein small bones were planted, standing an inch out from the said holes, which in his own country was reputed for a great bravery. He had also another hole in his nether lip, wherein was set a precious stone about the bigness of a pease: all his apparel, behaviour and gesture, were very strange to the beholder.

Having remained here almost the space of a whole year, and the king

10 In Latitude 5° 30' N, on the coast of what is now Liberia.

with his sight fully satisfied, Mr Hawkins according to his promise and appointment, purposed to convey him again into his country; but it fell out on the way that by change of air and alteration of diet, the said savage king died at sea, which was feared would turn to the loss of life of Martin Cockeram his pledge. Nevertheless, the Savages being fully persuaded of the honest dealing of our men with their prince, restored again the said pledge without any harm to him, or any man of the company: which pledge of theirs they brought home again into England, with their ship freighted, and furnished with the commodities of the country. Which Martin Cockeram, by the witness of Sir John Hawkins, being an officer of the town of Plymouth, was living within these few years.

The 'other commodities' in Guinea that Hakluyt mentions were spices while, in Brazil, Hawkins may have been after sugar as well as dyewood, for the Portuguese would soon be producing it extensively from cane plantations there. In exchange for such goods, he traded in the usual assortment of English ironmongery and textiles: a voyage the *Paul* made in 1540 laded 940 hatchets, 940 combs, 375 knives, five hundredweight of copper and the same amount of lead, three pieces of woollen cloth and nineteen dozen nightcaps. Twelve months later, she returned to Plymouth with a declared dozen elephant tusks and ninety-two tons of Brazil wood, but that could not have filled all the cargo space of a 250-tun vessel: there must have been other things undisclosed that would increase the voyage's profit without incurring taxation. As it was, Hawkins had to pay duty of £30 15s od on his imports, which was a modestly useful sum for the English Treasury. But Henry VIII rarely gave much in return to commercially minded mariners who set out on dangerous ocean-going voyages that increased his realm's prosperity – unlike those made by the Portuguese and the Spanish, which were all strongly backed by their royalty. The English monarch was rather more interested in the nautical skills that such seafaring developed and exercised. They were the expertise on which he was building his cherished navy for the purpose that excited him much more than any trade.

XI

A VANISHED GREATNESS

Warfare at sea did not take long to break out again, after the show of détente on the Field of the Cloth of Gold. As soon as that deceptive episode was over, and before returning to England, Henry held his second meeting with the Emperor, which Wolsey had provisionally arranged before the two parted company in Canterbury towards the end of May 1520. Now, just over a month later, he rode to Gravelines, spent a couple of days there becoming reacquainted with Charles, and then conducted him to Calais for forty-eight hours of serious discussion. The outcome was not a treaty (though that would come soon enough) but an agreement on where the pair of them stood, particularly in relation to France. Her name was never mentioned in the document that emerged from the talks, which was cloaked in generalisation, but there was no doubt at all whom the two monarchs were thinking of. The three clauses that mattered most of all were:

> 2 Both Powers to have the same enemies and the same friends. Offence or injury to the one to be repelled by the other as done to himself.
> 3 In case of invasion, neither party to desist until the aggrieved has recovered his rights. . .
> 5 Neither party to enter into treaty with any prince without the consent of the other; and if any treaties exist or hereafter be made contrary to the effect of this, they shall be invalid without the consent of both.

Neither participant would have expected this arrangement to last as long as each of them reigned, any more than any other act of diplomacy. It was nothing more than a bonding exercise – and only for the time being.

Others close to Henry would not be so circumspect in their language.

It was little more than a year before his secretary Richard Pace was telling Wolsey that 'His Highness thinketh that at such time as all things shall be concluded betwixt the Emperor and him...and a resolution taken for to invade France, then it shall be necessary for them both to provide for the destruction of the French King's navy.' Shortly afterwards, Pace was speaking of Henry recovering 'his right inheritance in France' and reporting that the King had taken 'very displeasantly' the capture of a Spanish vessel in the Thames by the French ('this presumptuous attempt used by the Frenchmen in his stream'). Meanwhile, Sir William Fitzwilliam was keeping an eye on Francis I's naval dispositions in his new capacity as ambassador at the Fontainebleau court, a position into which Wolsey had carefully put him on account of his naval experience and because he was 'keen, bold, sagacious, able to resist flattery and cajolery, and never lost his presence of mind'. In March 1521, the Vice-admiral signalled his patron that Francis had been speaking about the expansion of his fleet, which would soon include sixteen new vessels, the smallest not less than 350 tuns, 'and three great galleons that I never heard of such, for they draw so little water that he will bring them so near the shore that he may land out of them without a boat 500 footmen and...horsemen, and he will have a bridge that shall be ever carried with them, so as when they be aground...the bridge shall be put forth and so they shall land'. Francis was also building men o'war with unusually low decks, which were probably galleys, though the low decks may have been intended to carry guns rather than oarsmen. Five months later, Fitzwilliam reported that Francis expected to have forty or fifty ships ready for war within twenty days.

For the most part they were meant for imminent action off the Franco-Spanish frontier, in a move to take Fuentarrabia from Ferdinand of Aragon's successor, who was none other than Charles V wearing his alternative hat as a Spanish rather than an imperial ruler; and the vessel chosen to lead a blockade down there was James IV's old flagship *Michael*, now rehabilitated and translated into *la Grande Nef d' Ecosse*. Francis, in fact, had decided that he would have his very own seagoing pride and joy, which would outdo anything that either the Scottish or the English King had managed to build. In February, the finishing touches had been put to the *Grand François*, a vessel of 1,500 tuns which required a crew of 2,000 and which outclassed even *Henry Grâce à Dieu* in her lavishness, for she not only had her own shipboard chapel and a windmill for grinding flour to ensure fresh bread, but a tennis court for the recreation of her officers. She was, a Venetian noted, 'so magnificent that it looks as though she will be incapable of putting to sea'; and so she was, drawing so much water that she could not sail out of harbour after completion.

A meretricious self-indulgence *Grand François* may have been, but the other vessels Francis built were meant for serious business: the ones with the shallow draught and the special bridge for offloading soldiers were nothing less than landing craft for use in invasion which, in the assault on Fuentarrabia, was made over dry land and not seaborne. But Francis had, of course, been preparing himself for any eventuality against the old enemy across *La Manche* from the day he was crowned. An early act had been the construction of a new Channel port to supersede Harfleur, which was becoming silted up and would soon be unusable. He named it Havre de Grâce (though the English referred to it as Newhaven, and the world would one day know it as Le Havre), which received its first warship in the Bassin du Roi in 1518; and now, in spite of the peace between himself and Henry VIII, he began to improve its fortifications. One of the first things he did after the Field of the Cloth of Gold, was to call for a tally of all the shipping in Normandy.

By the beginning of 1522, the war clouds were drifting darkly over the Channel, and preparations for conflict were being made on both sides, even though the French were simultaneously embroiled in yet another Italian adventure, against imperial forces among others. If Charles and Henry had needed any excuse for joint action against Francis, he had just provided it by challenging the Holy Roman Emperor on two different peninsulas; and by now they had an official (though still secret) treaty to authorise their actions, a sharpened version of their preliminary agreement in Gravelines and Calais, which did not hesitate to name names. Among other clauses was one which promised that King and Emperor 'shall do their utmost to put down heresy and reform abuses in spiritual things, in such lands as they may conquer in France'. They also had the makings of a campaign strategy. If all went according to plan, Henry and his forces were to land at Calais in August and within the week they would be poised for a joint attack on Boulogne, with whatever army Charles could muster in Spain and the Low Countries. Both parties were to furnish a naval force with 3,000 men apiece, to make war upon France by sea. So that he could be involved in the invasion planning, Fitzwilliam was withdrawn from Fontainebleau to resume his naval duties as Vice-admiral and, in the Thames, Thomas Spert and eleven other mariners were overhauling *Henry Grâce à Dieu*'s tackle, as were the shipkeepers and their hands who were making ready nineteen other vessels in the river for active service: they included both *Mary Rose* and *Peter Pomegranate*, while the *Great Galley* (800 tuns) also had aboard, in addition to its skeleton crew of seamen, a couple of gunners who were checking out the ordnance.

On 7 January, it was reported to Wolsey from Calais that Frenchmen had attacked two English ships just outside the port and driven one of them ashore, that there were French men o'war lurking in the Downs so that 'no ships dare bring necessaries here from England', and that it was thought there might be a spy in Rye passing on naval intelligence. A memorandum of things needing to be done was drawn up, and at the top of the list was the despatch of 'the King's letters' to all noblemen and gentlemen of England, warning them to get themselves and their people in a state of readiness 'to serve at the King's pleasure'. The Master of Ordnance was sent to Valenciennes to prepare the King's artillery in the Low Countries and Sir Robert Wingfield, an old hand at diplomacy, had gone to ask Margaret of Savoy, Charles V's aunt and his Regent in the Low Countries, what assistance the English could expect from her. Even without it. Henry was thinking in terms of an English army of 16,000 foot and 2,000 mounted archers, plus 7,000 foreigners. 'Ships must be appointed with an army of 3,000 men, to guard the sea for the transport of victuals and men, and to prevent the enemy from annoying the realm.' And, oh yes, 'If the King pass the sea in person, someone should be appointed to govern the realm in his absence with a substantial council. . .' This was a question that should not have needed asking, given Katherine of Aragon's splendid fulfilment of that role the last time her husband went to war. But whispers around the court reckoned that the marriage was beginning to run into difficulties.

By February, the naval preparations were well advanced, and one of the ships recommissioned for hostilities was the *Swallow*, with 142 seamen and eighteen gunners on the strength. Another was the elderly *Mary and John* (*c.*180–200 tuns), which had been rebuilt after a fire and for which half the crew of 150 had been pressed into service in Suffolk. Fitzwilliam had drawn up his own list of things to be done at Portsmouth, which would cost a hefty £2,418 12s 8d: they included the provision of chains to seal the harbour entrance and the hire of boats to carry them into position, a dozen men working on the walls and ditches of the fortifications, the wages of sixty gunners, and 'Kettles for the ships, £20'. And in the midst of all this activity, arrangements were also under way for a second English visit by the Emperor on his way to Spain 'to obtain forces and money, the sinews of war'; when that was accomplished he would give Henry a month's notice of his readiness to go to war with France 'until each had recovered all that belonged to him'. Charles was expected in Dover during the last few days of May, after he had been entertained in Calais by the local Council at their own expense. The King was to meet him on the road to Canterbury and the two would stay one night in the Archbishop's palace there, another in Sittingbourne and a third in Rochester, before proceeding to Gravesend, where 'The barges of the King and noblemen must be ready...to take the King and Emperor to Greenwich. All ships in the Thames are to be laid between Greenwich and Gravesend, adorned with streamers and with ordnance ready to fire as the Emperor passes.' At Greenwich there was, naturally, to be a joust held over two days; also 'a meskeler [masque] and revels', for which the King's shoemaker was making twenty pairs of buskins for £5 and a Mrs Philips was supplying 'Red silk cordells, 91 oz at 14d...for bordering 8 Italian mantles, of crimson satin, with gold cyphers.'

Charles left Brussels on 23 May and embarked from Calais three days later for an uneventful four-hour crossing of the Channel, escorted by English vessels. Henry, impatient for the meeting, did not wait until his guest was on the road to Canterbury, but burst in upon him at Dover Castle 'just as the Emperor was about to sit down to supper. So sudden was the announcement of the King's arrival that the Emperor had scarcely time to meet him at the foot of the stairs of the palace, which is situated within the castle. The two sovereigns then doffed their bonnets and embraced, remaining thus for the space of two *Misereres*.' Charles may well have been surprised a second time by what happened the next day when, both of them having spent the night in Canterbury, Henry insisted on taking him back to Dover so that he could be given the now customary conducted tour of *Henry Grâce à Dieu* which, by then, was awaiting them just outside the harbour; so was *Mary Rose*, which was also inspected as an extra treat. Later they rode horses together along the shore, and received a number of dignitaries. It was 3 June before the two men reached their final destination where, in between the jousting and the revelling, 'wherein the King of England took part, and comported himself valiantly', they managed to fit in more talks.

Henry also made time to drop jovial hints to some Venetian diplomats that it would be best for them if the Serenissima detached herself from an existing alliance with France and came in with the English and the

Emperor. He sent Wolsey to twist their arms further and, in the middle of a dinner, the Cardinal 'commenced vituperating the French. He said that if peace was to exist in Christendom they must be exterminated, as they were always fomenting strife and discord among Christian powers. . . He said the King of England was better entitled to the crown of France than his most Christian Majesty and meant to possess himself of it.' Next day, he told the Venetians that he would take the field in person against the French, 'and raise 10,000 men with his own funds, selling even his sacerdotal garments for the purpose'. Wolsey was in an expansive mood that week. It had been agreed by Henry and Charles that in the carve-up of France, the Emperor should have the French part of Flanders to add to his own possessions just across the River Scheldt. This would include Tournai, and he had just promised Wolsey a pension of 9,000 crowns per annum, payable in half-yearly instalments, to compensate him for not being restored to the bishopric he had briefly enjoyed there before Henry's peace treaty with Francis.

It was during the imperial visit that Henry broke the treaty and declared war again on France, and at once his navy deployed itself for action. Charles was only midway through his second English experience when Thomas Howard issued a general order to the fleet:

1 When they set forth, no ship shall try to go before except the one my lord hath appointed, viz, the Vice-admiral's.

2 No ship to come behind except John Hopton's.

3 No ships, except those appointed, to give chase either to windward or leeward on pain of death.

4 No ship, at setting forth, to try to take the wind from one another coming, nor any danger wheresoever it be.

5 Every master to keep his lead, and sound at any danger, according to the old custom.

6 Every master and his company to attend on the Admiral, and no-one to go to harbour or road without orders.

7 Every master to keep safe the tokens given him, that each ship may know the other if separated by the weather.

8 Before sunset, every ship to come under the lee of the Admiral to know what course he will keep.

9 To every boat there must be a quartermaster and boatswain. When they land soldiers, the crew and gunners appointed to defend the boat must not leave it on pain of death.[1]

1 The tokens Howard mentions were probably prearranged flag signals, to ensure that friend was not mistaken for foe.

At the same time Howard allotted the areas that three separate flotillas were to patrol during any imminent hostilities. The *Katherine Galley* (60–80 tuns, Capt. John Cary) and three others were to keep the sea from the estuary of the Camber to Guernsey and Jersey; the *Christ* (300 tuns, Capt. William Gonson) and two others were to make sure nothing sailed between the Channel Islands and Scotland by the west-coast route; the *Sweepstake* (80 tuns, Capt. John Maryner) and three more vessels were to keep watch in the Narrow Seas between the Thames and the Camber and most especially between Calais and Dover. *Mary Rose, Great Harry, Peter Pomegranate* and the other ships over 400 tuns were not included in the list, for they were sailing under Fitzwilliam's direct command and had been lying off Dover since Charles arrived in England. One other notable absentee was Henry VII's old *Sovereign*, which had been declared unseaworthy and beyond redemption a few months earlier, after being once rebuilt (in 1509–10) and serving two kings for a total of thirty-three years; most Tudor warships could be kept afloat for a maximum of twenty-five years before they needed rebuilding.

The Emperor's departure for Spain was delayed for several days by bad weather, which did its usual mischief to all shipping it caught in the Channel. On 4 June, Fitzwilliam reported to the King that the wind had come from west-sou'west at his ships, 'so strainably that we were constrained to forsake that road [Dover] and go into the Downs, where we were fain to abide that night and Saturday and Sunday all day, for because the wind abode there continually and blew exceeding strainably'. They had set off for Hampton to take advantage of the tides when the wind came to the west on Monday, but it was a deceptive change, and 'when we were more near half seas over, the wind blew at south-west again so sore that we were forced to forsake the sea and come to the Downs again for harbour'. That little blow cost *Henry Grâce à Dieu* some timber and rigging, including her bowsprit and her main topmast. But at least Fitzwilliam made the best of his forced inactivity by sending two of his shipmasters from the anchorage in the Downs to take soundings in the Camber, in order to determine whether it might be a good place in which to lay up *Great Harry* for the forthcoming winter. They concluded that the water wasn't deep enough to take her safely and counselled further investigation in the West Country. Fitzwilliam told Henry that the masters also thought 'it is too great a danger to bring her into the Thames again'. They were presumably thinking of exposure to French attack.

By the end of the month, Thomas Howard was off the Devon coast in *Mary Rose*, seriously looking for somewhere to lay up all Henry's great ships when the campaigning season was over, and coming to the conclusion that Dartmouth was the right place, with a castle on either side of the harbour entrance complete with protective chains that could be laid between them very quickly. What's more, the River Dart was exceptionally deep and capacious, with five fathoms at low water as far as two miles upstream of the castles. Howard reported many other virtues in the port as well as these (he had discovered that within four miles of the anchorage were 2,000 'goodly oaks, which would furnish timber for repairs') and concluded that he 'Never saw a goodlier haven after all our opinions'. He was so enthusiastic that he sent his despatch to Henry for delivery by Dartmouth's Mayor, Nicholas Semer, 'a very wise man, who can tell you about this haven'.

Howard had just been made commander-in-chief of both the English and the imperial navies – some of whose ships were coming from Spain to take Charles to Santander, leaving others to render whatever assistance they could in the Channel. Maybe because he felt it important to make his mark while the Emperor was still on hand to take notice (for he was a fundamentally ingratiating man), Howard had it in mind to attack Havre, where eighteen or nineteen ships were said to be 'equipped for the wars', before sailing down to the Trade and assaulting Brest. Why he changed his mind about Havre is unclear, but instead he crossed the Channel from Dartmouth and raided Morlaix instead, going right up the long serpentine river to set fire to it and destroy seventeen vessels tied up at its quays: a dangerous enough exercise because it lay tight between steep and thickly wooded hillsides and there would have been no escape from the narrow little town had French men o'war come into the Morlaix River after him. He then decided against Brest because he was told that it was far too well defended for anything except a very large force to have any hope of success; but another consideration was doubtless the fact that he had looted Morlaix thoroughly before burning it, and returned to Southampton with much booty, including three ships taken as prizes that would be incorporated into Henry's fleet – as *Mary Grace* (90 tuns), *Bark of Boulogne* (80 tuns) and *Bark of Morlaix* (60 tuns).

Beacons had been prepared on the Isle of Wight in case they were needed to give Portsmouth and Southampton some warning of impending attack, and a couple of barks from the Channel watch had been detailed to keep a particularly close eye on anything that moved offshore there. But French warships never materialised and, by the end of June, the threat of serious naval engagement had receded so far that an English army crossed the straits to Calais to do battle ashore. Thomas Howard acquired yet another office to add to his two naval positions and was put in charge of these land forces, leaving Fitzwilliam in operational command of Henry's ships, though Howard seems to have reappeared more than once in his capacity as Admiral, to satisfy himself that his second-in-command was up to the mark. At the beginning of August, Fitzwilliam in *Mary Rose* told Wolsey that 'Yesterday, the lord Admiral left for Calais with a fair wind, and will probably be there tomorrow...has taken the *Maglory* with him to convey Lord Fitzwater's folks to Calais, but she is at liberty when they are disembarked.' The Vice-admiral had been told that he, too, would be required in Calais and was evidently reluctant to go, telling the Lord Chancellor that although he would not refuse to go wherever the King commanded, 'If he does order it, I wish to know it as soon as possible that I may send my folks thither, and provide what I need, and that you would write to the Admiral to keep the tent appointed for me. If I go, is Gonson to be Admiral...?'

Fitzwilliam appears to have reshuffled the vessels allocated by Howard to patrol the coasts, and recommended that the *Gabriel of Topsham* and *Trinity George*, both vessels on hire to Henry, 'would do better service in the West Sea, as well for the return of the fishermen from the New Found Lands, as for the going of the French into Scotland, than the others in the narrow sea'. Later in the month, having gone to Calais, he received a message directly from Westminster that he should, after all, stay on station with *Mary Rose*. He was clearly becoming irritated by one set of instructions contradicting another, if not also of being obviously super-vised, when he wrote again to Wolsey, hoping that, now he was ordered to remain at sea, 'he will be no more countermanded'. If he didn't already know it, Fitzwilliam had just discovered what every commander of forces ashore and afloat very quickly found out: that Henry VIII was perpetually changing his mind about which direction they should march or sail in and what they should do when they got there, wherever that was.

The Scots had entered the equation again, and it may have been because of this that Henry decided he would not go to France with his army, lest there should be a repeat of the invasion which ended, happily for him, at Flodden. Bearing in mind that whenever he warred with France the Scots invariably did what they could to live up to the Auld Alliance with England's other traditional enemy, he despatched a squadron up the east coast in May to keep them quiet. It was placed under the command of William Sabyn of Ipswich, one of a rising breed of ship-owning seamen whom the King was using more and more in his navy. He had captained his own vessel, converted for war, under Edward Howard off Brittany in 1512 and caught the eye enough then to warrant this promotion ten years later. His ships arrived off the Firth of Forth in the middle of the night and tried to land a party to burn a village near Tantallon Castle, but were driven off by a mixture of Scottish foot soldiers and horse. Two days later they attempted to burn some moored fishing boats but were repulsed again, and a couple of Sabyn's men were killed. So he went round to Leith and bombarded it, before crossing the firth to sail along its north shore and let fly at Kinghorn and Dysart as he passed them in turn. Encountering a Danish ship which the French had seized and were taking into Leith, he captured it and redirected it to Newcastle, together with its cargo of rye and twenty-four barrels of herring, and a covering note to the Customs officers, advising them to sell the grain as quickly as possible, because it was well past its best on account of the damp. The prize was then to be loaded with coal and sent down to Ipswich for his own use. Word of this reached Fitzwilliam, together with report of some other cavalier behaviour and, though the Vice-admiral wrote to Wolsey about it, there is no record of any reprimand. Sabyn continued his upward progress in the royal service: he was a man after Henry's own heart.

With four months left for campaigning, the English invasion was making little headway beyond the Pale of Calais. Howard's troops did nothing more than conduct a series of raids at various points in Picardy and Artois, and it became obvious that a much larger army would be needed to make any real progress into France, this time equipped with sufficient artillery to knock down a town's walls, which Howard's men lacked. So October arrived and the land forces dug themselves in for the winter, while only a token naval presence remained on watch in the Channel. *Mary Rose* and most of her consorts were laid up in Portsmouth or in the Thames, *Henry Grâce à Dieu* being anchored in the river off Northfleet, where some of her rigging was replaced. In spite of Howard's great enthusiasm for it (and, presumably, some glittering sales talk by Nicholas Semer at court), Dartmouth was rejected by Henry on the grounds that it was far too remote to be practicable: he was thinking of the money that would have to be spent on getting supplies so distantly to his fleet.

The year turned into 1523 and Charles Brandon took over command of the land army, taking with him reinforcements that meant he would have nearly 13,000 men to lead, and plenty of heavy guns. But then things stalled again, because the *Landsnechts* and cavalry the Emperor had promised didn't turn up until the end of September. While waiting for this assistance to materialise, Brandon abandoned the idea of besieging Boulogne and, far too late in the year, marched south-west instead. By the end of October he was on the other side of Amiens and well on the road to Paris itself after taking Montdidier. The weather turned nasty and his frost-bitten soldiers began to talk of going home; when a thaw left them sodden instead, they were even more determined to be done with it – some of them actually did desert, finding their own way across the Channel again – and late November saw a general retreat. Brandon himself was in Calais again by 12 December to find a blistering reprimand awaiting him from a sovereign who wasn't much interested in extenuating circumstances but only in triumphant outcomes. Henry had been humiliated by the Marquis of Dorset's withdrawal from Guyenne in 1512, and here was further ignominy. This was to be the last time for twenty years that English troops would seriously campaign on continental Europe. It has been described as 'the last campaign of the Hundred Years War' and the end of an ambition that began with Henry V's great French adventures – 'the last expression of vanished greatness'. It has also been suggested that the Middle Ages did not finish in 1485, as English historians have always conventionally insisted, but at the back end of 1523, when Charles Brandon had to turn away from Paris in Picardy's autumn mud.

Henry didn't have much to rejoice about that year at sea, either. The big French ships that had been blockading the Spanish coast spent the winter in Brest and there was no telling which way they would be sent when the fair weather returned. It was the Scots, however, who set off the first alarm when they began to blockade the Humber and then seized two small vessels off Yarmouth, and English vessels sailing to engage them were dispersed by a storm. Thomas Howard, by now a full-time Admiral again, heard that 'the Scots are going to set forth six or seven ships to the Islands, to intercept the Iceland fleet on their way home. If they (the Scots) succeed, the coasts of Norfolk and Suffolk will be undone, and all England destitute of fish next year.' He sent four of the ten ships he then had in the North Sea to escort the endangered merchant fleet home. There was an action a little later, but it involved a French vessel that was trying to steal into Leith and ended in disaster when Sir Henry Sherburn – a member of the Queen's household, close enough to Katherine to partner her at shuffleboard when he was at court, but serving as Howard's Vice-admiral in the North Sea – was killed in a bad day all round for the family, with his son Thomas permanently deafened by the gunfire of the two ships.

In the Channel, Sir William Fitzwilliam was charged with ensuring above all that the Scottish Regent Albany, who had been living in France these past nine years, didn't attempt to make for home with generous assistance from his hosts. At first he fulfilled his instructions admirably, when in August he encountered a dozen French and Scottish vessels with Albany (and the Archbishop of Glasgow) on board, together with 3,000 French troops, and chased them into Boulogne and Dieppe. He intended to destroy the Scotsmen inside the harbour at Boulogne in a surprise attack at midnight, but the wind suddenly changed 'so strainably' that he and his ships had to stand off towards the English coast to avoid disaster. When the weather improved he then had another thought, but this time it was an unfortunate one. Like every other English naval commander, Fitzwilliam found it difficult to resist the temptation to go raiding at the prospect of loot. In this case, the Norman fishing village of Le Tréport caught his attention, as it had Sir John Wallop's some years earlier; and having, as he thought, successfully seen off Albany, he took his squadron in for the usual sequence of burning and plundering, then went back across the water to unload before perhaps returning for more. It was while he was thus engaged in Hampshire that Albany seized his chance, rapidly got his people back aboard his shipping, and set off down-Channel to round the Lizard and continue up the west coast. The Regent even managed to avoid Sir Anthony Poyntz, who had replaced William Gonson in charge of the flotilla guarding the Irish Sea against just such an eventuality, and in September reached Kirkcudbright without having lost a single man. But then everything came to a standstill again because it was thought too late in the year for an invasion of England or any further activity.

In 1524 there was an early setback when the *Katherine Galley* was taken by half a dozen Frenchmen off Sandwich, together with a local vessel that tried to help her fight them off; but things improved within a month when two Frenchmen were captured in February as they were attacking a small fishing fleet off Rye. In May, Boulogne was bombarded and a landing party did some damage ashore; but that was about the sum total of naval activity, and nothing but a number of bloody little actions on the Scottish border, and between Calais and Boulogne, took place on land. For the most part this was a year of covert diplomacy and intrigue while, in its autumn, Francis I took another step towards disaster in Italy. Wolsey and Henry were at odds on how they should proceed in what was becoming for the English an impasse, with the King keen to go on fighting (he even talked of leading his army in person again) and the Lord Chancellor anxious to put an end to the high cost of warfare; he also had an ambition to succeed Clement VII as Pope and supposed that his masterminding of a peaceful Europe was a way to achieving this end.

Consistent with this aim, Wolsey entered into secret talks with the Queen Mother of France, Louise of Savoy, while her son was campaigning in the South, and these would have left the Emperor in the lurch if they had been successfully concluded that year. They were still in the balance when Francis and his army reached Pavia on the plain of Lombardy at the end of October. Two years earlier his soldiers – principally Swiss mercenaries on that occasion – had been thrashed by the imperial forces at Bicocca on the outskirts of Milan. Now, although his principal commanders advised against it, Francis was determined to take Pavia in person. He besieged it through the winter, in which his troops suffered so terribly from the cold and the rain that 6,000 mercenaries deserted, leaving him with vastly inferior numbers when the Emperor's army attacked. Francis himself fought bravely that day – as he had done at Marignano in 1515 – and had his horse killed under him before he was slightly wounded and captured, having seen much of the French nobility wiped out in a national catastrophe as great as the one at Flodden eleven years before. It was to be 1526 before he was released from a Spanish prison, after the French had paid a huge ransom to get him out.

When Henry heard that the Yorkist pretender to the English throne, Richard de la Pole, had also been killed fighting with Francis, he went into one of his great spasms of exuberance, exclaiming 'All the enemies of England are gone!', telling the man who brought the news to him that he was as welcome as the Archangel Gabriel was to Mary, and disbursing free wine all over London. He also recalled the treaty he had made with Charles V, and assumed that the carve-up of France would now begin, in which the Emperor would take Provence, Languedoc, Burgundy and French Flanders, while the English walked off with the rest of the country. Charles refused the proposition point-blank on the grounds that the English had made no contribution whatsoever to his great Italian victory, and had done very little anywhere else since the treaty was signed. Worse, he repudiated Henry's ten-year-old daughter Mary (fifteen years his junior), whom he had agreed to marry when she was old enough, and redirected his ardour at Isabella of Portugal, who was much nearer his own age and was on the market with a far bigger dowry than Henry could hope to raise. Once again, Great Harry had been humiliated very publicly; and this, as much as any other consideration, probably dictated the course of subsequent events.

There were other pressing matters to deflect him from further warfare, however. Anne Boleyn had recently caught his eye at court and Henry was beginning to compose love letters to her in French, the opening move in the matrimonial upheaval that would change the course of English ecclesiastical history within a decade. When his attention wasn't focused on her, it was heavily engaged by his financial predicament. He had, in fact, just about run out of money after spending his father's inheritance on some shipbuilding and on fighting the French, but even more on personal extravagance. He had become so strapped for funds that in quick succession since 1523 he had introduced two new taxes, the second of which was euphemistically called the Amicable Grant and took one sixth of everyone's income apart from that of the clergy, who had to yield one third. This produced such a volume of rioting and other forms of protest across the country that, unusually for him, Henry backed down; but that did nothing to remedy the basic problem. Humiliated, hopelessly lusting after a coquette who made it plain that she would settle for nothing less than becoming his Queen, and all but bankrupt, the King was in no condition to pursue grinding hostilities any further for the moment. Six months after Pavia, Wolsey's strategy prevailed when the Treaty of The More – named after the Cardinal's property in Hertfordshire, where it was signed – was concluded between England and France. Henceforth, the Emperor, as well as Francis, was to be Henry VIII's anathema.

XII

THE GREATEST FAILURE

On 27 June, 1522, Thomas Howard wrote a despatch to his sovereign from *Mary Rose*, which echoed almost word for word a signal his brother had sent to Henry ten years earlier, when he was preparing to attack the French off Brittany. The elder Howard was now mustering his task force for the full-scale invasion of France, and after his usual report on the state of the weather and the tides, he turned to something that needed resolving urgently. 'We have but little victual on board...' he said 'We want the rest of the victual in haste.' This was the third time that month on which the Admiral had brought up the subject, and each communication was more desperate than the last. In the middle of June he had emphasised to Wolsey the importance of making sure that the men who supplied the ships' provisions were paid £600 promptly, 'without which, undoubtedly, they shall not perform their victual...'; and he was particularly worried that not enough beer could be brewed in Portsmouth to keep his crews happy and willing while they were at sea: 'much more shift may be made at London than there'. Six days later, he spelled out the situation directly to Henry who, he told him, had 'been deceived about the victual. The whole complement for 5,000 men, the beer from Portsmouth and the rest from Hampton, was promised by the last of May; and now, the 20th of June, we have with much difficulty been provided with flesh, fish and biscuit for two months from Hampton, and we can get no more than one month's beer from Portsmouth.' He told the King that his Vice-admiral Fitzwilliam had been promised the full quota of provisions by now, but as things stood, few of his ships were victualled for more than three weeks, some for only eight days and most for a fortnight. He had been in touch with the victuallers, who 'say they have been hindered about the beer for want of casks, but are as far behindhand with flesh, fish and biscuit as with beer; which I think comes from negligence'. When nothing had yet been done a week later, Thomas Howard – who was always careful to control his resentments if they remotely involved the Crown – was more than a worried man.

A failure to supply his fleet with enough food and drink to keep it going through its immediate responsibilities can be taken as one indication of Henry VIII's need to tighten his belt; and Howard's predicament was certainly not eased by his monarch's awareness that his war chest was all but empty. But victualling the King's ships – or his soldiers fighting his battles ashore – had always been a major headache for English monarchs. Nothing else had to be found and organised repeatedly on quite so large a scale, for everything apart from pay and victuals had to be supplied from scratch only once, with the recurring cost and labour of replacement or repair being intermittent and comparatively small. What the sea captains needed for messing on board their ships were great quantities of four commodities in particular that had to be completely replaced very frequently, time and time again, as long as their vessels were manned. One was flesh ('meat' tended to mean everything and anything apart from drink), which required the slaughter of cattle and pigs, and their salting-down in barrels for the most convenient stowage. For the victualling of Edward Howard's fleet in 1512–13, animals from all the royal demesnes and parks in Hampshire were rounded up and driven to Southampton before being killed, their carcasses then being stored in sheds that in peaceful times accommodated merchandise; it was the next stage of getting the barrels onto his ships that was defective and caused Howard's great cry for help just before he went into battle.

Just as important as flesh was fish, which meant dried or salted stock-fish, and that might come from anywhere – or be in any state when the seaman finally sank his teeth into it. On one occasion, Thomas Howard reported that 'part of the ships lately come out of Iceland have not yet unloaded their fish and the rest stink so that no man not used to the same can endure it.' Seamen were expected to endure both fish and flesh that had been inadequately preserved on its way to them, which is why rotten food was responsible for repeated outbreaks of dysentery in the fleet. The third great standby – and it did require good teeth more often than not, consequently being known as hard tack among seamen – was the ship's biscuit of flour and water, a maritime substitute for bread, kneaded into flat discs before baking and liable to attract small black weevils when stored, but nevertheless always carried in great quantity: the *Anne of London*, hired to victual the King's ships in the Narrow Seas, conveyed to Dover '30,000lbs of biscuit in canvas bags, the freight of which, £6, is not paid for lack of money'.[1] Sometimes, however, biscuit must have been baked in the galley that *Mary Rose* and other ships had below deck. This fairly nutritious but extremely dull and often all but inedible diet of flesh, fish and biscuit was occasionally supplemented by the provision of cheese and even butter; and an imaginative captain could improve matters by carrying several score of fish hooks, so that in any convenient lull his ship's company could enjoy the rare treat of absolutely fresh food. But these were departures from the norm, which excluded vegetables or fruit – only officers enjoyed such things, by their private arrangement and at their own expense – and did no more than sustain working efficiency.

And then there was the beer, without which no naval commander would ever have dared put to sea. It was vital not only because it set men in good heart but also to slake their thirsts so that they wouldn't dehydrate. Fresh water was, of course, carried in barrels but that, too, ran out periodically and it was liable to go off, especially in hot weather, usually because the barrels had not been cleaned properly. The souring of beer occurred for the same reason or because the brewery had taken short cuts, but seamen would put up with that more readily than they would putrid water. Beer was of such importance that it invariably came first in any complaints naval commanders made about failures in victualling. Thomas Howard told the King's Council, when he was about to take on the Scots again in 1542, and was anxious that 500–600 tuns from the London breweries should be delivered to him on time, that he feared 'lack of nothing but beer'. Nothing else would do as a substitute for the English fighting man and soldiers certainly had come close to mutiny on foreign campaigns when, faced with the same dire shortage that seamen were so frequently threatened with, they were offered a local wine to pump them up for battle instead: this was a contributory factor to the failure of the Guyenne operation in 1513. There were rumblings from time to time in the fleet, and the collapse of morale after Edward Howard's death off Brittany was no doubt partly occasioned by the fact that the beer and other victuals were running out in spite of his repeated

1 The ship's biscuit had a very long shelf life of sorts, and was still being issued in the Royal Navy for some years after the First World War.

pleadings; but there appears to be no record of a ship's company actually refusing to work or turning against their officers because of such failures. They may well have thought they were far better-off than the soldiery, who sometimes had to forage for food instead of having it always provided for them. And when the system was working properly, they were well looked-after in the way that mattered to them most. Variable in quality, limited in its variety and unvarying in its tedium the seaman's diet may have been, but he could scarcely complain about the quantity of his rations when the daily allowance ran to a pound of biscuit, a pound of flesh, a piece of fish and a gallon (4.5 litres) of beer, plus occasional extras of cheese and butter.

A weakness in the system Henry inherited was that it was so open to abuse by people in the supply chain before the food and the beer actually reached the ships, and even as it came on board. It was supervised by men who had little or no knowledge of the sea and the requirements of mariners, and who were consequently less aware of inherent problems than they might have been. Bishop Fox directed such things in Henry's early days and in his latter years the key figure was Fox's successor in the see of Winchester, Stephen Gardiner, whose secular responsibilities were so notorious that he was known in the fleet as Simon Stockfish: both men quite obviously had been picked as much for their proximity to England's principal naval base as for their rank and social standing.

The system they were required to operate was known as purveyance, whereby the Crown obtained its supplies from civilian contractors at preferential rates, which were imposed without any option: when the government budgeted for the victualling of ten ships for twenty-eight days in the summer of 1522, it aimed to spend no more than 8s 4d on every man, at a total cost of £1,361 1s 8d. The price that anybody else would have had to pay for the same quantity of goods was obviously variable, depending on whether there was a glut or a shortage, but frequently it could be twice as much. The artificially cheap supplies may have made it easier to balance the Treasury's books (and were probably intended, as much as anything, to discourage profiteering), but they encouraged the contractors to practise various forms of deception that brought their returns nearer the going price in the market place. Barrels of salted flesh would contain much more salt than protein (and there were instances when they contained nothing but). Food that had been rejected as unfit for consumption by a civilian purchaser would simply be recycled for the King's ships. Less beer than had been ordered and signed-for actually arrived, the brewers complaining that they were short of barrels because the empties from the last victualling had never been returned. There were other ways of giving short measure and, often enough, supplies of every kind that were expected with confidence, simply didn't turn up at all.

It did not help, either, that the Crown – and Henry was particularly culpable in this respect – was always very slow to pay its bills, which meant that the victuallers defaulted on their own payments to farmers and other suppliers, who in turn became most reluctant to give of their best in any sense. And on top of all these defects there was always the possibility of a ship's purser fiddling the books in order to profit from some of the victuals that he sold on the side before the ship sailed or even after she had returned. One way and another, victualling was in a mess that would not be cleared up until a central authority was controlled by men who could give it their undivided attention, who knew what they were about and who could not be hoodwinked by the unscrupulous. But such an authority was not established until three years after Henry had gone. This was the one area of naval administration that he never did get round to setting on the right road.

And the seaman's life was hard enough without his having to face the recurring prospect of an empty belly or dissolving bowels. In spite of the various hardships, however, the sea was an attractive way of life to considerable proportions of the male population, and service in a man o'war, or in a merchantman converted for war in the King's service, was thought to be a much better option than the endless subsistence or downright poverty that most of his subjects endured. Seamanship was one of the very few professions in which a man could rise from the humblest beginnings to rank and prosperity: as at Newcastle in 1544, when ten of the city's twenty-eight shipowners were either ex-seamen or were still working as such. But even at the lowest level, a man was much better-off in the navy than ashore or even in the royal service as a soldier, for naval pay usually came through on time, whereas army commanders often had to find money out of their own pockets on the due date in order to prevent their men giving up and going home. An ordinary seaman was paid 5s a month in 1513 – which Henry raised to 6s 8d in 1545 – was given a coat and conduct money to cover the cost of getting from his home to his ship, and had to pay nothing for his bed or his board, whereas a labourer in civilian life could expect no more than 4d a day, and had to find food, lodging and everything else out of that.[2] Moreover, a seaman in the royal service could look forward to plunder or prize money if things went well for his ship, and was remunerated according to a recognised tariff for such bonuses: the captain received ten shares, the other officers anything between five and eight, the rest of the crew two. These were very considerable advantages in a country where unemployment was endemic and where failed harvests, plagues and other natural disasters were liable to devastate the already poor throughout Henry's reign. The principal drawback for most men, apart from the danger and hardship involved, was probably separation from their womenfolk, though female companionship seems to have been allowed up to a point while a vessel was in harbour. But a line was distinctly drawn by a standing order of the time – 'no woman to lie a ship board all night'.

The economic precariousness of life ashore would be a reason why parents were willing to see their eleven-year-old sons go to sea, though there were never as many ship's boys at this stage of naval history as became the case later on; none of Henry's warships was ever known to carry more than one or two at most, and in 1513 there was but a solitary child in the entire fleet. Merchantmen were a different case, however, often accepting the children of the somewhat better-off, who hoped that this might raise their sons even higher on the economic ladder by giving them the experience that would lead to a command. The crews of merchantmen were often cosmopolitan – in one London ship engaged in the Spanish trade early in the sixteenth century, the two quartermasters were Flemings, the master's mate was Italian and the bosun's mate was Dutch, as was the cook – which must have meant that sometimes the same mixture existed in the navy when merchant ships were required for war. For naval crews were mostly recruited from merchant seamen or fishermen, but in peacetime a majority of the King's ships would be laid up, almost all their people laid off, until hostilities broke out again. At that point it often became necessary to press landsmen into service, because it was axiomatic that ships should be overmanned to take account of losses through fighting, accident or disease.

2 When the seaman's and labourer's wages were as above in the first decade of Henry's reign, a neck of mutton cost 4d, eighteen rabbits 3s, eight marrow bones 16d, a goose 8d, six dozen loaves 20d, a pint of vinegar 2d, two haddocks 20d, a spade 8d and 200 nails 3d. The employer of a serving woman allowed 4s a year for her clothes, which was the same as the King spent on providing his sailors and soldiers with one coat.

The responsibility for raising the manpower fell upon Justices of the Peace or mayors – or upon the Lord Warden within the Liberty of the Cinque Ports – and always followed the same pattern. The men were pressed, they were given their conduct money, and they were told where to turn up for disposal round the fleet (significantly, it was not thought necessary to escort them there, unlike the infamous pressgangs of the eighteenth century), and for Londoners the usual mustering place was The Sign of the Gun in Billingsgate.[3] Desertion was rare in Henry's time, more prevalent in Elizabeth's, and that was probably due to the fact that she was even more penny-pinching than he, so that civilian pay rates rose faster than those she was prepared to authorise; and, while wages generally doubled under the Tudors, inflation pushed up the cost of living twice as much.

Seamen were naturally God-fearing men – they above all people had very good reason to be when they were exposed to powerful natural hazards every time they put to sea – and it was in everybody's tradition that a shrine should be maintained somewhere aft aboard every ship, more often than not to the Virgin Mary.[4] In English vessels the practice continued well into the sixteenth century and, for at least as long as Henry was devotedly Roman Catholic, every large man o'war habitually went to sea with a priest on board to say Mass and fulfil every other duty that was expected of him ashore. The spiritual welfare of seamen was bound to be a matter of concern in an age whose piety is almost unimaginable to the English mentality of our own day. Much less likely is the attention that was also paid to their physical health in Henry VIII's navy, which may to a large extent be attributable to the influence of Henry's personal physician, Thomas Linacre, whom he appointed as soon as he reached the throne and who was rarely far from the King's side until the doctor's death in 1524.

Linacre was an Oxford graduate who had studied medicine in Padua and who returned from Italy thoroughly committed to humanist ideals, which didn't stop him from becoming ordained and accepting a number of benefices (at one time he was the absentee Rector of Wigan in Lancashire) to supplement his official pay of £50 a year. Erasmus, who

---

3 Impressment had been a fact of life for centuries, and not only to provide a King's ships with crews. Carpenters could be pressed to build them, while glaziers had been pressed to work on the Chapel Royal, rope-makers and masons being others who might be recruited in this way.

4 The naval habit of saluting the quarter-deck when coming aboard is thought by some to have originated in the deference paid to the shrine by medieval seamen, though this is disputed by those who think it was a mark of respect to the captain of the ship and his officers.

became his close friend in England, thought him as deep and acute a thinker as he had ever met, and he seems to have been quite a polymath. Among other things, he was an ardent gardener who may have introduced the damask rose to this country. He was certainly behind the foundation of the Royal College of Physicians in 1518 and a medical Act of 1511, which attempted to eradicate the worst forms of quackery by requiring physicians and surgeons in all but the remoter country districts to be licensed by bishops if not by the King himself, and also united the ancient Fellowship of Surgeons with the equally old Barbers Company. This had the effect of introducing the academic rigour of the fellowship (whose members were more often than not university-trained) into the old profession of barber-surgeons, which had traditionally authorised anyone who could wield sharp instruments with dexterity after serving an apprenticeship just like a mason or a plumber. A product of the old system attempting to promote himself to the new was one William Garter of London who, in 1513, sought the King's new licence 'to work in and upon your loving subjects for the safeguard and preservation of their lives with the noble science and cunning of surgery, the which your orator hath been experted in this 16 year and above'.

The reforms meant that in future the King's navy was far better served than his army in terms of medical care – and we can only guess that this was a by-product of Henry's greater enthusiasm for ships and the men who crewed them. The improvements extended, after the 1513 disaster in Brittany, to gratuities for sixty wounded seamen from the *Mary James*, who were given tuppence a mile conduct money – four times the normal rate – to help them home from Plymouth, with another £20 to be shared between them; and if that sounds pitiful, it should be noted that it was £20 more than any similar group of soldiers received.[5] Seamen who fell sick were still kept on the strength and therefore continued to receive their pay, another benefit that soldiers did not enjoy. After the reforms, the recruitment of ship's doctors became the responsibility of the improved Barber-Surgeons Company, which played no part at all in the military intake. As a result, even in 1513 the fleet enjoyed the attention of thirty-two qualified surgeons, including Robert Sympson aboard *Mary Rose*, with Henry Yonge working as his junior, for which they were paid 13s 4d and 10s a month respectively. They and their colleagues in other vessels were expected to deal with a regular flow of patients suffering from head

5 This was the first step towards the establishment of the Chatham Chest, a regular charity started in 1590 by Drake and Hawkins, which paid benefits to disabled seamen.

injuries, closed and compound fractures, dislocations, wounds and serious burns, of which a fairly recent Medical Director-General of the Royal Navy has remarked that treatment was usually admirable, 'following sound surgical principles, and amputations were performed with minimal blood loss and emphasis upon cleanliness'. Surprisingly perhaps, venereal disease did not appear to be a big problem until much later in the sixteenth century, when the English had become accustomed to sailing regularly far beyond the waters of northern Europe.

Even more astonishingly, there is a degree of evidence that some ship's surgeons encouraged musicians – which every royal vessel carried, usually for their trumpeting abilities, though it is likely that they were also familiar with other wind instruments such as the oboe's ancestor, the shawm – to play soothing melodies while operations were going on, doubtless another effect of Thomas Linacre's benign presence. The surgical appliances, of course, were crudely primitive versions of those used today, though the biggest difference was probably that they were clumsier and they depended on manual power alone. And though the most influential treatise on medicine was still – but not for very much longer – that composed by Galen in the second century (which Linacre translated from the original Greek into more accessible Latin), some of its practices were no longer accepted by the English, who were beginning to take up the ideas coming out of Bologna and other advanced schools. They drew the line, however, at Italian advice that the best way to treat gunshot wounds was to pour boiling oil over them! Rather than cauterise such damage, they preferred to control haemorrhage by pressure, styptics or ligature. There was even a form of anaesthetic, based on opium, hyocyamus, hemlock, mandragora, lettuce, mulberry and ivy juice.

Sympson and Yonge occupied adjacent cabins on the starboard side of *Mary Rose*'s gun deck, which put them in the same class as officers for privacy and rest. Though such accommodation has been described as 'little cubbyholes' and was indeed more confined than the cabins enjoyed by the captain of a warship and his master, it was a great improvement on the sleeping arrangements of the ordinary seaman, who had no more than a thin and coarse mattress which he laid down in any available space on one of the lower decks.[6] The sailor also had his long wooden sea chest

6 Hence the still current expression 'the Lower Deck' to distinguish ratings of the Royal Navy from their commissioned officers, who are collectively referred to as 'the Ward Room'. The hammock, far superior to any other form of bed in a heavy sea, did not make its way into the navy until the 1590s, after the English had become well acquainted with South America.

in which he kept his private things. We know that aboard *Mary Rose* some of the crew played backgammon, and other items found in their sea chests included sewing gear, knives, spoons and combs. One man sailing in another vessel in 1535 kept a variety of garments in his chest, including two jerkins of 'fryse' (a coarse woollen cloth) and another of canvas, a couple of 'petycotes', two pairs of breeches, a shirt, a pair of 'short hosen' and an exceptionally long hand-line of ninescore fathoms, which must have been intended for cutting into shorter lengths for soundings: or was it a fishing line to improve the man's diet? He also possessed a pillow and 'a coverlet of beaver' (almost certainly a form of felted cloth rather than a pelt), which would have given him a modicum of comfort on his rough bed; and the inventory of his clothes represents the customary working dress of Tudor seamen, for whom the nearest thing to a waterproof was the canvas jacket, which would eventually be oiled and known as tarpaulin.

They normally wore a woollen cap, but there are drawings of the period and even earlier, which show men wearing a short garment with an attached hood, which looks very like the duffel coat favoured by the Royal Navy in World War Two. Non-commissioned (later known as petty) officers – the boatswain, the coxswain, the carpenter, the master gunner and one or two others – were slightly better-dressed, their seniors very much more so, according to their personal whims and the depth of their purse. We cannot be sure just how often a ship's company (or even part of it) was dressed in the Tudor colours which Henry enjoyed showing off on ceremonial occasions in particular, though it is hard to believe that it was a common rig for all conditions, given the expense involved: when *Mary Rose* and *Peter Pomegranate* made their maiden voyages from Portsmouth to the Thames in 1511 only the officers wore such coats, at a cost of 6s 8d apiece. But a Venetian reporting on the departure of Edward Howard's fleet for Brittany in April 1513 (with 'a double complement of sailors to work the ships') reported that 'The King had given a coat of green and white damask, his own colours, to each of the captains; a coat of camlet to each of the pilots, pinnaces and masters; and a coat of good woollen cloth, green and white, to each of the sailors and soldiers.' Given Henry's great taste for ostentatious display, could this simply have been part of ships being dressed overall for leaving harbour? Did the seamen change into the working rig of the day once they were well out into the Channel? It seems more than possible.

To work a ship efficiently required a rational organisation of her crew.

The watchkeeping that became standard practice in all navies – based upon a division of the twenty-four hours into periods when, except in emergency, some members of a ship's company were working on watch while others were resting down below – was no more than a specialised and more intensive variant of keeping the watch ashore, which had been practised by armies and civilian communities for centuries.[7] The first English naval document referring to watchkeeping appears to have been a fleet order of 1596, which was issued by Lord Howard of Effingham and the Earl of Essex at the outset of the Cadiz expedition in that year. Captains were instructed in Article XXIII that 'You are to take especial care of your watch by night, and that the soldiers do watch, as well in harbour as at the seas, one-third part of them every night…and that in harbour a certain number be appointed to keep diligent watch in the forecastle or the beak-head of your ships, for fear of cutting cables, which is a practice much used in hot countries.' The wording is ambiguous, raising the question whether the watchkeeping meant one (full) night on and two off, or one third of every night for each watch. Although we have no evidence of any specific rota for earlier in the sixteenth century, Henry's navy must have practised some form of it, if a list of action stations aboard *Henry Grâce à Dieu* is any guide. This records where some of her crew were expected to perform their duties when the ship was at sea and they were on watch:

The forecastle 100 men; waist 120

Main capstandard and main sheets 80

In the second deck for the main lifts 20

In the third deck to the topsail sheets 40

In the said deck for the trin and the dryngs 20

To the bonaventure and main mizen 20

To the helm 4 men

To the stryks of the mainsail 8 principal men

To the main top 12; to the fore top 6; to the main mizen top 6

To the bonaventure top 2

The little top upon the main top 2

7 Eventually, the Royal Navy's watches ran from midnight to 4 a.m. (middle watch), 4 a.m.–8 a.m. (morning watch), 8 a.m.–noon (forenoon watch), noon–4 p.m. (afternoon watch), 4 p.m.–6 p.m. (first dog watch), 6 p.m.–8 p.m. (second dog watch) and 8 p.m.–midnight (first watch). The purpose of the shortened dog watches was to create an odd number out of the twenty-four hours, so that everyone stood a different watch every day.

The little top upon the fore top 2	The little top upon the main mizen top 2
For the boat 40; the cok 20	The gellywatte 10[8]

Though the general perception of the seaman would change during the sixteenth century, such men as these, whether they were in the King's service or not, were generally reviled during Henry's reign by people above them on the social scale, who rarely saw them at their best; that is, working and fighting their ships. An English diplomat was disdainful of 'the ungodly manners of the seamen', and someone who sounds as if he may have had much closer contact with them reckoned that they were 'so unruly nowadays that there is no merchantman dare enterprise to take upon him the ordering and governing of the. . .ships.' And they could be a very rough crowd indeed, as the punishments listed by Thomas Audley indicate. Audley was an Essex lawyer, sometime Town Clerk of Colchester, who would finish up as Lord Chancellor, but who first came to the King's notice when he was acting as Charles Brandon's steward. The story goes that Henry asked him to draw up 'A Book of Orders for the War by both Sea and Land', a misleading title for something that was no more than fourteen folios which came in two parts. The first concerned 'wars on the land', the second 'Orders to be used in the King's Majesty's Navy by the Sea'. This was chiefly a set of fighting instructions for captains in the royal fleet, but it was preceded by a brisk summary of penalties for various crimes and acts of indiscipline on board ship. The principal clauses in this part of the document, which was to be copied onto parchment and nailed to the main-mast of every ship, 'to be read as occasion shall serve', went as follows:

If any man kill another within the ship, he that doeth the deed shall be bound quick to the dead man, and so be cast into the sea, and a piece of ordnance be shot off after they be thrown into the sea.

If any man draw a weapon within the ship to strike his captain, he shall lose his right hand.

If any man within the ship draweth any weapon or causeth tumult or likelihood of murder or bloodshed within the ship he shall lose his right hand as is before said.

If any man within the ship steal or pick money or clothes within the

8 'Dryngs' were halliards, the 'trin' was a wheel used with them in connection with the mainsail. 'Stryks' were ropes, 'capstandard' was the capstan, 'cok' was the cockboat, 'gellywatte' the jollyboat (both of them small craft used for harbour work, ferrying people between ships etc.).

ship duly proved, he shall be three times at the bowsprit, and let down two fathoms within the water, and kept on live, and at the next shore towed a-land bound to the boat's stern, with a loaf of bread and a can of beer, and banished the King's ships forever.

If any man within the ship do sleep his watch iiii times and so proved, this be his punishment: the first time he shall be headed at the main mast with a bucket of water poured on his head.

The second time he shall be armed, his hands haled up by a rope, and ii buckets of water poured into his sleeves.

The third time he shall be bound to the main mast with certain gun chambers tied to his arms and as much pain to his body as the captain will.

The fourth and last punishment, being taken asleep he shall be hanged on the bowsprit end of the ship in a basket, with a can of beer, a loaf of bread, and a sharp knife, choose to hang there till he starve or cut himself into the sea.

If any mariner or soldier depart from the King's ships without license of his captain, the same is felony by statute.

If any man within the ship be a drunkard, not being content with the victuals of the ship, nor as the rest be of the company, the captain shall imprison him in the bilboes while he think him duly punished that so offendeth.

Drunkenness was the most frequent offence, especially after seamen had enjoyed a good run ashore. An eventful consequence of such leave involved Richard Baker and three other members of the ship's company of *Mary Rose* in 1539, when she was anchored in the Thames. He and his shipmates, 'with divers other mariners...went on land to make merry at an honest man's house in Deptford...until 10 of the clock in the night, and then departed from the said house and came down to the water's edge and called to the *Mary Rose* for a boat.' Unfortunately, the watch-keepers didn't hear them, so Baker and his mates Robert Grygges, William Oram and Marmaduke Colman helped themselves to a wherry which began to drift downstream alarmingly on the ebbing tide towards Greenwich – they were evidently too sloshed to handle a pair of impro-vised oars capably – until it rammed a Portuguese vessel and roused its crew, who began to throw stones, one of which 'brake the said Oram's head'. The indignant Englishmen thereupon boarded the foreigner (Oram with a drawn sword), grabbed their three assailants, threw them down a hatch and slammed the cover on them, before withdrawing to the wherry and finally making it to St Katharine's, where they slept off their hangovers in a hay barn till ten the next morning: they had, Grygges allowed later, been somewhat 'overseen with ale'. There was another version of this intoxicating episode given by Gonsalianus Cassado, pilot, and Petro Falcon, merchant, in which the assault by the drunken English was wholly unprovoked and resulted in the theft of some Portuguese property. But whose account carried the more weight when the case came before the Admiralty Court and what action was taken we do not know, for only the witness statements have survived.

It has generally been supposed that Audley's fighting instructions were the first such orders issued to the navy (Thomas Howard's fleet order of 1522 scarcely counts, for it was a set of sailing directions and etiquette rather than battle tactics), though the long-accepted date of *c.*1530 has been questioned in recent times, as has the authorship. It included one or two points similar to those made by Howard – that no captain should go to windward of his admiral and no ship was to ride in the wake of another – but its principal aim was to indicate how captains were to fight their ships in the face of an enemy. The moment he was sighted, the weather gage was to be obtained. Only the admiral's ship was to make for the enemy's admiral, and every other vessel in the fleet was to attack an adversary of equal strength to its own. Boarding parties were not to go over the side until the smoke of cannonades had drifted away or until the enemy's decks had been cleared by small shot. A ship being pursued closely and under attack, should offer enough gunfire in return to produce a smokescreen for concealment while manoeuvring to advantage. When going into action, the admiral was to wear a flag at his fore- and main-masts, while other ships were to fly their bunting at the mizen. And so on. . . There was even a forbidding instruction that disobedient captains were to be put ashore.

Some of the practices – like gaining the weather gage and the convention that only admirals could attack other admirals – had been around for as long as men had fought each other in sailing ships and had attained such rank: they were nautical wisdom that everyone knew without even thinking about it. But there were other things of more recent origin, like an awareness that it was safer to let the gunsmoke clear away before going in for hand-to-hand combat. What mattered about Thomas Audley's 'book' was that someone had at last codified a great weight of naval experience which had been hard-earned across many centuries, and added to it knowledge gained only since guns became an increasingly important factor in naval warfare. The most remarkable thing about it, of course, in the absence of definite proof to the contrary, is the fact that it was at least supervised by a lawyer with no experience of the sea, but who made it his business to find out about such things from men who had. His findings about the new form of warfare did not by any means represent comprehensive knowledge, but they were a start. This was another small indication that Henry VIII was seriously intent on creating a more effective fighting fleet than any of his predecessors had attempted or even desired.

THE GATHERING STORM

The men expected to carry out these instructions were, as in the case of Sir Thomas Wyndham and Thomas Spert, *Henry Grâce à Dieu*'s first captain and master, from two different traditions. There were those like Wyndham who had been reared from birth to command other men in the service of their sovereign. They were courtiers who might fight his wars either ashore or afloat and who in peacetime often fulfilled diplomatic functions abroad or were put in charge of garrisons and other vital establishments at home. Otherwise, and when not fighting, theirs was often a merely decorative role in attendance on the King, which allowed them ample time to oversee their lands and properties and their often considerable retinues of household servants and tenants. Arthur Plantagenet (the Viscount Lisle from 1523) was such a one who, in spite of being sent home after grounding his ship at a crucial moment off Brittany – a mishandling that a man of lowlier birth might not have survived – continued in the royal favour for many years, to become Vice-admiral of England, Lord Warden of the Cinque Ports and Governor of Calais. Sir Anthony Poyntz, scion of a family whose line went back more than three hundred years, gained his knighthood for doing rather better than Plantagenet in Edward Howard's fleet, waited upon Henry at the Field of the Cloth of Gold, and was made Vice-admiral within two more years before abandoning the sea to become Sheriff of his native Gloucestershire. Sir Thomas Seymour, brother of Henry's third wife (and therefore uncle of the future Edward VI), divided his time between diplomatic missions to France and Hungary, army command in the Netherlands, and seatime in the Channel, and then outdid both Plantagenet and Poyntz by becoming Lord Admiral in 1547 (and, to cap the lot, by marrying Henry's widow). Sir John Wallop, who came from an old Hampshire family, fought on land in the Low Countries, Morocco and Ireland, at sea against the French, represented his King in several European capitals, and reached his professional peak as second-in-command of Calais. There were many others with backgrounds such as these, who at one time or another – but only for a part of their lives – commanded ships and flotillas and squadrons in Henry's fleet.

And then there were those like Thomas Spert, who were wholly of the sea. It was in his ancestry, both as mariner and shipowner, and after making his naval mark off Brittany and then as *Mary Rose*'s and *Great Harry*'s master, he advanced in the service by dividing his expertise between seatime and a supporting role ashore. This began with his responsibility for ballasting ships based in the Thames, an unglamorous but necessary job (also profitable, because it allowed him to pocket the tolls extracted from shipowners needing ballast from the river), and it led to his being made Clerk Comptroller of the King's Ships in 1524 and effectively the second most important figure in what was the beginning of an administrative apparatus such as English navies had never known before. Others in the same mould, though they avoided administration, were William Hawkins and William Sabyn, whom we have already met. Then there was William Woodhouse, from the Norfolk shipowning gentry, who went to sea at an early age, distinguished himself repeatedly against the Scots in the North Sea and was quite ruthless when he deemed it necessary, on one occasion casting adrift one of his own boats with seven men in her, so that he could be 'more speedy following the chase', which he gave up only after his bowsprit was broken. He was made Vice-admiral and Master of Naval Ordnance during the last few years of Henry's life, and went on to serve the King's son and both his daughters as Lieutenant of the Admiralty.

There was Lewis Sotheran from a family of Newcastle yeomen, who began his working life as a ship's apprentice, served as master aboard several merchantmen before the fifteenth century was out, owned at least two ships and greatly impressed Thomas Howard by the way he handled one of them, the *Elizabeth*, during Edward Howard's fatal action off Brittany, when 'good Lewis' was one of the few who came out of it with any credit, though he was elderly (perhaps rising sixty) by then. There was Christopher Coo, a flamboyant and very sharp shipowner from Lynn, much disliked by many of his contemporaries, for 'he is more in boasting than in any good feat', as one of them told Wolsey. Coo provided the King with many vessels, some of them sold and others hired, and was not averse to sailing them into action himself, especially if there was plunder to be gained. In 1524 he took *John Baptist* (400 tuns, which he had sold to Henry twelve years earlier) down the Channel and into the Trade, and reported on his return the taking of no fewer than nine prizes, only one of which he passed on 'for the King's service', though another was delivered 'by the Admiral's commandment to the mayor of Hull'. Something perhaps had gone to his head to warrant this cavalier behaviour because, only a few months earlier, Coo had succeeded Sir Henry Sherburn as Thomas Howard's Vice-admiral in the North Sea. Of all these men, Spert and Woodhouse were eventually knighted for their services to the Crown, while the others were unadorned commoners for the whole of their lives.

As also was William Gonson, who exemplified the rising breed of shipowning mariner merchants more completely than any other, and became perhaps the most crucial figure in the development of Henry's fleet. He has been rather witheringly described as 'a prosperous property-owning London grocer', and he was indeed Warden of the Grocers Company in 1525, but for many years before that he was making a name for himself in shipping and had sailed more than once as captain of a fighting vessel; he was, moreover, the founder of a dynasty that was still administering the Navy Royal at the end of the sixteenth century. His earliest recorded maritime connection was as a shipowner and one of the first men to run the risks inherent in trading directly with the Levant, which on one voyage resulted in two of his vessels being stuck in Venice for a couple of months, because the Emperor was blockading the Mediterranean east of the Straits of Messina in his campaign against Barbarossa and his Turks. It was for this hazardous trade that the prosperous grocer had the *Mary Gonson* built not later than 1514 and he was visionary enough to have her fitted with gunports: two on each side of the lower deck, two at the stern on the same level, and another pair on the upper deck. Among the King's ships, only *Mary Rose* and *Henry Grâce à Dieu* boasted full-size gunports (2ft 8in. wide by 2ft 4in. high) at that time, and *Mary Gonson* was therefore the first armed English merchantman to carry them. It is thought that Gonson probably owned eight vessels in all, and more than one of them, like the *Mary*, was named after a member of his family: there was certainly a *Christopher Gonson* (afloat in 1522) and a *Matthew Gonson* (c.1545) in addition to their predecessor. As well as these, he was also part-owner of at least one other vessel, the 400-tun *Nicholas*, which was sold to the King in 1512.

And he was a seaman who went to war in a number of different ships. He captained the *Katherine Fortileza* when she escorted the three vessels despatched to reprovision Edward Howard in 1513. He commanded the *Mary Howard* (240 tuns) in the following year's Channel patrol after Prégent de Bidoux's attack on Brighton, when a vessel named *Gonson's Bark* (80 tuns) had a Thomas Gonson in charge. In 1522, aboard *Christ*, William was keeping the sea between the Channel Islands and the west-coast route to Scotland with two other vessels until they were beset by storms that, the King was told, 'disgarnished of their masts, cables, anchors, boats and other tackling and habillements, in such wise that few or none of them can be sufficiently redubbed or furnished to do any service on the sea for this year, either for the guarding of your passages or impeaching of the Frenchmen's fishing': this was obviously the reason why Sir Anthony Poyntz was sent to replace him there. Seven years later, Gonson is found patrolling the Narrow Seas in command of *Minion* (180 tuns) and another vessel, which were continuously on station from the beginning of April till late June, when they received instructions to remain at sea. Within twelve months, Gonson's command had been enlarged to a squadron of ten with the grocer flying his Vice-admiral's flag aboard his own *Mary Gonson*. That he was valued more highly than most as a naval commander is clear from Sir William Fitzwilliam's query about whether Gonson should take charge of the entire fleet during his absence in Calais. But Gonson's true destiny lay elsewhere.

He had served as assistant to John Hopton (himself a merchant ship-owning seaman) when Hopton was occupying Robert Brigandine's old office of Clerk of the King's Ships, and in this capacity he is found taking delivery of guns from the Tower and then going to Holland to arrange naval stores, in the same year that also saw him down in the Trade aboard *Katherine Fortileza*. When Hopton retired in 1524, his function was separated into two parts, Thomas Spert becoming Clerk Comptroller and Gonson Keeper of the Storehouses. Spert's job when he acquired it was the more prestigious and it paid him £33 6s 8d per annum, whereas Gonson received no more than £18 5s, though there were various per-quisites on top of these sums for both men. Before long, however, it became apparent that Gonson's position carried the greater clout because it made him the navy's paymaster and therefore in control of everything from wages to equipment, from victualling to ship movements, while Spert became more and more sidelined with fewer and fewer respon-sibilities that were his alone, the supervision of fortifications at Portsmouth being one of them. The two men seem to have had a perfectly amicable working relationship, however, judging by the tone of a joint message they sent to Fitzwilliam as late as 1540: 'We have received your letter written yesterday at Hampton Court, and perceive the King is determined to buy certain masts of this bearer, Thomas Gigges'. The supplier had been asking £547 19s for twenty-six masts but they had managed to get his price down by £100, with which the King was later said to be well content. Gonson in particular was very quick to act when he thought the Crown was being overcharged: when Bridport's bills for cordage rose unreasonably in his opinion, he looked to the Baltic for an alternative supplier and reckoned to have saved the equivalent of rigging one ship as a result.

He may have become the dominant partner in administration because he was quite clearly a workaholic of some magnitude: on top of his job as Keeper of the Storehouses (openly referred to as Paymaster in due course), his naval commands at sea and his private interests, he was simultaneously an official of the Exchequer and a judge of the Admiralty Court who regularly suffered from gout, 'so pained...(that) he cannot move' on one recorded occasion. Fitzwilliam clearly had a lot of time for him, whether he was captaining ships or supplying them from his office at Deptford. 'In things concerning the sea', Sir William wrote to Thomas Cromwell, who succeeded Wolsey as Henry's chief Minister after the Cardinal's downfall in 1529, 'in my absence give credence to my fellow William Gonson.' This esteem was evidently shared by the King, who granted Gonson a number of lands belonging to people who had offended him in greater or lesser degree and had their properties confiscated as a result. So the grocer became even more prosperous and presently settled at Sebright Hall near Chelmsford. The highest mark of royal favour, however, came on the day in 1539 when he was handed £500 'to be by him employed about his Highness' affairs upon the sea'. Henry VIII could demonstrate no greater trust in anyone than by allowing them to spend his money unsupervised by either himself or his right-hand man, who was now Thomas Cromwell.

In so far as Gonson had a French counterpart, he was Jean Ango of Dieppe, though the comparison is inexact, because Ango was never a naval administrator in quite the same way; but Francis I came to rely on him both for the funds to conduct naval warfare and for the ships and captains fighting on his behalf, and on at least one occasion Ango also directed a naval operation. He was a man of medium build, with an aquiline nose and a high forehead, blond hair and beard and rosy cheeks, who had been born into a Norman family of banker/shipowners in 1480; one of his father's ships had been the first French vessel to reach North America. Shipowning was the basis of Ango's own wealth but he was deeply involved in everything that mattered in his home town, being Captain of Dieppe on behalf of the King and one of its civic leaders, the inspector of its salt stores, the Archbishop of Rouen's secular adviser there, and the local lieutenant to the Admiral of France. He was a well-rounded man, a classical scholar with a taste for the fine arts and *belles-lettres* that equalled his appetite for commercial and maritime speculation, and he had a particular gift for creating opulent buildings.[1] One was his town house down by the harbour, but even grander was the country manor he built in sandstone and flint outside the coastal village of Varengeville, some miles from Dieppe, in the Italian Renaissance style: its mullioned windows overlooked a courtyard, and a dovecote topped by a high weathervane towered above the roofline, while some of the inside walls were decorated with frescoes from the school of Leonardo da Vinci, and sculptures enlivened the colonnade running round the courtyard. It stood on a plateau with spectacular views out to sea and across the countryside, and here Ango would entertain his King, his Admiral, his captains, or the bankers from Genoa and Florence who had opened premises in Dieppe. He was a great friend of the Brunelleschis and the Centuriones, the Italian rivals of the powerful Fuggers of Augsburg, who kept Charles-Quint's imperial apparatus more or less solvent.

He sent his captains all over the known world, to Newfoundland and the Caribbean, to Brazil and to the East Indies, and if sometimes they behaved like pirates – and Francis licensed them to operate as privateers in 1530, after Ango had sweetened his Admiral with a huge diamond – that made them no different from anybody else.[2] One of them, Jean Fleury aboard *le Dieppe*, once ransacked seven Spanish treasure ships

1 It is notable that, whereas the French have retained a memory of Ango's appearance and of his 'other' life, the English haven't the faintest idea what William Gonson looked like or of anything about him unrelated to his family, his work and his prosperity.
2 The difference between piracy and privateering was largely technical on both sides of the Channel, with one vital qualification. The privateer operated under so-called letters of marque issued by his sovereign, which allowed him legally to take a foreign vessel in reprisal for injury done to himself, though this rule was often generously interpreted; whereas the pirate was a freebooter unsanctioned in any circumstances and therefore fair game to anyone who took him. The word 'privateering' did not appear in England until the seventeenth century, the 'letter of marque' in force earlier being, in fact, a 'letter of reprisal' which had existed since the thirteenth century if not before.

sailing home in convoy from Mexico and was finally beheaded on the orders of the Emperor, who had wearied of his plundering, while Jean Fain was twice taken by the Portuguese in *la Marie* and very narrowly escaped death himself. Silvestre Billes in *la Romaine* was captured alongside Fleury by half a dozen Biscayan boats but managed to escape and continued to sail wherever Jean Ango directed him. Pierre Crignon and Pierre Mauclerc took their ships more than once to the Indies on Ango's behalf. On one of these voyages Raoul Parmentier was in convoy with them in Sacre but died of typhoid in Sumatra on the way home with a cargo of spices. So did his brother Jean, captaining *la Pensée*, the most remarkable voyager of them all; for he was a translator of the classics, a map-maker and a poet as well as a fine navigator and seaman, who won gold trophies in literary competitions at Rouen and Dieppe, and used to compose verses which had been inspired by what he had seen at sea and upon foreign shores, his senses awake to everything he came across (after a voyage to Brazil, where he was excited by the sensuality of the young women, he wrote that they were 'colts who had never experienced a rein'). Jean Ango's own response to such exotica was to present the Dieppe church of St Jacques with a bas-relief, which depicted the natives of all the strange countries his captains had traded with. The ones who survived such long-distance voyages – Michel Féré, Guyon d'Etimanville, Cardin d'Esqueville-Bléville and others – he sent to fight wars when Francis I had need of them. They became the backbone of his Channel fleet.

As his own reign entered its third decade, however, Henry VIII was more concerned with the Scots than with the French. The peace between him and Francis was holding up well enough for him to cross the Channel for another meeting in October 1532, at which they renewed their treaty. Henry's lifestyle was beginning to take its toll and he was suffering from gout, but still felt like making the occasion just a little more special by taking Anne Boleyn – with whom he had progressed from love letters to an almost open affair – to France as a public demonstration of her role in his life: he had not yet received the papal dispensation that he sought, but had convinced himself that his remarriage and her coronation were not now far away. The couple spent ten days in Calais, mostly at leisure, though Henry made time to inspect the town's defences and ordered that these should be strengthened, with a new tower to be built on the harbour jetty, strong enough to bear the weight of cannon.

The two Kings eventually met six miles outside the town at St Inglevert (which the English knew as Sandingfield because it was within the Pale), but this was not to be another Field of the Cloth of Gold extravaganza, at Henry's special insistence. Nevertheless, he rode to the meeting with 140 lords and knights clad in velvet, in a retinue that required 600 horses all told, and Francis was similarly endowed. The rituals were as before, however. 'They embraced each other five or six times on horseback, and so did the lords. They rode hand in hand for a mile, then lighted and drank to each other.' And so they proceeded to Boulogne, their entrance announced by salvoes of artillery that could be heard twenty miles away. Various jollifications followed, at which it was noted that the French were far more lavishly dressed than the economising English. There was then a return visit by Francis to Calais, where he was lodged at the expense of the town's merchants, while the two Kings got down to serious business at last, discussing a joint crusade against the Turks and Henry's own Great Matter, the coded reference to his efforts to be rid of Katherine of Aragon; and Francis said he would do what he could to intercede on Henry's behalf with the Pope. Anglo-French co-operation could not possibly be in demonstrably better shape than that.

The Scots were another matter. They were blockading Henry's east coast more effectively than ever before and they had even begun to sail into the Channel with impunity. Much worse, before long they captured two English vessels, one of which was his. She was the very new *Mary Willoughby* (140–200 tuns), which had been sent up to the Western Isles to do some damage to Scottish pirates, but was taken by local galleys belonging to Hector Maclean of Duart instead, and incorporated into the navy of James V, who had come into his own at last in 1528 and eventually reaffirmed the Auld Alliance by marrying Francis I's daughter Madeleine.[3] For the next fifteen years this man o'war served both him and then Mary Stuart, Queen of Scots, once wafting a convoy of twenty-one ships northbound from France – nineteen of which had been taken at one time or another from the English – past an English squadron looking for it under Sir Francis Bryan, a courtier who had been wounded during Thomas Howard's attack on Morlaix (which earned him his knighthood), but would finish his naval career as a Vice-admiral in spite of his blunder off the east coast. An attempt was made to excuse this failure to intercept somewhere between Newcastle and Holy Island by pleading that his vessels had been 'very slenderly provided with gunners,

3 The consumptive Madeleine died only five weeks after reaching Scotland, whereupon James reaffirmed the alliance yet again by marrying Mary of Guise, who later bore him the Mary who became 'Queen of Scots'.

ordnance, shot and powder', which did not amuse the King when he heard of it. In time, the English recaptured and recommissioned *Mary Willoughby* into their own navy, where she continued to be a fighting force for several years more after being rebuilt in 1551. The other vessel taken by the Scots some months after her was the *Mary Walsingham*, a Yarmouth boat part-owned and captained by William Woodhouse, who was not cutting his usual dash in the North Sea at the time, but peacefully fishing off the Shetland Isles.

Bryan's excuse was, in fact, symptomatic of a wider failing in Henry's navy in these years. At the end of 1533 the imperial ambassador at his court, Eugene Chapuys, informed Charles that the King's Council had enquired about the readiness of his ships and had been told it would be impossible to have the fleet fully operational in less than twelve months. Two years later, Thomas Howard and William Fitzwilliam took him to Deptford to see the new *Sweepstake* (300–350 tuns) and the *Mary Willoughby*, one of them just off the stocks, the other almost ready to be launched. On what was obviously a propaganda exercise designed to counter any negative impression Chapuys might already have formed, Howard very heavily made the point several times that 'with these two, and four or five in the river before them, they could fight the whole world'. He was better than most at throwing dust into people's eyes.

The truth was that Henry, in these middle years of his life, was not properly engaged, either mentally or energetically, with the disposition and efficiency of his navy because he was almost totally preoccupied with domestic problems, all of his own making, and their wider implications. It was perhaps symptomatic of this diminished concentration clouding his judgement, that after Thomas Howard became the 3rd Duke of Norfolk in 1524 on the death of his father, his successor as Lord Admiral was the King's bastard son from Elizabeth Blount, the seven-year-old Henry Fitzroy, Duke of Richmond, which meant that the effective command of the fleet was held by Fitzwilliam, who was pronounced Admiral in his turn in 1536, after young Fitzroy died.[4] By then, Henry was in grave danger of losing his throne. He had justified his willing seduction by Anne Boleyn's coquetry on the specious grounds that his

---

4 Bessie Blount was one of Katherine of Aragon's ladies-in-waiting, and subsequently made a happy marriage. Rumour had it that Fitzroy was being groomed for kingship in Ireland, perhaps even for the English succession if Henry produced no legitimate heir. He married Thomas Howard's daughter only months before his death.

marriage to Katherine was invalid in God's eyes; more importantly to him, however, she had produced only a daughter, a series of miscarriages and deaths shortly after birth, but never the son and heir that he demanded of a wife. Three years after her marriage was brought coldly to an end in 1533, Katherine died (probably from cancer) and willed that her body should be buried in a house of the Observant Friars; but her husband had just caused it to be suppressed without her knowledge and so she was interred instead at the abbey church in Peterborough, soon to be a Reformed cathedral under the new dispensation.

Anne Boleyn herself didn't do any better as a spouse, mothering only another daughter, who one day would follow her step-sister as sovereign ('On September 7,' according to the birth notice of the new Princess Elizabeth three years before Katherine's death, 'between three and four o'clock pm, the Queen was delivered of a fair lady, for whom Te Deum was incontinently sung'; and at her baptism the silver font was 'surrounded by gentlemen who wore aprons and towels about their necks, that no filth should come into it'). Anne was shortly afterwards disposed of at the scaffold, on the grounds of infidelity; which was probably no more than the flirtatious behaviour she had shamelessly indulged in with Henry when she was Katherine's lady-in-waiting. He was now launched into his exhausting private life as a serial husband, but his third marriage ended tragically for him as well as for Jane Seymour, who died in bearing him the son who became Edward VI. Although he had been capable of great tenderness in his early years with Katherine, and particularly during her many pregnancies, this appears to have been the one union that combined genuine and continuous affection with the driving passion that came from his great carnal appetites.

There were three more wives yet to come, but already the repercussions of his behaviour were enormous and international as well as domestic. His lasting separation from the papacy in order to rid himself of Katherine had offended every obediently Catholic monarch across Europe and Henry became effectively friendless because of it, alienated even more from an Emperor who was Katherine's nephew. What followed in England from this previously unimaginable severance was an upheaval that came very close to a catastrophe. Thomas Wolsey had been unable to obtain the papal dispensation that would have legally annulled Henry's first marriage and had paid the penalty by being dismissed in disgrace. His successor Thomas Cromwell, another commoner (his father was a London fuller and blacksmith, and also kept a hostelry) who rose to become Henry's right-hand man, this time as Lord Privy Seal, was instrumental in solving Henry's problem but at a terrible cost, all of it issuing from the breach with Rome and some of it attributable to Henry's slide towards insolvency.

Cromwell, a calculating man as well as a skilful organiser and a ruthless opportunist, decided that the best way to tackle the government's growing financial difficulties was to plunder the wealthy religious houses; and so began the suppression of the smaller communities in 1536, followed by the dissolution of the greater foundations. And this did yield very fat returns. It was also the last straw for subjects who had been disturbed by Henry's treatment of Katherine and left aghast by his snub to the papacy. Some of them trimmed their sails according to the wind, inevitably, but an incalculable number were deeply offended and angered by what he had done. They wanted none of his new Church of England and they were appalled by his treatment of monasteries and convents which had represented both charity and stability to them far more than arrogance, corruption or sexual misdemeanour; religious buildings which had been as much a part of their landscape, emotionally and physically, as hills, trees and rivers for many generations, were being torn down before their eyes, and it drove them to action against their King. There were other grievances, including increasing taxation and a perceived remoteness of government, together with a number of very local matters, but it was the religious issue that inflamed them most of all.

In October 1536 an insurrection began in Lincolnshire and quickly spread across the North of England, where it became known as the Pilgrimage of Grace. It included a sprinkling of the northern nobility, many more of the gentry (its principal leader was an East Riding lawyer named Robert Aske), but most of the rebels were very ordinary folk: artisans, tenant farmers, labourers who lived from hand to mouth, their lives softened a little by piety and the consolations that only Mother Church could offer them. The speed with which they prepared to do battle with their King was breathtaking, with some 40,000 armed men across the North only three and a half weeks after the first clarion call had rung out from a pulpit in Louth. And Henry was dismayed by it, though he concealed this by blustering. Once more Thomas Howard stepped forward as a commander ashore, to do what he could with a raggle-taggle army of conscripts who had little incentive to fight rebel hordes fired up with zeal behind leaders who knew what they were doing, what they wanted (not the King's downfall, but his sympathetic hearing of their grievances) and how best to achieve it. The soldiers mustered against them suffered from all of Henry's great failings as a military leader. Their pay as often as not didn't turn up on time, nor did the victuals, and there were other failures of supply, as when a troop of horsemen had to gallop across country bareback because no saddles were available until their captain bought some out of his own pocket. On top of this, Henry kept changing his mind about how and where they should be deployed so that, before long, most of his people didn't know whether they were coming or going across a wide area of England.

On 26 October the two armies confronted each other at Doncaster and the Pilgrims outnumbered their adversaries by five to one. There can be no reasonable doubt that, had the battle been fought, the rebels would have swept aside the King's men and carried on down the country, picking up more support as they drove towards London. There they intended to confront Henry (if he had not already fled) and, unless he was prepared to reverse his most offensive policies and dismiss Cromwell, whom they saw as the arch-manipulator behind the throne, they would have unseated him and crowned his daughter Mary in his place: a dutiful Catholic like her mother Katherine and now twenty years old, she had been banished from court precisely because she might have been a rallying point for disaffection, and it was strictly forbidden to refer to her as Princess. But wily Thomas Howard saved the day for Henry. He persuaded him to negotiate with the rebels at Doncaster, to let them expect all sorts of concessions in due course, even if he had no intention of keeping his word. Robert Aske and the other leaders fell for the deception and their Pilgrim army was disbanded. A few months later some of their number, realising that they had been duped, decided to raise a new fighting force, and gave Henry the perfect excuse to put them down with great savagery before they had time to get properly organised. Howard also masterminded this operation and was as thorough in the punishment as in anything he ever set his hand to at sea. An unknown number of insurgents – 700 was the figure being touted in London – were massacred in a rout outside Carlisle, and 200 others were executed after trial, including Aske and all the old leadership. By midsummer 1537, Henry could at last breathe easily again. It was a haunting, tragic moment in English history, with Thomas Howard at centre stage from start to finish.

But there were also glimpses of other men whose names were or would be more associated with the sea than with civil war. William Gonson took some ordnance and £8,700 up to Grimsby for the hard-pressed garrison of Scarborough Castle, which he evidently intended to hand over himself, together with a despatch for the Yorkshire loyalists. Charles Brandon, who was in charge of operations in Lincolnshire, wanted him to remain there afterwards to assist in the examination of some prisoners already taken locally. But Brandon was told that he must 'return Wm Gonson to the King, who requires his services' and that one of Cromwell's agents should take over the assignment from Grimsby. This man was, in fact, Gonson's brother-in-law, Edward Water, who boarded a crayer there for the last part of the journey, but the boat was seized before it even docked by rebels who took all the cargo and the letter before sending it back to the Thames (Water, though, was retained as a well-treated hostage in extremely comfortable lodgings). A couple of weeks after this, with Gonson back in London, Brandon begged the King to let them have him in Lincolnshire again: 'we lack him both for putting things to order and in giving counsel', he said. One way and another, William Gonson was becoming indispensable.

Sir John Russell, before this a highly favoured courtier and diplomat who had served in the 1522 naval deployments (he lost an eye during Howard's raid on Morlaix and was promptly knighted in the same circumstances as Sir Francis Bryan) and would be Lord Admiral for a couple of years in the 1540s, was one of those who helped to put down the Lincolnshire rising, and months later he and Brandon arranged the executions there of the local rebels. The man who would follow Russell as Lord Admiral, Sir John Dudley, son of a Privy Counsellor and stepson of Arthur Plantagenet, brought a contingent of troops up from Sussex to the North and would have been involved in the battle at Doncaster had it taken place, but went south again without seeing any action and did not return for the great bloodletting. His naval career didn't begin until the year the Pilgrimage of Grace was put down but it was to be more important than anyone's, including Thomas Howard's. He became 'an innovative and distinguished Lord Admiral, at a time when the navy was undergoing one of the most important developments of the century'.

Dudley owned a ship by 1537, when it was trading with Calais and Flanders, but otherwise had no experience of or connection with the sea; yet suddenly he was made Vice-admiral in March that year and instructed to patrol the Channel between the Downs and Poole with four vessels. He must make sure that his activities did not breach any treaties, but he was 'to prevent unlawful taking of prizes, and do his best to compel restitution or apprehend offenders, taking the ship to one of the King's ports till he know further the King's pleasure, and having an inventory of all things signed by the captain and master, and setting the prize at liberty'. A week later he reported his first whiff of action, when he accosted a couple of Flemings lying at anchor in the Downs, after hearing that they had taken a French vessel laden with Brazil wood as she was sailing out of Southampton. He put a warning shot across the leading vessel's bows and she let him have one back in earnest, which 'brake down a great piece of the decks of my ship and hurt one of my gunners. I then trifled no more, but laid her aboard, and after a short fight she surrendered', while her consort slipped her anchor and sailed away, pursued by *Sweepstake* and by *Lion* (140–160 tuns), another of Henry's new ships which had only been launched the year before.

The purpose of Dudley's assignment was ostensibly to demonstrate Henry's current neutrality in the conflict between Francis and the Emperor. But there was at least one assault on an English vessel in March 1537, when the *Mary Fortune* of Hull was boarded by 'one Oliver of Boulogne', who searched the ship for Flemings and 'cruelly handled' Oswald Edwyn and John Langley in the process before making off with cloth and other goods, 'on the pretext that the cargo was Flemish'. And this exemplified the real reason for Dudley's commission, which emerged in a signal the Vice-admiral received at the end of July. If his squadron came across 'any merchantman, French or Imperial, who under colour of [traffic] has robbed the King's subjects, they shall see that he be punished as a pirate. For both sides have used themselves towards the King with such extremity that his honour can no longer suffer it.' For honour we may read pride, and nothing mattered more to him.

By August, Dudley was telling the King that 'In all the Narrow Seas, especially upon this coast, there is not one man-o-war of any nation.' But ten months later, Henry's situation changed significantly and he was obliged to concentrate on the defence of his realm again after thirteen relatively inactive years. In December 1538, Pope Paul III at last enforced the sentence of excommunication which had been hanging over Henry for the past three years; a month later, Francis and Charles patched up their quarrel in a *rapprochement* that was obviously threatening to the Englishman. Isolated and paranoid, Henry was seized with a fear that he was likely to be attacked soon by any number of foreign countries. He became so jumpy that when a convoy of Flemish vessels entered the Channel from the North Sea, and he heard that another fifty to sixty ships were off the coast of Zealand with 10,000 men on board, he assumed the worst was about to happen. Sir Thomas Cheyney, Lord Warden of the Cinque Ports, had woken up in Dover Castle one morning to find sixty-eight sails, 'all great ships', at anchor in the Downs, the leading vessel having 'the Emperor's arms painted on the stern, with the cross keys on the left side and the Burgundian cross on the right'. He signalled with three gunshots that he wished to come aboard, but 'they set a banner of truce in the poop'. Sir Thomas thought that 'they seem marvellous warlike' but didn't know whether or not to have beacons lit, before coming to the conclusion that starting the recognised cross-country chain of warning flares would 'be a great trouble to all the realm and a great bruit [rumour] might grow thereof throughout Christendom'; so he contented himself with telling his gentlemen to be ready for action at a quarter of an hour's notice, and declared that 'I shall light no beacons till I know more'.

At this news, Henry not only ordered that 150 English vessels should immediately be armed and made ready for sea, but decreed a general muster throughout the land of every able-bodied male capable of bearing arms. In fact, the Flemish convoy was simply sheltering from a contrary wind before continuing towards Spain en route to the Emperor's campaign against the Turks in north Africa, and this was the destination of any other ships getting ready to follow it; but the English reaction meant Francis himself then needed some assurance that Henry wasn't about to attack him. His new ambassador in London, Charles de Marillac, carefully explained his host's anxiety and assured his sovereign that 'all this preparation is only for defence, not for invasion'. To the Governor of Picardy, however, Marillac gave Henry's dispositions in some detail, doubtless to cover his own back if it turned out that he had misinterpreted what was afoot. He had seen new ramparts and bulwarks 'in the rock where the sea beats' when he arrived at Dover, well furnished with great and small artillery', and he had observed musters taking place at Canterbury and other places he passed through on his way to London. On the Thames he saw naval vessels being equipped with such diligence that it seemed likely they would have joined the rest of the fleet – making 150 vessels in all – at Portsmouth and Southampton within ten days. Five or six ships, he had discovered, 'do nothing but circle round the kingdom ...so that no foreign vessel could show itself without the whole country being warned'. And he added that 'The chief lords are at their posts as if the enemy were at the door.' He repeated what he had told Francis: that the preparations were for defence, not aggression, 'for at present this King has nothing so dear as to preserve by all means the alliance of France'.

The vessels in the Thames towards the end of January 1539 were in varying states of preparedness for action. The *Primrose* (which had just been considerably enlarged from her original 160 tuns to 240 tuns) and the *Sweepstake* would be ready to make for the sea within twenty days of the word being given, but the *Great Galley* (500–600 tuns), the *Less Bark* (another new enlargement, from 240 to 400 tuns), the brand-new *Jennet* (160–180 tuns) and the two-year-old *Lion* (140–160 tuns) could not possibly sail for thirty days, or the *Trinity Henry* (250–350 tuns) for forty days. *Mary Rose* (now 700 tuns), *Peter Pomegranate* (as was, now plain *Peter* and 600 tuns) and *Minion* (260–350 tuns), all of which had undergone extensive rebuilding which made them much bigger than they had been before, were said to be 'standing in their docks there, masts ready to be set up, who cannot be made ready to sail under three months' time after commandment given'. The delay in getting these vessels into fighting shape seemed, at least in part, to result from a shortage of skilled hands. According to a memo composed by some unidentified official (Gonson or Spert, probably), 'It will be hard to have shipwrights, caulkers and mariners to furnish all these ships at once, for they must occupy 500 persons.' To which a further cautionary note was added. 'The ships will also be in danger in great frosts, for which there seems no remedy but either to keep them in occupation or otherwise out of the Thames, or else provide docks before next winter.'

The lasting result of the unnecessary panic was that Henry strengthened and increased his coastal fortifications as they had never been improved before. In the first phase of construction, during 1539 and 1540, the defences were extended so that they stretched from Milford Haven in the West, right round the south and east coasts until they reached Hull: a map showing the state of things between Land's End and Exeter was drawn up in such detail that it was almost ten feet long. But the works didn't stop then: they continued right up to Henry's death in 1547, and in that time it has been estimated that they cost the King twenty-nine per cent of his ordinary revenue. For a start, Sir John Russell was told to survey the entire English shoreline and to report on the most inviting places for an invading enemy to land, while Henry issued new orders about the conduct of the coastal defence works. The captain of such a fortress must not be absent for more than eight nights in a month except with the express permission of the King. Every day, certain gunners and soldiers must keep guard during the day and watch through the night according to a rota drawn up by the Admiral. The captain must allow no more than two soldiers to be absent at once, and only for three days a month. The gate of every castle and fort was to be opened from 5 a.m. to 8 p.m. in summer, from 8 a.m. to 4 p.m. in midwinter and for different hours at times in between, but must always be closed from 11 a.m. to 1 p.m. 'No captains or others of the garrison are to make any exaction, or accept anything from ships passing or lying in the roads, nor trouble or hinder them to make them offer any of their merchandise.' None of the garrison was to hunt or course deer, hares or conies (rabbits), or hawk, take or shoot hawks, pheasants, partridges or shovellers. There were twenty-two specific injunctions, and one of them solemnly warned that 'The captain must not waste the King's powder'.

Based on Russell's recommendations, the work began, and a great deal of stone from the broken monasteries was used in the process, from Quarr and Netley and Beaulieu among others, the finance required for the whole project also being partly raised from the proceeds of the Dissolution. The Thames, which had been repeatedly attacked over the years by Frenchmen, Scots and others, increasingly so since the new dockyards appeared there, received due attention. A blockhouse went up at Tilbury and, facing it across the river, Gravesend was well fortified by more than one bulwark at a cost of £3,000. Even more vulnerable was the Channel coast, where the greatest proportion of new works were carried out. At the narrowest part, Dover Castle was augmented by a new bulwark mounting a battery down by the harbour; while, within a few miles and overlooking the Downs, new castles were built just above the shoreline at Sandgate, Deal and Walmer. There was a long history of French landings in the Camber estuary and so a fortification was now constructed behind the sea marshes between Rye and Winchelsea.

Hampshire was well taken care of in the new surge of activity, with Southsea Castle strategically placed at the entrance to Portsmouth harbour, and with Calshot and Netley castles on either side of South-ampton Water, so that any vessel attacking Hampton from the East Solent would first of all have to stay out of Southsea's range and then face a hammering from Calshot before passing beneath the guns of Netley in order to reach its target, which in theory was an improbable feat. In addition to these three fortresses, blockhouses were built on the Isle of Wight, at both East and West Cowes, where 170 men were put to work in the midsummer of 1539, supervised by Thomas Cannar, clerk, John Mowlton, mason, and John Russell, carpenter, who promised to have the work finished by Michaelmas 'or sooner with more men'. To guard the western end of the Solent, Hurst Castle was raised facing the island across the narrowest stretch of water, the work there being the responsibility of Thomas Bertie, who was probably a Frenchman and certainly the mason who had already created the vaulting of the nave aisles in Winchester Cathedral. The French ambassador remarked on the extent of the Hampshire fortifications, which he thought 'sufficient to make a good defence of that coast', though he had reservations about the work done at Portsmouth, where the defences 'are not very durable, being made of stakes filled with earth as if made in a hurry'.

In the West Country, Dorset was given castles at Portland and Sandsfoot, Devon a bulwark at the mouth of the Exe, a fort at Salcombe and improvements to the medieval defences guarding the entrance to Dartmouth's river, where both forts were enlarged and provided with new batteries at the water's edge; while Plymouth, which had been invaded periodically in its past (four times by the French between 1339 and 1403) similarly had its defences improved. In Cornwall, Henry decided that the chains intended to protect the approach to Fowey from unwanted visitors were inadequate, and put his faith in a fort at the harbour entrance instead. The Fal estuary was given castles, St Mawes and Pendennis, on either side of its celebrated anchorage.

Henry's new castles by the sea (but not the smaller forts and bulwarks he built) were a fresh departure in military architecture, though we do not know whose was the brain that masterminded it. There are a number of contemporary references to 'the King's device', as if he was personally responsible for the design; but it is thought that he did no more than originate some overall plan for the castles in Kent, possibly taking this a stage further at Southsea, where he may have expressed his usually strong views on how the keep should be shaped. The traditional English castle, of which Dover was a good example, was constructed with curtain walls and outlying towers around a high and rectangular keep, and any attacker was obliged to look upwards, both to see the defenders from ground level and to shoot at them. These sea defences, however, apart from Southsea, had circular keeps. Without any exception, they were built low, crouched squatly behind earthworks, so that they would be much harder to spot from offshore until they began firing their guns, especially as the invention of the telescope (by Galileo) was still three-quarters of a century away.[5] They would also present smaller targets; and it is at least conceivable, given his fascination with such matters even in the depths of peace, that Henry himself came up with this particular feature as a general principle for others to work out on the ground.

The masons and the commissioners overseeing them were charged with building military appliances for a specific and narrow purpose, with no comfortable accommodation or the other facilities that were customary in the normal castle household: only spartan conditions to sustain the gunners, the archers and the pikemen who were their sole residents. The castles had immensely thick walls – ten feet thick on the seaward side at Southsea, which was probably the general rule – and this was where they were most heavily armed, with sixty-six guns in four tiers in the case of the brooding castle at Deal. One other innovation was the sharply angled or semicircular outer bastions, which greatly increased the arc of fire for each gun. The castles were intended to be deadly at the short range necessitated by the heavy weapons then available: ships would have to come to within 400 and 600 yards to hit those walls and would not make much impression even then, whereas their own relatively flimsy construction could be smashed to bits by the garrison's artillery when they were that close.

Calais was not neglected in the new precautions. Defensive works were perpetually under way there, as they were at Dover, but in both cases they were almost always put in hand in order to protect these ports from the sea itself. The alarms towards the end of 1538, however, required reinforcements of a different order. A special commission was appointed to review the military defences of Calais and concluded that the Beauchamp and Dublin Bulwarks should be rebuilt and expanded, that every alternate tower on the town wall must be dismantled and replaced by a gun platform. The outlying fort at Rysbank was to be strengthened and the town's medieval castle must be drastically altered by lowering its walls and towers twenty feet, also to accommodate gun platforms. A great deal of work had to be undertaken at Guînes, so that it would be impregnable if an attack came from the direction of Ardres. Such was the sense of urgency in the reviewing commission, that the first thing it did after deciding what was needed was to send for a German expert, Stephen

---

5 Southsea Castle, which is still in much the same state as it was when Henry built it, is hard to pick out with the naked eye even from the high deck of a cross-Channel ferry approaching Portsmouth until the vessel is well inshore, unless you know what you are looking for.

Haschenberg, to design the new defences and superintend the whole operation.

The logistics were, as usual, much more complicated than they would be in England itself, with shiploads of stone coming from the dissolved monasteries at Faversham and Canterbury, and with timber brought in off the Kentish Weald; the unloading of all these things was made much more difficult than it ought to have been because Henry's recent inertia and cost-cutting had meant that the harbour was in a poor state, with its wharf dilapidated, its jetties beginning to collapse into the sea and, as woeful as anything, not one crane in proper working order. There was also a shortage of skilled labour, especially of bricklayers, a perverse situation when the only building material that Calais and its Pale could themselves supply was brick. Eventually, 200 Cornish miners were brought in to dig the necessary foundations and do other heavy work, together with a similiar number of labourers from Devon. 'All are tall men' reported Sir John Wallop, who was Captain of Guînes at the time, 'and with the tools they brought, cast as much at one time as other labourers do at three.' This was not the only place experiencing labour problems in the haste to counter foreign invasion. At Deal, where 1,400 were employed by May 1539, some workmen went on strike for more pay, and the dispute was only called off after Sir Edward Ryngeley, the commissioner in charge of the operation, put nine of their ringleaders in gaol.

No sooner had Henry's programme for improving his sea defences got under way, than he was minded to enunciate some grand principle which would convey the vital importance of shipping to the nation's well-being and prosperity, both for commerce and for defence. This appeared in 1540 as An Act for the Maintenance of the Navy, a rather misleading title to the modern reader, when it had nothing to say about the upkeep or running of the King's fighting ships for purposes of war. It began in the usual florid and breathless style of such documents:

> Forasmuch as it is evidently and notoriously known that the more part of this our sovereign Lord the King's realm of England and the confines and dominions of the same is and has been encompassed and environed by and with the great seas, so that neither the King's liege people and subjects of this his said realm, nor yet any other foreign realms or countries, can or may convey or transport their wares goods merchandise and commodities into and from the said realm by or across the said seas, but only by ships...

There was then an acknowledgement that merchant ships were 'also a great defence and surety of this realm in time of war, as well to offend as defend; and also the maintenance of many masters mariners and seamen, making them expert and cunning in the art and science of shipmen and sailing...' Not only that, but wives and children were supported by maritime endeavours, as were a whole host of bakers, brewers, butchers and craftsmen, to the extent that cities, towns, villages, havens and creeks owed their very existence to what came and went upon the sea. At the heart of the matter was the observation that 'the same navy and multitude of ships is now of late marvellously decayed, and by occasion thereof not only a great multitude of the King's liege people which thereby had their living is now diminished and impoverished, but also the towns and villages and habitations near adjoining unto the sea coasts have utterly fallen into ruin and decay'. There followed a reminder that Richard II had ruled that all trade between England and other countries should be conducted in English ships unless none was available, while Henry VII had decreed that the wine of Gascony should only come to these shores aboard 'ships of England, Wales, Ireland, Calais or marches thereof', and that Henry VIII himself had already ordained that the decrees of his predecessors still stood. Yet some people 'for their own singular lucre and advantage, have not feared nor dread to offend the said laws and good ordnance.' This, said Henry, had to stop. A comprehensive tariff of freight charges between England and various foreign ports was appended, with the particular rates for different cargoes. And that was that, in a piece of legislation which was characterised most of all by its long-windedness, and was unusually lacking in penalties for failure to observe the rules.

It was, nevertheless, a wake-up call to the nation, reminding the English of their dependence on the sea, and of the need for a flourishing mercantile marine to produce their fighting ships and seamen in time of war. Following as it did the regeneration of Henry's fleet, with some vessels rebuilt and others newly made, together with his sudden attention to coastal defence, it was another indication that he himself was feeling more vulnerable than he had ever been before.

THE LAST HURRAH

Though Henry's grief at the death of Jane Seymour appears to have been genuine, it took him only a few hours to get over it enough to start casting around for another wife. Jane died in giving birth to their son Edward towards the end of October 1537, and English ambassadors in France and the Low Countries were at once told to start making enquiries about suitable consorts for their King. Over the next two years a variety of possibilities were examined – including a French suggestion that Henry should marry Louise of Guise, while his daughter Mary was simultaneously united with Francis I's younger son – until no fewer than half a dozen Continental women were under review at the same time. Political alliance with some foreigner had become of such prime importance to the beleaguered King that no Englishwoman was considered (for the moment, that is) as a candidate. In the end, he settled for the German Anne of Cleves, whose brother-in-law was the influential Duke of Saxony, one of the seven princes who elected the Holy Roman Emperors. Henry's court artist, Hans Holbein, who had been busy painting one potentially new wife after another, moving from one country to the next until he must have been dizzy with travel, was therefore rerouted to Düsseldorf to produce a likeness of Anne for his patron to consider before taking the plunge again. Holbein was told that, while he was about it, he should make a portrait of her also available sister Amelia, too, just in case she became an even later starter in the marriage stakes. Early in October 1539, however, a treaty was concluded that would make Anne of Cleves the new Queen of England, and before the year was out the preparations for the marriage and coronation were well under way.

Once again, Henry's ships turned to for a state occasion. William Fitzwilliam (now Earl of Southampton) had just been made Lord

Admiral and in this capacity he took charge of getting Anne from France to England safely with an escort of fifty vessels. Everything was meticulously planned by Thomas Cromwell, down to a memo by one of Fitzwilliam's clerks which informed Henry of the expected state of the tides and what would be possible in any foreseeable weather. In December, he noted, the high tides at Calais would be at one on the afternoon of Friday the 12th and one in the morning on Saturday the 13th, so that 'if the wind be SW there can be no passage till 4pm, which will be very late, or 4am; if between NE and S, she [Anne] may ship in the haven and go her way by noon or 1pm'. For eight days after that the afternoon tides would not serve because it, would be night before any vessel sailing on them could reach England. There followed a schedule of the morning tides between 13 and 21 December.

With this in mind, Anne reached Calais from the Rhineland by way of Antwerp and Gravelines on 11 December, being greeted at the threshold of the Pale by Fitzwilliam and a medley of courtiers, while the English ships lying offshore saluted her with 200 rounds of cannonfire, which Calais itself bettered as she entered the town, with 300 pieces of ordnance. 'When she came to the Lantern Gate, she stayed and viewed the King's ships, the *Lion* and the *Sweepstake*, decked with 100 banners of silk and gold, wherein were 200 master gunners and mariners and 31 trumpets, and a double drum that was never seen in England before. . . At her entry, 150 pieces of ordnance let out of the said two ships such a smoke that one of her train could not see another.' She stayed in Calais for the next fortnight and Fitzwilliam taught her how to play cards to pass the time until the Channel calmed down, while Anne 'kept open household' throughout. On 27 December, she at last embarked to meet her prospective husband, as soon as the newly knighted Sir Thomas Spert, William Gonson and others, who had been keeping watch outside the town walls expressly for this purpose, reported that the weather was now suitable for a royal crossing. The vessels in the escorting fleet 'were trimmed with streamers, banners and flags, and men on the tops, shrouds and yard arms' and they set sail on the afternoon tide. They were in the Downs before seven o'clock in the evening, and Anne was then rowed ashore to be greeted by Charles Brandon and conducted to Dover, where a further galaxy of the nobility and gentry awaited her.

By New Year's Day she had travelled as far as Rochester, and there she and Henry set eyes on each other for the first time. As moments of truth go, this one took some beating. To Henry's dismay, she was not at all what he had been led to expect from Holbein's portrait, and even the gallant Charles de Marillac was reduced to the tactful observation that she was 'rather graceful than beautiful, of small stature &c'. Henry was, in fact, so perturbed by her appearance that he quickly retreated to Greenwich and postponed the marriage for some days while he tried to find a way out of it without humiliation. But that was impossible and so it went ahead, an unconsummated disaster in which he could not conceal his repugnance as he lay with her that night; and poor puzzled Anne, who was not only without the most tentative sexual experience but apparently lacking in any information on the subject, was left to assume that the English were always distantly polite on their wedding nights as a matter of national principle. Henry's inbred sense of chivalry ensured that the politeness endured, though he had little more to do with Anne after that first encounter as man and wife. Six months after they married, they were divorced and Henry ordered that 'She will be considered as the King's sister, and have precedence over all ladies in England, after the Queen and the King's children'.[1] Thomas Cromwell was awaiting execution by then; and though several things brought that about, including a plot by Thomas Howard and others of the nobility who detested the Lord Privy Seal, one element was most certainly Cromwell's part in negotiating the latest marriage, his responsibility for making his sovereign look a fool across Europe and probably a laughing stock among his own subjects. That Henry could never have countenanced without lashing out at whomsoever he decided to blame for it.

He was forty-nine years old, and his body was much less appetising than Anne's could possibly have been, partly because decades of gluttony had bloated it, partly because he had an ulcerated leg which periodically discharged pus.[2] He was now so corpulent that his bed had to be enlarged. More than once, Marillac recalled in one of his despatches, the King's life had been thought to be in danger, 'not from the fever but from the leg, which often troubles him because he is very stout and marvellously excessive in drinking and eating, so that people worth credit say he is

---

1 When that pronouncement was made, there was no Queen, though there would be a couple of weeks later. On the day Cromwell was beheaded, Henry married Catherine Howard (Thomas Howard's niece), who would herself go to the block in 1542, charged with the same offence as Anne Boleyn.

2 It was probably caused by the horse falling on him when he was jousting. Splinters from a damaged shin bone became embedded in the calf muscle of the left leg to produce a recurring cycle of burst ulcers, which healed and then swelled and then burst again (see p. 615 in *Six Wives* by David Starkey, London, 2003).

often of a different opinion in the morning than after dinner...' It was this illness that caused Henry in March 1541 to cancel a tour of the south coast for the purpose of inspecting the new defenceworks that were going up there. And it is a measure of his alarm at the prospect of invasion that he had already, five months earlier, gone up to London from Greenwich 'to see certain war machines and instruments for throwing fire, invented by Germans and Italians here'. At the time, Marillac understood that Henry 'intends before Easter next to prepare six swift galleys, similar to those at Marseille, for crossing to Calais and coasting'. The memory of Prégent de Bidoux, and the havoc he had wrought off Brittany in 1513, which he had then followed up with a successful raid on Brighton, still worked so powerfully on the King's imagination as to persuade him that a form of warship which sprang from and essentially belonged to the relatively tranquil Mediterranean, could have a long-term future in the much stormier northern seas. It evidently didn't occur to him that the French hadn't bothered to reconstruct their galley base at Rouen after Henry V destroyed it in 1418, for a very good reason: that when they needed galleys off their Atlantic coast or in the Narrow Seas for some specific purpose, in future they brought them up from the south, as when they summoned Prégent's squadron to Brest. There was talk of Henry sending to Italy for three shipwrights expert in making these craft but, in fact, five Venetians were eventually paid, 'as being more experienced in galley work' for their assistance in fitting out such vessels.

We need to read the word 'galley' with caution, however, because it was used without much discrimination in the sixteenth century, and this has led to confusion ever since; as has the word 'galleon', which can legitimately be applied only to some sailing vessels built between 1540 and 1570, constructed like galleys for'ard and like fully rigged ships aft, and notably longer and narrower in relation to their beam than was normal in sailing ships of the period. 'Galley' properly referred only to the long, low vessel chiefly propelled by oars and conforming to a design that originated in the Mediterranean; but it was often also applied to the galleass, which differed from the true galley in the amount of armament it carried, in having up to four masts instead of one and in positioning its rowers below the main deck, the only thing the two types had in common being the use of oars as well as sails. The galleass might be anything from 120 to the 450 tuns which made it more than half as large again as the genuine galley; and twelve of these vessels were built in an English shipyard while Henry was on the throne. A number of other craft propelled by oars also made their appearance during his reign, but these were rowbarges, small things of no more than 20 tuns with only a main deck and some superstructure; and if Henry really did try his hand at naval architecture, as the imperial ambassador Eugene Chapuys assured Charles V in July 1541, then the rowbarge was the most likely outcome of his efforts at the drawing board.

The one true Mediterranean-type English-built galley of his time was the *Galley Subtle* (200 tuns), which was laid down in 1541 and launched a couple of years later.[3] She was powered by twenty-five oars on each side of her flush open deck, and by a lateen sail whose yard was so extensive that it could only be fashioned by overlapping and joining two long spars together in the manner technically known as fishing. Her main armament consisted of two bronze sakers and a bronze cannon, but there was the usual assortment of smaller ordnance and bows, arrows, pikes and darts as well, and in addition she was built with an iron-shod prow for ramming an enemy, a throwback to the triremes of ancient Greece and Rome, though it may have been more gesture than anything. This meant that, although *Galley Subtle* flourished a serpentine figurehead, it was mounted on the stern, where it could only intimidate anyone pursuing her. She was manned by 242 mariners and eight gunners, and most of the seamen were clearly expected to work the oars, perhaps in watches and probably with more than one man pulling on each blade. A contemporary drawing shows someone standing over them and brandishing a stick, but whether that was used to beat the time or belabour rowers who weren't pulling their weight, it's impossible to tell. Some years after her addition to the fleet, criminals and captives were used to propel the oared vessels, but there is no conclusive evidence that this actually happened – though it was certainly threatened by public announcement – in Henry's time.

It is just possible that one other foreigner, apart from the Venetians, played some part in the final stages of fitting out *Galley Subtle*: it is certain that he at least offered ideas to Henry on the building of the later oared vessels. The man in question was none other than Prégent de Bidoux's nephew Pierre, Sieur de l'Artigue (a small town in Gascony), who included among his several accomplishments an advisory role in the French galley programme when he was in the service of Francis I. He had been with Prégent in the action which killed Edward Howard in 1513

---

3 Its name was an Anglicisation of the Italian *galea sottile* and the Old French *galere subtile* – the thin (or narrow) galley.

and he evidently made the most of the family name to prosper in the French navy, eventually becoming Vice-admiral of Brittany but with even wider influence: he was responsible for uncovering various forms of corruption in the fleet, to do with victualling among other things. He was a fine seaman and on no fewer than seven voyages since 1523 he had sailed past English blockades to reach Scotland. He was one of the French captains who evaded William Fitzwilliam when the latter was looting Le Tréport, successfully escorting 3,000 troops and the Duke of Albany, by the long west-coast route, and on another occasion taking the French-indoctrinated Cardinal David Beaton home to harden the hostility of Catholic Scots to the English. It was while he was on his way home from that mission in November 1542 that he was captured off Dartmouth aboard his vessel *La Ferronière* and put in the town gaol for piracy. After he had been missing for three months the French – still officially at peace with the English – made enquiries as to his whereabouts, and when they were told what had become of l'Artigue (as he was generally known) they insisted that he was no pirate but a perfectly honest gentleman. Not long after this they learned otherwise.

After several months in Dartmouth, l'Artigue persuaded the town's mayor (probably a successor to the diligent Nicholas Semer) to seek on his behalf an audience of Henry or at least of his Council, and when this was granted he offered a simple trade-off: his freedom in exchange for all sorts of information that probably stunned the English initially as much it did the French when they found out. The magnitude of his treachery was such that on the other side of the Channel it was still being referred to with exclamation marks more than three hundred years after the event: '*Et quel traître!*' wrote an eminent historian early in the twentieth century. The deal l'Artigue offered included a plan for the seizure of Brittany which would begin with a landing at Le Conquet; or, alternatively, an assault upon La Rochelle. He provided the names of forty-five French nobles and the number of men they commanded, together with those of six captains in Francis I's bodyguard, and the advice that 'in a company of 100 men at arms there are at least 600 horse'. He furnished a list of all the French strongholds with details of their arrangements. He told all there was to tell about current Franco-Scottish relations and he produced much first-hand navigational information about Scottish waters on both the east and west coasts. He gave advice on building galleys, suggesting that 'such galleys made a little higher than in the Levant would do great service'. And he asked in return only that he should be 'taken into the King's sea service, and to be examined as to his knowledge of sea matters, and other greater things which he will tell his Majesty'.

Pierre de Bidoux came as manna from above to the hard-pressed Henry, who at once granted him an annual salary of £50, which was subsequently raised to £75 when l'Artigue had proved his worth.[4] *La Ferronière* (140 tuns) was, of course, incorporated into the English fleet and served in it as the *Artigo* for the next four years. The vessel was overhauled for her new life under the supervision of William Gonson and she was made ready for action under the cross of St George just in time to go to war against her owner's native land, when hostilities broke out again between the two countries in July 1543, a particularly momentous month for Henry because in it he also made the twice-widowed Catherine Parr his sixth wife. For a year before that, however, he had been sparring with the Scots after James V had rebuffed his efforts to drive a wedge between Scotland and both Rome and France: James simply didn't turn up for a meeting in York at which his uncle – who had never travelled that far north before – intended to browbeat him into rejecting the Auld Alliance and suppressing the Scottish religious houses. Having been kept waiting fruitlessly in Yorkshire for nine days (yet another humiliation), Henry returned to London and shortly afterwards a series of raids across the Border began. In August 1542 a full army, which included continental mercenaries, was sent up under Thomas Howard's command, and defeated 20,000 Scots comprehensively at Solway Moss, taking large numbers of prisoners who were held as bargaining counters.

Although this was not another Flodden, James was dead before a month had passed, from grief, it was said; and Scotland was yet again left with an infant sovereign, Mary Stuart, who was scarcely a week old when she inherited the throne. Henry therefore began to negotiate with a new Regent, James Hamilton, Earl of Arran, and actually made a peace treaty with him which, among other clauses, agreed that when both children were old enough, Mary would marry Henry's five-year-old son Edward. The peace lasted less than six months, before Cardinal Beaton's

---

4 The grant of £75 per annum was made on 1 October 1545, but what became of l'Artigue after that is a mystery, to which not even the *Dictionnaire de Biographie Française* supplies an answer. Pierre de Bidoux is simply mentioned there as an appendage of his illustrious uncle and is last noted in 1537, when he was said to be busy conveying French prelates from Marseille to Rome for the papal conclave which elected Paul III.

faction persuaded Arran to join them and repudiate it, at the same time renewing all the treaties that had existed between Scotland and France. Henry's aim of getting the Scots off his back while he went to war again with his other old enemy had completely failed.

Since the end of 1541, he had been courting Charles V with a view to joint action against the French, and he had seriously planned a new offensive from the day in July 1542 when the French King and the Emperor ended their own treaty and started squaring up to each other once more. Henry and Charles came to a secret arrangement the following February under which, when they were ready to move, imperial forces would march into France through Champagne while Henry's army would head for the Somme and the road beyond to the French capital, which would be taken in a classic pincer movement: the English, indeed, referred to the entire operation as The Enterprise of Paris. On 22 June 1543, Henry presented Charles de Marillac with an ultimatum which Francis had to meet within twenty days or suffer the consequences. To avoid war he had to pay a large indemnity, yield Boulogne and three other towns just beyond the Pale, together with Normandy, Gascony and Guyenne, 'abstain from practises with the Scots and others to our Sovereign's detriment' and satisfy in a number of other respects an apostate English King who had the nerve to claim that he was taking this course of action partly out of 'his desire for the preservation of Christendom against the Turk'. It was flatulent humbug and Henry knew very well that it would be rejected out of hand even as he was composing it. But this did not mean that the great land campaign was launched without delay.

The rest of that year was limited to action at sea, and Henry's fleet went into the conflict under a new Lord Admiral. Fitzwilliam had relinquished the position (and later died on the march into Scotland with Thomas Howard), in favour of Sir John Russell, who handed over the golden whistle in his turn to Edward Seymour (Earl of Hertford and elder brother of the swaggering Sir Thomas) in December 1542, on becoming Lord Privy Seal. Seymour himself occupied the post for only a few weeks before being promoted to Great Chamberlain (another high office whose incumbent was, as custodian of the Palace of Westminster, traditionally entitled to the bed the sovereign slept in on the eve of his coronation, together with its bedding and his nightshirt). John Dudley was therefore made Lord Admiral on 26 January 1543, when he was thirty-eight years old and had recently become the 3rd Viscount Lisle on the death of his stepfather Arthur Plantagenet. Sir Francis Bryan, 'who has been vice-admiral before and is experienced in sea matters', was made Dudley's second-in-command.

Their first orders were to conduct a blockade to seal off the Scots from the French, which was easier said than done in a winter so bitter that only with difficulty had two of the King's ships been able to leave Newcastle and the Tyne for the open sea, because of ice 'which at the quay of this town is two fathoms thick'.[5] Dudley had been given half a dozen vessels for the blockade but claimed he could have pressed more into service from the north-east if it hadn't been for a local shortage of seamen and ordnance, and he asked for guns and powder to be sent up without delay. The big English worry was that Mary Stuart's maternal uncle, the Duke of Guise, would sail to Scotland and carry off the infant queen to France, and they had heard that at Havre the French had four vessels, augmented by a similar number of Scottish boats, ready to sail with just such a purpose in mind. So anxious was Henry at this possibility that he uncharacteristically told Dudley he cared not how much money it cost him so long as Guise was prevented from reaching the Forth. Bryan was instructed to make the ship in which the Duke sailed his own particular quarry 'and in any wise take it'.

At the beginning of February the little squadron thought Guise was approaching with a much bigger force than anticipated, when coast-watchers in Bamburgh reported seeing twenty-one great ships sailing northwards past Holy Island. It turned out, however, that this was the *Mary Willoughby* and the 300-tun *Salamander* (which had been part of the dowry Madeleine of France brought to her short-lived marriage with James V) convoying nineteen English vessels loaded with wine, which had been taken as prizes on their way home from Bordeaux; and, as we already know, Bryan allowed them to get away, to Henry's considerable wrath. The Vice-admiral appears to have been sidelined as a result of this failure (though it did his long-term career prospects no harm and he would finish up as King's Viceroy in Ireland); for it was from later this month that William Woodhouse was given command of four ships in the North Sea patrol under Dudley, with instructions to take any Scots

5 The temptation to assume that such extreme conditions were invariably more common in the sixteenth century than in modern times should be resisted. In the first two months of 1940 the weather was so severe that estuaries along the east coast were frozen up with ice that was also twelve feet thick in places. See *The War at Sea 1939–45* by S.W. Roskill (London, 1954), Vol. 1, pp. 141 and 147.

or French he might come across but not to 'meddle with any Fleming, Spaniard or Portingal' unless they had harmed English subjects or were carrying supplies to Scotland – 'but ships of the King of Denmark himself are to be searched for letters and news'.

Guise never did show up, in fact, and from the middle of the year the navy was also at work down in the Narrow Seas, where Sir Rees Mansell was made Vice-admiral. On 6 July he and his squadron of six ships came across sixteen French vessels and, after trailing them through the night, engaged them in action shortly after dawn the next day. Mansell's flagship *Minion* (260–350 tuns) and her consorts opened fire, which the French returned 'very freshly' and accurately enough to damage *Minion*'s main- and foremasts: Mansell said afterwards that not only was the enemy's gunnery of some quality, but that their vessels were good sailers into the bargain. The action continued for three hours, in which the *Sacré* of Dieppe was twice grappled by *Minion* and once by *Primrose* (240 tuns) before managing to break away from both and escape eastbound with all but one of the other Frenchmen as a storm began to blow up. In telling Henry of this 'great fight', Dudley pointed out that although most of the French got away, they would either have to turn and face Mansell once again in order to reach home, or they would have to sail on to Scotland and bide their time there as an alternative to continuing on the long westabout route round the top and down through the Irish Sea. This could therefore be construed as an advantage won by the English, when what they tangibly got out of the engagement was no more than the capture of a hoy with 120 men aboard, at the cost of certain damage to themselves, which left *Minion* in particular in need of new mainsails and foresails.

It was typical of the periodic and unspectacular naval skirmishes that took place off the east and south coasts of England during 1543. Typical, too, of the anxiety that always hung over the Channel Islands in time of war was the cry for assistance from the Captain of Guernsey in August after he heard that vessels in Dieppe, Honfleur, St Malo and elsewhere along the French coast were preparing to attack both his island and Jersey, 'and wishes some ships and Englishmen sent hither with speed'; but the attack presumably did not materialise, for nothing more was heard from the worried Governor. Ashore, the return of Anglo-French hostilities meant that Sir John Wallop marched 5,000 troops from Calais into the Netherlands, in order to guard the Emperor's flank when his invasion of France took place.

The first action of greater significance was a punitive operation north of the Border in April the following year. Angered by the repudiation of the treaty he had signed with the Regent and frustrated by the inability of his own placemen in Scotland to manipulate things there to his advantage, Henry resolved to make the Scots smart for their insolence. Edward Seymour was appointed commander-in-chief of a combined naval and military operation whose sole purpose was to do as much damage as possible to life and property, so that the Scots would be left reeling with the shock of it, as much as they had been after Flodden. Seymour and others close to the throne questioned the wisdom of this, but Henry was now in one of his most vicious moods and lusting for retribution. The Privy Council's instructions to Seymour specifically forbade him to consolidate his position after taking his objectives because the King wasn't interested in gaining territory or, indeed, in obtaining submission, but only in destroying everything in his army's path, with particular emphasis on symbolic Edinburgh. After he had accomplished this, Seymour was to withdraw his forces 'and, the King's journey into France approaching (before which the army must return to keep the Borders, the Lord Admiral to keep the Narrow Seas and others to attend the King's person), time cannot be spent on fortification, for fear of disappointing other purposes'.

The plan was to send a relatively small force of horsemen out of Northumberland into the Lowlands, to ensure that no Scottish reinforcements could reach their capital from that direction. The bulk of the army was to arrive by sea, sailing straight into the Firth of Forth and taking Leith, reducing it and then doing the same to Edinburgh. A considerable fleet of transports was mustered for this operation: twenty-seven sailed up from the Thames, some of them having been hired for the purpose from Dordrecht, Antwerp, Hamburg and even Lübeck, while from Ipswich came thirty-two vessels, Yarmouth twenty-eight, Lynn sixteen, with fourteen out of Hull, the entire convoy escorted by the very new *Pauncey* (400 tuns), the very old and twice rebuilt *Great Galley* (800 tuns), *Minion*, *Sweepstake*, and twelve other wafters, including the *Galley Subtle* (Capt. Richard Broke), which also played its part by attacking some coastal villages in Fife. By 6 May, the troops had been landed at Leith, sweeping aside a host of defenders led by Arran and the Francophile Cardinal, before continuing the few leagues into Edinburgh. They scaled its great rock and blew down the main gate of the castle with a culverin, but most of the damage was done to the rest of the city, which was plundered and then put to the torch; as was a great deal of Edinburgh's hinterland.

After ten days of rampage, Seymour and Dudley reported that they had 'daily devastated the country hereabouts and within six miles of Stirling, so that the enemies shall neither recover this damage whiles we live, nor assemble any power this year in these parts, whatsoever aid come to them from France or Denmark'. They were writing from Leith before leaving the scene of Henry's retribution, with enough loot to fill their ships and with the *Salamander* and other Scottish vessels taken as prizes from their berths there; and about to burn Edinburgh's port before marching home overland, leaving Woodhouse to convoy the transports south, after which all three would move on to serve the next part of Henry's ambitions. As combined operations go, theirs could scarcely be faulted, apart from the fact that the victuals almost ran out, as so often before. Henry was well pleased with their endeavours 'and gives them hearty thanks for their manly and discreet handling of their charge His enthusiasm was not shared by his ally. Charles V was so concerned that the wanton brutality might precipitate a coalition including the Pope against him, that from this moment he began surreptitiously to disengage himself from Henry, though he was not to sign a peace treaty with Francis for another four months. By then the English King, left in the lurch a second time by the Emperor, was heavily committed in France.

For him the invasion of 1544 was even more necessary than had been the campaigns of 1513 and 1522 because, in addition to the perpetual urge to conquer and dominate, to achieve glory and to spread his fame, there was one more imperative driving him: he was growing old and his body was beginning to decay, he had probably begun to count the years that might be left to him, and although it was now only with the greatest difficulty that his huge weight could be hoisted onto a horse, he needed to prove to himself and to the world that he was still a warrior King. So Henry would lead this expedition in person, at the head of his army. And such an army it was, of 4,000 cavalry and 28,000 of foot, mustered from all the shires of England and Wales, some of them having only just returned from the Scottish affair. This was far bigger than any other expeditionary force that had ever crossed the Channel before it, three or four times as many soldiers as Henry V had led to Agincourt. And on top of the native troops, foreign mercenaries were added across the water, providing more firearms than the English took with them. Transporting such unprecedented numbers meant that it took an unusually long time to get them all to Calais from a number of English ports, including Ipswich and Harwich as well as Dover and elsewhere on the south coast.

Thomas Howard began to lead the vanguard over on 6 June, with almost daily reinforcements arriving until Henry himself stepped ashore on 15 July. Howard and Charles Brandon were the chief commanders under their sovereign, and others in the invading hierarchy were John Russell and Dudley himself, in a further example of a Lord Admiral's ubiquitous role, with military as well as naval responsibilities: as soon as the army was safely across the Channel, Dudley was required to leave his ships and accompany his sovereign in the land campaign.[6] The joint strategy of the English and imperial forces was for the Emperor's troops to make for Luxembourg and St Didier in the first place, while Henry's headed for Boulogne and Montreuil, the combined armies meeting at the Maine by August and marching on Paris together. This never happened, because the by now half-hearted Charles was content to play out time at St Didier and because Henry was realistically happy enough to take Boulogne and by that much extend the English enclave in France. Howard's advance from Calais was excessively cautious and, bypassing Boulogne, which Henry had appropriated for his own display of the military arts, he settled into a siege of Montreuil which lasted two months before being abandoned because it was by then redundant.

Henry arrived outside Boulogne on 26 July, a week after Brandon had led his troops up to its outer walls. The King then began to direct operations in person, and his sheer adolescent enjoyment of this clearly did wonders for his failing constitution, for he stayed in the saddle day after day and people began to marvel that a man so obviously out of condition could still handle so deftly such a heavy lance as he carried; not to mention moving easily inside the favourite and highly polished suit of armour that he wore. Basse Boulogne, the lower town along the harbour, was quickly overcome but the heart of the community and the fortress itself was on a dominating ledge with steep slopes leading up to it on three of its four sides, which made it a far more difficult proposition. So much did the English confine their attack to the one obvious approach that, for much of the siege, the French were able to leave their sheep grazing on the rest of the hillside. The walls of the upper town were so

6 Not for many more generations would the two disciplines be completely separated. Even in 1627 George Villiers, Duke of Buckingham and Lord Admiral of England, personally led the siege of St Martin's on the Ile de Rhé, off La Rochelle. And in 1653, the first Commissioners of the Admiralty and Navy were all army generals or holders of other military rank.

unexpectedly resistant to Henry's artillery that, although a deal of damage was done inside them (including the demolition of the principal church's spire on 19 August) no serious breach was made in the defences themselves, and a major assault at the beginning of September also failed, as did an attempt to blow up the fortress by undermining it. Boulogne only surrendered two days after that, on 13 September, because its garrison had run out of powder, though its victuals were nowhere near exhausted. Francis had exhorted his soldiers to withstand the siege for six weeks and they had managed eight, during which time the English had put more than a hundred thousand cannon balls into and over their walls.

Five days after some 1,500 troops and 2,000 civilians had been allowed to leave their shattered town with all their private property, Henry was told that Charles V had just signed the Peace of Crépy; and so the Enterprise of Paris was reduced to the adventure of Boulogne. Dudley was appointed Captain of the new colony and Seneschal of the Boulonnais at a stipend of 40s a day, but he was anxious to retain his naval appointment as well, 'for it is an office of honour, estimation and profit': not only that, but he sought some arable land and pasture, a place in the country 'to lie in for a recreation in the time of peace' while he was in Boulogne, and he wanted his household goods shipped in from England without paying Customs dues. This was a short appointment – he would be back with the fleet within four months, and Sir Thomas Poynings succeeded him in the Captaincy – but the English control of the town lasted a full eight years.

Henry's last invasion was a costly adventure in many ways and financially it was nothing less than a disaster. The traditional method English monarchs employed to raise funds when their own resources ran out and revenue could no longer keep pace with their expenditure, was to lean on their wealthier subjects for loans at preferential rates; but the nobility, the merchants of great substance, and especially the Corporation of London, were no longer as amenable as they had once been, after many years of being milked. Henry was therefore obliged to start borrowing massively on the Antwerp money market at fourteen per cent interest, and two years later he owed the bankers there more than £100,000. It has been estimated that by then his spending on war and its preparations over a period of eight years had amounted to something in excess of £2,135,000, of which £265,000 had gone into funding his navy. But the money supply was only one of Henry's mounting problems; another was that his new acquisition placed a heavier burden on the fleet. By adding

Boulogne's servicing and other requirements to those of Calais he stretched his naval resources to the point at which they were in some danger
of breaking down. In the middle of November, Dudley signalled that his
garrison had eaten nothing but biscuit for six days, drunk nothing but
water and wine for fourteen, and was briskly told that he mustn't expect
bread and beer to arrive in the harbour once a week, that he must keep
'a more wary eye to your victuals, considering with what difficulty and
charge they are brought to you'.

Initially, the burden of supply fell on Sir Thomas Seymour, who was
in charge of naval operations in the Narrow Seas while Dudley was
otherwise engaged ashore. The fleet he had temporarily inherited was
widely dispersed in the Thames, in Dover and in Harwich, and it included
the newly acquired *Salamander*, the *Galley Subtle*, the *Artigo* (captained
by a Robert Garth and not by L'Artigue himself), the *Sweepstake*, the
Minion and a number of vessels on hire from Bremen and Danzig as well
as from Lübeck and Hamburg. One of Seymour's early concerns was
which of these groups should be given the job of supplying Boulogne,
what part Portsmouth was expected to play in the immediate future,
whether or not the navy should remain in the Narrow Seas after victualling the new colony or whether any ships should annoy the King's
enemies elsewhere – 'and how the same shall be sorted'. He himself
thought that the best thing would be for the whole fleet to muster
with the necessary supplies by the Isle of Wight, 'from whence, if the
Frenchmen would stop the passage betwixt Dover and Boulogne or
Calais, the King's ships may cut betwixt them and their own coast, and
so drive them to fight or else go to Flanders or Scotland'. He was told to
get the victuals to Boulogne 'with all speed' and then to send 'a convenient
number of small shallops and other vessels into the river to Etaples, to
burn and bring away the enemy's vessels there, or do them such annoyance
as the time will serve for'. After that, he should leave some of the fleet in
the Narrow Seas, while the rest made for Portsmouth to revictual and to
take aboard grain and other supplies which they should get over to
Dudley's people without delay.

Seymour's reply to these instructions was not encouraging. He himself
was aboard *Peter* (*Peter Pomegranate* as was), which had been laid down
in 1510 and rebuilt in 1536, and it had taken her eleven days to make way
from Harwich to the Isle of Wight, all the vessels under his command
having been hampered by winds which shifted from E to ESE ('as sore
a storm as ever I saw') and blew some craft so far to the west that he

expected they would not find a haven till they reached Dartmouth; the rest were arriving off Portsmouth in scattered groups. He reported that the *Mary James* of Calais had engaged the *François* of Dieppe carrying Scots among her crew, but had been obliged to share her cargo with a Flanders boat which was protecting the local fishing fleet off Dunkirk. He was severely rebuked by the Privy Council for failing to obey the order that would have sent some of his ships to Etaples and was told to get fourteen vessels over there 'with speed...if the wind will serve'. When he did as he was told, he found that awaiting him in the Canche estuary were seventeen French warships and he decided to give them a miss.

Later in the month his news was that Francis I had inspected four new French galleys in the Seine at Rouen and had ordered that six more should be built there, while a further twenty-five must be brought up from Marseille. That Mediterranean squadron had been bidden to take and bring north 'by fair means or foul' any great ships it encountered en route, of whatever nationality, and these were to be off the coast of Normandy by the beginning of 1545. Seymour also heard that Francis had been told by Charles that 'he will be friend to friend and enemy to enemy', that the French were going to put an army in and around a watch tower on the outskirts of Boulogne so that no English vessel would be able to use the harbour there, and that the renowned galley captain Leone Strozzi, a twenty-three-year-old Florentine in the service of Catherine de' Medici (Francis's daughter-in-law) had arrived in Marseille, which sounded ominous. The other depressing tale he had to tell was that the captain and all but forty-one of the 300 men aboard of one of the Bremen vessels attached to his fleet had been lost after all her anchors and cables parted 'and she brake all to pieces on the shore' of the Isle of Wight, that two other ships (including *Sweepstake*) had sprung leaks there. A fourth vessel had been smashed on a rock as it tried to enter Dartmouth, but all except three unfortunates were saved from that catastrophe.

Seymour, in fact, was going through a trying time with his interim command, attempting to follow a series of peremptory orders from his political masters, with the weather against him right through the onset of winter to the end of the year, constantly having to explain why he had not been able to carry out instructions precisely or as swiftly as was expected of him. In the end, this usually cocksure and extremely arrogant man was almost begging the Council to believe him when he said that anything they perceived as failure on his part was down to the awful weather: effectively he was saying that if you don't believe me then just ask the other captains and masters who went through it all, too. Meanwhile, up in the North Sea, problems of a different kind were coming to the attention of Francis Talbot, the 5th Earl of Shrewsbury, whose father had been one of Henry's principal commanders in putting down the Pilgrimage of Grace. Talbot had been sent up to replace Edward Seymour as overseer of the North when the latter was diverted to the invasion of France, and that autumn he was petitioned by the Aldermen and Brethren of Hartlepool after a Grimsby vessel on its way to Newcastle was chased into their port by 'a Frenchman or a Scotsman with two tops', so purposefully that the English crew had run her ashore and deliberately holed her before abandoning ship. Their pursuer, however, had sent a boat to mend the damage and had sailed her away, 'shooting many guns of which we have the gun stones'. The elders of the town told Talbot that they had fired every arrow they possessed at the boat, but were now afraid the intruders had noted that they had neither guns nor powder with which to defend themselves. The Frenchman (or Scot) was lying offshore at anchor as they wrote, and they were desperately afraid of what might follow at the next flood tide.

By almost the same post, the Bailiffs of Scarborough were rejecting an accusation that they had been remiss in supplying their quota of vessels for the defence of the realm, pleading that they had but four crayers under 50 tuns at their disposal 'and we are desolate of ordnance, shot and gunpowder'. If Talbot would but send them guns and ammunition they would put forth a couple of the crayers at once, and to demonstrate their sincerity they asked for the King's warrant 'to press mariners and fishermen' into naval service. Meanwhile, just up the coast at cliff-bound Whitby, the Bailiff and Burgesses were lamenting the fact that all their ships had been sold 'owing to the decay of the harbour', but promising that if the little port's facilities were repaired (implicitly with government assistance) it would not be difficult to find good ships to use them, as 'there is no such place for the safeguard of ships from Humber to the Forth'. They also made the point that their 'chief mariners are in the King's service in the South'.

Such was the bread-and-butter business of running Henry's navy and dealing with coastal alarms during the dwindling months of 1544, a constant battle to make ends meet one way or another with limited resources in the face of dangerous isolation again, of gathering intelligence, boosting morale and seizing opportunities, as well as making good losses, doing the best with what was available, improvising solutions; and always making plans, or trying to execute them. Almost the worst thing that could happen, in fact, occurred in London (or Essex?) at about this time, while Seymour and Talbot were coping with differing degrees of crisis upon the seas and along the coasts. William Gonson committed suicide, though just when and where and how and why we do not know: the fact was barely recorded – and not until January 1545 – when his lease of some land reverted to the King 'because the said William has now of late feloniously killed himself.' But it must have happened at least two months earlier because an inventory of 'the goods of Will. Gonson, deceased' appears in the official papers for 4 November; and it was probably after 25 June, when he billed a number of people for various payments, including £3 10s 8d owed by Robert Mott, master and owner of the *Margaret Bonaventure*.

The reason for his death remains a mystery, for although he would surely have been under the strain of his supporting role in the conduct of the war, he was familiar with such tension and had survived it often enough in the past. We can rule out embezzlement or some other serious form of corruption, because if Gonson had done something criminal, Henry would scarcely have handed his function over to his son Benjamin, who was temporarily his successor, and in that capacity presented his first account of financial and victualling transactions for the navy on 28 November. Benjamin Gonson would, in fact, prosper in the naval service of no fewer than four Tudor sovereigns, starting with his appointment as the fleet's first Surveyor in 1546 and ending only with his death in 1577, by which time he was Treasurer of the Navy and had lived to see his daughter marry the buccaneering Sir John Hawkins.

But William Gonson had other sons and a clue to his suicide may lie in the fate of the eldest, David, who had belonged to the English Chapter of the Knights of St John of Jerusalem. In October 1540 he was accused of treason 'on the sayings of one Philip Babington' some six years after the Act of Supremacy made Henry VIII the head of his new Church of England: this was one of the issues which led to the Pilgrimage of Grace, and criticism of the Act by those who preferred the papal authority was very dangerous when everywhere within earshot were informers prepared to tell tales that sooner or later reached Thomas Cromwell. It seems likely that David Gonson was shopped for talking unguardedly, though no transcript of his trial has survived; and he was executed the following July in London. It is at least conceivable that William Gonson's suicide was the result of pent-up grief, or shame, or a mixture of both, though why three years elapsed between the first tragedy and the second is another puzzle. The effect of William's death was something short of a catastrophe to the navy, but it did produce great confusion in the administrative machine that Henry was beginning to put together. This had, quite simply, suddenly lost its lynchpin.

XV

'OH, MY GALLANT MEN!'

One of Henry's last acts in 1544 was to announce that his shipowners and seafarers would henceforth be allowed to 'prepare and equip to the seas such and so many ships and vessels furnished for the war, to be used and employed against his grace's said enemies the Scots and Frenchmen, as they shall be able to think *convenient for their advantage* and the annoyance of his majesty's said enemies'. They were, in short, licensed to act as privateers from now on, and there would be no penalties. They could attack and plunder to the King's 'and their own proper use, profit and commodity all...such ships, vessels, munitions, merchandises, wares, victuals and goods of what nature and quality soever...without making account in any court or place of this realm...and without paying part or share to the Lord Admiral of England, the Lord Warden of the Cinque Ports, or to any other officer or minister of the King's majesty...' The only qualification was that the privateer must not presume 'to take anything from any of his majesty's subjects or from any of his majesty's friends'.

Inevitably, Henry's proclamation was loosely interpreted by those who saw profit in assaulting vessels that were neither French nor Scots. Most notoriously, on 1 March 1545, a young seagoing merchant and burgess of Southampton, Robert Reneger, plundered the *San Salvador* on her way home from Hispaniola, the first time an Englishman had ever attacked a Spanish treasure ship. She was carrying gold, silver and pearls, together with some less valuable merchandise, a few passengers and some official documents, and most of the cargo was bound for the merchants of Seville. The gold alone was subsequently valued at almost seven and a quarter million *maravedis* (about £4,300 sterling). According to the Spaniards, their vessel was taken by three English ships under Reneger when she was approaching Cabo de São Vicente, across waters where French pirates had long been in the habit of lurking, but one of that trio was a French vessel which Reneger and his people had seized some days earlier. When he got home, the privateer came up with a cock and bull story, involving the unjust arrest of one of his own ships in Spain, in order to justify his breach of Henry's new regulation, while Charles V's ambassador lodged a complaint that the specie in the *San Salvador*'s manifest actually belonged to the Emperor.

Probably because he was happy to frustrate the man who had let him down once too often, Henry seems to have turned a blind eye to the whole business, and the plunder was lodged in the Tower of London; but only for a couple of years, after which it was handed back to Reneger, whose actions had a long-lasting effect on Anglo-Spanish relations. Many English merchant shipowners, men like William Aphowell and John Cappes of Bristol, who had peacefully and beneficially traded with Spain over many years, and had established mercantile bases in Cadiz, San Lucár and other ports in Andalusia, turned to privateering themselves, partly because March '45 alienated them from their Spanish neighbours: this was one of the factors that shaped later events in the sixteenth century. There has always been a strong suspicion that a number of influential people at court helped Robert Reneger through his legal difficulties, from which it has been inferred that courtiers may have secretly backed his enterprise from the beginning. That is quite likely, for it is a fact that at about the same time Thomas Wyndham – a serving naval officer like his long-since dead father, who was *Henry Grâce à Dieu*'s first captain – went privateering in the *Mawdelyn Russell*, which was owned by none other than the Lord Privy Seal, John Russell.

As soon as Reneger's treasure was under lock and key in the Tower, he himself joined the fleet that Henry was gathering off the Isle of Wight, with three of his ships – the *Trinity Reneger* (160 tuns), the *James Reneger* (100 tuns) and the *Gallion Reneger* (100 tuns) – already under the Lord Admiral's orders by 19 April; though he himself captained the *Marlion* (70 tuns), which may have been the French prize he had already acquired before boarding *San Salvador* off Cape St Vincent. Another shipowner who had lately taken advantage of Henry's new licence was that venturesome old seadog William Hawkins, and he, too, put himself at the King's service under John Dudley, who had resumed his naval command at the end of January, when he found that he had several problems to solve. One of the most pressing was a shortage of manpower in the fleet,

Henry VIII in 1540, the year Anne of Cleves and Catherine Howard became his fourth and fifth wives. Also the year in which his Lord Privy Seal, Thomas Cromwell – held responsible by Henry for the unconsummated failure of the German marriage – was executed.

Henry Grâce à Dieu – otherwise known as the *Great Harry* – was one of the two most cherished warships in Henry's fleet. At 1,000 tuns she was his biggest vessel but she saw little action and couldn't even use Dover harbour because she drew too much water under her keel. An illustration from the Anthony Roll, the great inventory of the English fleet as it was in 1546.

A model of *Mary Rose* (*c.*700 tuns), Henry VIII's other favourite, which foundered off Portsmouth during an engagement with the French on July 19, 1545.

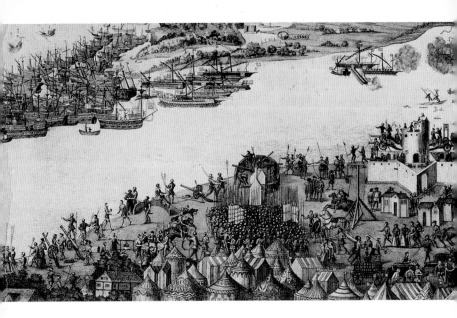

The sinking of *Mary Rose* off Portsmouth, with the French fleet to the left and the English to the right. The figures clinging to the foundered vessel's masts may not be totally fanciful, for she went down in less than 40 feet of water adjacent to the main channel in and out of the harbour. Southsea Castle is in the foreground and Henry can be seen on horseback riding past its wall (see inset, right).

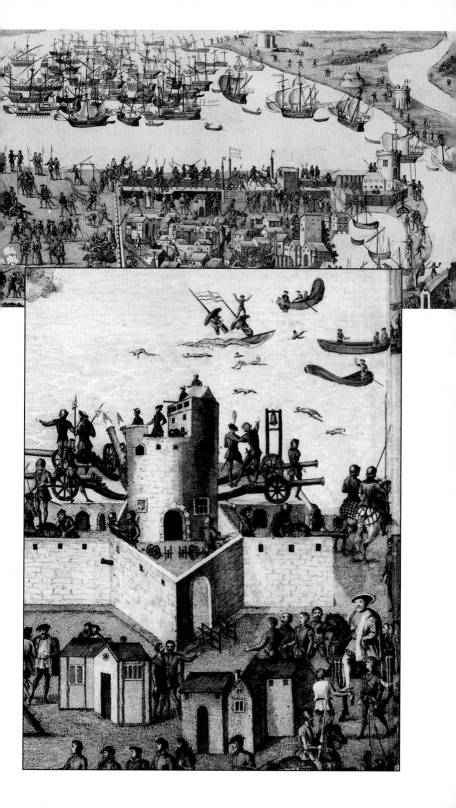

The galleass *Anne Gallant*, of 450 tuns, which was built during Henry VIII's last great expansion of the fleet to repulse an expected French invasion. She carried a crew of 220 seamen and 30 gunners. Another picture from the Anthony Roll.

The rowbarge *Rose in the Sun*, at 20 tuns and with a crew of 40, one of the smallest vessels in Henry's fleet. If he did try his hand at ship design, as some believed, then this was the likeliest outcome. This too is a picture from the Anthony Roll.

The Type 42 destroyer HMS *York* (5,200 tonnes) leaving Portsmouth harbour, seen from the battlements of Southsea Castle, where Henry VIII stood and watched *Mary Rose* sink in 1545. She went down some distance beyond the Spit Sand Fort which the destroyer is approaching, and which was built in 1860, against the threat of another French invasion.

which had been building up since at least August 1543, when Henry felt the need for an order which excused 'any shipman or mariner' from any other form of military activity.

The situation had become so much more disturbing by the beginning of 1545 that two other relevant pieces of legislation were pushed through on the same January day. The first threatened with the death penalty any who 'depart or go from their ships without testimonial signed with their captain's hands, to any place in the land, neither for victuals, water or any other necessaries, nor for any other lawful or unlawful occasion...' The second, rather more welcome, authorised a thirty-three per cent pay rise for seamen 'that shall be diligent and attendant in and about to serve his highness in his ships' from 5s a month to 6s 8d. Neither of these proclamations completely solved the problem, however, and at the beginning of summer it was announced that 'ruffians, vagabonds, masterless men, common players and evil disposed persons' were going to be pressed into working the naval galleys: London was thought to be an especially fertile ground for such recruitment, having a high proportion of ruffians and vagabonds 'able to work but living by theft and falsehood in play'. By then, the fishing fleets around the English coasts may have yielded more than their usual high quota of men to naval service in time of war. During the third week of August, when John Russell was inspecting the West Country, he reported from Exeter that 'As most of the fishermen here are taken from hence as mariners to serve the King, no fish is to be had; and women are going out fishing, and sometimes are chased home by the Frenchmen.' Similar stories were coming out of Dorset, too.

A key to much of what happened in 1545 was the capture of Boulogne the year before. Francis, whose temperament in many ways was much like Henry's, was so stung (and insulted) by this that he could not possibly be content until he had regained the town. While the English were still making their way home from Calais after their latest continental adventure, the Dauphin appeared outside its neighbour's walls with 30,000 troops and launched an attack on Basse Boulogne, which was quickly secured. The besiegers were busy looting what was left of the lower town, when the English garrison from the fortress above came thundering down on them and wrought such havoc that the attackers turned tail, leaving 800 men behind, most of them dead. The weather then turned nasty, the French rations were running out and, though October was not yet half spent, it was decided to postpone any further activity until the next campaigning season began in spring, to spend the winter building one or more fortified watch towers across the estuary of the Liane, from which a new siege could be launched in 1545. The *Landsnechts* and the Swiss mercenaries in French pay were therefore disbanded and sent home, as was almost all of the native soldiery under the Dauphin's command. Francis, however, would not be content with retaking the possession that Henry in person had stolen from him: he also needed to exact retribution on top of achieving his principal objective. And so he resolved to get even by invading England both across *La Manche* and from north of the Border. 'The King's final determination', according to one account, 'is to hold the sea and prevent victualling of Calais and Boulogne, attack England from Scotland, build two forts on the shore at Boulogne and sink six vessels laden with stone in the harbour mouth there', and his cross-Channel invasion force would 'join the Scots forces' somewhere above the southern counties, in a classical pincer movement. Whether or not he seriously envisaged total and long-term conquest is something for which we have no evidence.

Francis was, in fact, so ill at the turn of the year that he was thought likely to die 'of a thing swollen up beneath in his belly where he hath been cut once before', according to information which the Treasurer of Calais, Sir Edward Wotton, passed on to the King's secretary, Sir William Paget, but by the second week in January he was said to be on the mend. The English were also receiving reports from the beginning of the year that French troops were already on their way to Scotland and these were taken seriously enough for Francis Talbot to be given detailed instructions about the deployment of beacons in his bailiwick. Along the shores, three beacons were to be built at such short intervals that all could be seen from the adjacent three, and on each of the nearest hills two beacons must be visible both inland and out at sea; 'wise and vigilant persons' were to be posted by each beacon at all times; if the enemy landed in numbers that promised to overwhelm the defenders locally, all three of the shoreline beacons nearest the action must be fired to start a chain reaction across the area; and so on, in a comprehensive provision for any eventuality. When the Scots did march south in February, however, they went no further than Ancrum Moor, just beyond Melrose, in retaliation for a recent English raid in the same area; there they actually did beat their old foe for the first time within living memory, but it was a relatively small engagement and it was won without reinforcements from France. Not until the summer did Francis send 2,000 infantry, 500 horse and some money to Scotland by the west-coast route, after adulterating

10,000 crowns with copper and other metals so as to make up 150,000 crowns in wages for his troops.

Henry's problem in the spring of 1545 was that he was faced with several threatening options and didn't know which of them was the most likely to materialise, though a build-up of troops near Havre at the mouth of the Seine was certainly suggestive. But were these intended for invasion or simply for a fresh assault on Boulogne? The problem was not only one of uncertainty about Francis's overall intention, but also of not knowing just where he was going to strike if he pursued the first of those two alternatives. The Thames estuary, Margate and Sheppey were all considered as possible landing places rather than somewhere on the south coast. So was a stretch of East Anglia, which Thomas Howard inspected for weaknesses in May, returning to say that there were four miles between Yarmouth and Caister where there were 'as fair landing places, if it be no great sea winds, as ever I saw anywhere'; but he added that the French were unlikely to attempt anything with a main army this year 'because the coasts are so dangerous, with great sands as well near the shore...that I think they dare not adventure to go that way with their great ships'.

What the Privy Council actually did that month was to have more coastal beacons set up between the Downs and the Isle of Wight in pairs, with instructions that no watchman was to fire any of them unless he could see at least ten French vessels offshore, and was not to light two beacons until a landing took place. Trenchworks were dug behind the marshes of Kent, so that the local inhabitants 'may sustain attacks from the enemy until aid come'. Three separate defence forces had been mustered by the end of June, commanded by Charles Brandon, Thomas Howard and John Russell. Brandon's division of 32,394 men was drawn from the counties adjacent to London, from Hampshire, Wiltshire, Worcestershire and Herefordshire. Howard's 30,261 troops came from East Anglia and the east Midlands. The Lord Privy Seal led 27,476 conscripts from the four westernmost counties, from Gloucestershire and from Wales. At the same time, 5,000 soldiers were packed off to Boulogne, to stiffen any resistance that might be needed there. Any threat that materalised from Scotland or from the North Sea would be handled by forces that Talbot could raise from the northern counties. Henry was covering all eventualities as best he could.

The French preparations were taking shape, too, but more slowly than the English, largely because a vital part of their invasion force had faced a long voyage from the Mediterranean before it reached the Channel

assembly point. It was also late in setting off because the military authorities in Provence had been diverted by a campaign to put down the
Vaudois, a sect whose recently acquired Calvinism was regarded as heretical. Not until the middle of May, four months behind schedule, did
the twenty-five galleys from Marseille arrive in Normandy, and then
their oarsmen needed time to recover, the vessels themselves had to be
revictualled and rearmed before they were fit to sail on into battle. Leone
Strozzi came with them and so did his brother Pietro, but in spite of
their great experience and skill as galley captains, their appointment was
unfortunate in one respect. Leone had gained the enmity of Baron de la
Garde, his superior in the south, when Strozzi was given permission
(probably because of his connection with Catherine de' Medici) to keep
everything he took from captured Turkish vessels without yielding the
customary percentage to his Admiral; on top of this he had been put in
charge of the galleys when de la Garde – who was generally known by
his nickname of Polain and was regarded as the finest galley commander
since Prégent de Bidoux – was detached to the operation against the
Vaudois, which added to the Baron's resentment. The animosity between
him and the Strozzis would eventually reach the point where Pietro
accused Polain of cowardice and was challenged to a duel. But even
before that, the friction was beginning to affect other officers in the fleet
and this almost certainly played its part in a decision which influenced
the outcome of the approaching campaign.

The Admiral of France, Philippe Chabot de Brion, had died in June
1543 and eight months later Francis appointed Claude d'Annebault in his
place, leaving Polain (who may well have expected the promotion) to
make do with his inferior command. D'Annebault was a Norman, very
close to the King, and he had plenty of military experience as a captain-
general of light cavalry: he had been captured after the Battle of Pavia,
and again at Thérouanne, but had defended Turin successfully against
the imperial forces in 1536. He had been made Marshal of France two
years later and he was Governor of Normandy, too; but he had no naval
background whatsoever, and yet another appointment was an indication
of how far behind the English the French still were in this respect. By
July 1545 he had been a totally shorebound Admiral for seventeen months,
effectively holding a sinecure, with no reason at all (there were a number
of precedents, in fact) why he should not have retained this largely
ornamental role while the man with plenty of seatime under his belt
actually directed the forthcoming operation at sea. But at the last minute,

on 27 June, Francis – who had just undergone 'a 20 days' course of Chinese wood' for his ailment – decided that, instead of the highly qualified Polain, his favourite should lead the fleet into battle. The man d'Annebault was about to face, John Dudley, had been going to sea regularly for eight years by then, and this ageing French novice was expected to get the better of him with a complicated number and variety of warships at his disposal and no knowledge at all of how to use them most effectively.[1]

From his vantage point in Boulogne, Sir Thomas Poynings passed on a rumour that the French would shortly send an army across the sea as had never been seen before, and that an informant lately in Dieppe had come across a number of ships 'which had rooms in them like stables'. A spy whom he sent to check up on this reported that there were fifteen very new men o'war 'painted with black, yellow and green', together with a couple of great ships which carried three and four tops respectively, while a pair of galleys were anchored half a league offshore. He heard that the French task force was to muster at Havre at the end of June 'and some say they shall into Scotland'. In Rouen the same man noted three galleys, one of which was 'richly painted and gilt with the arms of France', but only 'pilots and slaves' were to be seen aboard them and their guns were on the dock; fifty other vessels were observed in the haven but none of them were men o'war. Charles V, meanwhile, was digesting information from his ambassador in France that d'Annebault would sail for Scotland with 25,000 troops, including the usual contingent of *Landsnechts* and Swiss mercenaries; but on this occasion these would be joined by 3,000 Spanish freelances.

The reality behind all these assessments was that in July the French Admiral found himself in command of 150 ships (many of them transports) and twenty-five galleys, which were assembling at Havre with an army of 50,000. The much smaller expeditionary force bound for Scotland under L'Orges de Montgomerie was well on the way to its destination by then. So Henry and his advisers had guessed correctly when they raised their principal defence forces to protect the south and south-east of England and concentrated their other preparations along the Channel coast. A number of patriotic pilots and shipmasters had added to these with a crafty idea that was all their own, based on intimate knowledge of the coastal waters. No stranger would dare approach the North Foreland with a view to rounding it, they said, if the navigation

1 D'Annebault's age is a matter of guesswork. The *Dictionnaire de Biographie Française* only tells us that he was born in the last quarter of the fifteenth century. He died in 1552.

beacon at the Spanish Knock was removed; and further defensive hazards could be created by shifting beacons which were intended to prevent mariners from being wrecked off Whitstable, Faversham and the Reculvers. These things, they reckoned, would only take a couple of hours to dismantle and they could easily be set up again in four.

John Dudley was expected to face a vastly superior force with no more than eighty vessels under his orders, but at least they were all fighting ships and a useful number were large: a muster of the fleet in April had amounted to no more than fifty-seven vessels, but of them fourteen were between 300 and 1,000 tuns and, although *Henry Grâce à Dieu* was in the tally, it didn't include the equally aged (and almost as big since her rebuilding) *Mary Rose*. Faced with a numerically superior enemy – and this had been a distinct possibility from the moment French preparations began – Dudley's first concern therefore was how to minimise the French advantage. He decided on a pre-emptive strike by sailing into the mouth of the Seine, where the French fleet was gathering, and doing as much damage to it as possible, pinning his hopes on the effect of surprise. On 19 June he notified Henry that thirty hulks had arrived in the Downs, mostly in ballast and bound for La Rochelle to load salt, though one was carrying a cargo of masts and spars; but he didn't say where they had come from. He proposed sending the one with the masts into Dover (it was a useful cargo, after all) but had other plans for the rest. He would strip them of their armaments and 'hire eight of the biggest of these hulks', which he proposed to use as fireships. He would sail them across the Channel with his own fleet in attendance, and when they reached the Seine – he had French pilots with him to do the tricky bit approaching the estuary – he would set them alight with rudders lashed in place and with their crews cast off in small boats, leaving the fireships to drift down on the biggest of the French vessels. In the confusion this caused, his own ships would then attack everything that wasn't ablaze. It was a bold plan which deserved to succeed, but it didn't quite come off. Realising that something unwelcome was afoot, the hulks sailed out of their anchorage in the night with Dudley's fastest vessels in pursuit. At the head of the chase, Sir John Berkeley in the *Less Galley* (400 tuns) 'thought to stop them by firing a saker, but it burst and he was stricken through the body with a fragment of iron', which hit him in the chest and came out through the shattered shoulder blade: it took him several weeks to die of the injury.

The hulks got away and the weather closed in, and not until much later in the month was Dudley able to make the crossing, to do whatever he could without the fireships. Perversely, the wind died down when the Englishmen needed it most, so that there was an inconclusive exchange of fire with the French; then it blew up again and threatened to put Dudley's ships onto the shoals, so they hastily withdrew from the estuary to the open sea. Having lost the crucial element of surprise against their original quarry, they cruised on down the Channel to make the best of a failing operation, while the weather continued to switch from one mood to another. Rounding Cap de la Hague, they encountered twenty-one galleys almost becalmed outside the treacherous rocks that surround Alderney, and opened fire. This was returned and, according to an officer who took part in the action, the French 'came within half a mile of us and beat at us continually with ordnance the space of five or six hours'. He added that this did little damage to the English ships, with only one man killed, a few more hurt, which sounds as if some of his figures were not quite accurate. The French eventually were put to flight 'with great loss of men and galleys', though these were probably not very big ships. Whatever the precise truth of the matter, the engagement seems to have done just about enough to redeem the earlier failure of Dudley's expedition and so his vessels turned for home, arriving in Portsmouth on 13 July.

They had left themselves with barely enough time to rearm, revictual and repair damage before d'Annebault and his main force sailed over the horizon. In many ways, they were not at all ready when he did show up off the Isle of Wight. As late as 22 July a letter was sent to Parson Levett at his gunfoundry in Sussex, requiring 300 cannon shot, 200 culverin shot, 300 saker shot and 300 fawcon shot 'or as many as he had ready', and he was asked to copy the letter and forward it to Anthony Anthony, Clerk of the Ordnance in London, so that any shortfall could be sent down from the Tower: this was the day after Anthony had received a direct demand from the Privy Council for large quantities of bows, arrows, bills and gunpowder. It is quite likely that this failure to be adequately supplied for something big and protracted which had been anticipated for weeks, and other shortcomings, were a by-product of the administrative disruption that lingered for some time after William Gonson's death.

France's Admiral had weighed anchor in the Seine on 12 July, but at once he had a crisis on his hands when his flagship, the 1,200-tun *le Philippe* (which had been a bequest to the King from d'Annebault's predecessor) caught fire as a result of an accident in the galley, always a hazard on wooden ships, and he had to abandon her. He took his flag over to *la Grande Maîtresse*, and three days later he proceeded to lead out of the river a fleet dressed in all the panoply of naval heraldry, with flags bearing images of the King's talismanic salamander as well as falcons, the fleur-de-lys and other devices. The different squadrons had just about cleared the estuary when *la Grande Maîtresse* ran aground so heavily that she started to leak, but after she was refloated, d'Annebault carried on undeterred, just as he would have done had he been leading a cavalry charge. Nevertheless, these setbacks meant that it was not until 18 July that he and his vessels reached the Sussex coast in the classic battle formation of line abreast, with all but two ships sailing flanked by a consort on either side. What happened immediately afterwards is not at all clear. According to the French, they attacked Brighton at this point for the second time in thirty years, but this has been questioned in modern times. Certainly, their fleet sailed westward for fifty miles or so until it appeared off the Isle of Wight the next day, by which time *la Grande Maîtresse* was taking water so badly that she had to return to Havre; so d'Annebault transferred his flag to a third ship (whose identity

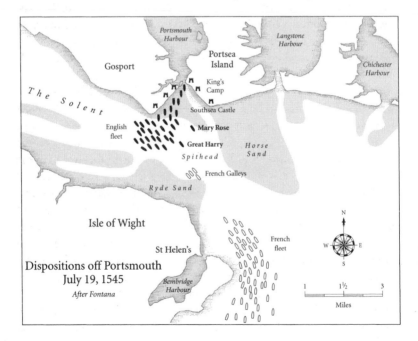

has been lost to us) and proceeded as planned with his invasion strategy.

To test the local defences and observe the deployment of the English fleet off Portsmouth, four galleys under Polain were detached from d'Annebault's squadrons and were rowed swiftly into Spithead, at the eastern end of the Solent, where they opened fire with their basilisks, mounted in the bows, as their course brought them through the channel between the Horse and the Ryde Sands. This appears to have taken the English completely by surprise. So disorganised were they that some vessels expected from the West Country had still not arrived when the action began. The sixty-three warships available to Dudley that day were at anchor inside Portsmouth harbour when the French turned up, some of them still undergoing repair of the damage that had been done off Alderney, and all their captains were otherwise focused on the visit of their King. Henry had gone down to Hampshire to inspect the port's defences, which had been giving concern for several months, and to lift his spirits as usual by going aboard his principal warships and cheering their people up. The new imperial ambassador, François Van der Delft, was in attendance and, although Henry seems to have been frosty to start with, he warmed up enough to give the Dutchman the obligatory tour of *Henry Grâce à Dieu*, which was now Dudley's flagship, before 'he bade me farewell more amiably than he had ever done before'. On Sunday, 19 July, a fine summer's day, Henry was aboard her again, dining with his principal officers and presenting Sir George Carew with his gold whistle of office.

Carew, whom Henry had just made Dudley's second-in-command with his Vice-admiral's flag in *Mary Rose*, belonged to an old West Country family (from Honiton, in Devon) with long and costly service to the Crown behind it. Sir George's grandfather, Edmund, was the luckless man whose head was blown off when he bent forward over the table at precisely the wrong moment, during Henry's 1513 invasion of France; and his uncle John had perished when the *Regent* went down after the explosion which took both it and *la Cordelière* to the bottom off Brest the same year. The Carews had also lost George's younger brother Philip not long before this, killed fighting the Turks on behalf of the same military religious order to which David Gonson had belonged. George himself had had a narrow escape in 1543, when he was in the contingent under Sir John Wallop which was sent ahead of Henry's last invasion force in order to back up the Emperor, and the man standing next to him was killed by a shot fired from the walls of Landrecy. And now, both he and the two other remaining men in the family were serving their King in Dudley's fleet, with George's uncle Gawen in command of the *Matthew Gonson* (600 tuns) and his youngest brother Peter captain of the *Great Venetian* (700 tuns).

All three were at the council of war which continued after they had finished eating the celebratory meal in *Henry Grâce à Dieu*, when news came that the French were in sight. Henry immediately called for someone to get aloft for a better view of the enemy and 'The word was no sooner spoken but that Peter Carew...forthwith climbed up to the top of the ship'. From there he called down that Polain's galleys were heading in their direction, with dozens of sails behind them on the horizon, abeam of the Isle of Wight. At this, 'the King hurriedly left the flagship' and was rowed ashore in a longboat to take up a position on the ramparts of Southsea Castle, where Sir George's wife, Lady Mary Carew, presently joined him and other watchers of what was about to unfold. As soon as the naval officers had returned to their own vessels, English anchors were weighed and Dudley's ships prepared to do battle. It was said that Portsmouth had never seen a fleet as large as this before.

In the confined waters of the anchorage there was a frenzy of move-ment, as the many ships manoeuvred tightly to avoid colliding with each other and worked their way towards the open sea; as sails were hoisted and set, orders were bellowed and trumpets blew, as men heavehoed on ropes, rigged the nets which would stop boarders from leaping onto their decks, raced up to the tops with their small arms, javelins, bows and arrows, brought up from below the shot and powder for the culverins and other ordnance, and doused the fires in the galleys before any powder was broached. In the largest ships, surgeons arranged knives and razors and saws and needles and thread and bleeding cups in their little cubby holes, and on every vessel the carpenters made whatever preparations would be necessary for running repairs. The business of getting under way was made more difficult for the English because there was scarcely a breath of wind when the manoeuvring began, which gave Polain's galleys a distinct advantage in trying to press home their attack: it was the reason why the bulk of d'Annebault's fleet stood well outside the anchorage and made no attempt to come in. But late that afternoon, as the tide began to ebb, a light wind at last stirred the sails and Dudley's vessels formed up to go out and fight.

The immediate task was to dispose of the lighter French oared vessels before they could turn back to their fleet, and *Mary Rose* (Capt. Roger

Grenville) was one of those that took the lead, possibly because she had the Vice-admiral aboard and was still handier in a narrow seaway than *Henry Grâce à Dieu*. She was as well armed as anything at Dudley's disposal since her rebuilding, with a total of ninety-one guns ranged along three decks except in the fo'c'sle, and with ordnance (small pieces probably) on four decks pointing astern. But she was heeling over in the freshening wind so much that it made Carew's uncle ask his own ship-master what he thought about it, and was told that, if *Mary Rose* canted any more than that, she might be in trouble. While she was taking up her position she passed the *Matthew Gonson* and, as she did so, Sir Gawen is supposed to have called across to Sir George, 'asking him how he did; who answered that he had a sort of knaves whom he could not rule' aboard his ship. If that is true, they are the last words the younger Carew is known to have spoken. When she was quite set, almost halfway between Southsea Castle and the edge of Ryde Sand, she fired a (probably) starboard broadside and then started to come about so that her ordnance on the other side could be brought to bear in turn. A gust of wind suddenly caught her, she heeled over again – and with terrible swiftness, as if she was being sucked under by some greedy maw, she sank. She went down so quickly that, of the 415 people aboard, no more than thirty survived; but Sir George Carew and Roger Grenville were not among them. It was said later that the frantic cries of men trapped under the boarding nets could be heard for the moment or two before they were silenced by the waves, and that the sound carried to the castle ramparts a mile away, where the King and the Vice-admiral's wife looked on appalled. He himself gasped 'Oh my gentlemen! Oh, my gallant men!' as *Mary Rose* settled on the bottom; then turned to comfort Lady Mary, who had just fainted from the shock of it.

The words attributed to her husband have been the subject of debate over the years, and are not now thought to carry much weight.[2] They implied that Sir George was having trouble with an insubordinate crew, which led to inefficient ship-handling; but a more plausible theory is that many of the men might have been weakened by sickness: there had lately been an outbreak of dysentery aboard *Sweepstake* and much worse was to follow in both the French and English fleets soon. In any case, Grenville and his shipmaster rather than Carew would have been responsible for

2 The only source for them is the Carew family biographer, John Hooker of Exeter, who was a friend and enjoyed the patronage of Sir Peter Carew: it is now held that Hooker was trying to clear Sir George of any responsibility for the tragedy.

the fatal manoeuvre, and the one description by a survivor has nothing to say about any indiscipline (which is not, of course, conclusive proof that it didn't exist). In his despatch to the Emperor, Van der Delft passed on his conversation with a member of the ship's company who was rescued, a Fleming who 'told me that the disaster was caused by their not having closed the lowest row of gun ports on one side of the ship. Having fired the guns on that side, the ship was turning in order to fire from the other, when the wind caught her sails so strongly as to heel her over and plunge her open gun ports beneath the water, which flooded and sank her.' The gunports in question were bound to let in the sea if left open, because they were no more than sixteen inches above the waterline even when the ship was on an even keel.

The French believed, and later claimed, that their gunfire was responsible for the sinking, though this was certainly not the case, as archaeological evidence gathered in the past few years has proved. But some of the English were not prepared to allow that it was a straightforward matter of bad luck, either. John Russell, writing to the King's secretary later that week, referred severely to 'such rashness and negligence' as had caused *Mary Rose* to be 'in such wise cast away'. A modern commentator has wondered whether 'the Captain's orders (to close ports on turning) had been deliberately disobeyed by a bloody-minded crew, perhaps the worse for drink', though it seems more likely that Sir George Carew and his captain, who had just been carousing with their King, were slightly the worse for wear if anybody was. Apart from the failure to close the gunports, it is possible that a poor distribution of weight around the decks had something to do with the accident.

The wind died again and in the ensuing calm the French galleys withdrew, leaving the stunned English to contemplate their loss; but the engagement continued on Monday when, Van der Delft reported, 'the firing on both sides went on nearly all day, and could be plainly witnessed from here. Some people say that at nightfall the English did some damage to a French galley.' On Tuesday, in an attempt to draw Dudley's ships out for a decisive battle between the two fleets, the French put men ashore at four or five places on the Isle of Wight and the fires they started, which burned some houses, could be seen from Portsmouth. The garrison eventually repulsed them with casualties on both sides, the Chevalier d'Aux being one of those killed; and a story which the Bishop of Ajaccio (who was in Picardy at the time) soon retailed to a Roman prelate, reckoned that it was not only soldiers who could claim the credit for driving off the enemy. He had heard tell that 'certain women fought and shot their arrows so swiftly that they did incredible hurt, and they ran like hares; and this because they hold these men here in no estimation, and every Englishman boasts that he can fight three Frenchmen'.

Dudley's reluctance to engage more fully in the prevailing weather is understandable, but there was another factor which made up his mind to hold back. It was thought that *Mary Rose* would be raised very quickly and, though it may seem ghoulish to modern sensibilities, the intention was doubtless to remove the corpses, put a new crew aboard and get her back to sea as soon as possible. Her loss meant a serious shortage of firepower in Dudley's fleet, quite apart from the effect it had on the morale of superstitious seafarers, some of whom might even have seen it as an act of God. Salvaging the stricken vessel rapidly would have been the best way to raise their downcast spirits.

Charles Brandon certainly didn't intend her to be on the bottom of Spithead very long, for on the last day of the month he told Paget that he would 'with speed set men to the weighing of the *Mary Rose*'. He had already hired thirty-one Venetians to undertake the salvage and the next day drew up a list of their requirements to get the job done, which included 'two of the greatest hulks that may be gotten' and four of the biggest hoys in Portsmouth, plus five of 'the greatest cables that may be had'. Henry, too, had been impatient and ordered a detention of every ship in the Thames until what was needed had been requisitioned, and by 2 August the hulks *Jesus* and *Sampson* were well on their way. By 5 August they had arrived, the *Mary Rose*'s sails and yards had been recovered, 'and on her masts there is tied three cables with other engines to weigh her up, and on every side of her a hulk to set her upright'. It was expected that she would be brought to the surface the following day, after which, Paget was informed, she would be 'discharged of water and ordnance, and gradually brought nearer the shore'.

The schedule was later put back twenty-four hours, but on 9 August Dudley had very bad news for the King's secretary. The Italians had told him that not only did they think it impossible to raise *Mary Rose* by the adopted method, but that they had managed to break her foremast with their first efforts. They asked for six more days, in which they would try dragging her into shallow water instead of refloating her where she lay. Although Dudley was loath to spare more time and resources on the recovery, he was mindful of the valuable ordnance that was lying on the seabed, as well as the place that *Mary Rose* occupied in his sovereign's affections: she was, in the language of our own day, Henry's signature ship, the original that had many years before heralded his arrival and his future plans. Because of this, Dudley appears to have given the go-ahead for the extension and the fresh approach; but how far this proceeded before it, too, was abandoned as impracticable we do not know, for the trail goes cold at this point and no more mention was made in the official papers of efforts to salvage the King's pride and joy. It would be 437 years before she was seen on the surface again.

XVI
D'ANNEBAULT'S GAFFE

Everything came more or less to a standstill while they were trying to raise *Mary Rose*. Dudley told Paget that all the shipwrights in Portsmouth had been so busy making the appliances required by the Italians 'that they have had no leisure for other things'. The Lord Admiral also had to cope with Henry, who had come down to Hampshire intending to stay for ten days or so, fussing and interfering at every turn, complaining about a lack of tools and even overriding Dudley's dispositions. He asked for a list of the ships' captains and shuffled many of the names about, at which Peter Carew, according to Dudley, 'with piteous moan besought me that he might not be shifted out of his ship'. The King went up Portsdown Hill, which gave a superb panoramic view of the anchorage, and when he returned to sea level he 'found fault with the lying of the ships, and wished that they should repair to the strait on this side St Helen's Bay.' This was, of course, done, though *Jesus* and *Sampson* remained in position above the wreck for the time being, and *Great Venetian* was also excused because she had to take in ballast.

There were other problems, among them the everlasting struggle to provision the fleet adequately. 'Are we to proceed with the victualling or not?' someone in the commissariat asked the naval command quite sharply. 'My master has commanded me, on the return of your answer, to cause 40 or 60 bullocks to be killed to refresh the fleet, so far as they will extend, with fresh beef, and the rest with salt beef, which I suppose is no worse than that you saw today.' And then there was the plague, probably caused by a combination of hot weather and rotting food: it was beginning to spread throughout the fleet, where an increasing number of people (including Sir William Woodhouse) were falling sick with 'swelling in their heads and faces and in their legs, and divers of them with the bloody flux'. Dudley's report of this on 1 August was 'Scribbled in the *Harry*', so hard-pressed was he by then. It's scarcely surprising that, with one thing and another, the Lord Admiral lost track of the French for a while, confessing to Paget on 5 August that 'it is not known where the French Fleet is at this present, nor what they do'. For all he knew, they might have gone home but, whether this was so or not, he advised staying put so that 'if they shall repair again into the Narrow Seas, then may His Majesty's army depart hence, to fight them to our most advantage'.[1]

D'Annebault and his armada had gone home, but only after a quick thrust at the Sussex coast. 'Twelve score sails of French ships' turned up off Seaford one morning and landed people, causing a terrified official of the town to beg the justices of Kent for urgently needed assistance: 'Haste, haste, post haste, for thy life, haste!' this Mr Gage implored. As well he might, when five or six cottages were set on fire. But after the alarm had been rung on church bells and all the beacons along that stretch of coast had been fired and the local militia had turned to, the panic subsided as the French pulled out, leaving some dead behind, and went back to Havre, to victual, to disembark troops who would reinforce those already outside the walls of Boulogne, probably to land the sick, and possibly to put ashore prisoners taken on the Isle of Wight. After that, they had returned to the Channel.

Henry had cleared off back to London on or about 2 August (fear of catching the disease probably propelled him as much as anything, for he had always been a hypochondriac) when reports came in that the French were nosing along the Sussex coast again. To engage them, Dudley ordered his fleet in a deployment that was new to English seamen, and may have been an adaptation of Spanish tactics learned during alliance with the Emperor. Instead of the traditional extended line abreast formation, the fleet was drawn up in three ranks of sailing vessels flanked by two wings of oared galleys and rowbarges, so that the overall pattern was that of a blunt wedge with its sharp end at the rear. In the first rank of eight vessels were the *Trinity* of Danzig and five other Hanseatic hirelings, big things that would bear the brunt of an initial encounter and make way for Henry's own men o'war to go in and do damage; but all of them were commanded by English officers. Dudley in *Henry Grâce à Dieu* led the second rank of eleven vessels, which also included *Peter*,

1 He was referring to the fleet, not to a force that did its fighting on land. The old habit of thinking in military rather than specifically naval terms still lingered enough to create ambiguity at times.

Matthew Gonson, Great Venetian, Sweepstake and *Minion*. Nineteen ships constituted the third rank, and among them was the *Mary James* (a new prize of 120 tuns and the second of Henry's ships to bear that name) and many hired vessels. The right wing of oared craft numbered the *Salamander* and eleven others; the left wing contained one of Robert Reneger's boats and nine others.

The potential for confusion among so many vessels was clear enough and to obviate this the Lord Admiral issued the first fighting instructions to appear since those produced by Thomas Audley in the previous decade. They are dated only 'August' but there is reason to believe that they were promulgated on the 3rd of the month. They emphasised the need for keeping 'such order in sailing that none impeach another' and they stipulated that vessels must stay half a cable (approximately a hundred yards) apart. The first two ranks were to lay aboard the enemy, each vessel choosing his own target, but leaving the French Admiral for *Henry Grâce à Dieu* to take care of, while the wings should enter the fray as wind and opportunity dictated. The King had decided that battle should be joined on Monday the 10th and, while it lasted, flags bearing the cross of St George were to be flown in a manner that distinguished one group from another. The instructions were relatively brief and they were clearly laid down.

By this time the laggardly West Country ships, fifty of them in all, had finally turned up, many of them very old-fashioned clenchers which were thought more likely to sink themselves than damage an adversary if they tried to grapple, so they were not considered for the engagement, though the others were incorporated into Dudley's command. The result was that the Lord Admiral put to sea with a fleet that had grown to 104, but with many ailing seamen aboard. On 10 August, he issued a new fleet order to cover the changed disposition, by which his ships were rearranged into a vanguard of twenty-four vessels, a main body (a 'battle') of forty, plus a wing of forty oared craft which could function in two divisions if need be. Sir Thomas Clere, who had been to sea since 1522, was made Vice-admiral in charge of the vanguard, flying his flag in the hired *Aragozia of Hampton* (700 tuns), Dudley himself in his flagship took charge of the main group, and Captain William Tyrrell, who would go on to serve all three of Henry's children at sea, was Vice-admiral in the brand-new *Grand Mistress* (450 tuns), commanding the oared vessels on the wing. The *Artigo* (Capt. John Merrick) was in the fleet and so was the *Galley Subtle* (Capt. Edward Jones), while Robert Reneger was aboard his own *Trinity*. Notable absentees were William Hawkins and Sir

William Woodhouse, who by then was seriously ill. A total of 12,675 men were committed to whatever lay ahead of them as the fleet sailed out into the Channel, and the modified instructions under which they were ordered went as follows:

1. First, it is to be considered that every of the captains with the said ships appointed by this order to the Vanward, Battle and Wing, shall ride at anchor according as they be appointed to sail by this said order; and that no ship of any of the said Wards or Wing shall presume to come to an anchor before the Admiral of the said Ward.

2. Item, that every captain of the said Wards or Wing shall be in everything ordered by the Admiral of the same.

3. Item, when we shall see a convenient time to fight with the enemies, our Vanward shall make with their Vanward if they have any; and if they be in one company, our Vanward (taking advantage of the wind) shall set upon their foremost rank, bringing them out of order; and our Vice-Admiral shall seek to board their Vice-Admiral, and every captain shall choose his equal as near as he may.

4. Item, the Admiral of the Wing shall be always in the wind with his whole company; and when we shall join with the enemies, he shall keep still the advantage of the wind, to the intent he with his company may the better beat off the galleys from the great ships.

5. Item, the Lord Admiral shall bear one banner of the King's Majesty's arms in his main top, and one flag of St George's Cross in his fore top, and every ship appointed to the Battle shall bear one flag of St George's Cross in his main top.

6. Item, the Admiral of the Vanward is appointed to bear two flags of St George's Cross, the one in his main top, and the other in his fore top. And every ship appointed to the Vanward shall bear one flag of St George's Cross in his fore top.

7. Item, the Admiral of the Wing shall bear a flag of St George's Cross in either of his mizzen tops; and every ship, galleass, pinnace and shallop, appointed to the Wing, shall have in their mizzen top one flag of St George's Cross.

8. Item, the Lord Admiral shall bear 3 lights in the night, one great light in the poop behind, and two smaller lights in the midst of the bonaventure mizzen shrouds.

9. Item, the Admiral of the Vanward shall bear two lights in the night, to be a knowledge to all that Ward, and those two lights to be borne in the said bonaventure shrouds without any other light in the poop.

10. Item, the Admiral of the Wing shall bear one light in his said bonaventure shrouds without any other light, for a token to all that Ward.

11. The watch words in the night shall be thus, 'God save King Henry'; the other shall answer 'And long to reign over us.'

The most striking thing about the two sets of orders, composed only a few days apart, is not that the second was the more elaborate, but that its predecessor also took account of the fact that 'There be, besides the said ships mentioned...50 sail of western ships'. We may wonder, therefore, why it was felt necessary to revise the original fighting instructions at all and change the formation of the fleet. Was this another example of a meddlesome King, whose latter years were characterised by the same intense interest in his navy as had been the case at the beginning of his reign? The fact that Henry had unrealistically ordered the fighting to start specifically on 10 August, even though the enemy's whereabouts were unknown, strongly suggests that this was so. More helpfully, he sent John Carter, Master of the King's barge, together with forty-four of the royal watermen, down from London to help man the galleys. He also required Archbishop Cranmer to arrange religious processions throughout the realm (with, very adamantly, choirs singing only in English, if you please) 'as victories come only at the appointment of God'. Nevertheless, Dudley must have been glad to have his lord and master off his back by the time he set sail.

The fleet put to sea on the morning tide of 12 August, by which time d'Annebault and his ships were cruising off Rye. Three days later the enemy was sighted and, for a time, the two foes did what they could to obtain the weather gage without firing a single gun, while the wind from ESE died almost to a flat calm. Dudley reported from somewhere off Shoreham that the French did not seem disposed to fight and said that the sea had become so nearly still that unless there was a wind he doubted they could work their way east of Beachy Head. This eerie manoeuvring in a silence broken only by the faintest breath of air and the gentlest slop of waves, continued almost all day until the French galleys suddenly plied their oars in attack and loosed off (so the English insisted) a couple hundred cannon balls, though this great expenditure of shot only managed to shatter three oars of Tyrrell's vessel. Dudley later commended the English galleys to the King, singling out *Grand Mistress* and *Anne Gallant* (very new and over 300 tuns) for especial praise, and telling Henry that they 'did so handle the (French) galleys, as well with their sides as with their prows, that your great ships in a manner had little to do'. As the light died that evening, the French galleys withdrew and the two fleets dropped anchor three miles apart to await the next day.

About midnight a wind began to ruffle the sea and rock the ships once more, and when daybreak came the English realised that 'our good neighbours were not to be found', so they raised sail and set off in pursuit, and a lookout in *Great Harry*'s maintop eventually spotted them almost out of sight to seaward; but then the wind died again, and a frustrated Dudley was reduced to complaining that unless the Almighty sent them something that blew without interruption for twenty-four hours they would be incapable of action. By then he was anchored in the lee of Beachy Head in order to hold his ground in an ebbing tide, intending with the next flood, about 4 a.m., to make way towards Dover. The Almighty then duly obliged, but so extravagantly that an easterly breeze soon became a gale so fierce that Dudley found himself sheltering under Beachy Head for two full days, quite unable to move into the Narrow Seas, and with storm damage being reported from various ships. *Grand Mistress*'s main-mast had worked loose and was liable to go overboard at any moment, while the cross-trestles on both it and the foremast were broken; so she ran before the storm to the safety of Portsmouth, with the shipwright who had made her ordered to get there from Rye as soon as possible. The Lord Admiral reported that several vessels were 'ill-appointed with anchors and cables, especially the merchants and the strangers'. Almost inevitably, the beer was running out, and Dudley could see the calamitous moment coming when 'a good many of this fleet may happen to drink water'.

At this point, the storm notwithstanding, he despatched a number of his smaller craft to go looking for d'Annebault in mid-Channel, and between Dieppe and Fécamp (which the English knew as Feckam) these came across a local fishing boat whose crew said that their fleet was now sheltering in the mouth of the Seine, while d'Annebault himself had gone ashore and was riding to Arques, inland from Dieppe, to see Francis. The little *Falcon* (80 tuns) was sent to check up on this and her captain, Thomas Harding, later reported that he had counted 200 French vessels in the estuary. He had also interrogated the master and merchant of a Flemish vessel he came across, who told him that when d'Annebault and some of his gentlemen landed at Havre 'there was no appearance of rejoicing'; what's more, the ships in the Seine had been disembarking great numbers of sick every day and the French seamen generally 'had rather be hanged than go forth again'. In fact, the local population greeted the Admiral with a stony silence as he stepped ashore, and he was pointedly not given the usual salvo of honour by the port's saluting gun. D'Annebault's unfamiliarity with naval custom may well have had something to do with their reaction. For, after withdrawing from the brief encounter which sank *Mary Rose* and either just before or after the trifling Seaford affair, the French had held a council of war to decide whether to ride at anchor until the English came out, and risk being beached if cables parted, or whether they should attack them where they lay between Portsmouth and the Isle of Wight, and risk being thrashed. In dodging both these options the French commanders were doubtless influenced by the fact that so many men were falling sick.

Another factor was that their Admiral was feeling rather unwell himself, not from the plague but from an ear infection, which he was having to endure on top of his regular gout. More than once he sent a signal to Francis, asking for permission to bring the fleet home, but each time he was told to carry on and fight. Refusing to take no for an answer, he headed back to the Seine so that he could get on a horse (which he doubtless found more congenial than a ship) and go and have it out with his sovereign in person. Francis was not at all pleased – he had, after all, just been forced to recognise that the invasion strategy was ruined – and promptly relieved him of his seagoing command, though d'Annebault retained his rank as Admiral of France. His adversary, John Dudley, was not impressed, either, taking the view that the French would never have a better chance of beating him than the one that came their way when *Mary Rose* went down and the English fleet was at sixes and sevens for a while. Their demeanour that day was shameful, he said. When the two men eventually met a few months later, d'Annebault told the Englishman that God had preserved them for a better purpose than fighting each other, such as an honourable peace; but Dudley's reply is not, alas, recorded. The charge of cowardice was not thrust at d'Annebault alone, however. This was the occasion when Pietro Strozzi aimed it at Polain for withdrawing after only damaging Tyrrell's oars on 15 August. Apart from being challenged by the Baron in return, Strozzi earned the enmity of a future French Admiral for his insolence. Gaspard de Coligny, who had also been aboard the galleys that afternoon, 'spat his contempt at the Florentine captain' and declared that he would rather be dead, yes, buried a hundred feet under the earth, than have anything more to do with him. It took the intervention of Francis himself to calm down his quarrelsome captains, for whom something more than personal honour was probably at stake.[2]

2 De Coligny also became a leader of the French Huguenots and perished in the Massacre of St Bartholomew's Day in August 1572, which is thought to have been instigated by Leone Strozzi's old patron and Henri II's (by then) widow, Catherine de' Medici.

By the time Harding brought his news to his commander, Dudley had withdrawn the fleet to an anchorage off St Helen's Point so that he would enjoy the shelter of the Isle of Wight. And there he remained for the best part of a week, fuming at the elements and longing for better weather 'in which to annoy the King's enemies', taking what comfort he could from an assumption that d'Annebault would be similarly frustrated, that some of his vessels, too, would be in need of serious repair after suffering damage from wind and wave. As for his own, he reported to the Lord Chamberlain that 'Divers ships after another storm will be unable to look abroad'. Just before the end of the month, he received fresh orders from the King's secretary, to the effect that if the French had gone home only to revictual, he should keep his fleet together 'and proceed as was before determined'. But if d'Annebault had decided not to come out and fight again, then Dudley would have to divide the fleet into two, one squadron being sent from Portsmouth to keep the Narrow Seas, victualled for a fortnight or longer, while the rest of his ships under the Lord Admiral himself must make for the French coast to 'burn towns and villages until his fortnight's victuals are spent'. When the victuals ran out they should come home, and most of this squadron must then be laid up in Portsmouth harbour itself or else in the nearby Hamble River. Another prospect awaited 'certain old hulks and merchants' ships', however. Four hundred men were to be retained from them for the defence of the naval base, while the remainder were sent with 'all the victuals that remain in Portsmouth' straight to Calais, to serve in the Narrow Seas until further notice. After Dudley had made these dispositions, he was to present himself to Henry at court, 'to know further of the King's Majesty's pleasure for his proceedings from Calais &c'.

Sir Thomas Clere was deputed to keep the Narrow Seas, which he was to traverse 'for the defence of the King's subjects, and endeavour to take the King's enemies, either Frenchmen or Scots'. If he came across anybody else's shipping, he must 'gently' board the vessel concerned and make sure it was not carrying anything that would benefit the enemy, before allowing it to go on its way. 'This is specially important', said the orders 'and any violation of it will be punished.' He must ensure that his capital ships – none of which was bigger than the 500-tun *Great Christopher of Danzig* – remained at all times in deep water, never venturing to the French coast, lest they became storm-bound there and unable to regain the English side. His people were strictly forbidden to go ashore anywhere, unless they were sick or were fetching and carrying necessities on his orders. His principal responsibility was to keep the Channel safe for English traffic crossing daily between Dover and Calais or Boulogne, for which he must provide wafters. He was informed, rather mysteriously, that the King's agent in Flanders would be sending by sea from Zealand to Calais 'certain things of weight and importance', obviously including despatches, which would also require an escort; and he was to send a pinnace to a rendezvous near Boulogne from time to time in order to pick up any messages the garrison might need to get out by sea. Clere was given one more task, which fell to his smaller craft. These were to be detached from his main squadron in order to raid Etaples and St Valéry – 'to burn or bring away ships laden with victuals; and doing this twice a week at the least'.

Dudley sailed out of Spithead within a day or so of receiving his instructions, set course for Normandy and did as he was told. On 2 September, he landed a large party to the west of Le Tréport and began marching towards it, 'skirmishing with increasing numbers of the enemy and dragging certain small pieces by hand'. He had divided his troops into two groups, one of which burnt the fishing port itself, including 'two or three gentlemen's houses and an abbey', as well as destroying eighteen or twenty boats in the harbour, while the other torched some small villages in the vicinity, before both withdrew with the loss of only three men. Enigmatically, Dudley reported that two of these 'wilfully cast away themselves, and more would have done so if they had not been looked unto'. He made a particular point of commending Peter Carew for his part in this action, but what he didn't mention was that, according to Jean de St Mauris, the imperial ambassador to France, his people had killed 'all the men and women they could catch.' The Lord Admiral was careful, however, when he had returned to Portsmouth, to inform Henry that he urgently needed money for the wages of his mariners, with £7,500 due on the next pay day, as he had already informed the King's secretary.

The English now dominated the Channel and the Narrow Seas, though the French had not completely given up in the wake of d'Annebault's great failure. On 14 September Dudley reported from Portsmouth that at least fourteen of their galleys were interrupting traffic, which meant that the five vessels under Clere's command might not be able to provide an adequate response. Henry therefore ordered that six more ships should be sent to join them. But by then Clere's problems were almost the least of the Lord Admiral's worries, when the plague was beginning to cripple his fleet. What had been no more than a matter of sporadic outbreaks in July, had become an overwhelming epidemic by September. Sir Thomas Seymour, who had been in Dover for several weeks to guard against invasion along the Kent coast, was summoned to Portsmouth to lead the reinforcements for Clere, but it was found that many of the ships he was to command were already infected, obviously ruled out 'because none will willingly enter them, and their mariners are not meet to be placed in other ship'. In a joint letter to the King, Dudley and Seymour reported that fresh cases were occurring every night, 'and some have died before me, the Lord Chancellor and the Admiralty, when they have come to receive their money full of the marks (of plague)'. Henry was told that there were very few 'clean' seamen available, compared with the number he had wanted remustering for the cross-Channel patrol; and the two officers questioned the wisdom of sending any ships at all to join Clere, given the state of things in Portsmouth on 11 September. A memorandum which they enclosed with the letter showed that on that day eleven vessels were infected, which meant that 1,882 men were already sick or at risk. Three days later a general roll-call of the fleet in Portsmouth indicated that only 4,888 men were still healthy, compared with the 12,000 or so who had been mustered at the beginning of the month. In other words, Dudley had lost well over a quarter of his manpower in less than a fortnight.

And the epidemic was still spreading, with the local garrisons of Portsmouth and the Isle of Wight beginning to lose people to 'agues and sickness', too. English naval medicine was somewhat ahead of that practised among the military, but there was still no concept of quarantine for such infections in either of the Tudor armed forces. This was a strange failure of the imagination, when it was well understood by everybody in the land that if you became leprous you would have to live apart from others for the rest of your life unless you could be successfully treated for it; and leper hospitals had existed for almost two hundred years in Plymouth, Dover and Sandwich among other places. Yet the Venetians, pursuing the logic that connected the treatment of leprosy with that for chronic dysentery and other forms of 'plague', had been isolating their infected ships since 1348 and Pisa had established the first quarantine station ashore in 1464. Marseille, too, had been placing plague victims out of bounds for forty days (hence the word *quarantine*) since the fourteenth century.

Henry's solution, however, was less sophisticated. He simply demobilised his fleet, in accordance with the instructions he had issued before

Le Tréport, permitting redundant seamen who were on the verge of sickness to drift off into the wider community. And so the disease lingered on into the following year. The Council was informed towards the end of April 1546 that men were dying in several ships, including the *Great Venetian* when, on the 26th of that month, 'two that were well at 7am died by 10am, and 14 fell sick'. The unfortunate Sir William Woodhouse, who was ill in mid-July, appears to have suffered a second bout nine months later when he was 'carried ashore very sore sick', and so was another of Henry's chief captains, Sir William Tyrrell, who was disembarked at Margate.

Dudley, as bidden, returned to court, to continue his duties as Lord Admiral ashore, and Seymour was left in operational command, such as it now was, wherever he might be needed. Early in October he received a signal from the Privy Council sitting at Windsor, telling him 'to enter some clean and uninfected vessel and sail with the whole navy to Portsmouth, there to lie within the haven or else between Chadderton's bulwark and the town, in case the enemy attempt anything thereabouts'. In fact, the danger was much more on the French side of the Channel and in particular it was the continuing threat to Boulogne. From the wreckage of his great invasion strategy, Francis still hoped to salvage something by repossessing his stolen property, which had been one of Europe's principal ports since the Romans were here and constructed the pharos – over a hundred feet high and known as the Tour d'Ordre to the sixteenth-century French, as the Old Man to the English – which helped to guide vessels safely across the Channel to Dover, where they had built its twin. Now the Old Man was fortified with a surrounding bastion and had significant military value for whoever occupied it.

A key to success or failure in any siege of the new English colony was not only the topography of the town itself, which was built on two levels, but the fact that both the Haute Ville and Basse Boulogne around the harbour were something over a mile from the sea, which meant that he who held the banks of the River Liane also controlled all shipping entering and leaving the port. That was why Francis had planned to sink blockships loaded with stone at the river's mouth, and why Sir Thomas Seymour must above all make sure it didn't happen. The defence of Calais was easier than trying to secure Boulogne because it was much closer to the sea, though both towns were protected to some extent by adjacent marshes and, in Boulogne's case, these so increased the range at which French artillery had to operate from the nearest high ground, that most of its fire was ineffective. 'The Frenchman's new fort', according to William Paget, when the first of their two watch towers went up across the river, 'shows proudly, but is so distant that there a white horse can hardly be discerned from a black, and their shot is only troublesome for the noise'.

For twelve months now, the English had been doggedly repairing the damage done during their own assault, and such gaps as there were in the walls had mostly been closed by earthworks held in place by stakes and hurdles; but what should have been a permanent solution was to become a long-standing headache because every winter, frost and other bad weather would damage the earthworks so much that work on them had to be done all over again in the spring. Henry, of course, took a very close and proprietorial interest in the refortification of the prize he himself had seized, insisting that every small plan must be submitted to him for approval before it was carried out, interfering at every turn in a manner that probably made John Dudley (now at his elbow in the Privy Council) grunt with recognition. When the question of covered galleries running inside the earthwork surrounding the Old Man came up, the supervisors were informed that

> his Majesty's pleasure is you shall make them of timber, and board them on the outside with board of two inches thick, and make so full of holes as a great number may stand and shoot out of them at one time, and to cover the roof of the same with board; which his Majesty doth not only take for a wonderful force but also a great commodity and strength for the holding up of your mounts, if special regard be had in the making of them so as you fasten the timber of your galleries with long timber into your mounts.

A master carpenter couldn't have put it more fluently.

It was on the King's orders that in July 1545 a new fortification was started halfway between the lower town and the Old Man, to minimise the risk of the latter being cut off in a surprise attack, and this was referred to as the Young Man. It proved to be a laborious process that would not be finished until a couple of years after Henry's death, because in its early stages it shared priority with an equally pressing need to build a stone mole that would stop the harbour from silting up, and to fortify the inlet at Ambleteuse (another Newhaven to the English) just along the coast towards Cap Gris-Nez. Lying at the mouth of the very minor but disproportionately deep River Slack, and protected by sandhills, it was picked out for use as an alternative haven if Francis did manage to blockade Boulogne. Though small to start with, it enjoyed more than two fathoms of water at high tide and its harbour proved to be a very safe refuge for shipping in the vilest weather. The following spring, it accommodated fifty vessels that had come across from Dover loaded with victuals, ordnance and tents for its growing garrison. Dudley was so impressed after inspecting it when the work was well advanced, that he told Paget it would be 'the handsomest tide haven that his Majesty shall have on that side of the sea'.

Although the broken walls of Boulogne were repaired by the mid-summer of 1545, other work proceeded slowly because it, too, was affected by plague. Its workforce was shipped over from England from the beginning of the year with an inducement of tuppence a day extra in pay for volunteers, but they were inadequately provided for from the start. The labourers were quartered in tents and their victuals left much to be desired, herring intended for consumption in Lent still being thrust at them two months later at Pentecost and, being by then half rotten at least, this was probably where the dysentery began. Of 1,200 workmen who had arrived in January, only 300 were still fit enough for duty six months later; the rest had either died or been sent away to recover and soldiers had been told to take their place. The sickness did not discriminate in choosing its victims, however. On the day that Dudley's ships were playing catch-as-catch-can with d'Annebault's off Shoreham, Boulogne's Governor, who had become Lord Poynings, was in bed with a serious bout of the bloody flux, and three days later he was dead of it.[3]

It was doubtless the epidemic that resulted in a great emphasis being placed on hygiene when the town acquired a set of English by-laws the following year, with their insistence that no-one must throw into the 'streets or other places (to the nuisance of his neighbours, or whereby any evil smell or corruption might ensue) any chamber pots', which must instead be taken to a place in the fields appointed by the constables; and anyone with a dead horse had to bury it seven feet deep. Nor was plague the only one of the town's domestic problems in 1545. By mid-August none of the garrison or the labourers had been paid for four months, and the Council of Boulogne which ran the place until Poynings' successor

---

3 Six days after that, Henry suffered a much greater blow, when Charles Brandon, Duke of Suffolk, his boyhood friend, his brother-in-law and his closest confidant, died suddenly from what sounds like a heart attack the morning after attending a meeting of the Privy Council in Guildford.

was named – he would be Thomas Howard's son Henry, Earl of Surrey – was having difficulty in staving off full-blown mutiny. Things were already bad enough to warrant the execution of 'one Sharpe, of the Guard, chief stirrer of the business' in the market place of the Haute Ville, which caused four of his mates to desert and join the enemy. To reduce the likelihood of further trouble, members of the Council began nervously to keep night watches themselves.

And then there was the perpetual menace of the French. German mercenaries who had been promised to reinforce the English garrison in August never appeared, because Francis offered them more money while they were on the way and they quickly changed step. By then, the enemy was said to have some 20,000 infantry and 1,000 of horse facing the town on the far side of its river, while pioneers made steady progress in building the Fort de Châtillon and its smaller outpost, the Fort d'Outreau, which would provide excellent springboards from which attacks could be laun-ched. At the same time, the Council was braced for more French to arrive on its doorstep, having picked up a rumour that the Dauphin would shortly be bringing another 12,000 footmen and 3,000 of cavalry to make an assault on the town. He never did turn up, but that didn't lessen the strain of expecting him. The French, in fact, appear to have spread an amount of disinformation in order to keep the English as anxious as possible. Ten of their horsemen who came within range were taken, and imparted the news that they were scouting out the ground for an extension of their existing camp, that someone had already been chosen to lead the burning of Boulogne, and that reinforcements would soon arrive in Etaples from the sea. And so the summer turned into autumn, which gave way to the onset of winter, and nothing much happened apart from sporadic cannon fire, which did no harm but kept everyone on his toes.

Henry Howard arrived to take charge in September, a swaggering young man, not yet thirty, who had all his father's arrogance but none of his astuteness. He very quickly made his mark with one or two sorties that impeded the French building programme, but then he got on the wrong side of his sovereign by suggesting that he ought to have his wife with him in Boulogne for the improvement of his morale, at which the King's secretary tartly observed that in the circumstances and in the foreseeable future, 'which will bring some trouble and disquietness unmeet for women's imbecilities', Howard had better forget it. Otherwise, the English waited and watched for signs of French movement, for their own reinforcements to arrive and, as ever, for their victuals to turn up: by

December, even fish was becoming scarce. But well before then, the Privy Council had come to the conclusion that Boulogne was costing much more in money and other resources than it was really worth: in fact, £47,166 18s 3½d would be spent on it and the works at Ambleteuse between its capture and Henry's death (and much more would be spent by his son before it was restored to France). The Council recommended relinquishing this extension of English territory because it was too expensive to maintain, for no return at all apart from prestige; but Henry would have none of it.

At least the threat of invasion by the Scots had receded. In early August 1545 they were reported to be closing in on the Borders, which galvanised Edward Seymour into getting in his retaliation first. He took an army up from Newcastle to Kelso and there was a nasty incident at its abbey, which was sheltering about a hundred non-combatants, only a dozen of whom were monks, but all refusing to surrender. So cannon was brought up to smash a way into the building and Seymour let loose some Spanish mercenaries he had with him, to drive the Scots into the tower, where they were confined overnight to ponder their fate. A small handful managed to climb down ropes at the back and escape, but in the morning the Spanish went in and slew all the rest. Seymour's troops then proceeded to Melrose, whose abbey they simply burnt; likewise the one at Dryburgh and over a dozen villages in the neighbourhood. Then they moved on to Jedburgh and incinerated the town, its abbey and every community within two miles. After that they marched home across good agricultural land at its harvest time, which they torched as they went along. Seymour compared this effort favourably with the punishment he had inflicted on Edinburgh seventeen months earlier. 'The country', he reported, 'is very fair, and so good a corn country and such plenty of the same as we have not seen the more plenteous in England; and undoubtedly there is burnt a wonderful deal of corn, for by reason that the year hath been so forward, they had done much of their harvest and made up their corn in stacks about their houses, or had it lying in shocks in their fields.' With their crops laid waste in ashes and the prospect of a hungry winter ahead, the Scots would not trouble the English again until after Henry was gone.

XVII
THE FINAL PIECES

The French and the English, in fact, were drifting towards peace again even before the beginning of the new year, although they continued to make threatening noises and move their forces around belligerently at the same time. Tentative feelers were extended by the French as early as October and both the Emperor and the German Protestants offered to mediate between Henry and Francis, but too many people were playing double games for headway to be made just then: Henry was even prepared to deceive his own negotiators, telling Paget (who was in contact with the Germans) not to inform his old friend Stephen Gardiner (who was talking to the Emperor) what was the state of play at his end of the table. The chief sticking point was the restoration of Boulogne at once, and neither the English nor the French monarch was ready to budge an inch on that. For the time being, therefore, Henry was content to let Gardiner make quite sure that Charles did not form an alliance with Francis, and this was achieved in January 1546, when a new treaty was concluded at Utrecht between the Bishop and his imperial counterparts, after someone floated the idea that the young Prince Edward and Charles's Spanish niece might make a marriage that would improve the stability of Europe.

But that month also brought a minor disaster for the English, when Henry Howard – still pining for his wife and composing verses to lament her absence – led 600 infantry and 200 of horse to St Etienne au Mont, beside the river a couple of miles upstream of Boulogne, to stop a French force that was said to be a reinforcement for the Fort de Châtillon. When the English attacked, their cavalry got the better of the French horse, but their foot soldiers took a beating and only managed to escape by making for the river and leaving 205 dead behind, together with several standards, which was considered even more disgraceful to their King's precious honour. As a result, Howard was recalled to England and Edward Seymour, having put down the Scots, was sent over the water to take charge in France, where he at once began planning to seize Etaples, a few miles down the coast in the estuary of the Canche. This was another fine haven where 'at full sea there is half a fathom more water...than at Dieppe', and both Seymour and Dudley thought it could be made even better by the installation of a mole to give protection against winds coming at it from NW or WNW. Even as it was, it dominated the coast between the Seine estuary and Boulogne so much that, according to the two Englishmen, without it the French could not victual from the sea their forces anywhere between Ardres (on the edge of the Calais Pale) and Montreuil (further up the Canche), 'nor keep an army in the field without aid of the Emperor's countries'. That was what they argued to Henry to justify its capture, adding that they wrote thus 'not to hinder an honourable peace, which seems the thing most necessary for Christendom', but so that their King might be better placed to annoy the French 'and thereby the sooner have peace'. This perfectly expressed the disingenuous mood in which the English approached the negotiating table when discussions took a more serious turn in the spring than they had done in the autumn.

Until that happened and even afterwards, while negotiations were still taking place, it was naval business as usual between the two countries, in the Channel and elsewhere. At the end of February a French vessel was lurking off the North Foreland, hoping to seize something in transit between the Thames and Zealand; and at the same time a report came in from the Continent that 'five small ships of war' were preparing to sail from Dieppe, to 'run into every creek and wait for our merchants' ships'. They had already taken a vessel conveying powder and ordnance from the Tower for the English forces under Seymour, as well as a rich cargo of general merchandise, and this 'has given them an appetite for more'. There was a lull in March, but by April the French were active enough along the East Anglian coast for the Privy Council to query Dudley about a shortage of wafters there, so he detailed the hired *Trinity Smith* (160 tuns, Capt. Gilbert Grice) as a permanent escort for the victuallers shuttling between the Thames and Dover, Calais and Boulogne, and he sent two other vessels to patrol the same area.

In quick succession a number of incidents filled that month and continued into May. Henry Howard's brother, Lord William Howard, was cruising off Beachy Head in *Great Venetian* when he came across a convoy that included some vessels of 500–600 tuns which he thought would be 'meet to serve the King', as well as an 800-tunner laden with pitch and masts on its maiden voyage. A strong nor'easterly drove them on to Portsmouth where they took refuge, and Howard made sure they didn't leave the anchorage, after requesting the Privy Council 'to send some men of skill to view the hulks' and decide which were worth pressing into the fleet. On the other side of the Channel, three French vessels laden with victuals for Etaples were seized and their crews were interrogated about the condition of the little port and any naval presence there. In retaliation, eleven French galleys appeared off Ambleteuse a few days later and bombarded it though, so Edward Seymour told the King, they did no damage to either people or ships, and after the English had fired back the Frenchmen stood out to sea and out of range. But he also had a less welcome tale to tell. One of Henry's newest pinnaces – probably *Saker* (60 tuns, Capt. John Burley) – was chased by three other French galleys further up the coast and grounded on the shore, whereupon her captain, master and entire crew of sixty 'like varlets shamefully forsook her'. Seymour himself led some troops to the scene 'and would have rescued her had they held out but half an hour; but they ran away towards Calais'.

Just as momentous, but much more acceptable, was a protracted series of actions across a couple of days, which began at three in the morning when a French foist sailed (or maybe pulled, for the type was a form of galleass) into the mouth of Boulogne's river and snatched three English hoys loaded with victuals. Four shallops which Henry had but recently built went out in pursuit and recaptured two of the prizes. Early the next afternoon, Lord William Howard and the squadron he was leading encountered ten French galleys in the vicinity but well out to sea. The English went in pursuit and fired a number of salvoes without doing any detectable damage; but then the wind died, they were becalmed, and the galleys rowed away. At eight the following morning, however, the two groups clashed again in an engagement where each side at one time or another was in pursuit of its enemy, the English having the final say as the day was drawing to a close when *Anne Gallant*, *Grand Mistress*, *Greyhound* (160 tuns), *Phoenix* (60 tuns) and *Salamander* – the first three all built within the previous twelve months, and *Phoenix* even more recently bought in Henry's last wave of naval expansion – closed in on one of the Frenchmen, the little *Phoenix* grappling with her until *Anne*

Gallant could come up and force a surrender. The prize was the *Galley Blanchard*, whose 140 rowers ('every man naked with his oar in his hand') may all have been prisoners of war or simply pressed men, with names indicating origins in Naples, Palermo, Biscay, Valencia, Majorca, Portugal and perhaps Genoa, which were not normal catchment areas for French naval recruitment. Her acquisition meant that Henry's navy for a brief space boasted two genuinely classic galleys in the Mediterranean tradition, though the English did not enjoy her as long as *Galley Subtle*, which was still in service in 1552, whereas the new vessel was returned to the French in 1547 and remained in their fleet until at least 1562.

That action took place on 21 May, when the two countries were only three days from declaring a ceasefire and less than three weeks away from signing their Treaty of Camp – appropriately close to the place where Henry and Francis had repeatedly hugged each other in fraternity over a quarter of a century earlier at the Field of the Cloth of Gold. The talks which might have started in October actually got under way after Dudley rather mysteriously used a Venetian merchant based in London, named Francesco Bernardo, to carry a message at the beginning of April to Claude d'Annebault, offering safe conduct to Ardres, where talks could then take place. The two men, each of them his nation's highest-ranking naval officer, thus became the principal negotiators and appear to have got on much better than might have been expected, given the hostile nature of their recent relationship. Dudley told Sir William Petre, one of Henry's Principal Secretaries of State, that he thought his counterpart was 'a right proper man, and very gentle and well spoken, and very fine in his apparel', while the Frenchman indicated that he had rather parley with Dudley than with anyone else. This did not mean that d'Annebault was anything other than a wily opponent, however: when Dudley pointed out to him that the King was better furnished with fighting ships this year than last, the French Admiral affected not to have heard and quickly switched the conversation to falconry.

As in October, so in May, the principal matter needing settlement was the future of Boulogne. The French offered 200,000 crowns for its return at once, but Dudley claimed that his King had spent 'eight millions of gold in the war', and they began to haggle over the price. 'All Christendom have not so much money', the scornful French replied when the figure was named, 'We may as well offer you again 100 crowns.' At this point a despatch arrived from London to say that sixty French vessels had put to sea, and Dudley told d'Annebault that, unless he recalled them, the

Englishman would have to leave the negotiating table to take command of his own fleet. D'Annebault prevaricated, so Dudley carried out his threat and spent several days with his ships, chasing some French craft into Dunkirk and taking one of them. This caused the Admiral of France to back-pedal rapidly, apologising for any offence and sending a fishing smack to tell his naval vessels to withdraw. He then made a great show of indignation at the capture of the *Galley Blanchard*, 'saying that his honour is more touched than ever it was', but he got a dusty reply from the Privy Council, which told Dudley to remind him of recent French infractions of normal negotiating etiquette, which included brazenly taking three victuallers at the entrance to Ambleteuse and burning houses ashore. 'These brags upon the seas', the Council concluded, 'and now of late upon the land, are not the ways to further this treaty.' Furthered it was, however, to an agreed compromise, in spite of French attempts late in the day to include a number of extra clauses, and Henry's meddling at long distance right to the very last word. The agreement was that the English would return Boulogne to its rightful owners in eight years' time, in exchange for two million crowns; and they would not make war on the Scots so long as these themselves didn't break the peace.

Amity was restored with the usual extravagant gestures. Three days after the treaty was made, Henry became godfather-by-proxy to Francis's new grandchild, and when Claude d'Annebault came to England to ratify the treaty in August he was treated not much less handsomely than royalty itself. He arrived in the Thames estuary in his flagship *Sacré*, which was escorted by twelve galleys, and off Queenborough the Lord Warden of the Cinque Ports and various gentlemen of Kent went aboard his vessel to greet him 'with French wines and viands', before he proceeded upstream to Greenwich. The order of the day detailing the arrangements beforehand specified that 'All castles and block-houses along the water where he shall pass to be furnished with ordnance and shoot triumphantly', and this was rigidly obeyed. After an overnight stay in Greenwich the Admiral sailed on up to Limehouse, where the Mayor and aldermen of London greeted him. There he spent another night before continuing by easy stages (that is, with another stopover, at Mortlake) to Hampton Court, where Henry was awaiting him. Nothing was overlooked in the preparations for this diplomatic fanfare, which included much more than half the nobility of both countries and many ladies from the English court, among them the two princesses and Anne of Cleves; it was made perfectly clear which horses should have footcloths, how many banqueting tables there would be and how many people should sit at each, also how many people would be serving them, what food they were to consume and what presents should be offered by the City of London to its guest ('two goodly pairs of flagons, one all gilt, the other parcel gilt, filled with...marchpanes [marzipan] sugar loaves, suckettes, wafers and spices to the value of £100'). Someone had even discreetly enquired well in advance, whether d'Annebault preferred to sit with all his entourage or 'apart, privately, with a few'.

It all went exactly according to what was a typically meticulous Tudor plan. *Sacré* was rowed serenely past the Tower of London, 'where was shot a terrible peal of ordnance', and at Hounslow the Admiral was greeted by the eight-year-old Prince Edward, who made a speech in fluent Latin and showed an impressive ability to handle a horse. On then to Hampton Court, where a rigmarole of greeting by the new Lord Chancellor, Thomas Wriothesley, and the Privy Council occupied d'Annebault's first day, before he was taken into the King's presence on the second. They attended Mass together and, indeed, signed the peace treaty in the palace chapel before embarking on the customary round of banquets, masques, dances, hunting trips and other pleasures. And when it was time to go home, Henry was as open-handed as ever in his disbursement of gifts, sending d'Annebault on his way with a cupboard full of plate worth £1,200 as well as horses and greyhounds, with smaller souvenirs for each of his staff: 'and thus they, laden with more riches than they had brought,' as Edward Hall carefully pointed out some years later, 'returned into France'.

At the age of fifty-five Henry was becoming old, and his health was failing steadily, bouts of fever being a normal and quite frequent occurrence now, though they did not always herald something more alarming: when he was indisposed in March he still felt able to pass the time by playing cards with Dudley and other cronies. Nor was he brought low enough to lose his appetite for naval expansion, which was greater in the last two years of his life than at any other comparable period. The sixteen new acquisitions he made in 1545 all but equalled the number of vessels that went into the royal service in the best previous year, 1512, while 1546 outstripped both of them, by seeing no fewer than twenty new craft added to the fleet. Nothing comparable to *Henry Grâce à Dieu* or *Mary Rose* was built in these years, the *Anne Gallant* (450 tuns) of 1545 only just surpassing *Grand Mistress* (420 tuns); while in the following year *Antelope* and *Hart* (both 300 tuns) went down the slips. These vessels were all four-masted galleasses, each with a bank of oars to augment their sails, each with most of its ordnance mounted for broadside gunnery, and each with a stubby metal spike on the end of its beakhead, which could in theory be used for ramming in the ancient tradition. The great majority of craft that left Deptford and other English shipyards at this time, however, were the thirteen rowbarges, none of them over 20 tuns (and all but two with a crew of forty), which made their appearance in the last full year of Henry's reign. There were also four pinnaces of 80 tuns and a fifth slightly smaller than that.

But in addition to those vessels which were newly built specifically for the King's navy, he also increased his fleet by buying ships that had already sailed in someone else's service. One was the *Matthew Gonson*, which was commissioned in 1545 after being purchased (or otherwise acquired after her owner's suicide) from William Gonson's heirs. Others were bought from Hanseatic traders and alternative sources, among them the *Jesus of Lübeck* (600 tuns), the *Struse of Danzig* (400 tuns), the *Mary Hamburg* (400 tuns) and the *Christopher of Bremen* (400 tuns), all of which had already been on hire for twelve months. Not all the deals that Henry was interested in making were finalised, however. The Bristol merchant John Smith was prepared to part with his *Trinity Smith* in April 1546 in exchange for 100 fother (cartloads) of lead and £200, but the sale evidently fell through, because the vessel never appeared in any subsequent list of the King's ships: perhaps she had not lived up to Dudley's expectations in her escort duties. A predatory eye seems to have been cast over certain foreign vessels berthed in English ports whenever something tempting turned up. Representations were made by a member of the Emperor's Council for the release of *le Salvator* (700 tuns), owned by some burgesses of Danzig and lying at Bristol, with a persuasive rider that 'She can do the King little service, as he has so many others, and she draws much water and is difficult to steer'.

The expansion of the fleet was only the most obvious manifestation of the English naval advance during Henry's declining years. Much more important for the future of naval development in England (and later in the United Kingdom) were the structural changes that were made at this time in the administration of the fleet. This was nothing less than 'the establishment. . .of a system of administration which remained essentially unchanged until 1832'. And although a highly respected voice from the end of the nineteenth century maintained that 'Of all others, the year 1545 best marks the birth of the English naval power; it is the year that most clearly displays the transition from oars to sails, and it was probably in this very year the first great sailing Admiral the world ever saw came obscurely into being' (he meant Francis Drake), modern experts put their money, rather less romantically, on 1546 because that was when the most significant administrative strides were made.

Historically, the business of organising and running the navy at the (usually erratic) whim of the monarch depended too much on people who had other pressing responsibilities which had nothing at all to do with maritime affairs. In Henry's time there was first of all Thomas Wolsey, his Lord Chancellor, who was so greedy for power and its emoluments that he maintained control of everything serving his purpose, whether or not he was good at or even interested in it. His successor as the power behind the throne, Lord Privy Seal Thomas Cromwell, was above all things an exceedingly efficient organiser across a much wider range of matters than Wolsey, very typically paying attention to the smallest naval detail that landed on his desk – and, vitally, making quite sure that nothing at all ever escaped his attention: William Gonson was made well aware that the Lord Privy Seal always kept track of what he was up to. But Cromwell often took the initiative himself: when he heard that part of the wine fleet was inexplicably detained in Bordeaux, he dashed off a quick memo to Stephen Gardiner to do something about it, and another to Arthur Plantagenet, Governor of Calais at the time (with some naval experience), to organise a wafter for a merchant who wanted protection for his ship in the Channel; though both instructions were written when Cromwell was almost single-handedly preparing the legislation and doing a lot of the other spadework necessary to begin the Dissolution of the Monasteries.

Two years later he personally appointed his friend Stephen Vaughan as the King's agent in the Low Countries, and charged him with the specific duty of procuring naval stores among other things. Just after the breach with Rome, when the question arose of what to do with the tax money that had hitherto gone into the papal coffers, it was Cromwell who quickly suggested that it should now be diverted into the provision of seaward defences. Characteristically, his painstaking mind drew up a list of all Henry's achievements since he came into the King's service, and in the middle of thirty-one items he noted that his sovereign 'new made the *Mary Rose*, the *Peter Pomegranate*, the *Lyon*, the *Katherine Galley*, the *Bark*, the *Minion*, the *Sweepstake*... He has purchased woods beside Portsmouth in Hampshire sufficient for the new making of the

Henry Grâce à Dieu and the *Great Galley*'.[1] He overlooked nothing, but some things had to be delegated, most notoriously in the use of Gardiner – whose heart, understandably, was more in saying the daily offices than in the provision of stockfish and beer – as the man in charge of victualling the fleet while he was still a functioning bishop and otherwise well out of his depth. Gardiner's predecessor in the see of Winchester, Richard Fox, had been saddled with the same secular responsibility under a similar handicap.

In such circumstances, naval administration could scarcely be other than a disjointed and very unreliable business. Under the traditional regime, even the long-standing office of Keeper (or Clerk) of the King's Ships was defined so vaguely that although Robert Brigandine – whom Henry inherited from his father – played a part in royal shipbuilding and in the allotment of naval expenditure, he had no role at all when the fleet was put on a war footing. The first signs of improvement, as we already know, occurred when Thomas Spert and William Gonson came into the royal service in the 1520s, bringing their different experience in maritime matters to bear on the navy. But even the division of responsibility between two such well-qualified officials had its limitations, which became increasingly obvious when, for reasons that are still not entirely clear, more and more real authority came into Gonson's hands, so that eventually the King's navy was effectively supervised except at sea by him alone; hence the crisis that followed his sudden death in 1544. It has, in fact, been proposed that what happened afterwards was largely pre-cipitated by the suicide, because John Dudley as Lord Admiral of England had to produce very quickly a substitute mechanism that did not contain the dangerously built-in flaw of too much power and respons-ibility in the person of any one man. What was needed was a body of knowledgeable individuals with well-defined and guaranteed separate roles, who collectively 'ran' the navy in collusion with its principal sea-faring officers.

In 1545 the first signs of such a development appeared, the earliest being the Governor of Hull's mention on 11 March that he had received letters 'from the Vice-admiral of England with other of the King's majesty's council of his marine'. At about the same time there were

1 Cromwell was not claiming credit for these things (as Wolsey almost certainly would have done), but simply noting them. Though he entered the royal service (on Wolsey's staff) very early in Henry's reign, he did not reach high office until he joined the Privy Council in 1531, two years after the Cardinal was deposed.

alternative references to 'the Chief Officers of the Admiralty', and in July a long and general memorandum to do with 'The War', annotated and corrected by Dudley, referred to seven individuals under the sub-heading 'For sea matters'. They were Sir Thomas Clere, Sir William Woodhouse, John Wynter, Robert Legge, William Broke, Benjamin Gonson and Richard Howlett. The qualifications of Clere, Woodhouse and Gonson are already known to us, while, of the others, Wynter was a seagoing Bristol merchant, Legge had spent thirty years in the Iceland fishery, Broke had commanded a squadron at sea, and Howlett had been Keeper of the Deptford Storehouse since January, after spending the previous three years as assistant to the Clerk Controller: so between them, they 'knew as much as anyone about the management of ships in port and at sea'. In their new lives as the Council for Marine Causes, Clere became Lieutenant (and so Dudley's deputy as the man in charge), Woodhouse was Master of the Ordnance for the King's Ships, Wynter was Treasurer, Legge was Clerk Controller, Broke was Surveyor and Rigger, Gonson was Clerk of the King's Ships, and Howlett was Clerk of the Store, working under the Controller; but the council had to be reshuffled after John Wynter died at the end of the year, as a result of which Legge became Treasurer, Broke became Controller, Gonson took over surveying and rigging, and Howlett became Clerk of the King's Ships.[2]

The original memo had spoken of these men's responsibilities as if they were required to function on no more than an *ad hoc* basis in order to prepare against invasion: having to decide what ships were ready to be 'trimmed and rigged' and whether this should be done at Portsmouth or elsewhere; having to send three more vessels to join the Dover patrol against the French, and to 'know what other ships be within the realm meet to serve'; having, inevitably, to make arrangements for their victualling. They also had to invigilate certain matters ashore – the state of blockhouses and their 'furniture', the positioning of beacons to warn of imminent landings, etc, – and they were expected to assess possible candidates for subordinate positions, 'men of reputation and such as shall be agreeable to them, to assist them in case of necessity'.

2 Master of the Ordnance for the King's Ships was a separation of naval responsibility from the Ordnance Board, whose headquarters were in the Tower of London and which had existed in some shape or form since the fifteenth century, though it had only acquired that name in the sixteenth. Until 1545 it was this body, under its Master of the Ordnance, which provided all the weapons for the armed forces of the Crown both on land and at sea. Afterwards, though the Tower was still the source of armament for the fleet, it was Woodhouse and his successors who decided what was needed and where it should be deployed.

GREAT HARRY'S NAVY

But by April 1546 the Council for Marine Causes was obviously seen as a permanent fixture, plainly implied in the patent appointing Robert Legge Treasurer. He was granted certain monies annually for the upkeep of his office and two assistants, together with a stipend of 6s 8d 'for every day that the said Robert Legge shall and be employed either by sea or land, only for such business as shall be needful and expedient to be used and dispatched in or concerning the same office of Treasureship'. Henceforth, he and his successors would handle all the naval accounts and be responsible for every penny spent. What's more, Wynter and Legge between them were allotted a total of £22,214 in the twelve months after May 1545, of which £19,000 was to be deployed as they in turn thought fit, with only £3,124 coming to the naval treasury with strings attached to it. They and the other members of the council were thus being given comprehensive responsibility for the first time, always keeping the overall state of the navy in mind within an agreed budget; and they could be sure that they need never dig into their own pockets to get a particular job done when necessary, but would always be guaranteed funds from the King's Treasury. None of them would ever need to claim, as William Gonson did in 1538, that the Crown owed him £2,142 10s.

And so the great step was taken, from which it would be impossible to return to the old ways. Importantly for the stability of this new organism, its officers were far better-paid than any past administrators of whatever rank, a powerful disincentive to even the milder forms of corruption. William Gonson had received an annuity of £18 5s and nothing more unless he invoiced the King for itemised sums to pay for particular tasks, but Robert Legge received £220 13s 4d in salary and day-to-day expenses. The best-paid official in the new order was obviously the Lieutenant, who received a stipend of £100 a year, 1s 8d each day for his two clerks, 10s a day travel expenses and £10 a year for 'botehire'. The Master of Naval Ordnance came immediately after him in the pecking order with £66 13s 4d for himself, 2s 4d a day for three clerks, 6s 8d for travel and £8 for boathire; and the pay scale diminished further until, at the end of the line, the Clerk of the Ships received £33 6s 8d in stipend and £100 for expenses. But even he was wealthy beyond any expectations that could have been entertained by anyone doing his job before 1545. Gone were the days when officials were paid a pittance and given certain perquisites, all based upon an assumption that they would profit hugely from their position in their private affairs. The only perk the new men enjoyed was the prize money they stood to collect whenever they put in

284

time at sea, which was no different from the expectations of any other ship's officer in the royal service.

The supervision of the navy would progressively evolve from this great turning point in its administrative history. By 1549 the council was meeting regularly at either Portsmouth, Deptford, Woolwich or in premises on Tower Hill, always with the Lieutenant sitting as chairman. The year after that, the one defect in the original establishment was remedied when a new position, General Surveyor of Victuals for the Sea, was added to the council, its first occupant being Edward Baeshe, who had long and honest experience of the business as a purveyor, and he held the appointment until his retirement thirty-six years later. Before long, the council was more commonly referred to as the Navy Board, as it still was in 1660, when Samuel Pepys became its Clerk of the Acts at a salary of £350 a year with a house thrown in and two men working under him, by which time the board met twice a week at its office in Seething Lane, just below Tower Hill. Essentially, Pepys's job at first was to keep the minutes of these meetings and to take charge of all naval records, but through sheer hard work and rapidly acquired knowledge of his new profession he subsequently became the board's most important official.

By the middle of the seventeenth century there was a clear distinction between the Navy Board and the Admiralty, the former being responsible for the administration of the fleet, for getting it to sea in a proper condition to fulfil its duties, the latter consisting of the Lord Admiral and his principal seagoing officers, who were in charge of naval policy, command and discipline; eventually there would simply be the all-embracing Admiralty. But whatever name it came under, at every stage of its transition from the Council for Marine Causes, this was an organisation without equal for almost two and a half centuries, certainly outside the Mediterranean's two great maritime nations. The English military had nothing like it and the Dutch, a growing naval power which possessed a national fleet funded by central government from 1653, would not know a similar organisation until 1795. Until the first Bastille Day in 1789 overturned their social order, the French navy continued to be run by men such as Claude d'Annebault had been before his appointment as Admiral, landed and cultivated *seigneurs*, often of an engaging eccentricity, who knew how to sit a horse and charge an enemy, but nothing at all of the sea until they were suddenly required to take more than a passing interest in it.

By the time the Council for Marine Causes was a fully functioning apparatus, it was apparent that Henry VIII's life didn't have much further to run. He had done some hunting after d'Annebault went home, but could only mount his horse with the assistance of blocks that were raised higher than usual from the ground; and when he set off for Guildford in September he cut short his journey because he was too exhausted to go on and had to return to Windsor. He was said to be suffering from a cold that month, though Van der Delft thought it was probably something more serious, and in October the King was so unwell that he was unable to greet the new French ambassador, Odet de Selve. In the middle of November he moved to his palace at Whitehall to take medicinal baths (part of his annual health programme in recent years, it was said) but by now his doctors were in attendance with unheard-of frequency: between August and December their charges for medicines and other necessities rose by 500 per cent.

It was in December that the final physical collapse began, after he took his last exercise on the 7th, though his mind and aggressive instincts still functioned as sharply as ever. He disputed a private land sale with Gardiner that month and, as a result, forbade the Bishop from ever entering the privy chamber again. He also approved of Henry Howard's downfall and that of his father Thomas Howard, who had served the King throughout his reign, including twelve years as Lord Admiral of England. The young man had at last overreached himself so much – by hinting that when the King died, a suitable replacement would be ready and waiting within the Howard clan – that he was charged with treason, not so much because of his preposterous ambition but because he had anticipated the monarch's death, which was an extremely punishable offence. He brought down his father with him, though Thomas's end was to be much delayed. The younger Howard was beheaded in January 1547 and the older man should have followed him to the block but the King's death, in the early hours of the very day he was due to be executed, caused the sentence to be suspended indefinitely: he remained in the Tower throughout Edward VI's reign, was fully rehabilitated during Mary's, and did not die (naturally, and at home in his bed) until 1554, when he was eighty-one years old.

Had it not been for his ability to rally from the depths, Henry might have died before 1546 was out. Three days after taking his last exercise, a crisis occurred in which he was fighting for his life, but the doctors pulled him out of it, and Van der Delft later reported that 'the King is so unwell that, considering his age and corpulence, he may not survive another

attack... If he succumb, there is slight hope of a change for the better.'
The court at Whitehall closed over Christmas, Catherine Parr and the
princesses having been instructed to spend it at Greenwich, with Edward
at another royal property in Hertfordshire. On St Stephen's Day, Henry
checked up on his will, in which he appointed John Dudley, Edward
Seymour, Thomas Cranmer and thirteen others as his executors and
Prince Edward's Privy Councillors, 'charging his said son to be ruled as
regards marriage and all affairs by the aforesaid Councillors until he has
completed his eighteenth year'. He also humbly bequeathed his soul to
God, 'Repenting his old life and resolved never to return to the like.'
There was another crisis in the New Year, and the doctors had to cauterise
his legs; but he surfaced from that painful operation, too, ordered saplings
for his garden, received both the French and the Spanish ambassadors,
and attended to some correspondence. In one letter he asked how 'the
new shallop' – possibly the *Trego Renneger* (20 tuns) – was handling at
sea; and one of the last communications he read was about weather
conditions in the Channel, where a vessel had just been overtaken off
Cap Gris-Nez by a sudden fog, which was so thick 'that they could hardly
see thrice the ship's length'.

The French had been nagging since the New Year for the return of
the *Galley Blanchard*, and only five days before Henry died, Paget
informed the Baron de la Garde that the King 'had ordered his admiral
to deliver the galley and the soldiers, but not the crew, who had been
promised their liberty, nor captain Pierre and three other gentlemen,
whose ransom had been promised to their takers'. Then Henry went into
his final relapse, after writing a farewell letter to Francis I, who was also
mortally ill, in which he couldn't resist telling his old rival that his time
was coming, too.[3] When the Englishman's end was clearly a matter of
days away, he said goodbye, weeping, to Catherine Parr, who was perhaps
the Queen he had been most comfortable with, though not excited by.
He died at two in the morning of Friday, 28 January, a few hours after all
the English ports were closed as a precaution against the movement of
any potential regicide, imposter or insurgent. News of his death was kept
from the country for a couple of days, until Edward Seymour had gone
to Hertford Castle to acknowledge the nine-year-old Prince Edward's

---

3 The French King's surprising (to say the least) response to Henry's letter was to authorise a
memorial service to him in Notre-Dame, which took place only ten days before Francis's own
death; and in it an orator 'praised his [Henry's] magnanimity, liberality and prudence, and
certain books published in his name'.

sovereignty and to bring him to the Tower, where he was publicly
proclaimed King.

Eighteen days before Henry died, de Selve and de la Garde had jointly
reported to Francis that 'Great war preparations (by sea chiefly) continue,
and are said to be against the Scots, although a great quantity of arms
and of pikes...is laden for Boulogne and Ambleteuse. The English may
attempt something upon the fort beside Boulogne, upon Ardres, or in
Normandy... In any attempt directed against Normandy, there will be
no lack of French pilots, for sixty are said to be in this King's service at
Hampton...' Next day, de Selve informed d'Annebault that he had been
approached by Jean Rotz, the Dieppois who had served Henry since 1542
as both pilot and Hydrographer Royal for 160 crowns (£40) a year, and
who now wanted to return home with his family. 'It would be useful', the
ambassador added, 'to obtain his services or at least deprive the King of
England of them.' Even in time of peace, the old Anglo-French reflexes
were still in good working order.

XVIII
THE LEGACY

Edward VI's inheritance did not give him the best start in sovereignty. His father had left him a financially crippled country, after spending between twice and three times his income for several years, after debasing the coinage to make ends meet, after exhausting all the considerable profit from dissolving the monasteries and still being deeply in debt, to the Antwerp moneylenders in particular. The religious issue which had rent the country a decade earlier was still a source of great tension within the realm, and the New Men of Reform – who had either helped to construct or merely applauded Henry's Church of England and were attracted to developments among the Continental Protestants – were not yet secure in their authority, which was still challenged by those who, while sometimes quite content to have parted from Rome, were still attached to many old ways of doing things: as, indeed, was Henry himself, with his enduring belief in transubstantiation. England was not quite the international pariah he had made her when he first snubbed the papacy, but she was still a country without reliable allies, a rather lost land which felt threatened by almost everyone. The French might turn nasty again at any moment, probably over Boulogne; the Emperor simply couldn't be trusted to keep his word, which meant that the Spanish, too, could easily become hostile. And then there were the everlasting Scots, who simply never gave up.

But at least Edward inherited a fine navy of *c*. fifty-four vessels supervised by men who understood what they were doing, from the moment a keel was laid down to the deployment of the fleet in time of war.[1] We know a great deal about these 'King's ships', including what each one of

1 See footnote to Appendix 1.

them looked like, because we can consult the Anthony Roll, a unique document which no-one even tried to emulate until the ebullient Fred T. Jane began to produce his *Fighting Ships* in 1897. The Roll's author was the Anthony Anthony who, as Clerk of the Ordnance, was expected to provide munitions quickly during the invasion scare of 1545. He was the son of a Fleming migrant who was granted denization, a limited form of citizenship, at the start of the sixteenth century, and he followed in his father's footsteps as a supplier of beer to Henry's forces before he became involved in ordnance: his life was consequently 'a combination of guns and beer', and he was still supplying the victual (from a brewhouse named The Ship) years after being appointed one of the Tower of London's gunners in 1533. He kept a chronicle of events from 1522 to Elizabeth's accession in 1558, which became valuable source material on which the historians John Stow and Raphael Holinshed later drew for some of their own work; but his major undertaking was the illustrated inventory of Henry VIII's navy which he presented to the King in 1546, probably in the hope that it might lead to some advancement, for Anthony had very early on in his career shown himself eager for royal approval. And it paid off when, in 1549, Edward made him Master Surveyor of the Ordnance for life, with authority in the Tower, in Calais, in Boulogne and elsewhere.

There were, in fact, three separate Anthony rolls, made from seventeen membranes of vellum, all including both text and pictures, all destined to survive the centuries.[2] Each of the fifty-eight ships Henry owned at the time of composition was surveyed in turn, with details of its tunnage, its complement, its ordnance, its munitions and its 'Habillementes for the warre' – which covered anything from coils of rope to nails 'of sundre sortes', and all of it (including the nails) very carefully counted. The illustrations were sketched with plummet (lead pencil) then painted in washes of many colours, and quite a lot of gold was also applied. The vessels are without exception pictured moving from left to right, or anchored in that direction, so that their sterns are prominently featured (a convention of marine art at this period because it showed off their heaviest armament to maximum effect). Each one is vividly dressed

---

2 The first and the third rolls were given to Samuel Pepys by Charles II and finished up in the Pepysian Library of Magdalene College, Cambridge, the second roll eventually finding a home in the British Library. But as a millennium project in 2000, the Navy Records Society produced, in association with both libraries, a most handsome illustrated volume which incorporated the material from all three inventories.

overall in a variety of flags, banners and pennants, and in the case of the galleys, rowbarges and galleasses it is possible to count the number of oars on the side facing the viewer; also the number of guns, though this feature of the illustrations in particular is thought to be 'of dubious reliability'. Anthony has also clearly flouted the rules of perspective for the sake of effect, he has painted to a formula which evidently developed as he went along, and some of the heraldry is probably a bit overdone. A modern expert opinion judges that the work is 'consistent with the abilities of a government official with a decent amateur grasp of form and colour'. Nevertheless, the Anthony Roll is an invaluable guide to the appearance and capability of Henry's warships in the dying fall of his reign.

The ships may now have been the juvenile King's Crown property, but they were at the disposal above all of Edward Seymour, whose brother Thomas (now Lord) Seymour succeeded Dudley as Lord Admiral of England a month after Henry's death. For Edward Seymour (now Duke of Somerset, an elevation he conferred upon himself) dominated the Privy Council, both as Edward VI's uncle and as Protector of the Realm and Governor of the King's Person: in short, he had become the English Regent. Protector Somerset would probably have liked to make peace with the Scots if only to reduce the financial burden on his exchequer, but he was confounded by the inexorable tenacity of the Auld Alliance, which was reactivated as soon as Francis died (probably of syphilis or gonorrhoea) at the end of March 1547; at whose funeral Claude d'Anne-bault was so upset that he could not bring himself to shout '*Vive le Roi!*', as he was supposed to do (solo and officially, as Admiral of France) after Normandy Herald had announced '*Le Roi est Mort!*', and the herald had to complete the exclamation for him.

Henri II, who succeeded Francis, did not share his father's obsession with Italian adventures, but only in what lay to the north; and a measurement of their different priorities is the way each reacted to Jean Rotz's desire to go home, and de Selve's endorsement of his request. Francis said Rotz could only return to Dieppe if the English and the French were at war again; Henri imposed no such restriction and England's former Hydrographer Royal was therefore back in France by the middle of June, having no doubt improved his chances by presenting the new French King with maps of England and Scotland, including charts he himself had made of their coastal waters. The situation in Scotland was ripe for French intervention by then, because eleven months earlier Cardinal

Beaton had been murdered at St Andrews by Henry VIII's Protestant sympathisers north of the Border, who then took possession of its castle and held it under siege. The murder had happened just as the English and the French were making their peace, which was still in place in the summer of 1547, when Henri II sent Leone Strozzi and a squadron of seventeen galleys up the North Sea to recapture the castle on behalf of the Catholic Scottish government. This they did, taking prisoners back to the Seine, one of them the preacher John Knox, who spent the next twelve months as a galley oarsman as a result, before being set free.

Neither the French nor the English were ready to go to war with each other over this incident, however, though both were after the same prize, for all the usual dynastic motives, in order to strengthen their political power: the English wanted Mary Stuart (then aged five) as a presumptive wife for Edward (aged nine); the French sought her for the new Dauphin, Francis (aged three). It was the English who made the first move in a clumsy attempt to bring about the union by forcing the Scots to submit. Edward Seymour personally led a force of 16,000 over the Border while, offshore, thirty-four warships and thirty-one other vessels cruised in support under the command of Edward Fiennes (Lord Clinton and Saye), who had been one of John Dudley's most efficient captains since 1544. Battle was joined in September at Pinkie, where the River Esk poured into the Firth of Forth near Musselburgh, and yet again the Scots suffered a crushing defeat, when their army of 23,000 received huge casualties and had 1,500 men taken prisoner. Three days later, Fiennes led his ships in an attack on the north side of the firth, where he pounded Kinghorn, captured the island of Inchcolm, and then sailed inland past Edinburgh along the narrowing channel to Blackness Castle and its attendant harbour, where he burned several vessels and recaptured two important prizes: one was the *Mary Willoughby*, which the Scots had taken from Henry VIII fourteen years earlier, the other the *Bark Ager* of Newcastle, which had been even longer in their hands.

This success was followed almost at once by the capture of Broughty Crag, much further up the Scottish coast, in the Firth of Tay, by warships commanded by Thomas Seymour and John Dudley's younger brother Andrew. An English garrison was installed there, but with the onset of winter it would have been retaken by the Scots if Thomas Wyndham had not sailed up from Newcastle with *Lion* (140 tuns), *Tiger* (200 tuns) and some smaller vessels in relief, forcing nearby Dundee to surrender while they were about it. But, so far from their bases, the English were in no position to hold onto these gains indefinitely and by the end of January 1548 Dundee was back in Scottish hands, shortly after seven French vessels had docked at Dumbarton on the west coast. They brought with them some soldiery, whose chief purpose was probably to turn raw moss-troopers – who had formed the bulk of the Scottish troops at Pinkie – into an efficient fighting force that would have some chance of defeating the English. The French were also there to press the Dauphin's claims on Mary Stuart in exchange for their own declaration of war. But although the betrothal was announced in July, followed by Mary's removal to France by the end of that month, full-scale hostilities between the French and the English were still a year away.

Instead, an undeclared state of war existed between them as they contended for Scottish submission on the one hand, and alliance on the other. There was a great deal of movement in order to reinforce the English garrisons at Broughty Crag and at Haddington, between Edinburgh and Dunbar, and a French task force of thirty transports escorted by nineteen men o'war managed to elude Fiennes's North Sea patrol and land some 6,000 troops at Leith. The English response to this was to muster 10,000 men in Berwick, ready to cross the Border again. But the rivals settled for stalemate on land, while things happened at sea. Fiennes was told to destroy the French shipping in Leith, and he did burn a dozen supply vessels there, though their consorts escaped yet again. A number of English vessels were captured off various coasts and in retaliation some West Country ships attacked French fishing boats homeward-bound from Newfoundland, seizing ten of them and driving others aground off Brittany. There was then the usual winter break, but the following spring brought more naval activity, with eleven warships ordered to patrol the Irish Sea, another eighteen in the Narrow Seas and a squadron under Thomas Wyndham stationed off the Tay estuary. Not until 14 August 1549 did the next step take place, but on that day the French made everything official by declaring war on their oldest enemy.

It lasted for barely seven months and in that time the focal point was no longer Scotland but the Channel coasts. A change in the English naval command also occurred, with John Dudley briefly resuming his role as Lord Admiral in succession to Thomas Seymour, who had just been executed for treason. One of two principal thrusts by the French consisted in a fleet of their galleys and transports commanded by Leone Strozzi sailing with 2,000 troops to attack the Channel Islands. To counter them, a much smaller squadron led by *Minion* (captained brilliantly by the late John Wynter's son, twenty-year-old William) left Portsmouth, engaged the French off Jersey, and as a result of superior gunfire destroyed or captured all Strozzi's galleys, killed 800 of his troops, and sent the surviving remnant of his fleet packing back to France. The French rather more than balanced this reverse, however, by successfully attacking Boulogne; and although the English brought in 3,000 reinforcements for the garrison and managed to keep open its access to the sea, they soon reached the conclusion Henry's Privy Council had come to four years earlier: Boulogne simply wasn't worth the cost, one way or another, of defending it. And so it was surrendered in March 1550, in exchange for 400,000 crowns, which was not a bad bargain for both sides. Peace was declared there (including Scotland in its terms) and it lasted for the rest of Edward VI's reign.

There was no peace at home, however, only turmoil and struggles for power behind the throne, often enough linked to the religious issues Henry had left behind, with the outcome for individuals sometimes even depending upon attitudes to what was evolving into the Book of Common Prayer. The young King was a cradle Anglican while his elder half-sister Mary, Katherine of Aragon's daughter, was devoutly Catholic, and the two quarrelled over her regular attendance at Mass, the strain being inevitably transmitted to their liegemen at court and in the country. There were riots in several areas and something much worse than that in East Anglia, when a rising at Wymondham in the summer of 1549 began on a feast day associated with St Thomas à Becket and cost (some reckoned) 3,000 lives before it was put down, followed by a number of executions. But Thomas Seymour was beheaded because he coveted the regency and was thought to have intrigued against his brother in order to become Protector in his stead. Edward Seymour shortly afterwards lost that position, and was succeeded by John Dudley as the dominant figure in the Privy Council, because he was judged to have mishandled too many things too expensively. 'He was vulnerable to what, in the different political culture of a later generation, would have been a vote of no confidence, but which in 1549 could only be a plot for his removal.' Three years later he, too, would go to the scaffold on suspicion of plotting a comeback which would have involved the assassination of Dudley, who now became Duke of Northumberland and indisputably the most powerful figure in the land; also extremely unpopular, for what was increasingly seen to be unprincipled ambition and arrogance.

In all this turmoil of peace and what preceded it, the Council for

Marine Causes proceeded diligently with the maintenance and management of the fleet, though the council itself underwent certain changes in personnel during Edward's reign. Robert Legge died in 1548 and Benjamin Gonson became Treasurer in his place, young William Wynter taking over as Surveyor (alternating his duties ashore with seatime, as did Gonson), while in 1552 Sir William Woodhouse succeeded Sir Thomas Clere as Lieutenant of the Admiralty, and Thomas Wyndham replaced Woodhouse at Ordnance; and, as we already know, Edward Baeshe joined the council in charge of victualling in 1550. The other big change in the command structure took place that same year, when Dudley, by then Lord President of the council, handed over the office of Lord Admiral to Edward Fiennes who (apart from most of Mary's short reign, when William Howard occupied it) would hold it for the next thirty-five years.

Most of the vessels these men controlled were – except in time of war or when hostilities seemed imminent, when Portsmouth became pre-eminent – based in the Thames or in the adjacent Medway, where Gillingham was being developed for servicing and repair, as (briefly) was Harwich at the mouth of the Stour, and a site on Essex's River Colne, though the most notable expansion continued to take place at Deptford, where expenditure in 1547 was well over five times that at nearby Woolwich. Dudley's continuing interest in the navy after he had left the Admiralty was demonstrated in 1550, when the Privy Council issued an instruction that all vessels after decommissioning were to be laid up at Gillingham, where there were extensive mudflats and a great tidal range, enabling vessels to be more easily cleaned of weed and other encrustations on their hulls, which everybody recognised as an annual necessity. Dudley almost certainly performed an even greater service to the fleet two years later, when a commission set up by the same Council to find ways of improving the Crown's financial position, which was still deplorable, decided that there must be certain naval economies, which would include getting rid of Baeshe's position. The proposal quietly foundered, and we may assume that it was the former Lord Admiral who scuppered it.

Meanwhile, the Council for Marine Causes had been getting on with its business, which included adjusting the composition of the fleet. In the year of Edward's accession, it had sold the *Artigo* and returned the *Galley Blanchard* to France, but it acquired the two Scottish prizes to balance the books. In 1548 it disposed of no fewer than ten of Henry's rowbarges because they were 'little and open and too weak', making a start in April, when four of these 20-tunners were sold to James Beck (who took two), Thomas Redmon and Thomas Hodge respectively; until, by December, only three such vessels – *Rose Slip*, *Gillyflower* and *Falcon in the Fetterlock* – were left, though not for much longer. But the same year also saw the building of *Flower de Luce* and *Seven Stars* (both 40 tuns) together with the *Double Rose* (50 tuns) and the *Moon* (80 tuns), all four of them pinnaces. Twelve months later these were joined by four more new vessels of similar tunnages (including the breathtaking 30-tun *Prickshaft*) and the large *Galley Mermaid*, which needed a crew of 300 and had been taken from Strozzi off the Channel Islands. *Gerfalcon* (140 tuns) and *Bark of Bullen* (60 tuns) joined the fleet in 1550, but *Merlin* (40 tuns) was sold and *Trego Renneger* disappeared from the records. The year after saw the rebuilding of *Mary Willoughby* and maybe also of *Primrose*; for if this wasn't a totally new ship of that name then she went back to 1523 and had been rebuilt once already after another fifteen years; 1551 also brought the sale of the old Hanseatic *Morian of Danzig* (500 tuns) to Evangelist Foule and James Pagatson, which was followed two years later by the disposal of her sister ship *Struse of Danzig* (400 tuns) which was sold to Robert Warner.

That was the last modification of Edward's fleet apart from one other loss. A few weeks after he died (on 6 July 1553, basically of consumption, though it was a common cold that took him in the end) the old *Henry Grâce à Dieu*, which had been renamed *Edward* when he came to the throne, was destroyed in a fire caused 'by negligence and for lack of oversight' as she lay at her moorings in the Thames off Woolwich. He would have regretted her loss in particular, for Edward seems to have inherited his father's interest in naval things: he regularly went to see the shipbuilding at Deptford, where the high street was paved so that he wouldn't have to walk through mud to reach the yard, and he noted in his journal the capture of the *Galley Mermaid* and many other naval incidents. And when the adolescent King was dying, only six years after his accession, he had himself carried to the window of his room so that he could watch the departure of three ships setting out hopefully for Cathay by what would later be known as the Northeast Passage round the top of Russia. They carried a letter of greetings from Edward to the Emperor of China himself, and this marked a tremendous departure from the attitude of his father, who never showed any interest at all in distant voyages of exploration.

When Henry VIII's first child reached the throne after thirty-seven years of waiting in the wings, she inherited a fleet not much smaller than that her brother had started with, and its supervisors were even more confidently in control of things than they had been in 1547. And Mary had need of both in her even shorter reign, which was dominated by her marriage to the Emperor's widowed son – soon to be Philip II of Spain on Charles V's abdication and retirement to the monastery of Yuste, south-west of Madrid, for the last two years of his life – and its consequences.[3] She was proclaimed on a wave of popular enthusiasm because the by then detested Dudley had attempted to forestall her accession by putting his daughter-in-law Lady Jane Grey in her place, which cost him and Jane and her husband their lives on the scaffold; and his long association with Dudley was the reason why Edward Fiennes was replaced by William Howard as Lord Admiral for most of Mary's reign. Six months after Dudley's fall, however, her popularity had been largely dissipated, perhaps less because of reprisals against the Protestant faction than the announcement of her marriage to Philip.

The reprisals followed on from Dudley's attempt at a *coup d'état* and particularly from the open rebellion it inspired, which was led by Sir Thomas Wyatt and others (including Sir Peter Carew) whose service to the Crown went back to the 1540s. These men tried to promote the Princess Elizabeth (another cradle Anglican) to the throne over Mary's head and such popular support as they drummed up in Herefordshire, Devon, Leicestershire and Kent at least partly came from hostility to the prospect of England being jointly ruled by a Spaniard. In fact, the discontent the conspirators acted upon produced less practical support than they had expected and the rebellion began to collapse after Carew's nerve went and he fled to Normandy, while Wyatt was still trying to muster some sort of army in Rochester. Wyatt actually marched on London with about three thousand supporters, but when he reached Ludgate to find the citizens within the city walls rather more sympathetic to the Queen than to him, it was apparent that the game was up. The government resisted the temptation to exact savagely widespread punishment for the fright it had been given, as Henry VIII had failed to do after the Pilgrimage of Grace: Wyatt was executed, but fewer than a hundred others went to the scaffold, while many more people than that

3 Charles was succeeded as Emperor by his brother Ferdinand and the position was subsequently occupied by other Habsburgs, but it became more nominal than powerful after the treaty which ended the Thirty Years' War in 1648, though the title was not abolished till the start of the nineteenth century.

were first convicted of treason and then pardoned.[4] One of them was William Wynter, who spent most of 1554 in the Tower before being freed under a general amnesty in January 1555: and, moreover, returning to his position as Surveyor of Ships. He would survive in that position, become Master of Naval Ordnance as well in 1557, and also be made Vice-admiral until his death in 1589, the year after the Armada was repulsed. Mary had inherited her father's shrewd ability to spot people of exceptional talent and make use of it, even if they were defective in some other way.

Nevertheless, the hostility to her Spanish husband never diminished: indeed, it intensified when it became apparent that the marriage was for him more than usually a matter of political convenience, entered into entirely to protect imperial interests in the Low Countries against any possible threat from France, which was now not only sheltering Carew and one or two others like him with seafaring experience, but actively encouraging them to commit piracy against anybody else's shipping in the Narrow Seas. This was certainly one reason why it was important to maintain the English fleet in good working order, as was the probability that Henri would sooner or later break the peace treaty, in which case the Scots would be on the warpath once more. And although the Privy Council was as unco-operative as it could be when Philip started to issue instructions as if he were the King of England instead of merely the Queen's consort, the navy was kept up to scratch in Mary's time. By the autumn of 1555, ships sorely in need of overhaul were being repaired in the Thames and two new big vessels were being built, *Philip & Mary* (500 tuns) and the second *Mary Rose* (600 tuns) which, in the remaining three years of Mary's life, would be joined by *Lion* (500 tuns), *Sprite* (40 tuns), *Bright Falcon* (60 tuns) and no fewer than eight vessels (of between 300 and 60 tuns) that were completely rebuilt. The keel was also laid down of an 800-tunner which was intended to fill the gap left by the fire which destroyed the old *Great Harry*, but she would not be launched (as *Elizabeth Jonas*) until the summer of 1559, when Elizabeth was Queen.

The running of the navy continued much as before, and William Howard proved to be a perfectly competent Lord Admiral, in the best seafaring traditions of his family; he was, moreover, a popular man in the fleet and ashore, a much warmer personality than his father Thomas had been. A similar figure from the landed seafaring gentry, whose star had

4 Mary reserved her savagery for those she deemed heretical, including Archbishop Cranmer and many others who were burnt at the stake.

been rising since the early 1540s, was Sir Thomas Cotton, who was now made Vice-admiral with special responsibility for the Narrow Seas. To strengthen the supervision of work in the dockyards, Peter Pett became a second Royal Master Shipwright, joining Richard Bull, who had held the position for almost a decade after succeeding James Baker, the first salaried occupant of the post. An adjustment was made to the purely administrative mechanism in 1557, when the Navy Board was placed under the direct authority of the Lord Treasurer, who was then William Paulet, Marquis of Winchester; but this should not be interpreted as a demotion so much as a consolidation of the arrangement that had existed for the past eleven years. For one thing, it was made plain that Paulet was to act only after taking the advice of the Lord Admiral and, for another, the change meant that the navy was still to be given a guaranteed annual allotment for the Admiralty's Treasurer to use as he thought fit, though initially this was rather less than had been granted in April 1546. Benjamin Gonson's first entitlement under the new rules amounted to £14,000, to be handed over in two six-monthly instalments of £7,000 each. But the intention behind the new regulation was sound and the effect was wholly beneficial. It helped that it was launched under the aegis of Paulet, who understood the reasons for, and was interested in, the development of the navy.

In April 1557 Henri II took the step that led to more war, when he sent troops from Dieppe to Scotland, his fleet pausing off the Yorkshire coast in order to land forty English dissidents, who were supposed to take Scarborough Castle and start a northern rebellion against the Crown, but who instead were quickly captured and left to their fate as the Frenchmen sailed on. A month later, twenty-one English warships were under sail with William Howard leading them in his flagship *Great Bark* (500 tuns), an elderly but still excellent seaboat which he had probably handled before, given that he took her out in preference to either of Mary's two brand-new big ships. This fleet took four French vessels off Dieppe, while seven others retreated rapidly to the safety of Boulogne, where a herald was landed by the English to make a formal declaration of war. In July Sir William Woodhouse, flying his Vice-admiral's flag, took over the fleet command from his superior, and William Wynter went to sea again for the first time since his disgrace, as Captain of the *Jesus of Lübeck* which was, in fact, the biggest ship in the Channel patrol that month.

Meanwhile, a squadron of eight vessels was detached to the North

Atlantic to escort the fishing fleet, which would shortly be homeward-bound from the waters off Iceland; but on the way back its commander (Sir John Clere in *Minion*) was rash enough to attempt a landing on Orkney, which was resisted so fiercely by the islanders that he and three of his captains were lost as they tried to get back to their ships. This, however, was but a trifling prelude to the real disaster which followed on New Year's Day, when the Duke of Guise led 30,000 troops in a strangely unanticipated assault on Calais: within a week, both the town and its surrounding little colony had fallen to the French, bringing to an end over two centuries of unbroken English sovereignty in a foothold that was not only commercially valuable and perfect for gathering useful intelligence, but strategically vital for command of the Channel at its narrowest point and for any military action that might be launched against France. Worst of all, perhaps, its loss was a particularly bitter blow to English morale and self-esteem.

No naval failure was responsible for this reverse, because the fleet was in its customary winter havens when it happened and never received an order to intervene until it was far too late to affect the outcome. The weather was foul on New Year's Eve when just five vessels were told by the Privy Council to leave Portsmouth, and though they tried to enter the harbour at Calais on the 3rd they were beaten back by the heavy guns of Rysbank Fort, which had already been taken by the French. The rest of Woodhouse's ships were ordered to follow them two days after the town itself had capitulated.

> But such terrible tempests then arose and continued the space of four or five days together, that the like had not been seen before in the remembrance of man; wherefore some said that the same was done by necromancy and the Devil was raised up and become French... But very true it is that no ship could brook the seas by reason of those extreme storms and tempests. And such of the Queen's ships as did adventure the passage were so shaken and torn with the violence of the weather as they were forced to return with great danger and loss of all their tackle and furniture.

All that could be done after this was a picking-up of pieces. One of the first things that happened was the recall of Howard to court, where his steadiness was desperately needed to restore shattered morale, and the consequent reinstatement of Edward Fiennes as Lord Admiral of England. It was in order to handle the suddenly increased workload of repairing the considerable storm damage to the fleet that Peter Pett was given his appointment, and it was then that the keel of *Elizabeth Jonas* was laid down.

By the end of June, Fiennes was flying his flag in the new *Lion* at the head of a joint Anglo-Flemish fleet of 140 vessels (thirty of them supplied by Philip from the imperial resources) which was assembling off the Isle of Wight for an amphibious attack on Brittany. A month later he had landed 7,000 men near the entrance to the Penfeld River, but Brest was well defended and the English were beaten off, so that they eventually went home after accomplishing nothing but burning Le Conquet and wasting its surrounding countryside. The Flemings returned whence they had come without asking Fiennes's permission to leave their Breton anchorage, before the English ships also left; and these were revictualling in Portsmouth when news arrived of another French expedition being prepared for Scotland. William Wynter was given a squadron of twenty vessels with which to patrol the Narrow Seas, while Fiennes himself took some ships to the coast of Normandy to forestall any attempt to reach the Scots through the Irish Sea. And either because the French had second thoughts in view of these defensive measures or because the intelligence was false, nothing more was heard of their latest Scottish plan. But the last English excursion of 1558 was, nevertheless, into the Irish Sea, when Sir Thomas Cotton sailed to attack the MacDonalds of the Isles, who had been threatening Carrickfergus and had, indeed, gained a foothold in Antrim. Cotton's remedy was very simple and very traditional. He landed troops on Kintyre at the threshold of the MacDonalds' home ground, torched the whole area, did likewise to the Isle of Arran and then to Cumbrae at the entrance to the River Clyde.

Two months later Mary died, childless, at the age of forty-two and a deeply frustrated woman for almost the whole of her life; and although it was cancer that took her, the loss of Calais almost certainly played a part in hastening her end. Effectively, she had been abandoned by Philip, whose absences had lengthened as the marriage wore on while he attended to his Spanish prospects and responsibilities. According to the coldly calculating nature of their betrothal, he had no incentive to do otherwise in a marriage of convenience which would bring him no advantage at his wife's death, for the treaty between them had specifically excluded him from succession to the English throne. Even if the Privy Council had not insisted on this provision, Philip could never have survived alone because of his unpopularity throughout the realm. The longer his union with Mary went on, the more it became obvious that he was only using his English position for the benefit of Spain, including the deliberate frustration of English trading opportunities where there was the slightest conflict of interest. The one commercial advance made during his time as consort was the foundation of the Muscovy Company, which was to prosper exceedingly on the sale of broadcloth; but that was the outcome of the voyage which began when the dying Edward watched three ships weigh anchor from his Thames-side window, from which one boat never returned, in which the others only got as far as Russia, and which produced an agreeable response to his letter not from from the Emperor of China, but from the Czar Ivan IV ('The Terrible') in Moscow.

XIX
THE PAYOFF

And so, with Mary's final blessing, even though she had felt sufficiently threatened by her half-sister to put her into the Tower for a couple of months after Wyatt's rebellion, Elizabeth came into her own at the age of twenty-five. Her reign is familiar enough to us and needs no recapitulation here, but it was characterised by the sheer willpower that overcame all manner of dangers and obstacles, by a sense of purpose that did not shrink from the execution of heretics (but a different sort of heretic from those Mary had incinerated) or of a Scottish Queen, by a genius for manipulating those who gathered round her, by an astute ability to outmanoeuvre conspirators at home and enemies abroad, by a gradual improvement of England's standing in the world (except among the Irish and, as always, the Scots) – and by a recognition from the start that the nation's security, no less than its prosperity, was inextricably related to and dependent upon the sea. It is striking that when we conjure Elizabeth's memory four centuries after her death, more often than not the moments that first spring to mind are maritime cameos: Elizabeth knighting Drake on the deck of *Golden Hind* after the great circumnavigation, Elizabeth presenting Raleigh with one of her ships before the expedition to Virginia (and also giving him £400-worth of gunpowder from the Tower), Elizabeth waving to Frobisher from her palace window as he left to find the Northwest Passage, Elizabeth sanctioning exploration and profitable ventures (often of questionable legality, and sometimes of none at all) on an unprecedented scale, Elizabeth presiding over the destruction of the Spanish Armada...[1] Hers was an expansive reign

1 It is also significant that when an exhibition was mounted in 2003 to mark the 400th anniversary of her death, the chosen venue was the National Maritime Museum; and not only because Elizabeth, like her father, was born in Greenwich.

in every sense, as well as an essay in the art of survival against considerable odds.

A very early decision after she reached the throne, however, was that the Navy Royal would be slimmed down in the interests of efficiency. The Queen herself appears to have initiated the Admiralty review that came to this conclusion, but right at the heart of the deliberations was William Wynter, wearing his three different hats. He it was who produced the document that emerged from the review in March 1559, entitled 'A Boke for Sea Causes', which has been seen as being 'the first attempt in England to plan naval requirements on first principles: the first piece of naval staff work'. It covered everything naval from an assessment of every ship and the costs involved in maintaining and manning it, to the performance of the dockyards and an outline of what the Navy Board had in mind for the future of the fleet. Some twenty-one of the existing vessels were reckoned 'meet to be kept and preserved', another ten were 'very much worn and of no continuance without great Reparation be done upon them', while three were written off completely as 'utterly decayed'. Those in the second group, in fact, had only a limited future 'during the doubtful time of peace' (which was agreed with France within days of the report's coming out), after which they should be either scrapped or sold and any savings or income from their disposal should be used to build replacements. It was estimated that in addition to the Queen's own warships, there were forty-five merchant vessels that could quickly be adapted for fighting if need be and, if war did break out again, it would take two months to work up all naval resources for, say, a five-month campaign, which would cost £71,377. The navy of the future would include four ships of 600 tuns or more, four of 500 tuns, four of 400 tuns, six of 300 tuns and six of 200 tuns-plus, augmented by four barks of 60–80 tuns and two pinnaces of 40 tuns – thirty vessels in all. There was never to be another *Henry Grâce à Dieu*, built chiefly to attract attention and impress visitors, and only one ship bigger than the newly completed *Elizabeth Jonas*: the 900-tun *White Bear*, which had started life in 1538 as the *Great Bark* (600 tuns), and would be rebuilt for the second time in its life in the very last year of the sixteenth century. Two more vessels, *Victory*, which appeared in 1562 and *Ark Royal* in 1587 (the first of five ships to bear that name up to the present day), were both, like *Elizabeth Jonas*, of 800 tuns.[2]

2 *Ark Royal* was built as *Ark Raleigh* by the Queen's Master Shipwright, Richard Chapman, but it was designed and owned by Sir Walter Raleigh, who sold it to Elizabeth shortly afterwards.

What all this amounted to was that although Elizabeth would own fewer ships than had Henry VIII at the height of his naval expansion, they would be in commission for much more of the time; there would be no more expensive laying-up of steadily rotting vessels during protracted periods of peace. The backbone of England's naval resources would henceforth consist of mostly medium-sized craft which were kept at all times in good repair and ready for sea at short (but not unrealistically so) notice: the Navy Board's intention was to get twelve to sixteen ships to sea from scratch within a fortnight of the order being given. As things turned out, Elizabeth built twenty-five warships between her accession and the Armada, eleven of them over 300 tuns, and in the 1580s she had, including armed merchantmen, at least 250 ships of over 80 tuns at her disposal for war. The emphasis, moreover, was weighted in favour of gunnery much more than earlier in the century. *Mary Rose*, which was heavily armed for Henry's time, had carried ninety-six guns, but only half a dozen of them were really heavy weapons. *Elizabeth Jonas* mustered seventy-six pieces, but thirty-four of them were demi-culverins or bigger, with barrels thirteen feet long, capable of firing cast-iron shot of between 10 and 15lb. *Revenge* (500 tuns), of 1577, mounted twenty-two such pieces of ordnance out of the forty-six guns she carried. The effect of these weapons could be impressive at a range of between 350 and 400 yards. In a famous action which Sir John Hawkins fought against the Spanish in 1568, aboard a vessel that had seen much better days, an entire squadron of enemy ships was held off long enough to allow a consort to escape, by bringing to bear sixty-one guns, twelve of them heavy, mounted on two decks, before his *Jesus of Lübeck* (which Henry had bought from the Hanse in 1545) was put out of action and taken as prize. The production of these weapons on the Weald of Sussex in particular had expanded so much since the early years of the century, that by now 'in England alone of all Europe, small and medium-sized battery guns were available cheaply and in quantity'.

Apart from advances in gunnery, certain technical innovations were made during these years and Hawkins himself is credited with one of them, by having horsehair sandwiched between a double thickness of planking below the waterline to protect the vessel against shipworm, which became a standard remedy until copper sheathing was introduced in the eighteenth century. Spritsails were rigged more than ever before in order to improve steering, and a better way of striking topmasts in exceptionally stormy weather was devised – though seamen would continue to experiment with refinements of this tricky operation well into the nineteenth century. Chain pumps were found to be less laborious and more effective than the traditional elm-tree pump and its plunger. William Wynter tried to have gravel ballast (which eventually stank after saturation with bilge water and other noisome substances) replaced with stone, and urged that the ship's galley should be built in the fo'castle rather than the hold, partly for the same reason and partly to reduce the risk of catastrophic fire; but he didn't get far with either proposal, the sixteenth-century mariner being as suspicious as any contemporary of too much change. As important as any change, however, was the developing ability of master shipwrights to commit their designs to paper, which could be followed in their absence or passed on to some other yard for repetition, instead of their having always to be at the dock in person, showing the workmen how this piece of timber should be cut and where that one should be placed, and exactly how much sheer the emerging vessel should be given. The age of the naval architect had arrived.

Deptford increasingly became the principal dockyard throughout the year: in 1562 it employed 214 shipwrights in building three new ships, when Woolwich had use for no more than a handful of storekeepers and labourers, and eight years later Deptford's main dock was reconstructed, with a new pair of gates to follow in 1578. But by then it was no longer used as an anchorage, a function which had been taken over in the Medway by Gillingham, whose promotion under Elizabeth was one of the most notable things in the naval infrastructure. William Wynter had decided that 'Gillingham water is the meetest harbour to keep the Queen's Majesty's ships in' and from then on it prospered and grew, that same year seeing a start made on Upnor Castle, where this could overlook the river and guard the anchorage. Though Gillingham's workforce seems never to have been as numerous as Deptford's, and though it wouldn't have a dry-dock until the seventeenth century, increasingly it was where ships were mended, which in summer meant that the artisans were 'repairing, ransacking, dubbing and caulking her Majesty's ships against the winter weather'. About thirty ships, including some of the biggest in the fleet, were in the anchorage consistently throughout 1562, and sixteen vessels were surveyed there in July alone. A mast pond was excavated at nearby Chatham, where trunks of spruce and other stocks of timber for spars could be kept until they were needed; and a further sign of the base's growing importance was the renting of a house on Tower Hill, Chatham, 'wherein the officers of her Majesty's ships do meet and confer from time to time touching her highness' weighty affairs'.

The Navy Board's offices, however, remained in Deptford during Elizabeth's reign, and there was surprisingly little change of key personnel in naval authority over long periods of time. Edward Fiennes, Benjamin Gonson, Edward Baeshe and William Wynter served in one capacity or another for thirty-five, thirty-one, thirty-six and forty years respectively. Naval dynasties and intermarriages began to take shape there, John Hawkins becoming Treasurer in 1578 after the death of Benjamin Gonson, whose son-in-law he was, and William Wynter's younger brother George following Richard Howlett as Clerk of the Ships, eventually being himself succeeded by a second Benjamin Gonson, the original's son; while Edward Fiennes was eventually succeeded as Lord Admiral in 1585 by Charles, the 2nd Lord Howard of Effingham and son of William Howard, who had held the post for the four years when Fiennes was out of the job... In spite of such affinities, there were sometimes quarrels within the Admiralty – the biggest involved Hawkins and the award of certain contracts – but these do not seem to have impaired the board's efficient prosecution of its duties very much. Young it may have been, but an administrative tradition had already been established, and that can be a difficult thing to disturb. Naval morale and continuity was further helped when William Paulet's sympathetic oversight as Elizabeth's Lord Treasurer was followed by that of William Cecil in 1572. The English establishment as a whole was waking up to the great benefits of seapower.

By then the Navy Royal had been well tested in the Queen's service. The first threat to her position came paradoxically just after the peace with France was signed, which gave the French the right to maintain garrisons in Scotland. Three months later, Henri II was killed in a tournament and his son, Francis II, was already married to Mary Stuart, who had inherited claims to the English as well as to the Scottish throne, being among other things Henry VII's great-granddaughter. The danger was obvious and in December 1559, therefore, William Wynter took fourteen ships from the Medway, with his flag in the new *Lion*, on an operation designed to cut the French lines of communication with Scotland – but his orders very cunningly distanced the Queen herself from whatever happened next: he was to proceed as though any action that might take place was not conducted in Elizabeth's name, but instead he must 'as of his own head, do that enterprise he shall see most hurtful to the French'.

It was the worst time of year to be out in the North Sea and the stormbound squadron was only a hundred miles up the coast after almost three weeks; had Wynter known it, a French fleet of thirty vessels under the Marquis d'Elbeuf was so mauled by the weather that it gave up trying to reach Leith and turned for home. But slowly the English butted their way north, fighting storms most of the way, reaching the Firth of Forth (minus half the squadron, which had been obliged to make for shelter at various havens on the north-east coast) on 22 January. There they took three French vessels and so dismayed a French garrison at Burntisland that these blew up their own guns and ammunition before retreating inland to join compatriots led by Henri d'Oysel, the French ambassador. Wynter then began a blockade of the firth, which was to continue right into the summer of 1560, when the English and the French agreed to withdraw all their forces from Scotland, and Mary Stuart renounced her claim to the English throne. The greatest reason for purely naval satisfaction, however, was the fact that the Vice-admiral had repeatedly been revictualled and resupplied well over two hundred miles from home for seven months and eight days. This was another important step forward in a progression that had started in 1545.

Francis II died only a few months after these events, whereupon Mary Stuart returned to her homeland, leaving the French with a ten-year-old Charles IX (Henri's second son) and effectively ruled by the dowager, Catherine de' Medici, a very hardline Catholic whose regency could only increase the religious tensions now tightening across the land. In 1562 the Protestant Huguenots offered Elizabeth the port of Havre in exchange for assistance against their internal enemies, and she seized the chance to obtain a bargaining chip that might help her recover Calais, or, failing that, become a very useful substitute at the mouth of the Seine. At the beginning of August, Sir William Woodhouse in *Hope* (500 tuns) took a squadron of five vessels cruising off the coast of Normandy for a month, during which he somehow damaged his hand and never put to sea again; and he died the following year. In October, more English vessels entered the Seine to help the Huguenots relieve Rouen from a royalist siege, but Elizabeth refused to allow troops which by then were garrisoning Havre and Dieppe to be used in the endeavour, as a result of which Rouen had surrendered by the end of that month. Dieppe became so difficult to sustain in the circumstances that it was abandoned, the English having so far lost two vessels in the enterprise.

They hung on in Havre throughout that winter but in March the French made peace with each other and the English suddenly became unwanted by both, though Havre was not surrendered for another four months. By the time that happened they had suffered another naval loss when *Greyhound* (200 tuns), which had only just been rebuilt, was wrecked on a sandbar as she was sailing past Rye and was lost with all hands, including one of the navy's most impressive captains, John Malen. He had first made a name for himself four years earlier, in the immediate aftermath of the loss of Calais, by sailing dangerously close inshore a few miles to the east of the port and bombarding French troops who were fighting Spanish soldiers on the beach, as a result of which he had been made Vice-admiral in charge of the Narrow Seas. A war which had never been officially declared was over by April 1564, after Elizabeth had spent £264,380 which she could ill afford on pursuing a persistent English chimera.

Officially the English were at peace with Spain, too, but the relationship was deteriorating fast, and this was mostly caused by the activities of certain West Country seamen – Drake, Hawkins and Frobisher most notably – who engaged in straightforward piracy, encouraged by a Queen who at the same time studiously looked the other way, just as she had done when sending William Wynter up to Scotland. She was somewhat discountenanced when a ship part-owned by John Hawkins and his brother William captured ten Spanish merchantmen in Plymouth Sound, which produced cries of outrage in Philip's new capital, Madrid; but this was nothing compared with what was in the offing, generally with Elizabeth's compliance. The great Spanish attraction for pirates of any nationality was their annual convoy which brought vast quantities of bullion from their colonies in the New World, and which for many years had been escorted by armed merchantmen. Spoiling a convoy was by no means a new phenomenon, however, one of Jean Ango's Dieppois captains having taken seven of these ships back in 1537.

But now the English were becoming the most prominent raiders of all and none was making a bigger name for himself than Francis Drake. And though he never did succeed in plundering an entire *flota* – nobody did until the Dutch managed it in 1628 – he began to wreak havoc in other ways. In 1571 he sailed for the Caribbean, with the intention of seizing silver as it was conveyed from the mines of Peru along the isthmus of Panama to the embarkation point at Nombre de Dios, the so-called Spanish Main. He failed in his initial attempt but, instead of leaving for home or some other target, he spent the winter waiting on an unfrequented part of the coast, where he made friends with escaped slaves who were waging guerrilla warfare on the Spaniards, and also with the great Huguenot navigator and cartographer Guillaume Le Testu, who had been a thorn in the flesh of the imperial power off South and Central America for years. In February 1573 they made a joint strike against a silver caravan and, although the Frenchman was killed, Drake made off with enough loot to set himself up for life.

Four years later he took the *Golden Hind* (100 tuns) on a much more extraordinary voyage, down the South American coast, through the Straits of Magellan and into the Pacific, which only the great Portuguese navigator had done before. On the coast of Peru he seized some silver and even more further north, before sailing home via the Moluccas (where he picked up a useful cargo of spices), rounding Penlee Point and sailing into Plymouth Sound in September 1580. He had been backed by some very influential investors including (off the record) the Queen herself, and between them these made a staggering profit of 4,700 per cent on the voyage, Elizabeth's cut being sufficient to pay off all her debts.

Philip by this time had just about had enough, though even worse was to follow when Drake sailed in 1585 for Cartagena on the coast of New Granada (modern Colombia) with a squadron of twenty-nine ships, two of which belonged to the Queen, taking a great deal of booty on the way, including much from the city of Santo Domingo on Hispaniola (which they captured), ransacking Cartagena itself, and then destroying a Spanish fort in Florida on the way back. Humiliated and robbed by the English more than once, Philip was nevertheless in something of a quandary, largely because the Protestant Netherlanders had been in revolt against Spanish rule since 1566; and although they had been savagely put down by the Duke of Alva, who commanded what were reckoned by then to be the best troops in Europe, the most belligerent rebels led by William of Nassau, Prince of Orange, had continued to fight on from exile in Germany and elsewhere. They had been particularly impressive in a number of sorties from the sea, in which their ships seized the principal Spanish North Sea naval base at Brielle, captured the deep-water port of Flushing and successfully besieged Middelburg on the island of Walcheren; and they had defeated three Spanish squadrons in the process until, effectively, there was no naval presence to protect Spanish interests in their Netherlands. A task force had been ready to set out from Santander in 1574 to remedy matters, but after it was assembled it was hit by yet another form of 'plague' (influenza this time) and never sailed. Philip's problem therefore was that, although by the late 1570s he loathed the English, he was dependent on their neutrality in order to maintain his line of communication by sea with his rebellious colony: without a degree of English goodwill, there was no way the colonial army could be supplied any more.

If Drake's plundering in the Pacific had first put into Philip's head the notion of invading England in order to stop all this (and it had), the Devonian's second escapade in the Caribbean was the moment when the Spanish King seriously began to plan war against the country whose throne he had (in a manner of speaking) so recently occupied. This was, in quite disparate ways, likely to be an unequal contest for, although Philip was the wealthiest monarch in the world with ten times Elizabeth's income, and though he was backed by a far superior army, his naval resources were much the poorer. Spain had long maintained a maritime academy as an offshoot of its Casa de Contratación, the mercantile guild based in Seville which operated the treasure convoys, and it had been modelled on Henry the Navigator's great school at Sagres.[3]

But outside the Mediterranean Spain lacked anything resembling England's well-organised Navy Royal, relying for transatlantic escort duties and any other purposes on armed merchantmen. Informed Spaniards themselves acknowledged that English warships were faster and handier than theirs and carried many more long-range guns. Even by 1588 there was no equivalent of the Navy Board, not even a naval dockyard, while all decisions were taken at the Escorial by Philip himself, who delegated nothing if he could help it. It was nevertheless Spain's most distinguished admiral, the Marquis of Santa Cruz, who had for several years been pressing upon the King the need to attack England. And when Philip reached the sticking point and at last decided to act he was, whether he realised it or not, embarking on an ambitiously risky venture, which was given an appropriately weighty title. The Spanish told themselves that they were bound for the Enterprise of England.

Twelve months before the Spanish invasion fleet set off, when it was already clear to the English what was brewing, Drake left the Channel with twenty-one ships to disrupt the enemy's plans. Seventeen days later his squadron sailed into the Bay of Cadiz without warning, spent three days there and destroyed twenty-four vessels without loss, setting fire to many of them before moving off again; he also wiped out a great deal of

---

3 Sebastian Cabot was the academy's principal during Henry VIII's time, but he had returned to England in 1548, bringing a great deal of information about the limitations of Spanish naval organisation.

stores and equipment that were being gathered for the invasion. He then made for Sagres, on the south-western tip of Portugal, which had been coerced into a union with Spain on the death of its King Sebastian seven years earlier. He destroyed the fort there, pitching its guns off the seacliffs, and unforgivably burned down the library of priceless charts and other documents which Henry and his successors had painstakingly built up across a hundred and fifty years. Having finished there, he sailed off into the Atlantic, meaning to attack the homeward-bound Spanish *flota* and any Portuguese shipping that might be en route to or from the Azores. A storm disrupted this plan dramatically, and he took only a single Portuguese prize with an extremely valuable cargo before turning for home. By Drake's standards, this was a paltry reward, but he had accomplished something much more valuable, by damaging Spanish self-confidence and disturbing their plans, by singeing the King of Spain's beard.[4]

If Santa Cruz had had his way, the Spanish Armada would simply have established a bridgehead in England's West Country or in Ireland, so as to maintain the easiest possible communications with home, and the invaders would have proceeded from there. Other voices came up with alternative suggestions and in the end Philip decided that his ships would sail the length of the Channel to support an invasion of Kent from the Spanish Netherlands which would be led for political reasons (particularly to keep Pope Sixtus V onside) by the Duke of Parma, who was in fact Philip's nephew, but was not a Spaniard. Parma was at first enthusiastic about the plan, especially after his troops took Sluys from the Dutch, for this would make an excellent embarkation point. But his ardour cooled rapidly when it became apparent that the naval planning was in a mess, part of which was Drake's doing because thirty-seven vessels had been despatched to look for him after his attack on Cadiz and Sagres.

Santa Cruz was trying to assemble the Armada in Lisbon, which took much longer than it should have done, with an impatient Philip snapping at his heels all the time. The victualling arrangements were in disarray, too, so seriously that by the time the fleet sailed, what had started as supplies sufficient to last eight months were only enough for half as long. There were shortages of everything, including guns, ammunition and

---

4 Drake may well have used the phrase (Francis Bacon certainly thought he did) but the copyright belongs to the Turkish Sultan Selim II, whose navy was destroyed by Christian forces at Lepanto in 1571. Of this catastrophe he said 'When the Venetians sank my fleet they only singed my beard. It will grow again.'

powder as well as food. Many of the ships were in poor condition, a plague of typhus was rampaging through their crews and, to top everything, Santa Cruz suddenly took to his bed and died. An unwilling Duke of Medina Sidonia (one of the wealthiest men in Spain and owner of San Lucár, the port of Seville) was told to take over, and his first act in command was to write to his sovereign to say that he thought the whole enterprise should be scrapped. This was not what Philip wanted to hear. Someone only a little more optimistic than the Admiral told a papal envoy that 'we are sailing against England in the confident hope of a miracle'.

And sail they did from the Tagus on 18 May 1588, with an Armada which began with 141 ships but which unseasonably bad weather and poor maintenance soon cut down to about 130 vessels, little more than a score of these being warships or armed merchantmen, most of them transports with 18,000 troops aboard. It took three weeks to plunge and beat their way through heavy seas as far north as Corunna and there Medina Sidonia had to pause while he collected his scattered fleet and replenished them with clean water after finding that most of what was in their old and faulty casks was foul: had Drake not destroyed stocks of seasoned wood in Cadiz the year before, that might not have been necessary. It was 11 July before the Armada weighed anchor again, but the weather had abated to a murky drizzle and the seas had subsided to a steady roll when an English pinnace, which had been sent out from Plymouth for this express purpose, spotted the invaders between the Scilly Isles and the Lizard a week later, with a south-westerly wind behind them. If Drake's own instinct had been followed they would never have got that far, for he had wanted to sail down to the Portuguese assembly point and destroy them before they even got going; and so, after some hesitation, had his superior, Lord Howard of Effingham. Three times the English had left port with this intent and each time they had been driven back by adverse winds, once within sight of the Spanish coast. It was therefore decided that squadrons led by Howard in *Ark Royal* and Drake in *Revenge* (500 tuns) would be ready for the Armada when it arrived at the entrance to the Channel, while other vessels under Howard's cousin and Vice-admiral Lord Henry Seymour in *Rainbow* (500 tuns) would be waiting for it at the eastern end.

When the Spanish were first sighted in the Western Approaches there were nineteen of Elizabeth's fighting ships in Plymouth, together with forty-six big and well-armed private vessels – thirty of them fitted out and paid for by the City of London – and forty smaller support craft, including victuallers. On station in the Narrow Seas were fifteen royal galleons armed with heavy bow chasers and a number of smaller craft, some of which were there at the Queen's expense, others funded by the Cinque Ports. And although all sixteenth-century statistics have to be treated with caution, the generally accepted figures for the relative strengths of the two adversaries during their passage of arms are 197 English vessels with 15,551 men aboard, facing 128 Spanish ships carrying 29,522 seamen and soldiers. The Spaniards may have regarded this above all as a punitive expedition, but for the defenders it was nothing less than a national emergency. That was why so much was put into it by private shipowners, municipalities and corporations as well as by the monarch. And that was why, when the enemy was sighted, beacons were lit the length of England, from the coast of Devon right up to the Scottish border, each one ignited as soon as flames from the one before it became visible. The news travelled all the way within an hour or two.

To begin with, the weather and the sea were against the English, a familiar predicament for fleets trying to get out of Plymouth Sound. When the alarm came, a strong flood tide was running, backed by a south-westerly, so there was little point in even trying to warp ships from the Cattewater until at least the tide had turned. If Drake really did say that there was time to finish his game of bowls on the Hoe and then beat the Spaniards, he was not so much swaggering (though he was very good at that) as patiently accepting the reality of his position: it was ten o'clock that night before the excruciatingly laborious business of towing the warships out to sea could begin, with men bending their backs to their oars like galley slaves. These small boats hauled the ships out to the lee of Rame Head, where they dropped anchor and waited for the wind to change or for the enemy to appear, whichever happened first. By next morning the wind was blowing off the land, exactly where Howard and his fleet wanted it and the weather gage which the Spaniards had held till then was suddenly lost to the English, who were scarcely without it after that for the next nine days.

Their enemy came up the Channel in a disciplined line abreast formation, with the big troop transports at the centre of a classic crescent shape and the fighting ships deployed on the wings, which was the way the *flotas* were always arranged. In the most exposed position was the Armada of the Levant, ten vessels commanded by Martin de Bertendona in *La Regazona* (1,249 tuns), with Medina Sidonia himself close behind in *San Martin* (1,000 tuns) at the head of the dozen ships constituting the Armada of Portugal. There were four other such squadrons, commanded by some notable seamen like Juan Martinez de Recalde in *Santa Ana* (768 tuns, Armada of Biscay), Miguel de Oquendo in another *Santa Ana* (1,200 tuns, Armada of Guipúzcoa), Diego Flores de Valdés in *San Cristobal* (700 tuns, Armada of the Galleons of Castile) and his cousin Don Pedro de Valdés in *Nuestra Señora del Rosario* (1,150 tuns, Armada of the Ships of Andalusia). In addition to these, there were twenty-three supply vessels led by Juan Gomes de Medina in *El Gran Grifon* (650 tuns).[5] Keeping station perfectly, these vessels ploughed on to the east when the English appeared, following their King's adamant instructions that they must sail to their rendezvous with Parma without being deflected by any other consideration.

From the outset, the Spaniards were outmanoeuvred in adverse conditions, in spite of the fact that the English were deeply impressed by their ability to hold their positions, which meant that an attacker could only engage with the extremities of the crescent, where the flankers were bristling with armament. The Spanish, for their part, seem to have been surprised by the adroitness with which the English changed tack, by the seamanship that enabled them to feint and move around the Armada like a swarm of wasps, choosing its moment to go for the kill. Howard made the first thrust, taking his squadron past the Armada's northern wing of Levanters, and fire was exchanged without doing much damage to either side. Drake, meanwhile, began harrying the other wing, but this one was led by Recalde, who aimed to grapple with the English (the last thing they wanted) and suffered some punishment from Drake's long-range guns before withdrawing into the protective heart of the Spanish formation. Medina Sidonia himself came to the rescue but the English had little difficulty in keeping him at bay. And so, inconclusively, the first day's engagement came to an end, having set a pattern which was to continue from the Sunday of that week until the Tuesday of the week following.

The Spanish doggedly tried to sail as close to the English coast as possible, past Start Point and into the wide ellipse that becomes Lyme

---

5 Of these men, Bertendona, Recalde and de Oquendo were Basques with a great deal of seatime behind them. Recalde was the designated second-in-command to Medina Sidonia, but Philip had ordered that if the Duke was killed, the command should pass to Don Alonso Martínez de Leyva, captain of *La Rata Santa Maria Encoronada* (820 tuns), which was part of Bertendona's squadron.

Bay as far as Portland Bill, and then on past the Isle of Wight, in the hope of gaining the weather gage again; but the English held their advantage almost all the way, the Spanish unable to close with them so that their lighter guns could be brought to bear. Yet although the English had the more effective firepower they were doing little damage with it and the only serious casualties at this stage were not the result of enemy action. *Nuestra Señora del Rosario* was so badly damaged in collision with other vessels that she was left behind (together with Pedro de Valdés and 50,000 ducats which were being carried for the next pay day in the Spanish fleet), while one of de Oquendo's squadron, *San Salvador* (958 tuns), was put out of action by an explosion of her own gunpowder, which may or may not have been sabotage by a Dutchman unwillingly pressed into her crew.

Next day, his appetite for plunder whetted enough to disobey Howard's orders, Drake doubled back to the limping *Rosario* and seized her as his personal reward for what he had so far achieved, which didn't endear him to his Admiral or to the rest of the fleet. What was left of *San Salvador* was also taken by the English but she foundered off Studland Point as she was being towed towards Weymouth. On Tuesday, the Spaniards briefly had the weather gage off Portland when the wind changed, and they might have captured one of Howard's ships if the south-easterly hadn't gone back to the south-west by dusk. After the Isle of Wight, the Spanish stood out to sea and the English rearranged their formation from two into four distinct squadrons under Howard himself, Drake, John Hawkins in *Victory* and Martin Frobisher in *Triumph* (1,000 tuns), the better to make their superior firepower pay by the squadrons attacking from different angles, with one ship after another loosing off their guns in line ahead. Not even that had the intended effect, and although the English did some damage and inflicted casualties, the Armada cruised on towards its rendezvous with Parma.

Medina Sidonia's fleet had dropped anchor in the Calais roads on the evening of Saturday, 27 July when a message arrived from the commander of the Spanish land forces – who was only a few miles away in Dunkirk – to say that he would not be ready to move until the following Friday: he was having trouble getting enough shallow-draught barges together to embark his troops, and without such craft there was no way he could get out of any port along the coast of Flanders. The Armada was therefore faced with the hazardous prospect of having to kill time for six days in a very exposed position, with the English also anchored to windward and the dangerous Flanders Banks to leeward. What's more, Howard's fleet had now been joined by Henry Seymour's squadron and the first thing the Admiral did was to call a council of war aboard *Ark Royal* to decide what to do next.

Medina Sidonia probably knew what to expect, for it was an old tactic in such a situation, and William Wynter, who was captaining *Vanguard* (500 tuns) in Seymour's squadron, is credited with the idea of suggesting it on this occasion. Eight fireships were prepared (which meant writing off over £5,000-worth of perfectly serviceable vessels of up to 200 tuns each) and, with flames beginning to lick at their rigging, were despatched about midnight on Sunday with a stiff wind and a spring tide in their favour and sails fully set. The Spanish Admiral had ordered a protective screen of small craft to take up position with grapnels at the ready, in order to tow the fireships off course, but this plan was disrupted when guns – which the English had double-shotted – began to go off as the heat mounted, spraying missiles in every direction, the vessels themselves now blazing furiously as they bore down on their target. Only a couple of the fireships were hauled aside, and for the first time since the two fleets had met, the Armada's discipline fell apart as panic seized most of the Spaniards. Some captains were so alarmed that they didn't wait to weigh anchor but cut their cables and scattered in the darkness, which led to a number of collisions and the stranding of a galleass with her rudder smashed. It was the opening the English had hoped for, the broken formation that could now be engaged with less danger to themselves.

Monday saw the Spaniards desperately trying to regroup, Medina Sidonia and the ships in his squadron fighting a rearguard action to buy time for the others, while Drake led the Englishmen, whose vessels bombarded the enemy at a far higher rate than they could manage in reply. Only one Spaniard (*Maria Juan*, 665 tuns) was, in fact, sunk by the endless gunfire but several more were so badly damaged that their crews ran them ashore or abandoned them to drift away helplessly: it is thought that at least 1,000 men had been killed and another 800 injured by then. And all the time the surviving Spanish vessels were being steadily chivvied by the pursuers, who had received little damage and few casualties themselves, towards the lethal shoals off Flanders. There was now not the faintest possibility of the Armada helping the Duke of Parma and his army to reach England; the only question was whether the elements or the English would effect its destruction, as the wind force rose and drove the Spaniards in the direction of the frightening Banks.

And then, as if by a miracle, the wind veered to the south just after dawn on Tuesday, 30 July and began to push the Armada away from the coast and into the North Sea. The English followed them, but at a safe distance now because they had almost run out of ammunition, their victuals were low and their seamen were beginning to fall sick. At first, Howard could not be sure what the Spanish intention was, but a possibility existed that they might make for some Baltic or Norwegian or Scottish haven where they could patch themselves up before returning for a second attempt at an invasion. By the time Medina Sidonia was sailing on past the Firth of Forth on 2 August, however, it was clear that he had abandoned the contest and was simply hoping to get home the dangerously long way round. Therefore most of the English turned back to replenish their stores and repair what small damage had been done to them, leaving a token number of pinnaces to shadow the enemy. What followed was an unmitigated disaster for the Spanish as weather that was variable in the North Sea became increasingly dreadful afterwards and steadily took its toll, while provisions began to run out, even though all the horses and mules were thrown over the sides of the transports in order to save water, and every man's ration was reduced to a mere eight ounces of biscuit, half a pint of wine and a pint of water a day. Their Admiral had decided that after rounding Scotland they should sail well out into the Atlantic in order to keep a safe distance from English-occupied Ireland before turning southward on course for Corunna. But from 4 August, more than a fortnight before that point was reached, ships began to go missing, having either foundered in the open sea or been wrecked upon some alien shore.

A diary which is thought to have been dictated to a subordinate by Medina Sidonia's second-in-command Recalde, whose first ship had been left behind on the French coast after being battered by the weather on the way to the Channel, and who was now flying his flag in *San Juan de Portugal* (1,050 tuns), conveys very well what the Armada went through during the back end of August and the whole of September 1588 in its struggle to reach Spain. On Sunday, 18 August, in latitude 59° N (the latitude of Kirkwall on Orkney) 'we had a very rough sea and a south-southeasterly wind which turned into a very strong gale'. Next day, 'dawn broke with...the same terrible sea, only more furious than the previous night'. Four days later they made their turn for Spain in the teeth of a sou'westerly after a night of strong wind and driving rain, and on 25 August the wind shifted to west-northwest, making the sea so rough that they had to reef in their sails. Twenty-four hours later everything suddenly calmed down and there was a lunar eclipse; but the respite was brief; by the 28th the storm was so furious that they were forced to lie-to until mid-afternoon, 'when the wind turned to the west, whereupon we steered south despite the rough sea'.

On the penultimate day of August, steering south-southeast towards Dursey Head, just above Bantry Bay, only eight other ships were visible from Recalde's. 'The recent storms had scattered the rest, which all together had numbered twenty-two'; but by 2 September, when *San Juan* had reached 53° 30' N, only six vessels were to be seen. 'At nine o'clock in the morning we turned seawards to the west and this night we sailed into a violent tempest, so that on the 3rd only the vice-flagship, one other ship and a pinnace remained together.' That night a comet flashed across the sky and with the dawn they spotted a hulk making distress signals because she was shipping a lot of water and the crew wanted to abandon her. 'But on account of the rough wind and sea we could not help her. . .' By now they were being blown back the way they had come, for at two the next morning Recalde and his crew found themselves in difficulties hard by The Blaskets, off the Dingle Peninsula, 'and nearly lost the ship because we came so close under full sail in the darkness and with a strong gale. And so we turned to seaward and in the morning landward again, trying to clear the headland, which we were unable to do; so we remained in great confusion as to whether we should turn seaward or search for a harbour to carry out repairs.'

Now began the most terrible time of all. A party went ashore on Great Blasket, where they found pigs and rabbits but very little fresh water, and they only managed to fill fourteen casks. Another great wind blew up ('one of the wildest storms we had ever seen') while *San Juan* was sheltering in the island's lee, where she was joined by a consort, but only for a couple of hours, before this vessel was seen to be dragging her anchor 'and suddenly sank, without a single man out of the four hundred that we knew she carried escaping or being seen'. *San Juan*, too, began dragging 'and it was a miracle that we escaped'. Another vessel sought shelter, arriving without her main-mast 'and in a very bad state'. For eight days Recalde barely managed to stay afloat there, while one storm after another threatened disaster but only took away an anchor and its cable. On 18 September he made to leave, but only with difficulty did the ship get away from the anchorage – 'We sailed so close to a promontory that at one point it was possible to jump ashore from the galleon and our deliverance from that was one of the greatest miracles ever seen. And so we got out to the open sea tonight with a fair wind.' They had been struggling along a very small stretch of the Irish coast for fourteen full days and it was not until the 22nd that they finally cleared Dursey Head, after which the weather alternated between calms and fresh breezes as they ploughed steadily onwards to the south, fortune at last on their side. Eventually, 'On the 28th, at dawn, we came within sight of land, which was the cape of Ortiguera, and at nine in the morning the wind turned moderate to the north-northeast, whereupon we steered towards the port of Corunna where we anchored at nightfall.'[6]

Recalde and the handful of vessels that had managed to stay close to him were among the last to reach Spain, and the only ones that survived landfall in Ireland. Sixty-seven ships finally made it home that year, bringing back only two-thirds of the men who had set out from Lisbon in May, and many of them half-dead from exhaustion and deprivation by the time they returned: one ship ran aground in Laredo harbour with the end of her epic voyage only minutes away because she didn't have enough crew left to man her properly. Of the vessels that came back, many were in such a dilapidated state that they were fit for nothing but the scrapheap: one had sailed all the way from the North Sea with cables bound around and under her hull, because her captain was afraid she might otherwise fall apart. Of the commanders who didn't return, Don Alonso Martínez de Leyva can be counted the most unfortunate, for when his ship began to sink he was rescued by another vessel, which shortly afterwards herself went down off Giant's Causeway with the loss of all hands. Recalde and de Oquendo returned sick and broken, and both were dead before October was done. Medina Sidonia survived and continued in the royal service for the fifteen remaining years of the Anglo-Spanish conflict, but everyone who subsequently met him said he was a changed and subdued man after the Armada.

Recalde set down on paper his opinion of what had gone wrong, as had de Leyva before he was drowned, and both blamed their Admiral and his closest adviser, Diego Flores de Valdés, for much of the failure. The accusers argued that Medina Sidonia had ignored the opportunity

---

6 The dates in this account have been adjusted to conform to the old Julian calendar still used in 1588 by the English, in which everything happened ten days before the dates recorded by Recalde, who was following the new Gregorian calendar which most of Europe had adopted by 1587. According to his calculations, therefore, the Armada began to leave Lisbon on 28 May and he himself returned to Corunna on 7 October.

to attack Plymouth when the English were still struggling to leave harbour, that he had rejected Recalde's advice to shelter in the Solent until they had found out whether the Duke of Parma was ready to receive them or not, had failed in his duty when he left the *Rosario* behind, had foolishly anchored off Calais and thus invited the fireship attack, was culpable in abandoning any vessel that could not follow his own up the North Sea or afterwards, had cravenly decided to sail for home instead of turning back for a second attempt to reach Parma and his troops, and had at one early stage even contemplated surrendering the entire Armada to the English. There was doubtless something to be said for some of these charges, and Medina Sidonia was certainly very defensive when Recalde's version was put to him. But King Philip should also take some of the blame for his insistence that the overall strategy he had devised must be followed inflexibly, for his failure to take into account the shallow waters off Flanders, which made it impossible for his great ships to come close inshore safely. Medina Sidonia could quite reasonably argue, too, that he sailed on past both Plymouth and the Solent because he was following the explicit orders of a sovereign who never countenanced disobedience.

And then there is the role played by the English, who enjoyed a number of advantages over their enemy. Their ships, as the Spanish themselves conceded, were superior in every way: better-founded, better-maintained, and adequately provided for so as to (just) last the course, all of which could be put down to superior naval organisation before they even set sail. They were handled better by seamen who had rather more varied experience of combat behind them than Spaniards who had mostly been limited to defensive actions against pirates, sailing in huge convoys across the Atlantic – though the Armada performed creditably enough so long as it maintained the formation which was comparable to that of the *flotas*. The English had guns with a greater range than those used by the Spanish, and they produced a much bigger volume of firepower, which has been partly attributed to compact four-wheeled gun carriages that were more manoeuvrable than the two-wheeled carriages (essentially land artillery) their enemy used: one of Medina Sidonia's own gunnery officers testified to the comparable rates of fire after a morning's action in which the English put 2,000 rounds into the Armada, which replied with only 750.

On top of all that, the English had the better battle tactics, which were varied and well practised enough to suit the changing circumstances of the running engagement, as in the subdivision of Howard's two squadrons into four at one stage, and his use of fireships at another; and when they attacked it might be in any one of two or three different formations, including circling movements or even figures of eight, whereas the Spanish appeared to be lost the moment their line abreast crescent was disturbed. These English advantages were not secured by naval habits formed only during Elizabeth's reign, but had developed slowly over many more years, most of them traceable to things that began to happen when Henry VIII was on the throne and aware that if he was going to achieve the virtue, glory and immortality that he craved, if he was going to defend his kingdom by the sea from its foes, his very first need was for ships and for men who would make of them a power in themselves.

Many human factors contributed to the failure of the Enterprise of England. The destruction of so much of the Spanish Armada, however, was not the work of its enemy but of the elements. As always in the days of sail, the weather had the decisively last word.

SHIPS INHERITED BY HENRY VIII

NAME	BUILT	CREW	TUNNAGE
Regent	1489	–	1,000
Sovereign	1488	–	600–1,000
Mary (and) John	bought 1487 or later	–	180–260
Sweepstake	1497	–	80 (?)
Mary Fortune	1497	–	80 (?)

SHIPS IN SERVICE AT HENRY VIII'S DEATH

NAME	BUILT	CREW	TUNNAGE
Trinity Henry	c.1530	220	250
Sweepstake	1535	220	300
Lion	1536	100	140
Less Bark	rebuilt 1536	250	400
Minion	rebuilt 1536	200	300
Peter (Pomegranate)	rebuilt 1536	400	600
Great Bark (Great Galley)	rebuilt c.1538	300	600
Jennet	c.1538	120	180
Henry Grâce à Dieu	rebuilt 1540	700	1,000

* The list of ships inherited by Henry VIII has been taken from R.C. Anderson's *English Men-of-war 1509–1649*. The longer list comes from Tom Glasgow Jr's compilation in *Mariner's Mirror Vol. 56/3*, 1970. However, it is as well to bear in mind something he himself wrote a little earlier (MM Vol. 52/4, 1966, p. 391) that 'no list of royal ships is likely ever to be compiled of this period which will not be subject to further corrections'.

NAME	BUILT	CREW	TUNNAGE
Dragon	1542	110	140
Pauncey	1543	300	450
New Bark	1543	130	200
Artigo	1543 prize	100	140
Galley Subtle	1544	300	200–300
Salamander	1544 prize	220	300
Unicorn	1544 prize	140	240
Swallow	1544	160	300
Less Pinnace	1544	44	40
Matthew (Matthew Gonson)	acquired 1545	300	600
Jesus of Lübeck	bought *c.*1545	300	600
Struse of Danzig	bought *c.*1545	250	400
Mary Hamboro (Hamburg)	bought *c.*1545	250	400
Christopher of Bremen	bought 1545	250	400
Grand Mistress	1545	250	420
Anne Gallant	1545	250	450
Morian of Danzig	1545	300	500
Greyhound	1545	120	200
Falcon	1545	60	80
Roo	1545	50	80
Merlin	1545	50	40
Saker	1545	60	80
Hind	1545	60	80
Brigandine	1545	40	40
Hare	1545	30	15
Bull	1546	120	200
Tiger	1546	120	200
Hart	1546	220	300
Antelope	1546	220	300
Phoenix	1546	60	70
George	1546	40	60
Trego Renneger	1546	25	20
Double Rose	1546	40	20
Flower de Luce	1546	40	20
Hawthorne	1546	40	20
Maidenhead	1546	40	20
Portcullis	1546	40	20
Three Ostrich Feathers	1546	35	20
Sun	1546	40	20
Rose in the Sun	1546	40	20

NAME	BUILT	CREW	TUNNAGE
Cloud in the Sun	1546	40	20
Rose Slip	1546	40	20
Gillyflower	1546	40	20
Harp	1546	40	20
Falcon in the Fetterlock	1546	45	20

APPENDIX II

INVENTORY OF HENRY GRÂCE À DIEU IN 1514

(Reproduced as it appears in the original MS, in which the descender 'j' represents single or final minims: e.g. j=1, iij=3, viij=8, xvj=16 etc.)

THE KYNGES SHIPP CALLED THE *HENRY GRACE DE DEWE*

Stuff tacle and apparrell of the seid ship delyverd by the seid commissioners into the charge of John Hopton by indenture, that is to sey:

Ffyrst the foremast of the seid shippe	j
Shrowdes to the same	xvj
Dedemens hyes to the same	xvj
Tacles to the foremast	iiij
Doble polles with shyvers of brasse	iiij
Single polles with shyvers of brasse	iij
Single pools with a colk of brass	j
Swyfters to the foremast	vj
Doble polles with colkes of brasse	iij
Polles with shyvers of wode	iij
Polles with v colkes of brasse and oone of wode	vj
Garnettes to the foremast with iiij poles	ij
Garnet with ij polles and shyvers of brasse	j
Garnet with a shever of brasse and an other of tymber	j
Trusses to the foremast	ij
Drynges to the same	j
Doble polles for the trusses with colkes of brasse	ij
Single poles of tymber	ij

Drynges with a double pole with a colk of brasse and oone single pole of wode	j
Halyers to the foremast	ij
Shyvers of brasse to the brest of the forecastell	iiij
Ramehedes with iv shevers of brasse	j
Shetes to the foresayle	ij
Pollies with shevers of brasse to the same	ij
Lyftes to the foresayle	ij
Doble polies with shyvers of brasse to the same	ij
Single polies with colkes of brasse	ij
Shetes to the toppe sayle	ij
Single polies with woden pynnes to the same	ij
Tackes to the foresayle	ij
Stodynges to the foreyerd	ij
Pollies to the same with woden pynnes	ij
Cranelynnes to the foremast	j
Single poles with a shyver of brasse	ij
Bowelynnes to the foreyerd with the poleis and dede manes hies and oone doble pole with a shever of brasse	j
Stayes to the foreyerd with iiij dedemens heies	ij
Sprete sayle yerdes	j
Halyers to the same	ij
Single poleis with shyvers of brasse to the same	ij
Lyftes to the sprete sayle with iij single polies and woden pynnes	j
Grapilles with the cheyne hangyng apon the bowspret with a pole having a colk of brasse	j
Knyghtes longyng to the lyftes of the foresayle with ij shevers of brasse	ij
The fore topmast	j
Shrowdes to the same	xij
Halyers with a doble polie and a colk of brasse ij single poleis with woden pynnes	ij
Bowlynes to the foretop sayle yerd with pawes and dedemens hyyes to the same	ij
Brasses for the foretopsayle yard ij single poles with pynnes of wode	ij
Lyftes to the foretopsayle yerd with iiij poleis with woden pynnes	ij
Shetes to the foretopsayle with ij woden poles	ij
Steyes to the foretopmast	j
Sayle yerdes to the foretop	j

Toppe Galant apon the foretopmast	j
Mastes to the same	j
Shrowdes to the same	viij
Halyers with ij single poles with woden pynnes	ij
Brasses to the same with ij single poleis and wodepynnes and dedemens hyes to the same	ij
Bowlynes to the topgalant yerd the power and dedemens hyes to the same	ij
Lyftes to the foretopgalant yerd with iiij single polies with woden pynnes	ij
Shetes with ij single poles with woden pynnes	ij
Stayes to the foretopgalant mast	j
Shevers of Brasse for the cattes in the forecastell	iiij
Davettes with iiij shevers of Brasse	ij
Smale davette with oone shever of Brasse	j
The mayne mast	j
Shrowdes with cheynes of yron and dedemens hies to the same	xl
Bote tacles of sterebord syde with iiij doble poles and viii single poleis with xvj shyvers of Brasse	iiij
Swifters on the same syde with vij doble poleis and vii single poleis with colkes of Brasse and ij poles of tymbes pynnes	viiij
Garnettes with ij single poles with shivers of Brasse	j
Garnettes with ij single polies with colkes of Brasse	j
Garnettes with oone single pole with a shever of Brasse and an other pole with a colk of Brasse	j
Stodynges with a single pole with a Shever of Brasse	j
Bote tacles oon ladbord syde with iiij doble polies and viij single polies with xvj Shevers of Brasse	iiij
Bretayn tacles with ij single polies and Shevers of Brasse to the same	j
Swyfters with vij doble polies with colkes of Brasse and viij single poles with colkes of Brasse	viij
Garnettes whereof oone with ij single polies and iv shevers of Brasse an other with ij single polies with ij colkes of Brasse and an other with a shever of Brasse	iij
Stodynges with a shever of Brasse	j
Tymber polies for the Shuts	ij
The mayne yerde with the mayne parell	j
Single poleis with a shever of Brasse to wynde up the mayne parell	j

Trusses with iiij doble polleis and iiij single polies with xij shevers of Brasse	iij
Drynges with ij doble polies and iiij shevers of Brasse	ij
Single poleis of tymbre to the same	ij
Tyes	j payer
Whele Ropes	j
Geers with vj single poleis whereof iiij with shevers of Brasse and ij of tymbre	iij
Knyghtes belonging to the same with iij Shevers of Brasse	iiij
Single poles for the topsayle	iiij
Shutes with iiij shevers of Brasse	ij
Knyghtes with ij shevers of Brasse	ij
The mayne yerd	j
Lyftes with ij doble poleis and ij single with vj Shevers of Brasse to the same	ij
Knyghtes with ij Shevers of Brasse	ij
Shutes	ij
Tackes	ij
Bowlynes with Brydelles and Dedemens hies	ij
Poleis to the mayne Bowlyne with ij Shevers of Brasse	j
Mayne Stayes with viij dedemens hies	iiij
Brasses with ij single poles and colkes of Brasse	ij
The mayne top	j
The mayne top mast and a coler of yron	j
Shrowdes to the same with dedemens hies	xiiij
The mayne top Sayle yerd	j
Tyes	j
Halyers with a doble and a single polie with ij shevers of Brasse	j
Brases with iiij poles	ij
Lyftes with iiij polies and colkes of Brasse	ij
Cranelynnes with a single pole and a colk of Brasse	j
Steyes to the mayne top mast	j
Bowlynes with dedemens hies	ij
The top Galant apon the mayne topmast	j
Mastes for the same	j
Rynges of yron for the same	j
Shrowdes to the same with dedemens hies	x
Sayle yerdes to the same	j
Stayes to the same	j
Bowlynes	ij

Brases with ij poles to the same	ij
Shutes	ij
Grabulles with cheynes to the same	ij
Poleys apon the mayne yerd for the grabulles	ij
Spare knyghtes standyng by the mast with ij shevers of Brasse	ij
The mayne meson mast	j
Shrowdes with xj doble poles and xj single poles, a doble and single polee with colkes of Brasse	xij
Swyftyers with vj doble poles and vj single poles with colkes of Brasse	vj
Tacles with ij doble poles of tymbre	ij
Single poles oone of tymbre the other with a colke of Brasse	j
Steyes	j
Shutes	j
Single poles oon of tre the other with a colk of Brasse	j
Cranelynes with a single polie and a colk of Brasse	j
Brases with ij single poles	ij
Teyes	ij
Halyers	ij
The rame hede	j
Kyghtes with iij Shevers of Brasse	j
The yerd to the meson Sayle	j
Lyftes with iiij poles and dedemens hies	j
Trusses with a doble and a single polie with colkes of Brasse	j
Toppe	j
Topmast to the same	j
Rynges of yron	j
Shrowdes with dedemens hies	x
The Sayle yerd	j
Tyes	j
Poles to the same	ij
Lyftes with iij poles and dedemens hies	j
The top Galant of the mayne meson	j
The mast to the same	j
Shrowdes to the same	vj
Lyftes with iiij poleis and dedemens hies	j
The Sayle yerd	j
Tyes to the same	j
Halyers	j
The boneaventure mast	j

Shrowdes with x Doble poles and x syngle poleis	x
Sayle yerdes	j
Tyes	j
Halyers with a doble pole	ij
Knyghtes with iiij Shevers of Brasse	j
Shutes with ij poleis to the same	j
The boneaventure top	j
Mastes to the same	j
Sayle yerdes	j
Shrowdes	viij
Steyes	j
In the storehouse of the Shippe viij single pendaunt poleis with shevers of Brasse	viij
Smale single garnet poleis with shevers of Brasse	j
Doble lyfte poleis with shevers of Brasse	iiij
Doble poleanker poleis with Shevers of Brasse	iiij
Snach polleis with gret Shevers of Brasse	iiij
Single poleis with Shevers of Wode	xiiij
Doble poleis with Shevers of Wode	ij
Doble poleis with a colk of Brasse	j
Single poleis with a colk of Brasse	j
Pottes called piche pottes	j
Ketilles to melt in pyche	j
Boyes for ankers	x
Boy Ropes	x
Shevers of Brasse without poleis	iij
Leddern bokettes	xij dossen
Love hokes	iiij
Lynch hokes	iij
Copper ketill not sett in turnes weying by estimacon ccc	j
CABLES AND CABLETTES OF	
xiiij ynch compass	j
xvij ynch compass	ij
xv ynch compass	ij
ix ynch compass	j
viij ynch compass	j—vij
HAWSERS OF	
iiij ynch compass	iiij
vj ynch compass	iij
v ynch compass	j
viij ynch compass	j
iiij ynch compass	j
ij ynch compass	j

v ynch compass	j
iiij ynch compass	vij
iij ynch compass	j
iij ynch di compass	j—xxij
Smale lyne	ij peces
Bygger lyne for lanyers	ij peces
Brayle Ropes with iij poles to the same	j
Grete doble Blockes ether of them ij Shyvers of Brasse	ij
Single blokes with ij Shevers of Brasse	ij
Long Ores for the Grete bote	ix
Tarre	ij barelles
Ores for the Cocke bote	xxiij
Standart Staves	lix
Stremers	viij
Lytle flagges	c
Top Armours	vij
Targettes	xx dossen
Farge fflagges	lx
To the mayne Sayle Acorse an ij bonettes doble	j mayne sayle
Mayne topsayles	j
Topgalant Sayle	j
The meson Sayle	j
The boneaventure Sayle	j
The foresayle Acorse and a bonet doble and bonet single an other corse and iij bonettes single in all	ij foresayles
The fore topsayle	j
The foretopgalant Sayle	j
The Bowspret Sayle	j
The mayne Sayle for the gret Bote, a corse and ij bonettes single	j sayle
The forsayle acorse and ij bonettes single	j
Top Seyle	j
The meson Seyle	j
The boneaventure Sayle	j
The old corse of a hulk Sayle	j

ANKERS CALLED

Sterbord bowers	ij
Ladbord bowers	ij
Destrelles of Sterbord	ij
Destrelles on ladbord	j
Shot ankers	j

Caggers	j
Spare ankers	ix—xix
Trene platters	iiij dossen
Trene cuppes	v dossen
Tankerdes	iij dossen
Lantrons	vj
Grete lantrons	j
Middellantrons	ij
Copper ketilles in turnes	iij
Lede in oone pece by estimacon	D [5cwt]
Grete belles in the seid Ship of Brasse	j
The grete botes mayne mast	j
Shrowdes to the same	xiiij
Polles to the same	xxviij
Tacles oone with a doble pole and colkes of Brasse the other with a single pole and a Shever of timbre	ij
Single poles with a shever of Brasse	j
Mayne yerdis and the parell	j
Trusses with ij poleis and Shevers of timbre	j
Tyes	j
Halyers with a doble pole and Shever of Brasse	j
Single poleis on of them with a Shever of brasse and other of timbre	ij
Shutes	ij
Tackes	ij
Bowlynes with a pole and Shever of tymbre	ij
Lyftes with ij Single poleis	ij
Topsayle Shows with ij single poleis	ij
Yerde Ropes	ij
The meyne Stay with ij doble poleis	j
The toppe	j
The topmast	j
Shrowdes to the same	vj
Sayle yerdes	j
Tyes	j
Parell to the sayle yerd	j
Bowlynes	ij
Lyftes	ij
Cranelynes	j
Brases	ij
The foremast	j
Shrodes to the same	vj

The Sayle yerd	j
The parell	j
Teyes	j
Syngle halyers with a polie to the same	j
Shetes	vj
Tackes	j
Lyftes with ij poleys	ij
Steyes	j
Bowlynes with a polie	j
Single Trusses with a polie	j
Bowspretes	j
Mayne meson mast	j
Shrowdes to the same	vj
The Sayle yerd	j
The parell to the same	j
The Tye	j
Single halyers with a pole	j
Trusses with ij poles	j
Lyftes with iij poles	j
Brases with ij poles	ij
Steys with ij Smale poles	j
The boneaventure mast	j
Shrowdes to the same	iiij
Tyes	j
Single halyers with oone pole	j
The sayle yerd	j
The parell to the same	j
Ankers for the seid bote	iij
Cablettes of v ynch compass	ij
Cocke bote	j
Mastes to the same	j
Sayle yerdes	j
Shevers of Brasse	ij
Ores to the same	xij
Bote hokes	j
The skyff otherwise called Jollywatt	j
Mastes to the same	j
Sayles	j
Ores to the same	vj
Shevers of Brasse	j
Shevers of Brasse called a Wyndyng Shever for the Rame hede	j
Hawsers of v ynch compass	j

Hawsers of vj ynch compass	di [half a] hawser
Hawsers of v ynch compass	iiij
Cables of ix ynch compass	j
Hawsers of vj ynch compass	di hawser
Soundyng ledes	vj

Ordnance, Artillarie and habillements for warr delyvered to the charge and custody of Thomas Spert, master, and William Bonython, purser of the seid shipp by Indenture as aforeseid, that is to sey

Serpentynes of yron with miches boltes and forlockes	cxxij
Chambers to the same	ccxliiij
Stone gonnes of yron Apon trotill wheles and all other Apparell	iiij
Chambers to the same	iiij
Serpentynes of Brasse upon wheles shod with yron	iij
Serpentynes of Brasse apon wheles unshod	j
Grete peces of yron of oon makyng and bignes	xij
Chambers to the same	xxiiij
Grete yron gonnes of oon sort that come owt of fflaunders with myches bolts and forelocks	iiij
Chambers to the same	iiij
Stone gonnes apon Trotill wheles with miches boltes and forelockes to the same	xviij
Chambers to the same	xxxiiij
Smale vice peces of Brasse apon shodd wheles of Symondes makyng	j
Long vice peces of Brasse of the same makyng	iij
Ffawcons of Brasse apon Trotill wheles	vj
A fayre pece of Brasse of Arragows makyng	j
A Slyng of yron apon Trotill wheles	j
Chambers to the same with other apparell	j
Grete Stone gonnes of yron	ij
Chambers to the same	iiij
Grete culverynes of Brasse apon unshodd wheles of Symondes making	ij
Grete bumberdes of Brasse appon iiij trotill wheles of herberd makyng	j
Grete curtalles of Brasse apon iiij wheles and of the same makyng	j
Hakebusshes of yron hole	clxxxxiiij
Hakbusshes of yron broken	vij

Shott of yron of Dyverse Sortes	Dclx shott
Stone Shott of Dyverse Sortes in the balist of the ship A grete number not told	
In the Grete Bote of the seid ship Remayning first Serpentynes of yron with muches boltes and forelocks	viij
Chambers to the same	xxv
Serpentynes of Brasse apon shodd wheles	j
Ffawcons of Brasse apon shodd wheles	ij

IN THE STOREHOUSE OF THE SHIP

Bowes of Ewe	cxxiiij
Chestes for the same	ij
Hole chestes of Arrowes	iij
Billys	cxliiij
Moryspykes	lxxx
Backes and Brestes of Almyne Rivettes of ether	cc
Splentes	clxxxviij payer
Salettes	cc
Standardes of mayle	cc
Chargyng ladylles for Gonnes with staves	vj
Staves withowt ladelles	viij
Spare miches for Gonnes	xiij
Spare boltes	ij
Javelyns	ix dossen
Dartes	lvij dossen
Hamers for Gonnes	xiiij
Crowes of yron	iiij
Stonepykes of yron	xiiij
Lynch pynnes	iiij

BIBLIOGRAPHY

ABBREVIATIONS

AA   *Archaeologia Aeliana*
EHR   *English Historical Review*
EcHR   *Economic History Review*
HJ   *The Historical Journal*
IHR   *Institute of Historical Research*
LP   *Letters and Papers, Foreign and Domestic, of the Reign of Henry VIII*
MM   *The Mariner's Mirror*
NH   *Northern History*
NRS   *Navy Records Society*
RP   *Royal Proclamations*
TRHS   *Transactions of the Royal Historical Society*
SNR   *Society for Nautical Research*
SPH   *State Papers of Henry VIII*
SPS   *Spanish State Papers* (Vol. VIII)
SPV   *Venetian State Papers* (Vols II & III)
SPE   *State Papers (Domestic) of Edward VI*

Adair, E.R., 'English Galleys in the Sixteenth Century' (EHR Vol. LXXXV, 1920)
Albion R.G., *Naval and Maritime History: an Annotated Bibliography* (Newton Abbot, 4th edn, 1973)
Anderson, R.C., 'Henry VIII's "Great Galley"' (MM Vol. 6/8, August 1920); *List of English Men-of-War 1509–1649* (SNR Occasional Publication No. 7, 1974 rev. edn); 'The Mary Gonson' (MM Vol. 46/3, 1960)
Arenhold, L., 'Ships earlier than 1500 AD' (MM Vol. 1/11, November 1911)
Awty, B.G., 'The Continental Origins of Wealden Ironworkers, 1451–1544' (EcHR 2nd Series Vol. XXXIV, 1981)
Balteau, J., et al. (eds), *Dictionnaire de Biographie Française* (Paris, 1936–)

Beer, E.S. de, 'The Lord High Admiral and the Administration of the Navy' (MM Vol. 1/13, 1927)

Bennell, J.E.G., 'English Oared Vessels of the Sixteenth Century' (Part One MM Vol. 60/1, 1974: Part Two MM Vol. 60/2, 1974)

Bernard, J., *Navires et Gens de Mer à Bordeaux 1400–1550* (3 vols, Paris, 1968)

Blomfield, R.M., 'Man-of-War Boats' (MM Vol. 1/9, September 1911); 'Naval Executive Ranks: Admiral, Lord Admiral, and Great Admiral' (MM Vol. 2/4, April 1912)

Bonner, E., 'The Recovery of St Andrews Castle in 1547; French Naval Policy and Diplomacy in the British Isles' (EHR Vol. CXI, 1996)

Boulind, R., 'Ships of Private Origin in the mid-Tudor Navy' (MM Vol. 59/4, 1973); 'Tudor Captains: the Beestons and the Tyrrells' (MM Vol. 59/2; 1973)

Brewer, J.S., Gairdner, J. and Brodie, R.H. (eds), *Letters and Papers, Foreign and Domestic, of the Reign of Henry VIII 1509–47* (21 vols plus addendae, London, 1862–1932)

Bridbury, A.R., *England and the Salt Trade in the Later Middle Ages* (Oxford, 1955)

Brooks, F.W., 'A Wage-Scale for Seamen, 1546' (EHR Vol. LX, 1945); 'The Cinque Ports' (MM Vol. 15/2, 1929)

Burwash, D., *English Merchant Shipping 1460–1540* (Toronto, 1947)

Byrne, M. St C., *The Lisle Letters* (6 vols, Chicago, 1981)

Callender, G., 'Wyngaerde's Map of London' (MM Vol. 2/7, July, 1912)

Carus-Wilson, E.M., 'The Origins and Development of the Merchant Adventurers' Organisation in London as shown in their own medieval records' (EcHR Vol. IV/2, 1933) *Medieval Merchant Venturers* (London, 1954)

Carus-Wilson, E.M. and Coleman, O., *England's Export Trade 1275–1547* (Oxford, 1963)

Casson, L., *The Ancient Mariners: Seafarers and Sea Fighters of the Mediterranean in Ancient Times* (Princeton, 1991)

Childs, W.R., 'The Commercial Shipping of South-western England in the Later Fifteenth Century' (MM Vol. 83/3, 1997)

Clowes, W.L., *The Royal Navy: a History from the Earliest Times Vol. I* (London, 1996 edn)

Colvin, H.M. et al., *The History of the King's Works* (6 vols, London, 1963–73)

Connell-Smith, G., 'English Merchants Trading to the New World in the Early Sixteenth Century' (IHR Bulletin Vol. XXIII, 1950); *Forerunners of Drake; a Study of English Trade with Spain in the early Tudor period* (London, 1954)

Corbett, J.S., *Drake and the Tudor Navy: with a history of the rise of England as a Maritime Power* (2 vols, London, 2nd edn, 1899); (ed.) '*Fighting Instructions 1530–1816*' (NRS Vol. 29, 1905); 'The Lord Admiral's Whistle' (MM Vol. 3/12, December 1912)

Crossley, D.W., 'The Management of a 16th-Century Ironworks' (EcHR 2nd Series Vol. XIX, 1966)

Cruickshank, C., *Henry VIII and the Invasion of France* (Stroud, 1990)

Davies, C.S.L., 'The Administration of the Royal Navy under Henry VIII: the Origins of the Navy Board' (EHR Vol. LXXX, 1965); 'Provisions for Armies, 1509–50; a Study in the Effectiveness of Early Tudor Government' (EcHR 2nd series Vol. XVII/2, 1964)

Dasent, J.R. (ed.), *Acts of the Privy Council of England; Vol. I 1542–1547* (London, 1890)

DeVries, K., 'The Effectiveness of Fifteenth-Century Shipboard Artillery' (MM Vol. 84/4, 1998)

Dietz, B., 'Dikes, Dockheads and Gates: English Docks and Sea Power in the Sixteenth and Seventeenth Centuries' (MM Vol. 88/2, 2002)

Doubleday, H.A. et al., *The Victoria County History of Hampshire* (London, 1900–12); *The Victoria County History of Norfolk* (London, 1901–6)

Edler, F., 'Winchcombe Kerseys in Antwerp' (1538–44) (EcHR Vol. VII, 1936–7)

Ewen, C.L.E., 'Organized Piracy Round England in the Sixteenth Century' (MM Vol. 35/1, 1949)

Fisher, F.J., 'Commercial Trends and Policy in Sixteenth-Century England' (EcHR Vol. X, 1939–40)

Field, C., '"The Santa Anna"; an Early Armour-clad' (MM Vol. 9/12, December 1923)

Fox, H.S.A., *The Evolution of the Fishing Village: Landscape and Society along the South Devon Coast, 1086–1550* (Oxford, 2001)

Friel, I., *The Good Ship: Ships, Shipbuilding and Technology in England 1200–1520* (London, 1995)

Fudge, J.D., *Cargoes, Embargoes and Emissaries: The Commercial and Political Interaction of England and the German Hanse, 1450–1510* (Toronto, 1995)

Gairdner, J. (ed.), *The Paston Letters* (Stroud, 1983 edn); 'On a Contemporary Drawing of the Burning of Brighton in the Time of Henry VIII' (TRHS Series 3/1, 1907)

Galliou, P. and Jones, M., *The Bretons* (London, 1991)

Glasgow, T. Jr., 'The Navy in Philip and Mary's war 1557–58' (MM Vol. 53/4, 1967); 'The Navy in the first Elizabethan undeclared war 1559–60' (MM Vol. 54/1, 1968); 'The Navy in the Le Havre Expedition 1562–64' (MM Vol. 54/3, 1968); 'Maturing of Naval Administration 1556–1564' (MM Vol. 56/1, 1970); 'List of Ships in the Royal Navy from 1539–1588' (MM Vol. 56/3, 1970)

Goodman, W.L., 'Bristol Apprentice Register 1532–1658; a selection of enrolments of mariners' (MM Vol. 60/1. 1974)

Goring, J., 'Social Change and Military Decline in Mid-Tudor England' (*History* Vol. 60, 1970)

Greenhill, B., *The Evolution of the Sailing Ship 1250–1580* (London, 1995)

Hakluyt, R., *The principal Navigations, Voyages, Traffics and Discoveries of the English Nation, made by Sea or Over Land* (Vols V and VIII, 1903–5 edn)

Hall, E., *Chronicle; Containing the History of England. . .* (London, 1548/1809)

Harland, J. and Myers, M.R., *Seamanship in the Age of Sail* (London, 1985)

Hattendorf, J.B., et al. (eds), *British Naval Documents 1204–1960* (NRS Vol. 131, 1993) and Unger R.W. (eds), *War at Sea in the Middle Ages and Renaissance* (London, 2003)

Heath, P., 'North Sea Fishing in the Fifteenth Century: the Scarborough Fleet' (NH Vol. 3, 1968)

Hobbs, D., 'Royal Ships and their Flags in the Late Fifteenth and Early Sixteenth Centuries' (MM Vol. 80/4, 1994)

Hodges, H.W., and Hughes, M.A., *Select Naval Documents* (Cambridge, 1922)

Hollinshed, J.E., 'Chester, Liverpool and the Basque Region in the Sixteenth Century' (MM Vol. 85/4, 1999)

Hoskins, W.G., *The Age of Plunder: King Henry's England 1500–1547* (London, 1976)

Howard, F., *Sailing Ships of War 1400–1860* (London, 1979)

Hughes, P.L. and Larkin, J.F., *Tudor Royal Proclamations; Vol. I The Early Tudors 1485–1553* (New Haven and London, 1964)

Hull, F., *A Calendar of the White and Black Books of the Cinque Ports 1432–1955* (London, 1966)

Humpherus, H., *History of the Origins and Progress of the Company of Watermen and Lightermen of the River Thames 1514–1859* (Vol. 1, Wakefield, 1981)

James, N.D.G., *A History of British Forestry* (London, 1981)

Johns, A.W., 'The Principal Officers of the Navy' (MM Vol. 14/1, 1928)

Keevil, J.J., *Medicine and the Navy: Vol. I 1200–1649* (Edinburgh, 1957)

Kemp, P. (ed.), *The Oxford Companion to Ships and the Sea* (Oxford, 1979)

Kitson, H., 'The Early History of Portsmouth Dockyard 1496–1800' (MM Vol. 33/4, 1947)

Knecht, R.J., *Francis I* (Cambridge, 1982)

Knighton, C.S., *Calendar of State Papers Domestic Series of the Reign of Edward VI 1547–1553* (London, 1992)

Knighton, C.S., and Loades, D.M., *The Anthony Roll of Henry VIII's Navy* (NRS Occasional Publications Vol. 2, 2000); *Letters from the Mary Rose* (Stroud/Portsmouth, 2002)

Ladourie, E. Le Roy, *The French Peasantry 1450–1660* (trans. A. Sheridan, Aldershot, 1987)

Lane, F.C., 'Tonnages, Medieval and Modern' (EcHR 2nd series Vol. XVII/2, 1964)

Laughton, L.G.C., 'Early Tudor Ship-Guns' (MM Vol. 46/4, 1960); 'The Burning of Brighton by the French' (TRHS 3rd series Vol. X, 1916)

Leyland, J., 'A German Pirate of the Sixteenth Century' (MM Vol. 2/8, August 1912)

Lewis, M., *The Hawkins Dynasty: Three Generations of a Tudor Family* (London, 1969)

Loades, D.M., *The Tudor Navy* (Aldershot, 1992); John Dudley, *Duke of Northumberland 1504–1553* (Oxford, 1996); *England's Maritime Empire: Seapower, Commerce and Policy 1490–1690* (London, 2000)

Macdougall, N., *James IV* (East Linton, 1997)

Mackie, J. D., 'Henry VIII and Scotland' (TRHS 4th series Vol. XXIX, 1947)

Manwaring G.E., *A Bibliography of British Naval History* (London, 1970 edn); 'The Whistle as a Naval Instrument' (MM Vol. 5/3, September 1919)

Marcus G.J., *A Naval History of England: Vol. I The Formative Centuries* (London, 1961); 'The Mariner's Compass: its influence upon navigation in the later Middle Ages' (*History* Vol. XLI, 1956) 'The First English Voyages to Iceland' (MM Vol. 42/4, 1956)

Masson, P. and Vergé-Franceschi, M. (eds), *La France et la mer au siècle des grands découvertes* (Paris, 1993)

Menzies, G., *1431: The Year China Discovered the World* (London, 2002)

Michaud, J.F., (ed.), *Biographie Universelle, ancienne et moderne* (45 vols, Graz, 1966–70)

Miller, R., 'Early Medieval Seamen and the Church: Contacts Ashore' (MM Vol. 89/2, 2003)

Milne, G., *The Port of Medieval London* (Stroud, 2003)

Mollat, M. 'The French Maritime Community; a slow progress up the social scale from the Middle Ages to the Sixteenth Century' (MM Vol. 69/2, 1983)

Moore, A., 'The Snow' (MM Vol. 2/2, February 1912); and Nance, R.M., 'Round-Sterned Ships' (MM Vol. 1/4, April 1911, Vol. 1/11, November 1911); 'Rig in Northern Europe' (MM Vol. 42/1, 1956)

Morris, M., 'The Rise of the English Sailcloth Industry 1565–1643: Coastal Trade Records as an Indicator of Import Substitution' (MM Vol. 84/2, 1998)

Murray K.M.E., 'Dengemarsh and the Cinque Ports' (EHR Vol. LIV, 1939); *The Constitutional History of the Cinque Ports* (Manchester, 1935)

Nance, R.M., 'The Kraek of WA' (MM Vol. 2/8, August 1912); 'Stone-Carved Ships in Brittany' (MM Vol. 2/3, 1925)

Oppenheim, M., *A History of the Administration of the Royal Navy and of Merchant Shipping in Relation to the Navy from MDIX to MDCILX* (New York, 1961 edn)

Oman, C., *A History of the Art of War in the Sixteenth Century* (London, 1937)

Outhwaite, R.B., 'The Trials of Borrowing: the English Crown and the

Antwerp Money Market in the mid-16th Century' (EcHR 2nd Series Vol. XIX, 1966)

Owen, D., 'The Black Book of the Admiralty' (MM Vol. 1/10, October 1911)

Padfield, P., *Guns at Sea* (London, 1973)

Page, W., (ed.) *The Victoria History of the County of Cornwall* (London, 1906); *The Victoria History of the County of Devon* (London, 1906); *The Victoria History of the County of Dorset* (London, 1908); *The Victoria History of the County of Kent* (London, 1926); *The Victoria History of the County of Suffolk* (London, 1907)

Page, W., et al., *The Victoria History of the County of Sussex* (London, 1905–37)

Parker, G., 'The Dreadnought Revolution of Tudor England' (MM Vol. 82/3, 1996)

Patterson, A.T., *Portsmouth: a History* (Bradford-on-Avon, 1976)

Perrin, W.G. (ed.), *The Autobiography of Phineas Pett* (NRS Vol. 51, 1918)

Pollard, A.F. (ed.), *Tudor Tracts 1532–1588* (New York, 1946)

Potter, D., *A History of France, 1460–1560: the Emergence of a Nation State* (London, 1995)

Prockter, A. and Taylor, R., *The A to Z of Elizabethan London* (London, 1979)

Rackham, O., *Trees and Woodland in the British Landscape* (London, revised edn 1990); *Ancient Woodland* (London, 1976); *The History of the Countryside* (London, 1996)

Rawlinson, H.G., 'The Flanders Galleys' (MM Vol. 12/2, 1926)

Reed, A.W., 'John Rastell's Voyage in the year 1517' (MM Vol. 9/5, 1923)

Robinson, G., 'The Development of the Capital Ship' (MM Vol. 4/1, January 1914); 'The Great Harry' (MM Vol. 20/1, 1934)

Rodger, N.A.M., 'The Naval Service of the Cinque Ports' (EHR Vol. III, 1996); 'The Development of Broadside Gunnery, 1450–1650' (MM Vol. 82/3, 1996); *The Safeguard of the Sea: a Naval History of Britain Vol. 1 1660–1649* (London, 1997); (ed.), *Articles of War: The Statutes which Governed our Fighting Navies 1661, 1749 and 1886* (London, 1982)

Roncière, C. de la, *Histoire de la Marine Française* (Vol. 3, Paris 1923)

Rose, S., 'Bayonne and the King's Ships, 1204–1420' (MM Vol. 86/2, 2000)

Ruddock, A.A., 'The Flanders Galleys' (*History* Vol. XXIV, 1940); 'Alien Merchant in Southampton in the Later Middle Ages' (EHR Vol. 61, 1946); 'London Capitalists and the Decline of Southampton in the Early Tudor Period' (EcHR, 2nd Series Vol. II, 1949); 'The Trinity House at Deptford in the Sixteenth Century' (EHR Vol. LXV, 1950)

Rule, M., *The Mary Rose: the Excavation and Raising of Henry VIII's Flagship* (London, 1990 edn)

Salisbury, W., 'Early Tonnage Measurement in England' (MM Vol. 52/1, 1966)

Salter, F.R., 'The Hanse, Cologne and the Crisis of 1468' (EcHR Vol. III, 1931–2)

Scammell, G.V., 'English Merchant Shipping at the end of the Middle Ages: some East Coast evidence' (EcHR 2nd series Vol. XIII/3, 1961); 'Shipowning in England c.1450–1550' (TRHS 5th series Vol. 12, 1962); 'War at Sea under the Early Tudors' (AA 4th series Vol. 38, 1960 and Vol. 39, 1961); 'Manning the English Merchant Service in the. Sixteenth Century' (MM Vol. 56/2, 1970); 'Shipowning in the economy and politics of early modern England' (HJ Vol. XV/3, 1972); 'The English in the Atlantic Islands c.1450–1650' (MM Vol. 72/3, 1986)

Scarisbrick, J.J., *Henry VIII* (New Haven and London, 1997 edn)

Senior, W., 'The History of Maritime Law' (MM Vol. 38/4, 1952)

Spont, A., *Letters and Papers relating to the war with France 1512–13* (NRS Vol. X, 1910)

Starkey, D.J., Reid, C. and Ashcroft, N. (eds), *England's Sea Fisheries: the Commercial Sea Fisheries of England and Wales since 1300* (London, 2000)

Stottas, J., *Guillaume Le Testu and His Work* (MM Vol. 2/3, 1912)

Stow, J., *A Survey of London* (London, 1598–1971 edn)

Straker, E., *Wealden Iron: a Monograph on the Former Ironworks in the Counties of Sussex, Surrey and Kent* (Newton Abbot, 1969; reprint of 1st edn 1910)

Taillemite, E., *Dictionnaire des marins Français* (Paris, 1982)

Taylor, E.G.R., *The Haven-Finding Art: a History of Navigation from Odysseus to Captain Cook* (London, 1971 edn); *Tudor Geography 1485–1583* (New York, 1968 edn)

Thomas, H., *Rivers of Gold; The Rise of the Spanish Empire* (London, 2003)

Touchard, H., *Le Commerce Maritime Breton à La Fin du Moyen Age* (Rennes, 1967)

Twiss, T. (ed.), *The Black Book of the Admiralty* (4 vols, London, 1871–6)

Unger, R.W., *The Ship in the Medieval Economy, 600–1600* (London, 1980); *Ships and Shipping in the North Sea and Atlantic 1400–1800* (Aldershot, 1997)

Vaughan, H.S., 'Figure-Heads and Beak-Heads of the ships of Henry VIII' (MM Vol. 4/2, 1914)

Wagner, J.A., *The Devon Gentleman: The Life of Sir Peter Carew* (Hull, 1998)

Wallis, J.A., 'Cartographic Knowledge of the World in 1492' (MM Vol. 78/4, 1992)

Warner, G. (ed.), *The Libelle of Englyshe Polycye; a Poem on the Use of Sea-Power 1436* (Oxford, 1926)

Watt, J., 'Surgeons of the Mary Rose: the practice of surgery in Tudor England' (MM Vol. 69/1, 1983)

Waters, D.W., *The Rutters of the Sea: the sailing directions of Pierre Garcie* (New Haven and London, 1967)

Webb, J.G., 'William Sabyn of Ipswich: an Early Tudor Sea-officer and Merchant' (MM Vol. 41/3, 1955)

Weir, A., *Henry VIII; King and Court* (London, 2002)

Willan, T.S., 'Some Aspect of English Trade with the Levant in the Sixteenth Century' (HER Vol. LXX, 1955)

Williamson, J.A., 'The Geographical History of the Cinque Ports' (History Vol. XI, 1926); *Hawkins of Plymouth* (London, 1949)

Winton, J., *The Naval Heritage of Portsmouth* (Southanpton, 1989)

Wood, A.B., 'The Laws of Oleron' (MM Vol. 4/6, June 1914); 'The "Libre de Consolat"' (MM Vol. 8/1, 1922)

Youings, J., *Sixteenth-Century England* (Harmondsworth, 1984); *State Papers of Henry VIII; Vol. I Parts I and II* (London, 1830); *State Papers of Edward VI* (London, 1861)

SOURCES

(In quotations from *Letters and Papers*, the figures refer to documents, not pages, except where indicated otherwise)

FOREWORD

p. xii   'at some indeterminable' Tom Glasgow Jr, MM Vol. 56/3, 1970, p. 299
p. xii   'an Act for the Encouragement' The Rodney Papers Vol. I 1742–1763, D. Syrett (ed) (NRS 2005), p. 426
p. xiv   'As far as the limitations' *The Command of the Ocean: a Naval History of Britain 1649–1815* by N.A.M. Rodger (London, 2004) p. xlv

CHAPTER I Business in Great Waters [pp. 1–7]

p. 5   'The lord Howard' Hall, p. 525
p. 6   'by command of the lords' LPI (1), 855

CHAPTER II The Inheritance [pp. 8–30]

p. 8   'when he moves' SPV II, 219
p. 9   'He was banqueted' Ruddock, 'The Flanders Galleys', p. 516
p. 10   'On the Thursday' LP II (1), 1113
        'advertise the King's majesty' LP XVII, 899
        'he will not set them' LP XVI, 1005
p. 12   'yeoman of the Crown' quoted Oppenheim, p. 36
p. 13   'virtue, glory, immortality' LP I, 51
p. 15   'The old story' H.A.L. Fisher, *A History of Europe* Vol. I (London, 1960 edn), p. 490
p. 17   'as a country which' Mackie, p. 95
p. 18   'renowned for its efficacy' Macdougall, p. 51
p. 20   'achieved less than' quoted Macdougall, p. 232
p. 24   'will shoot a stone' LP I (1), 1504
p. 25   '469 pokes of wool' Ruddock, 'London Capitalists,' p. 141
p. 26   'to put ready four' LP XVIII (1), 59

p. 28   'The chroniclers of the Middle Ages' Brooks, 'The Cinque Ports',
         p. 145
p. 28   'they were simply the nearest' ibid., p. 174
         'nets called "flewys"' LP II (2), 3650
p. 30   'probably the first English' Loades, England's Maritime Empire, p. 11
         'As far as the keeping' ibid., p. 12

CHAPTER III A Nation Defined by the Sea [pp. 31–54]

p. 32   '200 women carders' Cambridge Economic History of Europe Vol. V, p. 471
p. 32   'to the people and chief men' quoted Carus-Wilson, p. 109
p. 38   'A remembraunce for the advancing' LP I (1), 1005
p. 42   'The commodity that ariseth' quoted Hoskins, p. 187
p. 43   'letters to that effect' ibid., p. 185
p. 46   'with brooks running through' Stow, p. 374
p. 47   'large, fair and beautiful' 'bid., p. 190
p. 53   'Sail on so west' quoted MM Vol. 16/4, 1930, p. 333

CHAPTER IV The Enemies [pp. 55–70]

p. 55   'if there be a storm' quoted Corbett, Fighting Instructions, p. 5
p. 57   'On Friday last' LP III (2), 2302
p. 58   'a good road' LP XX (2), 27
         'No-one passes the Raz' quoted Rodger, The Safeguard of the Sea, p. 50
p. 59   'some feasting, bowling' quoted MM Vol. 15/3, 1929, p. 269
         'the very front door' quoted Pevsner, The Buildings of England: North-
         east and East Kent (Harmondsworth, 1969), p. 276
p. 62   'Although that seems' LP XVI, 712
         'the King's grace' quoted Byrne, Vol. I, p 424
         'of long time, and yet is' RP 3 Henry VIII, c 63
p. 63   'mere English' ibid., c 64
p. 66   '1. The master may not' quoted MM Vol. 4/2, 1912, pp. 197–8
         'The mariners of Brittany' Black Book of the Admiralty Vol. III, p. 23
p. 69   'Indentures and instructions' LP I (1), 1080
         'as the tin of England' ibid., 325
         'to the number of' ibid., 1081
         'to be admiral of the forces' ibid., 1170 No. 6

CHAPTER V Disaster off Brittany [pp. 71–87]

p. 71   'men of war, over and above' LP I (1), 1132
         'half the prizes' ibid.

p. 72   'and yet, when they saw' quoted Spont, p. xviii
p. 74   'at last rescued' Spont, p. xxv
p. 76   'la Cordelière s'ouvrit' Roncière, p. 100
          'The French were losing' LP I (1), 1403
p. 79   'poldavys' LP I (2), 1994
p. 80   'from certain Staplers' LP I (1), 1385
          'on Saturday morning' ibid., 1698
p. 81   'Bedell the carpenter' ibid., 1748
          'I pray God' quoted Spont, p. 97
          'for God's sake' LP I (1), 1748
          'Wherefore send a proportion' ibid., 1772
p. 82   'le magnifique capitaine' Roncière, p. 58
          'who fled like cowards' LP I (1), 1771
p. 83   'wrote to the King' Holinshed quoted Spont, p. xxxviii
p. 85   'commanding him to accomplish' ibid.
          'never did seaman' quoted MM Vol, 65/3, 1979, p. 242
          'were protected on both sides' LP I (2), 1844
p. 86   'Sirs, I assure you' quoted Spont, p xl
p. 87   'if it be such as they report' LP I (2), 1851
          'did their part very ill' quoted Spont, p. 160

CHAPTER VI A Quest for Glory [pp. 88–104]

p. 89   'making an enterprise' LP I (2), 1869
          'Sir, I doubt not' ibid., 1870
p. 90   'this is the worst haven' ibid, 1875
          'which prevents him from' ibid., 1883
          'this day at 10 o'clock' ibid., 1886
          'Your new cables' ibid., 1894
          'warping with much pain' ibid., 1907
p. 91   'found him so kind' ibid., 1965
          'or some town nearer Bruges' ibid., 1848
          'saying they will go no more'. Ibid., 1971
p. 92   'The King should command' ibid., 1978
          'We are here strong enough' ibid., 1991
p. 93   'after long struggling' ibid., 2391
p. 94   'was a chance of war' quoted Wagner, p. 26
          'such as Neptune' LP I (2), 2391
p. 95   'practising archery' ibid.
p. 96   'He is of middle height' ibid.
p. 97   'for some days' ibid.
          'le chevalier sans peur' quoted Oman, p. 165

p. 98 'girls offered crowns' ibid.
p. 99 'artillery and other' SPV Vol. III, 174
p. 99 'facts which sound' ibid., 283
p. 102 'the contest was' Oman, p. 320
p. 103 'no great man' LP I (2), 2246
'did not trouble' ibid., 2283

CHAPTER VII Creating a Fleet [pp. 105–119]

p. 107 'Before the ship can be' quoted Harland, p. 187
p. 108 'and weathered them all' quoted Knighton and Loades, p. 84
p. 109 'grew up round' Oppenheim, p. 69
'the making of a pond' quoted Hattendorf et al. in *British Naval Documents*, p. 121
p. 111 'and in at least one instance' Oppenheim, p. 73
p. 112 'seven tiers, one above' LP I (2) 3018
'stuff tacle and apparel' quoted Knighton and Loades, *The Anthony Roll*, p. 113
p. 114 'dedicated with great triumph' LP I (2), 3018
p. 115 'a poore village' Hall, 568
p. 116 'which seeing, Prior John' ibid., p. 269
'my cousin Wyndham' LP I (2), 2946
'fled with sails' ibid.

CHAPTER VIII The Gunnery Revolution [pp. 120–139]

p. 121 'Victory would go' Casson, p. 76
p. 123 'it not only saved' ibid., p. 214
p. 124 'a certain iron instrument' quoted Friel, p. 152
p. 126 'As so often, the excellence' Padfield, p. 23
p. 128 'by the way of a reward' quoted Knighton/Loades, *Letters from Mary Rose*, p. 64
p. 129 'the conveyance hither' Dasent, p. 346
p. 130 'towards new stocking' LP I (2), 3608
'one of the King's gunpowder' LP II (1), 362
p. 132 'Hogge was the owner' quoted Straker, p. 147
'born in the City of London' quoted Rule p. 165
p. 133 'simply because it' Friel, p. 92
p. 134 'they enter in no bigger' quoted Hodges and Hughes p. 9
p. 135 'has viewed the timber' LP Addendae Vol. I (1), 10
'restrain waste of' ibid., 415

p. 136 'They whose woods' James, p. 306
'The King our Sovereign' 35 Henry VIII, c 17
p. 138 'to cause to be made' quoted in *Victoria County History of Dorset*, p. 345
'The whole effect' H.E. Fitzrandolph and M.D. *May in Rural Industries of England and Wales Vol. I* (London, 1926), p. 210
p. 139 'the most part of all' *Victoria County History* op. cit., p. 346
'for the true Makynge' 21 Henry VIII, c 12
'much decayed' quoted in *British Naval Documents* op. cit., p. 113

CHAPTER IX Henry Meets His Match [pp. 140–155]

p. 140 '*Le roi est mort*' quoted Potter, p. 42
p. 141 'to me a thing incredible' ibid., p. 83
p. 143 'a sight very gorgeous' LP II (1), p. xiv
p. 145 'Beyond that of' ibid., p. liii
p. 147 'idiot, ill-intentioned' quoted Potter, p. 257
p. 149 'to scour the seas' LP III (1), 704
'8 loads of knees' ibid., 558
p. 150 'for making cabins' ibid., 1009
p. 151 as high as the highest' ibid., 870
'fifty gentlemen' ibid., 869
'the front and sleeves' ibid., 870
p. 152 'Both hosts were well supplied' ibid., 869
'the most beautiful' ibid.
p. 153 'midsummer games' quoted Weir, p. 228
'retired to the Admiral's tent' LP III (1), 870
'1. In consequence' ibid.
p. 154 'who also declined' ibid.

CHAPTER X A Small World [pp. 156–173]

p. 160 'the thin inner rind' *The Travels of Marco Polo* (London, 1926 edn), p. 202
'a certain kind of earth' ibid., p. 319
p. 161 'no fewer than' ibid., p. 202
'to guard against' ibid., p. 322
'having been on a voyage' ibid., p. 323
p. 162 'proceed all the way' quoted Menzies, p. 37
'consisted of some' *Science and Civilisation in China* by Joseph Needham (Cambridge, 1954), Vol. 4, p. 484
p. 165 'As for his skill' *The Canterbury Tales*, trans. into modern English by Neville Coghill (Harmondsworth, 1965 edn), p. 30
p. 167 'You will see south of' quoted by Waters, p. 21

p. 168 'perhaps the most remarkable' Taylor, *The Haven-finding Art*, p. 170
p. 169 'Coleta his wife' LP XVII Supplement 20
'for the safe conduct' LP XVI, 220/41
'knowledge of the secrets' the full text is in Ruddock, 'Trinity House', pp. 460–2
p. 170 'shall take upon him' ibid., p. 464
'somewhat learned in' quoted Taylor, *Tudor Geography*, p. 46
p. 171 'to adventure there' quoted Oppenheim, p. 90
p. 172 'Old Mr Hawkins' Hakluyt (Everyman edition), p. 18

CHAPTER XI A Vanished Greatness [pp. 174–187]

p. 174 '1. Both Powers to have' LP III (1), 908
p. 175 'His Highness thinketh' SP I (1), XVII
'his right inheritance' ibid., XXIII
'keen, bold, sagacious' *Dictionary of National Biography*
'and three great galleons' LP III (1), 1198
p. 176 'so magnificent that' quoted Rodger, *The Safeguard of the Sea*, p. 204
'shall do their utmost' LP III (2), 1508
p. 177 'no ships dare bring' ibid., 1935
'the King's letters' ibid., 2012
'Kettles for the ships' ibid., 2073
p. 178 'The barges of the King' ibid., 2288
'a meskeler and revels' ibid., 2305
'just as the Emperor' SPV Vol. III, 463
p. 179 'commenced vituperating' ibid., 467
'1. When they set forth' LP III (2), 2355
p. 180 'so strainably' ibid., 2302
p. 181 'Never saw a goodlier' ibid., 2355
'equipped for the wars' SP I (1), LVIII
p. 182 'Yesterday, the Lord Admiral' LP III (2), 2419
'he will be no more countermanded' ibid., 2463
p. 184 'the last campaign' Rodger, op. cit., p. 175
'the Scots are going to' LP III (2), 3071
p. 185 'so strainably' ibid., 3237
p. 186 'All the enemies of England' quoted Weir, p. 249

CHAPTER XIII The Greatest Failure [pp. 188–202]

p. 188 'We have but little victual' LP III (2), 2351
'without which, undoubtedly,' ibid., 2320
'been deceived about the' ibid., 2337

p. 189 'part of the ships' LP XVII, 753
p. 190 '30,000 lbs of biscuit' LP XX (2), 430
'lack of nothing' LP XVII, 753
p. 193 'no woman to lie a ship' quoted Davies, MM Vol. 48/3, 1962, p. 224
p. 195 'to work in and upon' LP I (2), 1898
p. 196 'following sound surgical' Surgeon Vice-admiral Sir James Watt, MM Vol. 69/1, 1983
'little cubbyholes' Knighton & Loades, *Letters from Mary Rose*, p, xviii
p. 197 'fryse ... short hosen' quoted Burwash, p. 78
'a double complement' SPV Vol. II, 237
p. 198 'you are to take especial care' quoted Clowes, p. 432
'the forecastle 100 men' quoted Oppenheim, p. 80
p. 199 'the ungodly manners of' ibid., p. 79
'Orders to be used in' quoted Hodges and Hughes, p. 4
p. 200 'with divers other mariners' quoted Knighton and Loades op. cit., p. 101

CHAPTER XIII The Gathering Storm [pp. 203–223]

p. 204 'more speedy following the chase' quoted Scammell, 'War at Sea under the early Tudors', p. 192
'good Lewis' quoted Spont, p. 156
'he is more in boasting' LP III (2), 2374
p. 205 'for the King's service' LP IV (1), 83
'a prosperous property-owning' Scammell, 'Shipowning in England', p. 117
p. 206 'disgarnished of their masts' SP I(1), LPXIII
p. 207 'We have received' LP XV, 313
'so pained' ibid., 325
'in things concerning the sea' LP XIV (1), 726
'to be by him' quoted Rodger, op. cit., p. 223
p. 209 'colts who had never' quoted Thomas, p. 441
p. 210 'They embraced each other' LP V, 1484
'very slenderly provided' LP XVIII (1), 10
p. 211 'with these two' LP VIII, 48
p. 212 'On September 7' LP VI, 111
p. 215 'return Wm. Gonson to' LP XI, 1061
'we lack him both for' ibid., 1239
'an innovative and distinguished' Loades, *John Dudley*, p. xiii
'to prevent unlawful' LP XII (1), 601
p. 216 'brake down a great piece' LP XII (2), 416
'one Oliver of Boulogne' LP XII (1), 612
'any merchantman' ibid., 393

'In all the Narrow Seas' LP XII (2), 416

p. 217 'all great ships' LP XIV (1), 728
'all this preparation' ibid., 669
'in the rock' ibid., 670
'do nothing but circle' ibid., 770

p. 218 'standing in their docks' ibid., 143
'It will be hard' ibid.

p. 219 'No captains or others' LP XIV (2), 785

p. 220 'or sooner with' ibid., 899
'are not very durable' ibid., .35

p. 222 'All are tall men' LP XVI, 759
'Forasmuch as' 32 Henry VIII c 14 1540

CHAPTER XIV The Last Hurrah [pp. 224–242]

p. 225 'if the wind be SW' LP XIV (2), 674
When she came to the' LP XV 14
'were trimmed with' LP XIV (2), 677

p. 226 'rather graceful than' LP XVI, 12
'She will be considered' LP XV, 899
'not from the fever' LP XVI, 590

p. 227 'to see certain war' ibid., 269
'intends before Easter' ibid., 1005
'as being more' quoted Oppenheim, footnote to p. 51

p. 229 'Et quel traître!' Roncière, p. 403
'in a company of' LP XVIII (1), 663
'such galleys made a little' LP XVIII (2), Appendix 15

p. 231 'abstain from practises' LP XVIII (1), 754

p. 232 'who has been vice-admiral' ibid., 19
'which at the quay' ibid., 75
'and in any wise' ibid., 57

p. 233 'meddle with any Fleming' ibid., 225
'very freshly' ibid., 849
'great fight' 'ibid., 867
'and wishes some ships' LP XVIII (2), 24

p. 234 'and, the King's journey into' LP XVIII (1), 348

p. 235 'daily devastated' LP XIX (1), 510
'and gives them hearty' ibid., 508

p. 237 'for it is an office' LP XIX (2), 338

p. 238 'a more wary eye' ibid., 629
'and how the same shall be' ibid., 501
'with all speed' ibid., 588

'as sore a storm' ibid., 580
p. 239 'with speed ... if ibid., 588
'by fair means or foul' ibid., 597
'and she brake' ibid., 601
p. 240 'a Frenchman or a' ibid., 514
'and we are desolate' ibid., 620
'owing to the decay' ibid., 621
p. 241 'because the said William' LP XX (1), 125 (7)
'the goods of Will. Gonson' LP XIX (2), 550
'on the sayings of' LP XVI, 132

CHAPTER XV 'Oh, my gallant men!' [pp. 243–258]

p. 243 'prepare and equip' 36 Henry VIII 243 1544
p. 245 'any shipman or mariner' 35 Henry VIII 221 1543
'depart or go from' 36 Henry VIII 244 1545
'that shall be diligent' 36 Henry VIII 245 1545
'ruffians, vagabonds' LP XX (1), 812
'As most of the fishermen' LP XX (2), 190
p. 246 'The King's final determination' LP XX (1), 1069
'of a thing swollen up' ibid., 45
'wise and vigilant' ibid., 52
p. 247 'as fair landing places' SP I (2), CCX
'may sustain attacks' LP XX (1), 671
p. 249 'a 20 days' course' ibid., 619
'which had rooms' ibid., 880
'painted with black' ibid., 925
'richly painted' ibid., 925
p. 250 'hire eight of the' ibid., 987
'thought to stop them' ibid., 1023
p. 251 'came within half a mile' ibid., 1184
'or as many as he had' ibid., 1244
p. 253 'he bade me farewell' SPS VIII, 101
p. 254 'The word was no sooner' quoted Wagner, p. 75
'the King hurriedly left' SPS VIII, 101
p. 255 'asking him how' *Hooker's Life of Sir Peter Carew*, quoted Knighton and
Loades in *Letters from Mary Rose*, p. 137
'Oh, my gentlemen' quoted Weir, p. 485
p. 256 'told me that the' SPS VIII, 101
'such rashness' SP I (2), 216
'the Captain's orders' Lewis, p. 81
'the firing on both sides' SPS VIII, 101

p. 257 'certain women fought' LP XX (2), 260
'with speed set men' LP XX (1), 1325
'two of the greatest' LP XX (2), 2
'and on her masts' ibid., 38

CHAPTER XVI D'Annebault's Gaffe [pp. 259–273]

p. 259 'that they have had no leisure' LP XX (2), 39
'with piteous moan' ibid., 62
'found fault with the' ibid., 16
'Are we to proceed' ibid., 5
'swelling in their heads' ibid., 5
p. 260 'it is not known' SP I (2), CCXXIII
'Twelve score sails' LP XX (1), 1245
p. 261 'such order in sailing' Corbett, *Fighting Instructions*, p. 22
p. 262 '1. First, it is to be considered' SPI (2), CCXXVI
p. 263 'There be, besides' Corbett, op. cit., p. 23
'as victories come only' LP XX (2), 89
'did so handle' ibid., 158
'our good neighbours' ibid., 142
p. 264 'ill-appointed with' ibid., 174
'a good many of this fleet' ibid.
'there was no appearance' ibid., 185
p. 265 'spat his contempt' Roncière, p. 429
p. 266 'in which to annoy' LP XX (2), 185
'and proceed as was' ibid., 229
'for the defence of' ibid., 264
p. 267 'skirmishing with' ibid., 261
'two or three gentlemen's' ibid., 307
'all the men and women' ibid., 493
p. 268 'because none will' SP I (2), CCXXVII
'agues and sickness' ibid., CCXXXVIII
p. 269 'two that were well' LP XXI (1), 679
'carried ashore' ibid, 563
'to enter some clean' LP XX (2), 513
p. 270 'the Frenchman's new fort' ibid., 919
'his Majesty's pleasure' LP XIX (2), 592
p. 271 'the handsomest tide haven' LP XXI (1), 520
'streets or other places' LP XXI (2), 402
p. 272 'one Sharpe, of the' LPXX (2), 200
'which will bring some' LP XXI (2), 356
p. 273 'The country is very' LP XX (2), 400

CHAPTER XVII The Final Pieces [pp. 274–288]

p. 275 'at full sea' LP XXI (1), 693
'nor keep an army' ibid.
'five small ships' ibid., 283
p. 276 'meet to serve' ibid., 676
'like varlets shamefully' ibid., 779
p. 277 'every man naked' LP XXI (2), 319
'a right proper man' LP XXI (1), 837
'eight millions of gold' ibid., p. xxviii
'All Christendom' ibid., 749
p. 278 'saying that his honour' ibid., 890
'These brags upon' ibid., 899
'with French wines' ibid., 1384
p. 279 'where was shot' *Hall's Chronicle* p. 867
'and thus they' ibid.
p. 280 'She can do the King' LP XXI (1), 695
'the establishment . . . of' Hodges and Hughes p. 1
'Of all others' Corbett, *Drake and the Tudor Navy*, Vol. I, p. 59
p. 281 'new made the *Mary Rose*' LP X, 1231
p. 282 'from the Vice-admiral' quoted Davies, 'The Administration of the Royal Navy under Henry VIII,' p. 273
p. 283 'The War' LP XX (2), Appendix 27
'knew as much as anyone' Rodger, *Safeguard of the Sea*, p. 226
p. 284 'for every day that' Hattendorf et al, *British Naval Documents*, No. 58, p. 95
'botehire' quoted Loades, *The Tudor Navy*, p. 82, from which all these figures have been taken
p. 286 'The King is so' LP XXI (2), 606
p. 287 'charging his said son' ibid., 634
'the new shallop' quoted Oppenheim, p. 62
'that they could hardly' LP XXI (2), 680
'had ordered his admiral' ibid., 743
'praised his magnanimity' Knecht, p. 416
p. 288 'Great war preparations' LP XXI (2), 684

CHAPTER XVIII The Legacy [pp. 289–302]

p. 290 'a combination of' Knighton and Loades, *The Anthony Roll*, p. 3
p. 291 'of dubious reliability' ibid., p. 13
'consistent with' ibid., p. 20
'*Vive le Roi!*' quoted Knecht p. 421
p. 294 'He was vulnerable' Loades, *John Dudley*, p. 129

p. 295   'little and open and too weak' quoted Glasgow, MM Vol. 56/1, 1970,
             p. 14
p. 296   'by negligence and for lack' Loades, *The Tudor Navy*, p. 158
p. 300   'But such terrible' quoted Pollard, p. 294

CHAPTER XIX the Payoff [pp. 303–322]

p. 304   'the first attempt' Rodger, *Safeguard of the Sea*, p. 230
             'meet to be kept' quoted Loades, *The Tudor Navy*, p. 179
p. 305   'in England alone' Rodger, op. cit., p. 214
p. 306   'Gillingham water' quoted Loades, op. cit., p. 180
             'repairing, ransacking'/ ibid., p. 189
             'wherein the officers' ibid., p. 187
p. 307   'as of his own head', quoted Glasgow, MM 54/1, 1968, p. 26
p. 312   'When the Venetians' quoted Mattingly, p. 108
p. 313   'we are sailing against England' quoted Rodger, op. cit., p. 259
p. 318   'we had a very rough sea' MM Vol. 90/3, 2004, p. 332 *et seq.*

INDEX

Malocello, Lanzarotto, 157

Mansell, Sir Rees, 233

Maplin Sand, 54

maps/charts, 166–9

Margaret, 23, 24

Margaret, Queen of Scotland, 17, 24, 105

Margaret Bonaventure, 241

Margaret of Savoy, 98, 177

Margate, 247, 269

Maria Juan, 317

Marie, 209

Marignano, Battle of (1515), 143–4, 146, 147, 186

Marillac, Charles de, 217–18, 226, 227, 231

Marlion, 244

Marseille, 67, 117, 239, 248, 268

Martyn, William, 25

Mary I, Queen, 296–7, 298, 301, 303

  as Princess, 148, 187, 214, 224, 294

  reign of, 286, 295, 296–302

Mary, Queen of Scots *see* Mary Stuart

Mary and John, 12, 72, 177, 323

Mary Barking, 5

Mary Fortune, 12, 216, 323

Mary George, 116

Mary Gonson, 205, 206

Mary Grace, 181

Mary Guildford, 171

Mary Hamburg, 280, 324

Mary Howard, 206

Mary James, 74, 195, 239, 261

Maryner, John, 180

Mary Rose

  and Edward Howard, 71,73–4, 80, 81, 84, 108

  and Fitzwilliam, 108–9, 182

  and George Carew, 253, 255

  and Spert, 108, 113, 170, 204

  and Thomas Howard, 89, 92, 116, 181, 188

  building of, 68, 105–6

  crew, 197, 200

  guns, 127, 128, 132, 205, 255, 305

  inspected by Henry VIII and Charles V, 178

  maiden voyage, 108, 197

  medical staff, 195, 196

  sinking and attempted salvage of, 254–8, 259

  brief mentions, 13, 76, 101, 107, 112, 119, 135, 149, 177, 180, 183, 190, 218, 250, 265, 279, 281

Mary Rose (second), 298

Mary Spert, 113

Mary Stuart (later Mary, Queen of Scots), 210, 230, 232, 292, 293, 307, 308

Mary Tudor (Henry VIII's sister) (Queen of France, then Duchess of Suffolk), 118, 119, 142–3, 148, 150

Mary Walsingham, 32, 211

Mary Willoughby, 210, 211, 232, 292, 296

Massif Central, 131

Master of Ordnance, post of, 130, 283n2

Master of the Ordnance for the King's Ships/Master of Naval Ordnance, post of, 283, 283n2, 284

Matthew Gonson, 205, 254, 255, 261, 280, 324

Mauclere, Pierre, 209

Mawdelyn Russell, 244

Maximilian I, Emperor, 16, 93, 95, 96–7, 98, 100, 143, 144, 147

May, Isle of, 23

Mayfield, 132

Mechlin (Malines), 130

Medina, Juan Gomes de, 315

Medina Sidonia, Duke of, 313, 314–15, 316, 317, 318, 320–1

Mediterranean

  Prégent de Bidoux in, 82, 117

  navigational aids, 166

  ships/boats, 51, 52, 67, 227

  trade, 9, 31, 37, 38, 160

  weapons and battle tactics, 121, 123, 125

  brief mentions, 29, 34, 156, 164, 167, 205, 239, 247

Medway, River, 50–1 (map), 295, 306, 307

Melrose, 246, 273

Mercator, Gerhardus, 166

Merchamestone, John, 22

Merchant Adventurers, 12, 43–4, 64

Merchants of Iceland, The, 32

Merchants of the Staple, 63–4

Mexico, 16, 209

Michael (later known as *Grande Nef d'Ecosse*), 23–4, 92, 104, 105, 109, 175

Middelburg, 310

Midlands, 12, 247

Milan, 15, 68, 117, 143–4, 186

Milford Haven, 218

Minion, 206, 218, 233, 234, 238, 261, 281, 293–4, 300, 323

Moluccas, the, 170, 310

Mombasa, 159

Montauban, 34

Montdidier, 184

Montreuil, 236, 275

Moon, 296

Morbihan, 58

More, Sir Thomas, 48, 170

More, Treaty of The (1525), 187

Morea, John, 29

Morian of Danzig, 296, 324

Morlaix, 3, 73, 181, 210, 215

Morocco, 169, 204

Mortlake, 49

Mother Bank, 92

Mott, Robert, 241

Moustier, M. de, 155

Mowlton, John, 220

Muscovy Company, 302

Nagasaki, 160

Namur, 131

Nanking, 162

Naples, 15, 68, 277

Narbonne, 67

Narrow Seas, 28, 54, 58, 59, 61 (map), 62, 67, 77, 92, 166, 180, 190, 206, 216, 227, 233, 234, 238, 264, 266, 267, 293, 298, 299, 301, 309, 314

naval administration, 280–5, 307

Navarre, 88, 146

navigational aids, 166–9

Navy Board (formerly known as Council for Marine Causes), 285, 299, 304, 305, 307, 311 *see also* Council for Marine Causes

Needham, Joseph, 162

Needles, The, 44

Nef de Dieppe, 68, 74

Nef de La Rochelle, 68

Nef d'Orléans, 68

Nelson, Lord, 127

Netherlands, 16, 49, 203, 233, 310, 312 *see also* Dutch, the

Netley, 219

New Bark, 324

Newbridge, 132

Newbury, 32

Newcastle, 26, 31, 43, 102, 183, 192, 204, 232, 240, 273, 292

Newfoundland, 77, 168, 171, 208, 293

New Granada (modern Colombia), 310

Newhaven, 19, 23, 24, 109

Newneham Bridge, 62, 64

Nicaragua, 157

Nice, 117

Nicholas, 83, 205